Table of contents

VANDALISM

BEHAVIOUR AND MOTIVATIONS

VANDALISM

behaviour and motivations

Claude Lévy-Leboyer
editor

1984

NORTH-HOLLAND
AMSTERDAM · NEW YORK · OXFORD

© ELSEVIER SCIENCE PUBLISHERS B.V. – 1984

ISBN 0 444 86775 9 ✓

Publishers

ELSEVIER SCIENCE PUBLISHERS B.V.
P.O. BOX 1991
1000 BZ AMSTERDAM
THE NETHERLANDS

Sole distributors for the U.S.A. and Canada

ELSEVIER SCIENCE PUBLISHING COMPANY, INC.
52 VANDERBILT AVENUE
NEW YORK, N.Y. 10017

Library of Congress Cataloging in Publication Data
Main entry under title:

Vandalism, behaviour and motivations.

    Bibliography: p.
    Includes index.
    1. Vandalism--Addresses, essays, lectures. I. Lévy-
Leboyer, Claude.
HV6666.V36 1984   303.6'2   84-4083
ISBN 0-444-86775-9

PRINTED IN THE NETHERLANDS

Vandalism and the social sciences

Cl. LÉVY-LEBOYER

This book is one of the outcomes of a colloquium which took place at the Université René Descartes in Paris on October, 1982, thanks to the financial and moral support of the Ford Foundation. The *raison d'être* of both the colloquium and this collective publication lay in my wish to bring together the demand emanating from researchers seeking a clearer understanding of vandalism as well as from workers and organisations in the field requiring workable solutions to the problem, and the response of the social sciences, i.e. not only the theoretical advances and the results of monitored vandalism control projects, but also the information stemming from psychological and sociological analysis. In other words, both colloquium and book arose from the fact that there is a demand for this type of research, that the market is poorly informed as to the real contribution which the social sciences can make in this respect, and that social scientists, if they are to roll back the frontiers of knowledge in this field, must take stock of hitherto localised, little known research and project findings whilst, above all, they must become aware of the theoretical weaknesses and gaps in our knowledge which are still extant.

There can be no doubt that demand is high. Vandalism has increased dramatically over the last ten years, as may be seen from the national and sectorial statistics and estimates quoted for a number of countries in Europe and the Americas in the pages of this book. Vandalism costs society dear and is a major factor in the deterioration of built and institutional environments. Moreover, the fact that vandalism is often described as 'unmotivated behaviour' constitutes a challenge for the social sciences. In reality, no behaviour occurs without motivation. The fact is that it is difficult to expose and analyse the motivations behind vandalistic behaviour because they are often unconscious or not immediately apparent; such behaviour may also be the, at first sight, illogical outcome of a number of conflicting motivations. In short, it may be said that the desire to understand the motivations behind vandalistic behaviour and the wish to explain its current increase stems as much from scientific considerations as from the need for practical applications of such knowledge.

A great deal of research, project work and project monitoring has been carried out in this domain – as shown by the number of contributions to this book, which itself constitutes only a small sample of the literature currently available. In many cases, research has been carried out by or on behalf of bodies which have suffered from vandalism and which have sought effective means of protection against it. This explains why the bulk of research has consisted of case studies which have not always been widely circulated and which have lacked a real theoretical basis owing to limited time and resources. Furthermore, the very nature of the problem posed means that practitioners from a large number of different disciplines are involved, notably geographers, architects, planners, sociologists, criminologists, clinical psychologists and environmental specialists, as well as workers in the field of every type and description, e.g. maintenance engineers, public relations specialists, headmasters, security personnel and mayors.

The fact that people from such a broad range of backgrounds were able to meet for three days, to take stock of the diversity of approaches to vandalism related problems and to compare their hypotheses and assumptions had two main effects. Firstly, it became clear that neither pure research nor its applications will make progress if there is no agreement with respect to a precise definition of vandalistic phenomena. Secondly, it became clear that current research has, over the last few years, been characterised by an original orientation coloured by the transactional paradigm and by the application of the social sciences to the study of the environment.

It is self-evident that the study of any phenomenon is impossible in the absence of a clear definition, so that further discussion of this point would appear to be superfluous. Nevertheless, the problems encountered in seeking to furnish an adequate definition of vandalism do give rise to difficulties. It is possible, in theory, to reach agreement with respect to certain characteristics of acts of vandalism, viz. aggression with respect to the environment, absence of personal gain or profit for the perpetrator of the act in question. However, despite the general acceptance of these points, there remains a considerable degree of uncertainty, probably because it is wrong to view the word vandalism as referring to a homogeneous type of behaviour: there are several types of vandalistic behaviour and it must be accepted that these can flow from a variety of motivations. In fact, vandalism is playful or dramatic 'limit' behaviour bordering on violence, theft and political activism, as well as on curiosity, boredom and negligence, while it is also not clearly distinguishable from wear and tear or lack of maintenance: it is in fact a ragbag in which highly diverse types of behaviour are to be found under one and the same name. Ten years ago Stanley Cohen, in the book published by Colin Ward, drew up the definitive list of vandalism types from which I shall cite merely the main headings: "Vandalism as institutionalised rule-breaking, vandalism as a label, ideological vandalism, conventional vandalism (acquisitive, tactical, vindictive, play vandalism and malicious vandalism)" (Cohen, 1973).

The analysis contributed to this book by Stanley Cohen fills out the picture by reminding us that the definition of vandalism varies from one culture and from one time period to another. The modest veiling of the half-naked statues of Renaissance virgins may appear today to be an act of vandalism, as may the iconoclastic destruction of holy images viewed as symbols of idolatry. On the other hand, each year, on the fourteenth of July, the French officially celebrate with great pomp and ceremony the historic act of vandalism which was the destruction of the Bastille.

In the following pages various attempts are made to define the common features of acts of vandalism, to specify the characteristics corresponding to a particular group of behaviour types and to provide typologies on the basis of field observations. Even though these goals have not always been reached, everyone agrees that a rational definition and classification must be found if the heuristic approach is not to be paralysed from three points of view. Firstly, it becomes impossible to compare investigations when it is unclear whether they are dealing with the same subject. Secondly, it becomes impossible to evaluate the effects of vandalism prevention or control projects since it is not known what it is that one is seeking to prevent or control. Thirdly, it becomes difficult to develop statistical indices and to make use of international comparisons and longitudinal studies.

Furthermore, vandalistic acts vary in terms of their degree of seriousness. Research into the norms applied to such acts and into their perception and evaluation by different sectors of society is seen to be of more than purely sociological and historical interest, when one recalls that much vandalism takes place in public and that public tolerance in this respect is a factor which can encourage or restrain the increase in such acts. It is for this reason that one of the sections of this book is devoted to the attitudes of the public with respect to vandalism. While the work on vandalism presented in the various chapters of this book does raise problems of synthesis and theoretical modelling as well as complex questions concerning definitions, norms and typologies, it must be borne in mind that research in the field has greatly expanded and that advances have been made over the last ten years, to such an extent in fact that an important turning point has been reached with respect to the general orientation and the viewpoint of investigations into the phenomenon. This evolution may be outlined as follows. Initially, three relatively straightforward hypotheses were advanced to account for vandalistic phenomena. More recently, it was realised that these hypotheses explained only a small proportion of the behaviour classified under the common heading of vandalism. Consequently, a new approach to vandalism has appeared, one which has taken form in the shape of different research, and control efforts of a different type. In order to describe this evolution, I shall begin with the classical hypotheses, present the facts which they are incapable of explaining and specify what appears to be a new theoretical framework for the study of vandalism.

Vandalism has traditionally been described as absurd, unreasonable or even pathological behaviour in as much as it procures no advantage to its perpetrator and, indeed, even has a negative impact upon him/her by reducing the quality of the environment in which he/she lives or works. Consequently, vandalism is frequently referred to as senseless behaviour. Traditionally, three hypotheses have been advanced to attempt to explain the motivations behind this apparently pointless behaviour.

(1) Clinical psychologists have taken the view that irrational behaviour of this sort is pathological, that those characterised by it are delinquent and that they are probably not very different, in terms of their personality and social background, from the juvenile delinquents whom these psychologists are frequently called upon to examine.

(2) Sociologists have emphasized the fact that vandalism is social behaviour, since (a) it is more commonly perpetrated by groups than by individuals acting alone and (b) it represents the expression of a revolt against adult and institutional authority. It is a fact that vandalism would appear to be more serious and more common in areas occupied by mixed social classes where locals often refuse to accept new arrivals. In such circumstances, gangs of adolescents form and develop a subculture which justifies aggression against the physical and social framework by which they are rejected. Furthermore, vandalism has been observed to be more deep-rooted where the ability of families to meet the needs of their members is limited: this is particularly the case when socio-economic standards are low, when unemployment is present and when immigrants are involved.

(3) Another approach to the analysis of the causes of vandalism has been put forward by Oscar Newman who has pointed out that vandalised environments are more fragile than others. Fragile in this case refers not only to the destructible nature of the building materials employed but also, and above all, to the difficulties of guarding such environments owing to their architectural design and the social life style to which this gives rise. The large communal, anonymous zones used by all residents of certain large-scale housing developments represent 'barren' areas which are impossible to keep under surveillance and with which residents do not identify since they neither own nor are concerned with them. Such zones constitute choice targets for vandals.

The clinical, social and architectural factors would appear at first sight to cover all aspects of the problem. A fragile, poorly guarded built environment, inhabited by people from the underprivileged strata of society or from the increasingly anomic groups associated with migration, unemployment, cultural assimilation problems or broken families, provides the setting for the more delinquency prone elements to resort to large-scale vandalism. Seen from this viewpoint, then, vandalism constitutes a symptom of a sick society, one that is 'mal dans son environnement' much as a human being may be 'mal dans sa peau'. *

All the above is probably true in part, but only in part. There remain a great many disturbing points. The clinical psychologist's idea that the deviant behaviour of vandals stems partially from their personality and partially from their social and family background is based only on the examination of the small numbers of vandals arrested by the police. Such a sample is probably not representative of the population of perpetrators of vandalistic acts. Moreover, a number of anonymous self-report surveys of adolescents have shown that extremely high proportions of 'normal' young people admit to having recently committed one or more acts of vandalism (Gladstone, 1978; Stace, 1978). It should also be borne in mind that juvenile delinquents are more critical than their non-delinquent counterparts in their assessment of the seriousness of such acts. Furthermore, notwithstanding the undoubted causal role of social and socio-environmental factors in the generation of vandalistic behaviour, it must be remembered that single individuals also perpetrate acts of vandalism and that the phenomenon is also to be met with in areas where residents and users do not correspond to the 'sociological' definition of poorly integrated, alienated, lazy vandals hostile to the adult world or to the social system in which they are compelled to live. Finally, the architectural design view, based on the assumptions so brilliantly presented by Oscar Newman, has encountered widespread criticism since its application has failed to produce the anticipated results: designing space to be 'defendable' in Newman's sense of the word, has not often led to a reduction in the amount of vandalism (Mawby, 1977; Mayhew, 1979).

Above all, if, instead of relying on *a priori* hypotheses with respect to vandals, their socio-economic motivations or their tactics, the problem is tackled by observing vandalised environments, a whole set of facts emerges which the clinical psychological, sociological and physical environmental approaches do not explain. These facts may be categorised under four main headings.

(1) Vandalism and type of environment

All environments are not vandalised to the same extent. A link has been observed to exist between the social characteristics of residents or users and the amount of vandalism occurring. However, social variables of this nature are insufficient to explain this inhomogeneity in the presence of vandalism which really is characterised by environmental variability. What is going on here?

---

* 'Mal dans sa peau' and 'mal dans son environnement' may be literally rendered as 'having an ill-fitting skin' and an 'ill-fitting environment' respectively.

First and foremost, public property is more frequently vandalised than private property while, even within the former category, vandals do not choose just any target: it has often been remarked upon, for example, that one school may be badly vandalised while another, apparently similar in terms of design and student body, is left relatively untouched. Similarly, one call box may be repeatedly ruined while another, 100 metres away, in the same neighbourhood, is completely spared. It would appear that, over and above the personal, social and physical environmental factors mentioned earlier, certain spots are particularly prone to being vandalised. This gives rise to a problem, viz. what are the features characterising vandalised environments?

(2) Newness and vandalism

Those responsible for designing areas for public use have often had occasion to observe that novelty attracts vandalism. For example, new playgrounds in housing estates are often ruined very shortly after their appearance. If they are subsequently repaired it may well be that they will be vandalised a second time. It is most unusual, however, for this to occur a third time. This endows the study of vandalism with a time dimension, raises the problem of resistance to change and suggests the idea, inspired by work psychology, that participation in the environmental modification process could bring about conditions propitious to a decrease in vandalism. More generally, this second observation highlights an important problem, to wit, what determines the attitudes to territoriality in terms of public and semi-public space?

(3) Vandalism and vandalism

It is commonplace to say that in public buildings or housing developments vandalism leads to more vandalism. For example, if graffiti are left on a wall for 24 hours, that wall will be completely covered with them two days later. Again, if the cleaning and maintenance of public facilities are cut back, vandalism will immediately begin to develop. Why? Here we have a third problem for the environmental specialist: what is the significance of the first graffiti on a wall, or of the shoddy state of inadequately cleaned facilities? In what way does the initial deterioration modify the individual–environment relationship so as to lead to the rise of vandalism?

(4) Small-scale vandalism

Some destructive acts take place on a massive scale and are often collective in nature. Examples of such behaviour would be the smashing up of an underground station, a train, a recreation area or an exhibition. Nevertheless, vandalism is also frequently the result of an accumulation of small-scale aggressive acts such as kicking open a tube car door handle a hundred times a day, continuously leaving a telephone receiver dangling off the hook or endlessly slamming a classroom door shut with one's shoulder. Similarly, vandalism can stem from inappropriate behaviour or the wrong use of every-day objects and facilities, e.g. supermarket trolleys for scooters, lawns for parking, flower beds for ball games, bicycles propped up against fragile walls, etc. What determines such negligent or careless behaviour with respect to the environment? Why does an individual eschew negligent behaviour in his immediate, personal work or home environment and yet inflict minor damage on other environments?

In a word, these observations oblige us to look at the problem of vandalism in the framework of the relationship between individuals and their environ-ment: the clinical psychological, sociological and physical environmental ex-planations are seen to be inadequate despite their partial observational con-firmation. Specifically, the four sets of observations presented above lead to the formulation of three hypotheses or, rather, three research paradigms.

Firstly, there are heavily vandalised environments, which can be dis-tinguished from unvandalised or little vandalised environments: in terms of the transactional paradigm, environmental features exist which give rise to a person/environment relationship such that aggressive and destructive be-haviour is triggered off.

Secondly, social norms determine our behaviour with respect to the environ-ment, i.e. for each environment, some behaviour is accepted, some is tolerated and some is repudiated. For example, an act such as stepping on a cigarette stub will be accepted in the street, tolerated in a public place and perceived as vandalistic when it takes place on private property.

Thirdly, social and institutional life and the use of the physical environment in which the former takes place are closely linked. Just as work psychologists speak of sociotechnical systems here we must think in terms of a socio-environ-mental system.

Although these three paradigms are not always explicated in these terms, they frequently constitute the effective framework for the various investiga-tions presented in this book. This is the case, for instance, with respect to those studies seeking to accurately determine the environmental features of heavily vandalised locations, as well as those attempting to define environmental use norms or describe the influence of life in society on environmental behaviour. While it is clearly impossible to go into these investigations in detail at this point, let alone their findings, I should like to present a few examples with a view to clarifying my position in this regard.

It has often been stated that vandalism is the manifestation (or rather one of the possible manifestations) of an organisational dysfunction, or even of a lack of social cohesion. For example, when relationships within a teaching body are at a low ebb, as are those between teachers and the school administration, and when this is combined with lack of contact between school maintenance personnel and users, the amount and seriousness of acts of vandalism is much greater than when all school workers form a cohesive social group, through which information flows, within which communication of all sorts takes root and wherein opinions can be expressed and defended. Similarly, in housing estates high rates of vandalism appear to be associated with extremely mediocre quality social life. Where vandalism holds sway residents are constantly changing, have little or no contact with each other or even argue about a whole series of problems such as noise and the use of communal facilities. Interviews with residents in such estates have proved most interesting. Where communal activity does occur, the physical environment constitutes both the backdrop and the symbol of such activity. As such, it belongs to the whole group and consequently to all its members, each one of whom identifies (to a greater or lesser degree of course) with the communal areas or facilities and therefore feels partly responsible for their improvement and protection. When social life is of a low standard, when institutions have little status in the eyes of those who work in them and provide them with no satisfaction, then indifference with respect to the physical environment is the immediate expression of the poor relationship with the social system and of indifference with respect to the group. Under these circumstances, interviews have shown that no-one cares about school buildings or communal areas in the particular development or in the neighbourhood as a whole. In a word, the link up between an active communal life and environmental protection takes place by belonging to a vibrant community living in and through its communal areas and facilities.

As a corollary to the above, it should be borne in mind that participation in the planning and upkeep of communal facilities may represent one of the consequences of social cohesion or constitute one of its building blocks, but it cannot form the starting point for its generation. Any attempt to eliminate vandalism by 'artificially' encouraging participation in the planning and maintenance of a given environment will fail if the social terrain is not already characterised by adequate cohesion, i.e. if the group involved does not already share common goals and interests. This probably accounts for the failure of certain endeavours to create participatory environmental planning in communities which did not have such a group identity. Groups must exist as such if participatory environmental planning is to succeed, i.e. there must be a consensus with respect to aims, activities, norms and regulations: it is impossible to improvise participation where the social fabric is non-existent.

From the point of view of the vandalism problem it must be emphasised that, in every case, vandalistic behaviour stems from contempt for the environment, and not from the particular features characterising the vandals or those specific to the environment itself. It is very much a question of an individual/environment *system*, with the environment being viewed as a sociophysical whole, and not one of individuals on the one hand and the environment on the other.

Let me describe a second example. When a particular environment is inadequate, i.e. when it prevents a person from implementing his plans, either by constituting an obstacle to those plans or by not providing the appropriate means to bring them about, a chain of events occurs which has frequently been described by psychologists. The person prevented from carrying out his project (e.g. parking his car, playing ball, making a phone call, crossing the street) becomes frustrated and, under certain circumstances, this frustration triggers off aggressive behaviour. These other conditions are as yet poorly understood, but it appears that sensory overload, i.e. the presence of a large number of sensory stimuli (noise, words, traffic, posters, illuminated hoardings, etc.) encourages aggression with respect to the environment. The type of frustration experienced also plays a part. In the case of telephones, for example, aggression is more violent and more frequent when the apparatus not only fails to work but also withholds the would-be caller's money. Under these circumstances, ordinarily peaceful citizens who are not, as a rule, particularly young or of standard delinquent or marginal appearance, can be seen to strike the apparatus with the receiver if necessary, shake it and roughly handle supports and buttons.

The preceding example shows that numerous factors are involved in determining aggressive behaviour and that it characterises all members of society, not just a group of deviants (70% of respondents in another survey admitted that they had forcibly struck out of order telephones); such behaviour takes place in public, is determined by cognitive factors and is motivated, above all, by the lack of *congruence* between an individual and his environment. In general it is to be expected that an inadequate environment will be subject to aggression. The more important the project which is prevented from being carried out then the stronger the aggression will be. And all members of society will react aggressively, not just those belonging to a deviant minority.

A third example enables the clinical psychological and sociological positions to be modified. The proposition that it is deviants and antisocial citizens who perpetrate acts of vandalism as a protest against society, adults or a system which rejects them does not explain *why* they resort to this particular way of protesting which, in any case, backfires as it lowers still further the quality of their living environment. An analysis of the individual/environment relationship helps to clarify the debate. One of these poorly integrated people's sources of profound dissatisfaction certainly seems to be their passive dependence on a society which presents them with a series of bans rather than with support. As they are unable to control their own destiny, they seek, through breaking things, to reassert a feeling of power and control over their environment. The act of breaking, in fact, represents riskless conduct in as much as it has every chance of being brought to a successful conclusion. It poses no difficulty as such to rip open the seats on a tube train, to smash a windowpane or to break up a public bench. Nevertheless, such acts constitute a source of satisfaction precisely because they are a sure way of asserting oneself, of dominating one's hostile environment and of leaving one's mark upon it. People who do not feel themselves to have a clear social identity find, in attacking their environment, a means of building one up. Also, by pulling off an act with easily visible consequences they simultaneously rise in the esteem of the marginal group who are united by their common experience of alienation and by their positive attitudes towards challenging rules laid down by adults and by society. The analysis of data from surveys of perpetrators of acts of vandalism has clearly shown that the choice of public, rather than private property, and communal areas which 'belong to no-one' as targets renders such aggression quite moral since, from the aggressors' standpoint, nobody in particular is harmed by it. Similarly, the apparently pointless nature of the damage done removes any perception of it as wrongdoing since its perpetrator draws no personal benefit from acts carried out for their symbolic value only. To sum up, it is clear that the relationship between vandals and their physical environment cannot be understood without reference to that existing within their social environment. But, once again, the social environment of vandals does not suffice to explain either their acts or their choice of targets.

Vandalism is not just a social problem; it is wrong to limit it to a type of delinquency or to a particular personality problem; it is not simply a manifestation of an inadequate environment and of the lack of social norms. In fact, it is all these things at one and the same time. This is why the study of vandalism and its control, or rather the control of its multifaceted forms, must take into account all these factors and adopt a system viewpoint. As a consequence, this book is organised around three basic themes: the variety of vandalistic behaviour, the multiplicity of motivations behind it and the importance which must be attached to the individual/society/environment-system.

Following a review of the current literature, the volume is divided into five parts, each one being introduced by a brief account of the discussion that went on during the symposium. The first part deals with attempts to model and synthesise the phenomenon, the second looks at it from the social angle and the third examines its behavioural aspects. The fourth part of the book brings together investigations into public attitudes towards vandalism and their *raison d'être*. The fifth and final part draws together, as a provisional conclusion, the results of monitored vandalism projects, since the lesson to be learned from them appears to be quite clear and reads as follows: vandalism control must be based, firstly, on a better understanding of the significance of the environment for the individuals and groups living therein and, secondly, on modifications of the psychological relationship between man and his environment.

It would not be fair to end this introduction without reminding the reader that this book could not have come to fruition without the generous support of the Ford Foundation. It was the assistance of the Foundation coupled with the large measure of autonomy extended by its officers to those responsible for the organisation of the colloquium, which made it possible to hold the conference and to publish its proceedings. The editor is also deeply indebted to Dr. James Brougham, who translated or revised many of the contributions, for his forbearance and understanding, and even more so to Catherine Isacco, who shouldered responsibility for the colloquium secretariat and the preparation of the manuscript.

References

Clarke, R.V.G., ed., 1978. Tackling vandalism. Home Office Research Study no. 45. London: Her Majesty's Stationery Office.

Cohen, S., 1973. Property destruction: Motives and meanings. In: C. Ward, 1973, pp. 23–54.

Gladstone, F.J., 1978. Vandalism among adolescent schoolboys. In: R.V.G. Clarke, 1978, pp. 19–39.

Mawby, R.I., 1977. Defensible space: A theoretical and empirical appraisal. Urban Studies 14, 169–179.

Mayhew, P., 1979. Defensible space: The current status of a crime prevention theory. The Howard Journal of Penology and Crime Prevention 18, 150–159.

Newman, O., 1969. Defensible space. New York: Macmillan.

Stace, M., 1978. Vandalism and self-report studies: A review of the literature. Occasional Papers in Criminology no. 6. Victoria University of Wellington.

Ward, C., 1973. Vandalism. London: The Architectural Press.

CHAPTER 1

Vandalism: an assessment and agenda

W. VAN VLIET

The purpose of this chapter is to review the 'state-of-the-art' on vandalism. It aims to bring some order in the rather diverse literature, to distinguish the several different perspectives on vandalism while considering their relative merits in addressing the problem and, further, to suggest some work that needs to be done next. This review, therefore, is necessarily broad in scope, providing an organizing framework for the more specific theoretical, methodological, and substantive issues which are treated in greater detail in the contributions comprising the remainder of this volume. [1]

Below, the extent of the problem is indicated first in terms of young people's involvement in vandalism, the range of environments affected, and the magnitude of economic and socio-psychological costs. This is followed by a review of approaches taken to study and combat vandalism. Different programs are assessed with respect to their effectiveness in specific cases, and two general strategies are distinguished. The conclusion points out future directions for work on vandalism.

1. Involvement, targets, and costs

Vandalism is an activity primarily engaged in by young people. Statistics for the United States indicate that about 90% of all arrested vandals are white males under 25 years of age (U.S. Bureau of Federal Investigation, 1979). Figures reported by the Pennsylvania State Police (1980: 65ff) show that those under 18 account for some 60% of the vandals arrested, whereas four out of every five juvenile offenses are cases of vandalism. Marshall (1976) found ten years to be the most common age group among arrested vandals. Participation in vandalism by youths appears to be widespread. Clarke (1978) noted "extensive involvement" among urban boys, aged 11 to 15, without mentioning a precise figure. Such figures are hard to obtain, of course, as vandalism is very much an anonymous offense: some 90% of the reported incidents remains

[1] This chapter benefited from contributions by Stuart Mann and a literature search conducted by Susan Knasko and Maria Onestini aided by Linda Rambler. A supporting grant of the school for Continuing Education at the Pennsylvania State University is gratefully acknowledged.

unresolved (Pennsylvania State Police, 1980: 70). Nevertheless, in a few instances students have been asked for self-reports. Marshall (1976) cites a study conducted by Francis Gladstone in which between 30% and 40% of secondary school boys in Liverpool, England, admitted engagement in vandalism. Phillips and Bartlett (1976) found involvement by more than 50% of a sample of mid-western American teenagers. Similar outcomes are described by Richards (1979) for a sample of nearly 2,000 middle-class American adolescents and by Donnermeyer and Howard (1980) in an investigation of sophomore and junior-high students in five rural Ohio schools.

From the above one may conclude that vandalism, while variably defined, is a fairly common activity among (pre-)adolescents. Moreover, data for the U.S.A. point out a 70% increase in reported incidents during the 1970–79 period (U.S. Bureau of Federal Investigation, 1979, 1980; see also Bayh, 1977, for school vandalism). Although acts of vandalism are primarily committed by young people, the stereotypical profile of the vandal as a 'working-class, inner-city male adolescent' has been invalidated by various studies. Vandals come from urban and suburban as well as rural areas, from working-class and middle-class as well as upper-class families, and are of different ethnic origins (Herbert, 1980; Torres, 1981; Levine and Kozak, 1979; Richards, 1979; Bates and McJunkins, 1962).

Thus, vandalism is increasing and is not limited to specific socio-economic milieus or spatial locales. Consequently, a wide range of environments is affected, including private and particularly public property. A summing up of all vandalized settings and objects would result in a rather meaningless, long list. However, principal categories which subsume more specific environments are: [2]

(1) *parks and playgrounds* (e.g., Peuleche, 1976; Burall, 1980; Christensen, 1978; Damron, 1978):
(2) *educational facilities* (e.g., Mayer and Butterworth, 1979; Bayh, 1978; Arlan and McDowell, 1980; Howard, 1978);
(3) *public transportation* (e.g., U.S. Department of Transportation, 1980; Glazer, 1979; Bartholo and Milte, 1979; Klein and Feiner, 1980);
(4) *institutional settings* such as dormitories, libraries, correctional institutions, military installations, places of worship, museums, etc. (e.g., Sleep, 1982; Brill, 1977; Graham, 1981; Griffith, 1978);
(5) *housing* (e.g., U.S. Department of Housing and Urban Development, 1973; Newman, 1980; Jephcott, 1971; Larsson, 1982); and,
(6) *street furniture* (e.g., Zimbardo, 1973; Bennett, 1969; Torres, 1981; Ley and Cybriwski, 1974a)

---

[2] For a more complete list of references, see *Vandalism: a selected bibliography*, no. 118, Chicago: Council of Planning Librarians.

Table 1. Indications of financial cost of repair and replacement of vandalized equipment.

YEAR	AMOUNT OF DAMAGE	PLACE	ENVIRONMENT	SOURCE
1967	1,941,000	New York City	Schools	Zimbardo (1973)
1967	100,000,000	New York City	Public Phones	Zimbardo (1973)
	4,400,000	U.S.	Cars	Goldemeir (1974)
	722,000,000	U.S	Construction sites	Goldemeir (1974)
1968	5,000,000	New York City	Public Trans.	Zimbardo (1973)
1968/9	870,000*	Liverpool, England	Corporation Housing	Pullen (1973:259)
1969	30,000	small U.S. city	Schools	Zimbardo (1973)
	61,000*	City of 500,000 in England	Schools	Burall (1980)
	122,000*	Berkshire Cnty in England	Schools	Burall (1980)
1972	2.55, (monthly cost per unit)	U.S.	60 federally sub-sidized limited dividend housing projects	HUD Challenge (1978:28)
1975	1 to 5 billion $	U.S.	Schools, parks, recreation areas, public housing, & transit systems	U.S. Senate Judiciary Sub-committee (1975)
1976	114,000,000*	England/Scotland/Wales	General	Ward (1978:203)
1978	460,000,000 or $13 per/student	U.S.	Schools	Commission on Crime and Delinquency (n.d.)
1978	14,000,000	U.S.	Small businesses	Commission on Crime and Delinquency (n.d.)
	853.08**	Canada	Small Univ. Library	Sleep (1982)
	44,000*	City of 500,000 in England	Housing	Burall (1980)
1979	1,000,000,000	U.S.	General	Anonymous (1977) Commission on Crime & Delinq. (n.d.)
1979	100,000,000	England/Wales	General	Burall (1980)
1979	$15.00 per resident	PA small town	General	Pietro (1980)
1982	130,000	U.S.	Dormitories in a state university	Gailey (1983)

All amounts are in U.S. dollars unless otherwise indicated
*English pounds
**Canadian dollars

Incidents in these different types of environment include such acts as throwing rocks at passing cars, smashing windows, ripping off wires from and urinating in public phone booths; 'soaping' creeks with detergent; shooting street signs; pilferage of building sites; slashing tires; squirting ink and glue on or cutting out pages of library books; smashing marble statues; trampling flower beds; and countless more devious acts. The list could go on and on.

There have been few systematic attempts to estimate the financial costs resulting from repair and replacement of vandalized equipment. Such efforts are further confounded by the absence of unequivocal criteria as to what constitutes vandalism. [3] Nevertheless, some figures do exist (see table 1).

While reflecting on the data contained in table 1, several points should be borne in mind. To begin with, the figures are often estimates; it is seldom specified how they are calculated, and there is little possibility here to evaluate their accuracy. Further, the figures may be inflated by including as vandalism what is really negligent maintenance (see fn. 2); at the same time they are deflated by the rate of inflation and incomplete information. Therefore, the above data should be interpreted cautiously. However, even if taken only as indications of the financial implications of vandalism, the costs appear to be staggering.

In addition to the economic aspect, it is important to consider the less tangible socio-psychological costs and suffering in health. In this connection, some have been concerned with the effects of school vandalism. In a study of high school students, aged 16 to 18, in four schools in Michigan and Illinois, U.S.A., Rose (1978) failed to find a correlation between the official drop-out rate and an index of suspensions due to "depreciative behaviors" such as thefts, fights, and assaults. However, in another investigation of 321 students (about 13–14 years of age) in a large midwestern city, vicitimization – inherent in an atmosphere of violence and vandalism – was found to be related to lower self-esteem and stronger feelings of anonymity (Blyth et al., 1980), suggesting that the performance of the educational system may suffer qualitatively. In another context, Burall (1980) mentions accident records in Great Britain for 1978, indicating tens of thousands of injuries requiring hospital treatment as a result of accidents involving faulty and often vandalized playground equipment. Other unintended consequences may be elderly people and mothers with young children stranded in or out of their apartment because of an out-of-order

---

[3] For example, in educational settings maintenance tasks may be classified as being the result of vandalism rather than regular wear and tear, so that they can be charged against students' general deposits, thus inflating the cost figure. Also, possible other beneficiaries on the benefit side of the ledger should be noted, as repair and replacement needs create an additional demand for labor and materials. Further, tax legislation often allows deductions for the cost of restoring property losses, thus shifting the burden from the private to the public domain. However, there are indications that much vandalism goes unreported, suggesting that the actual figures are much higher.

elevator; loss of life or property because of a vandalized fire-alarm; delay of medical help due to a vandalized public phone; traffic fatalities and injuries from accidents attributable to vandalized lighting, road decks, tires or navigational aids; lack of investment by financial institutions and refusal of insurance companies to cover losses in areas of high vandalism; increased turnover, vacancy rates, fear to leave the home, and distrust of neighbors; and so forth. In a nation-wide study in Ireland, the problem of vandalism, as perceived by a sample of 2,019 residents, was found to be the second most important predictor of neighborhood satisfaction (Davis and Fine-Davis, 1981).

Clearly, vandalism does not stand alone as a factor contributing to undesirable situations as those named above. This point will be argued later. For now, it suffices to note that vandalism, broadly defined, appears to be increasing and is associated with high monetary and social costs, mental anguish, and suffering in health. It comes as no surprise, therefore, that numerous programs and strategies have been formulated in order to combat vandalism. Before reviewing these, we will take a brief look at the various perspectives on and definitions of vandalism which underlie such programs.

Recapitulating the main points of this first section, the available data indicate that (1) acts of vandalism are increasing and predominantly committed by youths under 25 years of age; (2) many youths engage in vandalism at one time or another – more than 50% according to some self-report studies – and participation is not restricted to particular socio-economic milieus or spatial locales; (3) a broad range of environments is affected, the chief categories being parks and playgrounds, educational facilities, public transportation, institutional settings, housing and street furniture; (4) direct financial loss due to repair and replacement is very high and in addition to perhaps more important intangible socio-psychological costs and suffering in health.

2. Perspectives on vandalism

The literature on vandalism shows little consensus as to what constitutes vandalistic behaviour. To begin with, there is a judicial perspective. In the U.S.A., for example, the FBI has defined vandalism as "the willful or malicious destruction, injury, disfigurement, or defacement of any public or private property, real or personal, without consent of the owner having custody or control, by cutting, tearing, breaking, marking, painting, drawing, covering with filth or any such other means as may be specified by law or ordinance" (U.S. Department of Housing and Urban Development, 1979). According to the British Criminal Damage Act of 1971, a vandal is "a person who without lawful excuse destroys or damages any property belonging to another, intending to destroy or damage any such property or being reckless as to whether

Table 2. Types and definitions of vandalism.

SOURCE	TYPES OF VANDALISM
Cohen (1973)	Ideological: Property destruction characterized by (1) rulebreaking toward some explicit and conscious ideological end, and (2) challenge of content of the rule being broken;
	Acquisitive: Damage done in the course of or in order to acquire money or property;
	Tactical: To advance some non-material end in a planned fashion. May be inspired by ideological motives (e.g., slogan painting) or personal ones (e.g., sabotage to relieve job monotony or get a rest);
	Vindictive: As a form of revenge;
	Play: Form of institutionalized rulebreaking without malicious intent, inspired by curiosity and a spirit of competition and skill;
	Malicious: Hostile actions enjoyed for their own sake at the victim's expense, inspired by feelings of boredom, despair, exasperation, resentment, failure and frustration.
Farmer and Dark (1973)	Smashing things with considerable strength and determination for the sheer satisfaction of smashing them.
Zimbardo (1973)	Mindless, wanton destruction of property. Prototype of a behavior pattern characterized by deindividuation, assaultive aggression, senseless destruction and efforts directed towards shattering traditional norms and institutionalized structures.
Goldmeir (1974)	Retaliation by a person who believes he had been done wrong. Wanton vandalism involves property destruction purely for excitement, usually without an ulterior motive.
Pablant and Baxter (1975)	Number of forcible entries with consequent theft and/or damage to school property or equipment reported to the security officer of the district.
Greenberg (1976)	Editing simple worded letters to the editor.
Zeisel (1976:11-12)	Malicious vandalism: Instantaneous damage demanding immediate attention. Conscious motive. Primarily (part of) social, educational and legal problems. Designer can do little.
Zeisel (cont.)	Misnamed vandalism: Accidental damage identical to malicious vandalism with one crucial difference: no purposefulness. Could be avoided by better prediction of use of the environment and designing accordingly.
	Non-malicious property damage: Conscious modifications of the environment without malicious intent, e.g., in the course of a game.
	Hidden maintenance damage: A cumulative condition not resulting from intentional acts, but requiring eventual attention, e.g., wear and tear. May be avoided by materials and designs accommodating frequent and rough use.

Table 2 continued

SOURCE	TYPES OF VANDALISM
Cornacchionne (1977)	Predatory: damage caused during stealing; Play: No intent to destroy; Vindictive: motivated by revenge; Wanton: variety of motives
Mawby (1977)	GPO records on incidents of kiosk vandalism. Definition of vandalism left to repairmen.
U.S. Dept. of Justice (1979)	The willful or malicious destruction, injury, disfigure-ment or defacement of any public or private property, real or personal, without consent of the owner having custody or control, by cutting, tearing, breaking, mark-ing, painting, drawing, covering with filth or any such other means as may be specified by law or ordinance.
Becker (1980)	Damage (in university dormitories); may be the result of purposeful destruction as well as neglected maintenance.
Griffiths and Shapland (1980:11)	According to the British Criminal Damage Act of 1971, a vandal is "a person who without lawful excuse destroys or damages any property belonging to another, intending to destroy or damage any such property or being reckless as to whether such property would be destroyed or damaged."
Wilson (1980:20)	Damage to property owned by others (whether or not they are perceived to "belong" to someone), and to be mended by others.
Graham (1981)	The breaking of cell windows at a remand centre.
Mayer and Butterworth (1981:499)	The presence of broken glass, equipment theft, fire damages, and property damage such as graffiti or damaged furniture.
Torres (1981:21)	Destruction of property, or the mischievous marring, painting, or defacing of same with willful malicious intent.
Sleep (1982)	Mutilation and theft of library periodicals.
Wise (1982:31)	Alteration of the physical environment without consent of its owner or manager.

such property would be destroyed or damaged" (Griffiths and Shapland, 1980: 11). Quite clearly, formal circumscriptions such as these are open to multiple interpretation; statistics collected on this basis may mirror as much of the behavior of law enforcement personnel as activities of vandals, and they convey no information regarding the motives for and meaning of engaging in vandalism. The usefulness of a judicial perspective is limited because it focuses on legal aspects of vandalistic incidents rather than on their social context and their behavioral and psychological antecedent circumstances. This focus may be problematic because differences in these factors may require a different classification of an identical outcome. For example, an unearthed shrub may in some instances be the result of malicious intent of teenagers, whereas in other instances it may be due to exploratory behavior of toddlers. This ambiguity in classification is a perennial problem in the compilation of vandalism statistics, since a large majority of the reported offenses goes unwitnessed and few offenders are apprehended.

A large portion of the literature on vandalism is opinionative and characterizable by a lamentable lack of scientific rigor. The divergent conclusions and recommendations are, in large part, based on ad hoc interpretations and attributable to differences in (or the absence of) definitions of vandalism and the operationalization of contributing factors, the variety of data gathering techniques employed (if any), the lack of control for influences of extraneous variables, and the absence of systematic considerations concerning theory, research design, and sampling procedure. The evidence brought forward in support of a given viewpoint is more often than not informal in nature and based on casual observations and personal professional experiences of, for example, educators (Irwin, 1976), police officers (Cornacchione, 1977), administrators (Stormer, 1979), and civic leaders (Torres, 1981).

Apart from a judicial perspective and attestations of concern as referred to above, a third perspective is provided by concentrating on the vandalized environment. While narrowing down the environmental dimension, this kind of approach has so far not produced a coherent explanation of vandalism. In the extensive literature on schools, for example, vandalism has been attributed to such diverse factors as deficient design and construction materials, lack of discipline, bureaucratic anonymity, and administrative incompetence and mismanagement. Clearly lacking is an integrated theory capable of explaining the phenomenon of school vandalism.

Similarly, one might focus on types of vandalism such as arson or graffiti. However, then also there is ample room for widely different views. Graffiti, for example, has been seen as a phenomenon to be curbed by setting loose police dogs (New York Magazine, 1977), as an established means of expressing one's identity (Brown, 1978), as territorial markers functional in the regulation of a social system (Ley and Cybriwsky, 1974b), and as semantic cues to different sex-role perceptions (Bruner and Kelso, 1980; Bates and Martin, 1980). Again, a unifying theoretical explanation of graffiti is lacking.

A number of authors have recognized the diversity of vandalistic acts and have come up with different typologies. Zeisel (1976:11) distinguishes between malicious vandalism (where conscious acts cause instantaneous damage demanding immediate attention), misnamed vandalism (not purposely done, but otherwise identical), and, further, non-malicious property damage and hidden maintenance damage both of which are cumulative conditions demanding eventual attention; a distinction which suggests that vandalism really subsumes a set of rather different behaviors. Cohen (1973), who has perhaps presented the most considered approach, identifies six different types of vandalism including, among others, acquisitive vandalism aimed at obtaining money or goods, vindictive vandalism of a selected target for revenge on the owner or representative, play vandalism occurring in the context of a game, and ideological vandalism intended to advance some ideological cause (see table 2).

The above review of perspectives on vandalism is certainly incomplete and excludes some attempts at more theoretical approaches (e.g., Allen and Greenberger, 1978, 1980; Abel and Buckley, 1977; Arlan and McDowell, 1980; Fisher and Baron, 1982). However, the purpose here was not to be exhaustive, but to indicate the mixed taxonomy and lack of unanimity in defining vandalism. The broad spectrum of views found in the literature as to what vandalism is has given rise to a corresponding variety of approaches intended to reduce or eliminate vandalism. These anti-vandalism programs and strategies are reviewed in the next section.

3. Programs and strategies

The literature abounds in recommendations on how to combat vandalism. They include suggestions to improve building lay-out and design (Leather and Matthews, 1973); to use enhanced construction materials (Miller, 1973); to install indestructible play equipment (Burall, 1980), and better locks (Spalding, 1971) and lights (Dukiet, 1973); to upgrade schooling and leisure opportunities (Gladstone, 1978); to develop participatory management in housing for low-income residents (Pietro, 1980) and students (Becker, 1980); to institute block watches (Burich, 1979) and tenant patrols (Miller, 1979); to increase the effectiveness of surveillance by security personnel (Graham, 1981); to implement juvenile restitution projects (Oswald, 1981) and family therapy programs (Reilly, 1978); to set stricter limits on the number of destructive acts shown in films (Fuellsgrabe, 1978); and to organize 'smash-ins' (McCann, 1980) (see table 3).

The diverse approaches to vandalism represent different levels of generality at which the problem may be tackled. They range from overall strategies (e.g., target hardening) to more specific tactics and techniques that may be derived from such strategic frameworks (e.g., installing locks). At the more general level, it seems possible to divide the available strategies into a global dichotomy: one strand oriented to various planning and design aspects of the *physical* environment and the other directed at a range of personal, behavioral and organizational facets of the *social* environment. The former is typically characterized by an emphasis on short-term solutions and has resulted in, for example, the development of detailed checklists and guidelines intended to alert architects and planners to designs and site plans likely to evoke vandalism (Zeisel, 1976; Sykes, 1980). In the second major approach, which concentrates on individual and socio-structural factors, the solutions tend to be more

Table 3. Programs and strategies against vandalism.

SOURCE	STRATEGY OR PROGRAM	SETTING	EFFECTIVENESS
Leather and Matthews (1973)	Extensive architectural design guidelines	Liverpool, England, especially housing	No information on implementation
Reid (1975)	1. Legislation of basic sanitary and maintenance standards and monthly inspections of residences' interiors; 2. Occupants with inadequate cultural level must be trained or rejected; 3. Security force	USA, low income housing	No information on implementation
Graf and Roberts (1976)	Two-way radio communication for bus and subway, and helicopter track surveillance for commuter rail	Trenton, NJ, USA, public transit system	No information on implementation or evaluation
Petty (1977)	Security force	Dallas, USA, 3 public housing projects	$1,000 reduction weekly in losses due to vandalism and theft. Problem: Funding.
Broski (1978)	Exterior and interior lighting; unbreakable glass; night custodians; electronic detectors	Ohio, USA, 360 schools	Not reported
Christensen (1978)	Increased user involvement by encouraging through verbal and printed appeals to intervene in or report rule violations	USA recreation and camping ground	After appeals, 3 reactions to (staged) littering increase: reporting (10%) intervention (7%) litter pick up by witness (17%)
HUD Challenge (1978)	Conversion to co-operative form of management	1,523 housing units in Baltimore, USA	Reduction in extensive teenage vandalism (also less vacancies, turnover, and rent delinquency)
Sensenig et al. (1978)	Environmental: security personnel, alarm systems, unbreakable glass, etc. Social: contingency fund for vandalism repairs, surplus for students; offenses tried by jury of peers; police officers teaching courses to improve ties with students. Psychological: making students or parents pay for damage; enhancing self-esteem by professional peer couseling & extracurricular activities.	Urban schools	Not reported
Becker (1980)	Increased involvement of students in procedures regarding maintenance, damage reporting; awareness meetings. Faster response by administrators and repairmen to requests for information and repair	Dormitories at The Pennsylvania State University, USA	One year after implementation 45% reduction in vandalism cost in target buildings with cost in non-target buildings going up. Problem: sustaining student interest.

Table 3 continued

SOURCE	STRATEGY OR PROGRAMS	SETTING	EFFECTIVENESS
Sykes (1980: 95-99)	Checklist of improved design features and construction materials	England, educational buildings	No information on implementation
Graham (1981)	Increasing detection rate to near 100% while maintaining small punishment only	Low Newton, England remand center	Reductions in broken window panes after experimental period from 60% to 85%. Results sign. at $p < .001$ (X^2). Concern: possibility of displaced vandalism
Mayer and Butterworth (1981)	Visits and counsel to project classrooms by trained teams of graduate psych. students, model teachers, and principal. Teams plan and assess school needs, e.g., cafeteria, playground, community relations, based on social learning and operant theory	20 elementary and junior high schools in Los Angeles County, USA	Average monthly vandalism cost per 100 students decreased sign. In Treatment Group as compared w/Non-Treatment Group in 1st and 2nd year of 3-yr. program. Savings maintained in 3rd year. Effects generalized from model teachers' classrooms throughout project schools. Also decrease in students yelling, hitting, throwing objects, not doing assigned work, etc.
Torres (1981)	Poster & slogan contest among 6-18 yr. olds w/ monetary prizes; certificates of achievement and increase community recognition by involvement of police, parents, school administration, small business, and civic organizations	Montville, NJ., USA; suburb of 16,000 primarily residential w/ small business and little manufacturing	Reduction in 1980 Halloween vandalism as compared to previous year. No specification.
Sleep (1982)	Inserting sensitized strips in periodicals as part of electronic theft prevention security systems	Library of Brock University, Canada	Two years after implementation of the system the periodical loss rate was basically the same and mutilations had increased

long-term in nature. Here, gradual processes such as changes in values and attitudes with respect to the environment and the people with whom this environment is shared are stressed as being important (U.S. Department of Housing and Urban Development, 1978, 1979). Corresponding to the distinction between a 'physical' and a 'social' tack is a distinction which contraposes a 'product' with a 'process' approach. Architects and planners naturally attempt to produce a perfect environment, a ready-made, vandal-proof package (see fig. 1) delivered to the user and meant to last a lifetime or more. In

"The council were worried it might get vandalised"

Figure 1. Target hardening and an emphasis on delivering 'vandal-proof' products (reprinted with permission of *Private Eye*).

comparison, proponents of a process approach (not necessarily excluding design professionals) stress the significance of social organization, arguing that no building or neighborhood can ever be guaranteed to be free of vandalism without continuous user concern about and involvement in the environmental maintenance and management process.

The two general strategies sketched above – directed at the physical and social environment, respectively – and their more specific derivatives are not, of course, mutually exclusive or contradictory. Like many environmental 'real world' problems, vandalism too is a multifaceted problem; therefore, it would be myopic to cut up its composite elements along 'artificially' set boundaries delimiting the domains of design professionals and social behavioral scientists. Instead, it would be more profitable to view the alternative perspectives on vandalism as supplementing each other, each in itself providing potentially valid, yet *partial* answers to the questions asked. Unfortunately, there is little evidence in the extant literature for such theoretical and methodological triangulation of the problem.

4. An agenda

While at times commenting upon the literature, this review has so far been a predominantly descriptive ordering of available data and existing research on vandalism. This last section will pull together the previous parts of this paper and point out remaining lacunae and gaps in the literature. What follows is not intended as a complete research agenda or an ideal anti-vandalism program but rather a listing of some issues which need to be addressed in further work on vandalism.

4.1. Triangulation

The complexity of the problem indicates a need to experiment with the simultaneous adoption of various supplementary anti-vandalism measures. By way of illustration, the background and nature of one proposal along these lines are described below.

In recent years, the cost of damages due to vandalism in dormitories has become of serious concern to the administration of The Pennsylvania State University. To combat the problem, a damage reduction model program was instituted. It is based on a theory of residence 'hallativity' according to which students view the university as a large and impersonal structure, "ripping you off if it can find a way to do so" (Becker, 1980). Frustration generated by the inability to make an impact on this bureaucracy would manifest itself in aggression against the most immediate and direct extension of the university, the dormitory environment. The damage reduction model attemps to reduce vandalism by increasing, in a variety of ways, student involvement in the maintenance of dormitories.

In an initial evaluation of the effectiveness of the program, a senior class of students majoring in Man–Environment Relations at Penn State identified several more specific components and various other factors which seemed relevant but which had not been included in the original model. For example, the model had appeared to be oblivious to the role of the physical environment and the composition of the dormitory population. The students also deemed it important to develop some form of dormitory self-management in addition to the implemented more limited participation in maintenance of the dormitory environment. In recognition of the need for a broad-based approach, including these and other considerations, the students formulated recommendations for the simultaneous adoption of multiple interventions in the physical and social dormitory environment. Numerous specific measures were proposed as derived from general strategies addressing generic 'social' issues such as user participation in environmental decision making, behavior modification of vandals, and increasing social cohesion in dormitories in conjunction with environmental attitude restructuring. These social strategies were to be implemented in tandem with physical strategies such as 'target hardening' and developing 'defensible space' characteristics. Also, Merry (1981) and the U.S. Department of Housing and Urban Development (1978, 1979), have recently stressed the need for coordinating social and physical factors in achieving residential safety. While the effectiveness of the proposed measures has to await their implementation, they represent a rudimentary but orchestrated attempt illustrating triangulation of the problem of dormitory vandalism.

Experimentation with this kind of approach is warranted, but it should be noted that triangulation may not be appropriate in every case. More systematic and comprehensive assessments than those contained in table 3 should clarify which programs are most effective alone and in combination and under which conditions.

4.2. Evaluation

An extension of the last point is the need for sound evaluation research. There is certainly no lack of recommendations on how to deal with vandalism. [4] The problem is that a substantial number of proposals does not reach the stage of implementation and that a still smaller number is ever assessed with respect to their effectiveness in reducing vandalism. However, systematic evaluation of anti-vandalism programs should be an integral component of such programs and may take several forms (cf. Freeman, 1977; Schnelle et al., 1975; Suchman, 1967). First, the *program itself and its implementation* need to be scrutinized. What are the objectives of the program? Has the appropriate target population been selected? Have the intervention efforts been undertaken as specified in the program? These and similar questions serve to assess the soundness of the organization of the program and to determine whether it has been implemented in accordance with stated guidelines and criteria. A second type of evaluative questions concerns the *impact* of the program. Did it achieve its goals? In which ways are changes attributable to the program? Could an alternative program be more effective? And what are possible side effects, negative (e.g., simple displacement of the problem to another area) as well as positive (e.g., recreation functions which are legitimate and worthy in and of themselves without necessarily also reducing vandalism – the provision of recreation facilities, for instance).

The above two types of evaluation research are rather technical in nature. In comparison, a third set of questions is more value-laden. It identifies the ideological system and values from which the program's principles are derived and examines these vis-à-vis the available evidence. For example, anti-vandalism programs may center on fostering social cohesion among adolescents by

---

[4]   In the U.S.A., an extensive listing of proposals and projects is available from the Smithsonian Information Exchange and the National Criminal Justice Referral System.

establishing a neighborhood community center on the assumption that a lack of local ties leads to alienation manifesting itself also in vandalism (Byrne, 1977; Mergen, 1977). Such programs raise at least two critical issues. First, there is the question to what extent social cohesion inhibits vandalism. Criminal mischief by delinquents is often committed by close-knit gangs (Herbert, 1980; Bogert, 1980); Phillips and Bartlett (1976) report that 93% of the cases of vandalism they studied were group actions. It is likely that promoting social cohesion is effective only to the extent that it reinforces concurrently transmitted 'right' values. Second, the function of the local neighborhood for the social integration of adolescents would need to be examined. Some studies indicate that adolescents' social frame of reference may extend far beyond the neighborhood (Bernard, 1939; Heinemeijer and De Sitter, 1964).

4.3. Theory

A large majority of the vandalism programs and studies lacks theoretical underpinnings and is simply based on spontaneous reaction to, and ad hoc interpretation of, a given vandalism problem. However, vandalistic incidents do not, of course, occur in a vacuum as if they were episodes in and of themselves which can be studied in isolation from the broader behavioral context surrounding them. Reade (1982: 37) has rightly argued that vandalism is best understood not as a phenomenon *sui generis*, but as merely one aspect of, or even as a consequence of, a wider syndrome of attitudes and behavior. This point has been noted by several authors (e.g., Griffiths and Shapland, 1980: 16; Wilson, 1980: 21; Blaber, 1980: 41) and indicates the need to go beyond purely empirical observations and narrow positivistic explanations, instead situating vandalism within a more encompassing theoretical framework. One such framework is provided by a developmental perspective according to which vandalism and related behaviors may be seen as responses of young people to a normative system which denies them opportunities for engaging in responsible and constructive social and environmental tasks. Theory indicates that the 'fourth environment' outside the home, school, and playground, fulfills important functions regarding, for example, the development of a self-concept and the acquisition of skills facilitating children's gradual integration into the adult world (Van Vliet, forthcoming). There are indications in the literature that chances to become involved in and help shape one's social and physical environment heighten one's sense of responsibility toward it (e.g., Turner, 1976). The question for planners and designers then becomes to understand children's developmental needs and to deduce from them guidelines for the provision of opportunities for meaningful participation. [5] The concept of the adventure playground fits in here (Bengts-

---

[5]   Also pertinent to the issue of participatory development is the notion of (perceived) control

son, 1972), as does the contribution of children to the design of a school yard (Moore, 1980), and the self-management of dormitories (Becker, 1977).

This participatory development approach is premised upon suppositions concerning children's competence and the total community repertoire of social, political, and economic roles deemed appropriate for them. Therefore, this approach cannot remain confined to 'patches' set apart specifically for young people but, quite to the contrary, has to concern itself explicitly with ways of integrating settings which accomodate young people's special needs in the 'real' world. A developmental perspective on vandalism seems worthy of further exploration for two reasons. First, because a large proportion of vandalism is committed by teenagers and adolescents and, second, because vandalism is so common in these developmental stages.

Earlier it was already stressed that vandalism really is an umbrella label covering a set of widely different behaviors. Consequently, the foregoing conceptualization which relates developmental needs to developmental opportunities in the environmental and community context (see sections 4.4 and 4.5 below) can supply a partial view only. At quite another level of analysis, vandalism can be seen as a reflection of changes in social order resulting from interactions between broad societal processes such as industrialization, urbanization and bureaucratization (Pearson, 1978). In this view, vandalism is not mindless, wanton destruction characterized by de-individuation (Zimbardo, 1973), but instead it is a pattern of *purposeful* and *organized* behavior protesting against prevailing institutional structures and inequalities generated by existing resource allocation mechanisms (Tilly, 1978).

This is not the place to develop these theoretical perspectives on vandalism more fully. The aim here is to offer some thought on starting points for possible conceptualizations of the problem, not excluding alternative views (see, e.g., Allen and Greenberger, 1978; Abel and Buckley, 1977; Arlan and McDowell, 1980; Richards, 1979; Fisher and Baron, 1982). Testing of theoretically derived hypotheses is essential to develop these and alternative notions further so as to avoid narrow anti-vandalism programs directed at symptomatic manifestations of much broader issues.

4.4 Environmental context

To the extent that studies of vandalism have examined environmental aspects of vandalistic behavior, the concern has commonly been with the environment

---

which has been more fully addressed in research on density effects (e.g., Rodin, 1976), and which seems to underlie findings in the literature linking vandalism to age-status conflicts (Richards, 1979), attempts at identity expression (Brown, 1978) and territorial control (Ley and Cybriwsky, 1974b), and engagement in passive recreation (Csikszenkmihalyi et al., 1977). See also Allen and Greenberger (1980) for a useful discussion of the relation between destruction and perceived control.

where the incident occurred. Thus, features of defensible space and target hardening have been subjects of research (Booth, 1981; Mawby, 1977). It would seem worthwhile to expand the environmental focus of research on vandalism by including fuller consideration of the environment of the offender(s). In this regard, the neighborhood in particular is important to the extent and in the ways that it provides opportunities for alternative preferential behaviors. Environmental analyses of offender neighborhoods, such as inventories of land uses and available behavior settings, are beset by such difficulties as the small proportion of offenders that are actually apprehended and hindrances in obtaining access to confidential data. Nonetheless, such research may well be worth the effort because the *spatial* shift from the environment of the vandalized object to the environment of the vandal(s) also means a *temporal* shift from the product of vandalistic behavior to the producer(s) of that behavior, suggesting a little explored but potentially fruitful locus of environmental intervention. It should be noted, however, that the offender's local environment acts mostly as an intervening variable between the offender and a more encompassing social, economic, and political system which produces an unequal distribution of environmental opportunities for both socially desirable and undesirable behaviors.

4.5. Community context

It appears that, by and large, studies of vandalism have given passing notice at best to possible effects of community characteristics on vandalism. This level of analysis may be quite relevant, however, in directing attention to contextual variables which form an essential component of the total constellation of factors that need to be considered in explanations of vandalistic behavior. Support for this viewpoint is provided by a number of studies which have found property crime to be related to such community characteristics as composition of the population (Bates, 1962), per capita income (Blaber, 1979), transportation routes and pattern of commercial land uses (Hakim, 1980), population density (Cohen et al., 1980), number of permanent residences (O'Donnell and Lydgate, 1980), and proportion of female-headed households (Phillips and Bartlett, 1976). In a related vein, in a number of cross-sectional studies various socio-economic and demographic community characteristics have been found to define ecological contexts associated with child maltreatment (Garbarino and Crouter, 1978) and Steinberg et al. (1981) have shown in a longitudinal study how increases in child abuse were preceded by increases in the unemployment rate. A more intangible, but certainly no less important contextual factor is the value system embraced by a community and the norms embodied by its members, making up an essential component of the macrosystem surrounding growing children (Bronfenbrenner, 1978).

While it is quite clear that vandalism is not an exclusive function of community characteristics, there can be little doubt that supra-individual conditions such as those named above increase or reduce opportunities for vandalism and influence young people's propensity to 'use' those opportunities. Furthermore, community characteristics may be seen as parameters defining the range of feasible anti-vandalism strategies and as enhancing or decreasing the effectiveness of more specific ameliorative measures.

5. Conclusion

This chapter has reviewed the state of the evidence on vandalism. It has indicated that vandalism is a pervasive and costly problem. Different approaches to this problem were pointed out and an agenda outlining remaining issues was proposed. The chapters that follow will provide a fuller coverage of several of the questions that were identified as salient ones and will add insights from case studies. In reflecting upon the foregoing review, two related matters stand out as meriting special attention.

The first concerns the circumstances under which a given behavior gets classified as vandalism. For example, grounds, shrubs and trees in an urban park may get damaged within the context of games, largely because of a lack of adequate opportunities for play elsewhere; the children and teenagers doing the damage may be considered criminal offenders and be punishable as such (Harvey, 1982); however, within the context of urban renewal vastly more destructive acts (often depriving children of play space) are officially sanctioned. This issue of what gets labelled as vandalism, and what does not, is nicely captured in the observation: 'If a car hits a child, that is an accident, but if a child damages a car, that is vandalism',[6] and discussed more extensively by Cohen elsewhere in this volume.

Questions regarding *who* defines vandalism, and *why*, lead to the second point which concerns the increasingly accepted view that vandalism is *not* meaningless, senseless, wanton and willful damage and destruction. Rather, vandalism may be seen as constituting purposeful conduct, devoid of a mature vocabulary of interaction; put otherwise, vandalism is often a manifestly destructive behavior as well as a 'political statement', a latent form of an attempt at communication and participation. Therefore, relevant questions ask about ways to create opportunities and to develop procedures for more appropriate behaviors to achieve objectives of social interaction.

---

[6] *Fair play for children*, National Playing Fields Association, England; cited by Patricia MacKay, p. 21 in: W. Michelson, S.V. Levine and E. Michelson (eds.), *The child in the city: today and tomorrow*, Toronto, University of Toronto Press, 1979.

References

Abel, Ernest L., Barbara A. Buckley, 1977. Handwriting on the wall – Toward a sociology and psychology of graffiti. Westport (Conn): Greenwood Press.

Allen, V.G., D.B. Greenberger, 1978. Aesthetic theory of vandalism. Crime and Delinquency 24 (3), 309–321.

Allen, V.L., D.B. Greenberger, 1980. Destruction and perceived control. In: A. Baum, J. Singer, eds., Advances in environmental psychology, vol. II. Hillside (N.J.):Erlbaum.

[Anonymous,] 1978/79. The heavyweight thieves. Journal of American Insurance 54 (4), 26–30.

Arlan, J.P., C.P. McDowell, 1980. Vindictive vandalism and schools – Some theoretical considerations. Journal of Police Science and Administration 8 (4), 399–405.

Bartholo, A.A., K.L. Milte, 1979. Psychiatry and the railway vandal. Australian and New Zealand Journal of Criminology 12 (3), 175–176.

Bates, J.A., M. Martin, 1980. The thematic content of graffiti as a non-reactive indicator of male and female attitudes. Journal of Sex Research 16 (6), 300–315.

Bates, William, 1962. Caste, class and vandalism. Social Problems 9 (4), 348–353.

Bates, William, Thomas McJunkins, 1962. Vandalism and status differences. Pacific Sociological Review 5 (2), 89–92.

Bayh, Birch, 1977. Challenge for the third century: Education in a safe environment. Final Report of the Subcommittee to Investigate Juvenile Delinquency, 95th Congress, 1st Session. Washington, D.C.: Government Printing Office.

Bayh, B., 1978. School violence and vandalism – Problems and solutions. Journal of Research and Development in Education 11 (2), 2–7.

Becker, F.D., 1977. User participation, personalization, and environmental meaning: Three field studies. Ithaca (NY): Urban & Regional Studies Program, Cornell University.

Becker, T.M., 1980. Report on the residential damage reduction model. Unpublished report. The Pennsylvania State University, Association of Residential Hall Students.

Bengtsson, A., 1972. Adventure playgrounds. New York: Praeger.

Bennett, J.W., 1969. Vandals wild. Portland: Bennett Publishing Co.

Berk, Richard A., Howard E. Aldrich, 1972. Patterns of vandalism during civil disorders as an indicator of selection of targets. American Sociological Review 37 (5).

Bernard, J., 1939. The neighborhood behavior of school kids in relation to age and socio-economic status. American Sociological Review 4, 652–662.

Blaber, A., 1980. The Cunningham Road scheme. In: J. Sykes, ed., Designing against vandalism, pp. 30–53. New York: Van Nostrand Reinhold.

Blyth, D.A., K.S. Thiel, D.M. Bush, R.G. Simmons, 1980. Another look at school crime; student as victim. Youth and Society 11 (3), 369–388.

Bogert, V., 1980. Freaking people out and other acts of vandalism. Childhood City Newsletter (special issue on 'Adolescents and vandalism') November 21, 4–6.

Booth, Alan, 1981. The built environment as a crime deterrent: A reexamination of defensible space. Dept. of Sociology, University of Nebraska. An abbreviated version appears in Criminology 18, 557–570.

Brickman, W., 1976. Vandalism and violence in school and society. Intellect 104 (2374), 503 (April).

Brill, M., 1977. Concepts for reducing vandalism and destruction of Navy military occupant quarters. Port Hueneme (CA): U.S. Dept. of Defense, Navy Civil Engineering Lab.

Bronfenbrenner, U., 1978. The social role of the child in ecological perspective. Zeitschrift für Soziologie 7 (1), 4–20.

Broski, David J., 1978. Ohio school vandalism: Characteristics and preventive measures. Dissertation Abstract International 38, 11-A, 6409.

Brown, Waln K., 1978. Graffiti, identity and the delinquent gang, International Journal of Offender Therapy and Comparative Criminology 22 (1), 46–48.

Bruner, Edward, Jane Paige Kelso, 1980. Gender differences in graffiti: A semiotic perspective. Women's Studies International Quartely 3 (2-3), 239–252.

Burall, P., 1980. Children's playgrounds. In: J. Sykes, ed., Designing against vandalism. New York: Van Nostrand Reinhold.

Burich T., 1979. New Haven anti-crime consortium. New Haven (Conn): New Haven Boys Clubs Inc.

Byrne, S., 1977. Nobody home: The erosion of the American family. Psychology Today 10 (2), 40–43, 45–47.

Christensen, Harriet H., 1978. Bystander reaction to illegal behavior in a forested recreation area. Dissertation Abstracts International 39, 6-B, 2588.

Clarke, R.V.G., ed., 1978. Tackling vandalism. Home Office Research Study no. 47. London: Her Majesty's Stationery Office.

Cohen, L.E., M. Felson, K.C. Land, 1980. Property crime rates in the United States: A macrodynamic analysis, 1947-1977; with ex ante forecasts for the mid 1980s. American Journal of Sociology 86 (1), 90–118.

Cohen, S., 1973. Property destruction: Motives and meanings. In: C. Ward, ed., Vandalism, pp. 23–53. New York: Van Nostrand Reinhold.

Commission on Crime and Delinquency. Vandalism: How to protect your home and property from vandals. Harrisburg (PA): Governor's Office, CCD., N.D.

Cornacchione, Frank, 1977. Juvenile vandalism: A typology. Police Chief 44 (July), 64–50.

Csikszentmihalyi, M., R. Larson, S. Prescott, 1977. The ecology of adolescent activity and experiences. Journal of Youth and Adolescence 6 (3), 281–294.

Damron, Thomas C., 1979. A survey of practices used to reduce and eliminate vandalism in municipal parks and recreation areas in Kentucky. Comprehensive Dissertation Index, Supplement, p. 110.

Davis, Earle E., Margret Fine-Davis, 1981. Predictors of satisfaction with housing and neighborhoods. Social Indicators Research 9, 474–494.

Donnermeyer, J.F., Ph. G. Howard, 1980. The nature of vandalism among rural youth. Paper presented at the 1980 annual meeting of the Rural Sociological Society, August 19–23, Cornell University, Ithaca (NY).

Dukiet, K.H., 1973. Spotlight on school security. School Management 4 (17), 1–9.

Farmer and Dark, 1973. The architect's dilemma: One firm's working notes. In: C. Ward, ed., Vandalism, pp. 112–116. New York: Van Nostrand Reinhold.

Fisher, J.D., R.M. Baron, 1982. An equity-based model of vandalism. Population and Environment 5 (3), 182–200.

Freeman, H.E., 1977. The present status of evaluation research. In: M. Gutentag et al., eds., Evaluation studies, vol. 2, pp. 17–52. Beverly Hills: Sage.

Fuellgrabe, V., 1978. Die psychologische und soziologische Analyse des Vandalismus. Kriminalistik 32 (2), 56–61.

Gailey, T., 1983. Directors dispute dorm damage. Collegian Magazine 2 (13) 26.

Garbarino, J., A. Crouter, 1978. Defining the community context for parent-child relations: The correlates of child maltreatment. Child Development 49, 604–616.

Gladstone, F.J., 1978. Vandalism amongst adolescent school boys. In: R.V.G. Clarke, ed., Tackling vandalism. Home Office Research Study no. 47. London: HMSO.

Glaser, D., 1979. Economic and sociocultural variables affecting rates of youth unemployment, delinquency, and crime. Youth and Society 11 (1), 53–82.

Glazer, Nathan, 1979. On subway graffiti in New York. The Public Interest 54, 31–11.

Goldemeir, H., 1974. Vandalism: The effect of unmanageable confrontations. Adolescence 9 (33), 49–56.

Graf, C.R., A.W. Roberts, 1976. Transit crime study. Trenton (N.J.): State Bureau of Operation Research.

Graham, F., 1981. Probability of detection and institutional vandalism. The British Journal of Criminology 21 (4), 361–366.

Greenberg, B., 1974. School vandalism: Its effects and paradoxical solutions. Crime Prevention Review, January, pp. 11–18.

Greenberg, P., 1976. To edit – or not to edit. The Masthead 28 (3), 3–5.

Griffith, J.W., 1978. Overdue – of vagrants and vandals and library things. Wilson Library Bulletin 52 (10), 169.

Griffiths, R., J.M. Shapland, 1980. The vandal's perspective: Meanings and motives. In: J. Sykes, ed., Designing against vandalism, pp. 11–19. New York: Van Nostrand Reinhold.

Hakim, S., 1980. The attraction of property crimes to suburban localities: a revised economic model. Urban Studies 17, 265–276.

Harvey, J., 1982. Vandalism in the residential environment. Monograph no. 3, Children's Environments Advisory Service. Ottawa: Canada Mortgage and Housing Corporation.

Heinemeijer, W., L. de Sitter, 1964. Buurt, jeugd en vrije tijd. Amsterdam.

Herbert, D.T., 1980. Urban crime: A geographical perspective. In: D.T. Herbert, D.M. Smith, eds., Social problems and the city, pp. 117–139. New York: Oxford University Press.

Howard, J.L., 1978. Factors in school vandalism. Journal of Research and Development in Education 11 (2), 53–63.

HUD Challenge, 1978. Comparison of operating costs (March), p. 28.

Irwin, James R., 1976. Vandalism – Its prevention and control. NASSP Bulletin 60 (400), pp. 55–59.

Jephcott, P., 1971. Homes in high flats. Oliver & Boyd.

Klein, S.M., J.S. Feiner, 1980. Vandalism as cultural conflict: New York graffiti war. Childhood City Newsletter, November (special issue on 'Adolescents and vandalism') 21, 7–10.

Larsson, N.K., 1982. The nature of child-related maintenance and vandalism problems in CMHC housing projects. Research Project no. 3, Children's Environments Advisory Service. Ottawa: Canada Mortgage and Housing Corporation.

Leather, A., A. Matthews, 1973. What the architect can do: A series of design guidelines. In: C. Ward, ed., Vandalism, pp. 117–172. New York: Van Nostrand Reinhold.

Levine, E.M., C. Kozak, 1979. Drug and alcohol-use, delinquency, and vandalism among upper middle class pre-adolescents, and post-adolescents. Journal of Youth and Adolescence 8 (1), 91–107.

Ley, D., R. Cybriwski, 1974a. The spatial ecology of stripped cars. Environment and Behavior 6, 53–68.

Ley, D., R. Cybriwski, 1974b. Urban graffiti as territorial markers. Annals of the Association of American Geographers 64, 491–505.

McCann, T., 1980. Auto takes beating as WDFM holds 'smash in'. The Daily Collegian, October 16, p. 3.

Marshall, T., 1976. Vandalism: The seeds of destruction. New Society, June 17, 625–627.

Mawby, R.I., 1977. Kiosk vandalism: A Sheffield study. British Journal of Criminology 17 (1), 30–46.

Mayer, G.R., Th. W. Butterworth, 1979. A preventive approach to school violence and vandalism: An experimental study. Personnel and Guidance Journal 57, 436–441.

Mayer, G.R., Th. W. Butterworth, 1981. Evaluating a preventive approach to vandalism. Phi Delta Kappa 62 (7), 498–499.

Mergen, A., 1977. Der jugendliche Staftater. Kriminalistik 31 (7), 298–301.

Merry, Sally E., 1981. Defensible space undefended: Social factors in crime control through environmental design. Urban Affairs Quarterly 16 (6), 397–422.

Miller, A., 1973. Vandalism and the architect. In: C. Ward, ed., Vandalism, pp. 96–111. New York: Van Nostrand Reinhold.

Miller, M., 1979. Project security self-help. Brooklyn (NY): Tompkins Houses Tenant Association, Inc.

Moore, Robin C., 1980. Generating relevant urban childhood places: Learning from the 'yard'. In: Paul F. Wilkinson, ed., Innovation in play environments, pp. 45–76. New York: St. Martin's Press.

New York Magazine, 1977. The graffiti 'hit' parade. In: William E. Arnold, Jerry L. Buley, eds., Urban communication: Survival in the city, pp. 2–5. Cambridge (Mass.): Winthrop (orig. publ. 1973).

Newman, O., 1980. Community of interest. Garden City (NY): Anchor Press.,

O'Donnell, G.R., T. Lydgate, 1980. The relationship to crimes of physical resources. Environment and Behavior 12 (2), 207–230.

Oswald, T., 1981. Washington County juvenile restitution alternative. Washington, D.C.: U.S. Dept. of Justice, Law Enforcement Assistance Administration.

Pablant, P., J.C. Baxter, 1975. Environmental correlates of school vandalism. Journal of the American Institute of Planners 42, 270–279.

Page, C., 1977. Vandalism – it happens every night. Nation's Cities, Sept., pp. 5–10.

Pearson, G., 1978. Goths and vandals: Crime in history. Contemporary Crises 2 (2), 119–139.

Pennsylvania State Police, 1980. Crime in Pennsylvania: 1979. Uniform Crime Report. Harrisburg: Bureau of Research and Development, PA State Police.

Petty, Ann E., 1977. Concentrated security program. Journal of Housing 34 (8), 388.

Peuleche, T., 1979. Vandalism as a design consideration in urban parks and plazas. Doctoral dissertation, Dept. of Architecture, University of Georgia.

Phillips, G.H., K.F. Bartlett, 1976. Vandals and vandalism in rural Ohio. Wooster (Ohio): Ohio Agricultural Research and Development Center.

Pietro, L., 1980. State College establishes anti-vandalism campaign. Clearfield Progress, March 6.

Pullen, D., 1975. Memoirs of vandalism. New Society, February 6.

Reade, Eric, 1982. Residential decay, household movement, and class structure. Policy and Politics 10 (1), 27–45.

Reid, John B., 1975. No fault vandalism. Best's Review H/L 75 (10), 54–56.

Reilly, Dennis, H., 1978. Coping with vandalism in family, school and community. Hackensack (N.J.): National Council on Crime and Community.

Richards, P., 1979. Middle-class vandalism and age status conflict. Social Problems 26 (4), 482–497.

Rodin, J., 1976. Crowding, perceived choice, and response to controllable and uncontrollable outcomes. Journal of Experimental Social Psychology 12, 564–578.

Rose, Floyd S., 1978. The effect of violence and vandalism on the completion of the education process. Diss. Abstr. Intern. 1978, no. 7A, 3865.

Schnelle, J.F., R.E. Kirchner, M.P. McWees, J.M. Lawler, 1975. Social evaluation research: the evaluation of two police patrolling strategies. Journal of Applied Behavior Analysis 8, 353–365.

Sensenig, B., T.L. Sensenig, B.R. Spykerman, 1978. Environmental, social and psychological approaches to the prevention of school vandalism. Society for the Study of Social Problems (SSSP 1978 1026).

Severino, M., 1972. Who pays or should pay when young vandals smash things up in your schools. American School Board Journal 159 (12), 33–43.

Sleep, E.L., 1982. Periodical vandalism – A chronic condition. Canadian Library 39 (1), 39–45.

Spalding, T.L., 1971. Door hardware to check vandalism. School Management 15 (10), 30–31.

Steinberg, L.D., R. Catlano, P. Dooley, 1981. Economic antecedents of child abuse and neglect. Child Development 52, 975–985.

Stormer, D.E., 1979. Catch the vandal. Daily Collegian, December 12.

Suchman, E.A., 1967. Evaluative research: Principles and practice in public service and social action programs. New York: Russell Sage Foundation.

Sykes, J., ed., 1980. Designing against vandalism. New York: Van Nostrand Reinhold.

Tilly, Ch., 1978. From mobilization to revolution. Reading (Mass.): Addison-Wesley.

Torres, D.A., 1981. Vandalism prevention. The Police Chief, March, pp. 21–23.

Turner, J.F.C., 1976. Housing by people: Towards autonomy in building environments. London: Marion Boyars.

U.S. Bureau of Investigation, 1979. Crime in the U.S. Washington, D.C.: U.S. Gov't Printing Office.

U.S. Department of Housing and Urban Development, 1973. Las Vegas housing evaluation. Washington, D.C.: U.S. Gov't Printing Office.

U.S. Department of Housing and Urban Development, 1978. Crime in public housing: A review of major issues and selected crime reduction strategies. 2 vols. Washington, D.C.: U.S. Gov't Printing Office.

U.S. Department of Housing and Urban Development, 1979. Planning for housing security: Assessing the social environment. Washington, D.C.: U.S. Gov't Printing Office.

U.S. Department of Transportation, 1980. Railroad vandalism. Washington, D.C.: Federal Railroad Administration.

U.S. Senate Judiciary Subcommittee, 1975. Our nation's schools – A report card; 'A' in school violence and vandalism. Report to the Senate Subcommittee to investigate property damage, 67-589-0-76-2, 1–39 (cited in Fisher and Baron, 1982).

Van Vliet, W., forthcoming. Exploring the fourth environment: an examination of the home range of city and suburban teenagers. Environment and Behavior (Sept./Nov., 1983).

Ward, C., 1978. The child in the city. London: The Architectural Press.

Wilson, S., 1980. Observations on the nature of vandalism. In: J. Sykes, ed., Designing against vandalism, pp. 19–29. New York: Van Nostrand Reinhold.

Zeisel, J., 1976. Stopping school property damage. Boston: American Ass. of School Administrators and Educational Facilities Laboratories/City of Boston Public Facilities Department.

Zimbardo, Philip G., 1973. The human choice: Individuation, reason and order vs. deindividuation, impulse and chaos. In: John Helmer, Neil A. Eddington, eds., Urban man: The psychology of urban survival, pp. 196–238. New York: The Free Press.

Abstract: W. van Vliet, Vandalism: an assessment and agenda

The literature shows little consensus as to what constitutes vandalism and how it might be dealt with. Numerous reports have been written and conclusions formulated without the benefit of knowledge of other studies on the topic. Research has been scattered rather than cumulative, and a synthesis of the work on vandalism is lacking. This chapter attempts to address this gap. After a brief prelude – indicating the extent of the problem in terms of young people's involvement in vandalism, the range of environments affected, and the magnitude of economic and socio-psychological costs – various perspectives on vandalism are reviewed.

It appears that much of the work on vandalism is opinionative and lacks scientific rigor. The divergent and often inconclusive statements are, in large part, attributable to differences in the definition of vandalism and the operationalization of contributing factors, the variety of data gathering techniques, the lack of control for influences of extraneous variables, and the absence of systematic considerations regarding research design and sampling procedure. The evidence brought forward in support of a given viewpoint is more often than not informal in nature and based on casual observations and personal professional experiences.

Two general approaches to vandalism are distinguished. The first is primarily concerned with features of the physical environment (e.g., locks and lights); the second focuses especially on characteristics of the social environment (e.g., peer interaction and housing management). These approaches are seen as leading to different ameliorative strategies based on the delivery of environmental products for social groups and the organization of social groups vis-à-vis their environment, respectively. Following a discussion of future directions for work on vandalism, the chapter's conclusion raises questions concerning the definition and functions of vandalism.

PART ONE

Theoretical approaches to vandalism

Vandalism: speech acts

J. SÉLOSSE

It may seem almost provocative to publish a collective volume on vandalism when one remembers that the very definition of the concept is far from clear. It is enough to read through the literature to see that the scope of the term varies considerably from author to author according to their discipline (e.g. sociology, law, planning, etc.) and to their principal preoccupations: explanation, prevention, negotiation, etc.

Furthermore, the concept has many meanings. It covers a multitude of behavioural sins ranging from the daubing of graffiti on a wall to the pillaging of a public building whilst including the destruction of parking meters or the removal of road signs. It is applied to the multiform activities involved in games, pranks, reactions of frustration and ideological protest, whether undertaken single or in groups.

Moreover, while the occurrence of vandalism is quite obvious owing to its material effects – to such an extent in fact that its social costs affect the estimation of local authority budgets – it must be admitted that very little is actually known about the vandals themselves. In other words, the functions which the various types of vandalistic behaviour are reputed to fulfil can only be conditional and ambiguous. They depend mainly on the interests of those affected by such behaviour, but, in the way they are depicted, they give rise to representations and reactions which encourage collective feeling of disapproval and which contribute to the maintenance of group solidarity in terms of emotions.

The diversity of vandalism gives rise to varying interpretations according to the thresholds of tolerance to deviations from the norms in question: daubing walls, changing the import of hoardings, upsetting the workings of automatic dispensers or damaging telephone booths do not meet with the same degree of disapproval from all witnesses of such acts. In other words, vandalism, just like any other problem behaviour, affects only certain people and consequently its definition depends largely on those who are the most inconvenienced by it. Vandalism raises, firstly, the question of identifying the norm and the function whose working has been disturbed. These then influence the type of reaction generated and therefore the social group aware of the phenomenon. Following this, a process of vandal identification and penalisation builds up.

While the study of vandalism results in it being considered as a form of social deviance, it is in the researcher's own interest to try and pick out specific aspects of it. Among these, it seems reasonable to state that vandalised objects are mainly of a communal nature: visibility is certainly one of the dimensions of vandalism.

The areas and facilities providing the backdrop to vandalistic activity are also communal, while a goodly portion of the damage constitutes a challenge to the normative organisation of power and to solidarity in terms of both communal and private interests.

Vandalism constitutes deviance with respect to others as opposed to deviance affecting oneself, such as theft, or deviance as such, like drug addiction. Just as with any other public form of deviant behaviour, however, its analysis raises questions with respect to the reactions manifested as a result of its occurrence. When such reactions are publicly displayed, involving social solidarity, the feelings to which they correspond will vary according to the degree to which individuals are directly affected by the trouble caused. Reactions of this sort will, like all collective social manifestations, be in search of a code of legitimacy with a view to presenting a united front to such difficulties. This approach calls for a determined attempt to define, explain, put down and prevent vandalism. As a general rule, collective reactions are expressed in polarised, dichotomous terms on a scale of value judgements consisting of 'good' and 'bad'.

This involves the whole of society, or certain categories with similar interests or of the same age or sex, resorting to an attributive function connected to various frames of reference (e.g., legal, ethical, aesthetic, utilitarian) on which the interpretation of deviance is based. In this way, the problematical phenomenon finds itself locked into the categories of concepts and judgements which are supposed to be used to understand it. It is known that concepts model and structure analyses undertaken in this way and that the instrumentalist study of a behaviour or situation affects the information which is being dealt with. This is why one of the basic questions, arising inexorably from the study of social problems and inevitably influencing them, is whether or not there can be agreement between what may be termed scientific legitimacy and a code of legitimacy. This would appear to me to constitute one of the main points raised by the colloquium: a full definition, however, lies outside its scope.

Van Vliet's analysis of the main themes of the international literature on vandalism (ch. 1) enables us to distinguish a certain number of the characteristic features of this social phenomenon.

Vandalism is a fundamentally destructive, world-wide phenomenon which is tending to increase. Perpetrators of acts of vandalism are generally young and correspond to all social backgrounds. Targets are mainly parks, playgrounds, school buildings and facilities, public transport facilities, public buildings and

roads. The damage caused gives rise to considerable costs in terms of refurbishment.

Although the effects of vandalism are obvious, its definition varies considerably according to the laws bearing upon it and the subjectivity involved, which
is particularly apparent in terms of its formulation. This variation corresponds
to the ambiguity which lies at the root of any assessment or justification of
social control faced with the questioning of its own implementation or inadequacies.

A more ecological approach is adopted by those who describe the damaged
environments and proceed to infer motivations as a function of the likely
relationships between a given context and the social actors involved. The
typologies which have been drawn up vary considerably from one researcher to
another.

This spectrum of opinions and definitions has led to great diversity in terms
of strategies and vandalism control projects. At this juncture, it should be
pointed out once again that, when society stands face to face with a problem
which questions its organisation and operation, it tends to seek to eliminate the
problem rather than investigate it. It is easier to condemn than to try and
understand the origins and significance of such manifestations.

The organisation of vandalism control varies according to whether or not
targets are clearly demarcated, whether the strategies adopted are defensive or
preventive, and to what extent its aims concern the materials or social aspects
of the phenomenon.

Van Vliet suggests that a third term be inserted in between the two poles of
material and social aspects. He feels that they should be connected by taking
into account the position and involvement of the individuals implicated by
their participation in a situation. Moreover, the assessment of vandalism
control projects must be based not only on technical criteria but also on the
social values that may be involved (e.g. social cohesion). The theoretical bases
of these projects must go beyond the immediate effects of acts of destruction
and examine their significance as part and parcel of a vast syndrome of
attitudes and behaviour.

I would also stress most strongly the appositeness of the developmental
paradigm in the analysis of the behavioural problems of young vandals. This
paradigm enables us to grasp the range of the protest of certain adolescents
who are less able than adults to transform their material and relational
surroundings, owing to their temporal helplessness and their transient inequality of status. The spatial context has a direct effect on behaviour while the
study of vandalism falls within the purview of transactional psychology in as
much as perceptions and behaviour adjustments depend on personal and social
criteria which can modify the way connections with one's material and
relational surroundings are negotiated. However, it is the social context with its

diverse demographic, sociological, economic, cultural and also ideological criteria which gives meaning to the deliberations of juvenile courts.

Longitudinal studies are still too few and far between to provide the information which is vitally needed to understand the origins of problem behaviour and should highlight the importance of certain factors associated with its appearance.

The fact that it is not possible to put forward a general explanation of this polysemous and polymorphic phenomenon, and thereby to propose a method of prevention workable for all forms of vandalism, means that the public develops feelings of fear and gives rise to repressive attitudes. It is important that researchers take care not to encourage this spiralling growth of insecurity and helplessness.

The empirical study of vandalism has been aimed mainly at finding the causes and assessing the consequences of the phenomenon. Baron and Fisher (ch. 3) propose a new model for looking at the phenomenon from a psycho-sociological standpoint. Given that vandalistic activity is significant, they believe that society's refusal to recognise that this type of behaviour has a structural basis stems from the fact that it refuses to question its system of disparity. If the principle that social activities seek to maintain equality in all relationships is accepted, behavioural motivations are seen as seeking to restore this equality when it has disappeared. This search for a transactional equilibrium applies as much to economic exchanges as to any other socially regulated activity. And when discriminatory practices are perceived as unjust, they can give rise to anti-social responses. The environment itself may be seen as a cause of inequality while the built environment can come to symbolise contrasts and disparities. A normative model of equity based on the theory of reciprocal relations between social partners should be able to account for acts of vandalism, which do not constitute a homogeneous phenomenon. In order to do this, the model's matrix must allow for several factors, notably the perceived control level and the degree of disparity present. When one of these parameters varies, the way in which vandalism manifests itself also changes. Other factors concerning the intensity and specificity of certain types of activity are also involved, viz. the physical state of the environment, apparent signs of appropriation and wear, the symbolic values of objects and buildings and the degree of group cohesion.

When these factors are combined they can either determine or modify vandalism. Interaction among them also makes it possible to assess the short- and long-term effects of vandalism, whilst, above all, making it possible to predict the various types of behaviour perceived as reactions to social malfunctions or disparities. Thus, vandalism is associated with distortions of the communications among social partners.

This view is a stimulating one in that it takes in the whole of the social structure and implicates all participants, not just those who have been driven to reactional conduct, which is often judged externally and unequivocally by social control personnel and generally seen in a context of illegality.

Notwithstanding the foregoing, criminologists consider vandalism to be one of the vaguest phenomena with which they have to deal. Legal definitions are imprecise and vary from one legislature to another. The term 'vandalism' in fact covers a whole range of behaviour. Frequently, this heading corresponds to a sort of residual ragbag characterised nevertheless predominantly by destruction, damage to public and private facilities and breaches of the peace.

Vandals themselves are slightly better known (although noticeable differences have emerged from the various surveys). Most researchers believe them to be between ten and 20 years of age, to act in groups and to be males rather than females.

Official legal or police figures are not particularly reliable as they are either too fragmentary or too inclusive. In France, for example, police figures show that the percentage of solved crimes of damage to public or private property is around 16%. Between 1971 and 1981, the number of these acts almost quadrupled, rising from 42,611 to 175,177 (Commission des Maires, 1982: 20). The vandalism which is readily apparent is therefore by no means the same as that which is tracked down and punished by the law. Surveys of victims of vandalism are inadequate as they cover mainly private property or certain public facilities only, such as transport and telephone systems. Self-report surveys of delinquents have hitherto been of a limited and fragmentary nature but nonetheless appear to constitute an appreciable source of information, provided they adopt a temporal perspective with a view to highlighting vandalism fluctuation with age: such an approach makes it possible to assess changes in the phenomenon over time, notably its disappearance with increasing age and its transformation as a function of repetition. One consistent finding of these surveys has been so stable that it is worth drawing attention to: theft, and indeed all forms of appropriation, is more common at all ages than are acts of vandalism.

Furthermore, acts of vandalism are part of the same latent behaviour continuum as that defining a single dimension covering the whole of juvenile delinquency (Dickes and Hausman, 1982). Acts of vandalism, just like any other misdoings, share the same common denominator independently of the effects of the reactions of society.

It is, however, the meaning of such acts which calls most strongly for examination. Why is no reason put forward for the conduct of vandals – perceived as senseless and useless – while other wrongdoers are attributed justifications and explanations? Cohen was among the first to criticise the interpretation of vandalism as irrational, senseless behaviour. He sought to throw light on the motivations hidden behind certain regularities observed in the conduct of vandals. Thus, he came to propose that preferential vandal targets (such as schools, transport facilities, etc.) should be studied and that one should steer clear of erroneous interpretations such as: vandalism equals the first step down the slippery road of delinquency or is an opportunity to learn about violence, etc. Cohen looked at the selective perceptions which feed such a phenomenon as vandalism. His aim was to place this type of deviant behaviour squarely within the whole set of social interactions linked to the organisation of society. This led him to criticise the emphasis placed on the aetiology of vandalism which can result in neglecting to study the phenomenon as such. This was why Cohen, from 1970 onwards, has been recommending that attention be directed towards the relationships existing between social reactions and the forms in which ideological violence is expressed.

A few years later, Cohen (1973) put forward a descriptive typology which brought together both the motivations for and the significance of property destruction. This typology featured acquisitiveness, vindictiveness, tactics, play, malice and ideology and is still one of the most frequently used in the study of vandalism.

Currently, interest centres on the examination of the processes by which this social problem is created. The problem is expressed in terms of deviance and concerns the attribution of a certain number of criteria to a social object constructed outside and beyond its objective reality. This object construction relates to a political ideology in the broadest sense of the term, an ideology which provides the reasons for the justification, forgiveness, neutralisation or normalisation of this conduct.

To sum up, the question of defining objects that are subject to social control also involves the way in which any deviant behaviour can be given a socio-political interpretation. The wrongdoer in question may have no political views in mind, but society may attribute one to him willy-nilly. On the other hand, a person may wish to draw attention to a political plan by his activities and yet find society discrediting it and describing his behaviour as senseless, incidental and therefore of no importance.

However, as vandalism is being portrayed, the examination of the social and physical features of its appearance in given contexts suggests the necessity to investigate the underlying motivations in relation to the individual characteristics of its perpetrators, where these are known. The instrumental and expressive aspects of these acts call for a social and interpersonal interpretation of the situations giving rise to them. Cohen sees them as demands which should be interpreted in the appropriate terms. Allen (ch. 4) and Noschis (ch. 5) have rendered us a great service in drawing our attention to the emotional and symbolic dimensions of vandalism, while stressing the role of fantasy and imagination therein.

There can be no doubt that destruction is endowed with a play dimension which children discover when seeking to respond to the way things are. Taking things apart and breaking them not only helps the child to learn but also evokes the search for the laws of operation and use. However, stressing the importance of the aesthetics of vandalism Allen points out that psychological interaction is closely linked to the activities of destruction and construction. He highlights the provocative nature of modern art which deforms the functional nature of all sorts of machines and devices in such a way as to render them useless with respect to the purposes for which they were originally designed. It is this unexpectedness, originality and lack of logic which creates aesthetic surprise and invites us to join in the very dynamics of object transformation. Allen also states that the pleasure arising from such changing appearances flows from visual, auditory and kinaesthetic processes which are enriched by new sensations and which link up progressively before, during and after the act of destruction, according to the unexpectedness of the degree of modification of the objects in question. Thus, hedonistic responses are seen to reinforce destructive activity and encourage its repetition.

Exploratory interviews and experiments have revealed that subjects prefer to break objects which are perceived to be complex: complexity stimulates this type of activity. Moreover, destruction is more fun when the outcome is not the one expected. Finally, the sensation of play resulting from destructive activity is correlated with the sensory features of the act of breaking which affect the excitement obtained.

While vision is the main parameter reinforcing the actual act of destruction, all the senses, particularly smell and touch, have an effect on the stimulation and excitement resulting from it. These aesthetic factors are, nevertheless, an integral part of the stimulus itself. The outcome of this original approach to vandalism would appear to be a suggestion to increase the number of breakable objects, to the point where they are perfectly standard environmental features and that hedonistic experiences, which do not occasion damage to society, be made available.

It is thus not impossible to envisage the cathartic possibilities of creative activities being made available in adventure playgrounds or in workshops for artistic expression. But we can also reflect on the therapeutic value of creative activity for vandals.

Turning now from aesthetics to ethics and the work of Heller (1979), Noschis points to the image of quality associated with Switzerland which has grown up around the equation: physical health = mental health and, along with the promotion of the cleanliness ethic, the concept of order and a certain internalisation of these values. Here, human and social conduct take place in a certain framework which supposes a degree of congruence between the environment and the behaviour of Swiss citizens. The development of national identity would also appear to constitute a variable in the study of vandalism which may be perceived as a manifestation of non-congruence with respect to a dominant sociocultural image.

The explanation of vandalism by reference to the animism of Piaget and to autistic thought, where no distinction is made between the psychic and the physical and where objects are used as substitutes for constraints and frustrations, suggests a different paradigm and correspondingly different tools for the analysis of the phenomenon.

By forsaking the rationalist perspective for the symbolic dimensions of vandalism, Noschis brings in the subconscious mechanisms of projection. Vandalised objects may act as a support for subconscious drives and thereby exteriorise people's inner conflicts, desires and ambiguities. This may lead to some people becoming aware of these sensations (and this may account for the disappearance of vandalistic behaviour, without social control, noted in self-report surveys of delinquents).

Furthermore, it would appear that 'animist-vandal' behaviour constitutes a reversion to egocentrism, i.e. to a sort of 'dissociation of subjective and objective phenomena' and to the deformation of reality according to the individual in question.When these mechanisms are invoked with respect to the development of Swiss identity, they suggest different interpretations of vandalism which show their value in comparative perspectives. They point to new sets of relations in harmony with cultural heritage or with general or specific sociocultural environments which endow objects, places, situations and the behaviour of certain groups with special significance. Instances of this are afforded by the vandalistic behaviour of immigrants and by the cultural symbol conflicts which this represents.

In order to round off this overview of theoretical approaches to vandalism it is worthwhile to point to a number of specific aspects of particular interest arising from surveys of developmental psychology, particularly self-reported juvenile delinquency.

During a recent study (1975–1980) of a population of young (12–18) city dwellers of both sexes, it appeared that provocative behaviour was frequently engaged in by 55% of these adolescents. This was categorised as vandalism since no benefit could be gained from it. Nevertheless, using the self-report questionnaire followed by an interview it was possible to highlight the transient nature of acts of vandalism: they decrease with age as young people become able to take advantage of material goods and to take up gainful employment (Sélosse, 1983).

In addition to the foregoing, there is no direct link between vandalism and delinquency. Vandalistic behaviour is not the same as theft. Adolescents distinguish between destroying a fruit machine and taking the change which it contains. They refuse to be linked to possessions and the alienation and material dependency which these stand for. Vandalising does not mean appropriating.

Lastly, damage caused by the younger adolescents (under 14) stemmed from impulsiveness rather than from subversive organisation. Their acts were not premeditated, they were essentially unpredictable. As they grew older, their acts of vandalism diminished in number: they developed a utilitarian relationship with objects and the exchange and use of values, not to mention the symbolic value of objects call for other motivations and other behaviour.

These observations (taken from the study) suggest a few comments with respect to the dimension of 'senselessness' which is often invoked by public opinion when confronted with vandalism. While the world of adults is built on a delusory sentiment of self-assurance, due to a vast panoply of economic and technical protective systems expressed in terms of justificatory rationalisations and the enjoyment of material benefits, vandalism calls into question this model of relationships to things. The disrespectful behaviour manifested in the mutilation and destruction of objects gives rise to reactions based on an economic and political interpretation of the phenomenon. However, these youngsters of less than 14 years of age have no access, be this of an intellectual or a factual nature or by right, to this level of analysis. They interact at the symbolic level and downgrade the material, monumental or commercial objects in question by endangering their impressive functional aspects and the relationships of dependency or alienation which they evoke.

It is in terms of symbolic exchanges that vandals act, as though the disorder they cause gives rise to new 'flows' between people and things. There can be no doubt that acts of vandalism perpetrated by the under 14's are so many acts of provocation to a society of greed. In as much as they are publicly displayed, they cry out to be interpreted, decoded and deciphered. They play on disturbance and remind us that the relationship between 'consumer goods' and 'consumable goods' is not just an analogous one. Some adolescents indulge in this with great skill and cheek.

Vandalistic behaviour takes on a new orientation between the ages of 14 and 16 and increasingly involves rule breaking. It then becomes a matter of relationships to rules rather than relationships to objects. Adolescents now seek to provoke prohibition. They test just how far they can go in terms of stipulated, accepted, tolerated and prohibited behaviour.

This is statutory vandalism. Adolescents seek to test the flexibility of relationships of dependency, of submission and of social constraint. They try out their power and react to any humiliation. Destructive acts are less random, targets are more carefully chosen and, behind the targets, the individuals and the powers that are to be attacked.

Adolescents at puberty, who have no access to objects, assimilate the material world into themselves. Their vandalism evokes the signs of a forgotten, poorly understood presence seeking paths towards the juvenile sociality which is lacking in the technological world. After the age of 16, vandalistic behaviour becomes more clearly reprehensible. It challenges power and value hierarchies. It readily sees itself as protest behaviour and righting wrongs. It deforms objects and the working of organisations in derisory and sensational ways. Acts take on a more aggressive colour while the destruction becomes less multiform, more selective and more directed. Notions of peer group solidarity or social belongingness start to give a category dimension to behaviour. Power relationships thus become more clearly antagonistic and, as the objects and symbols are more fully integrated into an opposition life style, vandal behaviour develops a more negative impact. It is now no longer a matter of games getting out of hand but of carefully thought out destructive activities.

The preceding diachronic interpretation of acts of adolescent vandalism, as revealed by an anonymous self-report survey, shows that young people of all social backgrounds are often powerless in terms of the things and beings around them and that this can result in them going too far. Smothered by the background noise to communication, outrage becomes a language. The words of youth fail to penetrate the walls of indifference and justification and consequently they carry out acts which, although they prove nothing, are at least striking in their effects.

Since no one listens to them, adolescents exchange the audible register for the visible. In this way they leave their mark, create events and have apparent adventures. Young vandals refuse to remain dumb, i.e. with no way of expressing themselves: they seek to communicate at all costs. Behind the marks left by their activity, they are the ones who need to be looked at and, above all, listened to.

As a conclusion, it seems to me that vandalism covers a vast range of essentially juvenile, multiform, collective and individual behaviour. This behaviour is characterised by challenge, disturbance and provocation: it questions the symbolic and functional world of the technological society along with its mechanistic logic and its myth of security.

Since the effects of vandalism are far more clearly visible than are its perpetrators, one supposes that its 'senselessness' is largely due to the 'mystery' surrounding them. Although the marks of vandalism remain, those who left them behind rarely are apprehended.

Unlike UFOs which are seen but which leave no objective sign of their visits, vandalism does leave traces but, as the vandals themselves are generally unknown, the interpretation of these traces leads to rumours, projections and fantasies of all sorts while simultaneously scapegoats are dreamed up. In a word, the collective unconscious and its sacrificial needs are well catered to.

Vandalistic behaviour is a feature of malfunctioning, inegalitarian communication channels. It constitutes the speech of the dumb, the powerless and of minorities. There can be no doubt that it is a striking form of interrogation – and that it calls for an appropriate response.

References

Cohen, St., 1971. Images of deviance. Harmondsworth: Penguin.
Cohen, St., 1973. Property destruction: motives and meanings. In: C. Ward, ed., Vandalism. London: Architectural Press.
Commission des Maires, 1982. Rapport au Premier Ministre sur la sécurité. Paris: La Documentation Française.
Dickes, P., P. Hausman, 1982. Définir et mesurer la délinquance. Comportements délictueux, no. spécial du Bulletin de Psychologie, Paris.
Heller, G., 1979. Propre en ordre. Lausanne: Editions d'en Bas.
Sélosse, J., 1983. La délinquance des adolescents. Paris: PUF.

CHAPTER 2

Sociological approaches to vandalism

S. COHEN

A personal introduction about my own involvement in the study of vandalism is, I hope, not just a matter of self-indulgence, but of some wider interest in understanding vandalism.

When I first started researching and writing about vandalism some 15 years ago, I confess that the 'substance' of vandalism itself was of little interest to me. Influenced by the labelling theory of deviance, I was more interested in the audience than in the actor or the act. That is to say, the important question seemed not the *behavioural* one ('why do people do these bad things?') but the *definitional* one ('why are these things defined as bad, deviant or socially problematic in the first place?'). I am still convinced that this is the best starting point for the study of vandalism – or of any other form of rule breaking, misbehaviour or deviance which becomes classified as a form of crime, delinquency or social problem.

But then, as now, I had to stop a long way short of the extreme position which many simple-minded critics have accused labelling theory of implying: namely, the notion that if no action is intrinsically deviant, then there is really 'nothing' out there and that everything is a matter of definition, awareness, reaction, selective perception, labelling, social control. Besides the theoretical and common-sense reasons for avoiding such extreme relativism, there always remained for me an intrinsic curiosity about vandalism as a form of behaviour. Why and under what circumstances do people continue to damage, destroy and deface property? What type of property is chosen as a target? Are any of the offenders distinctive 'kinds of people'? In particular, the question of motivation became central – precisely because the dominant societal stereotype of vandalism was (and is) that vandalism is the archetypal instance of 'motiveless' action: senseless, wanton, random, meaningless.

Gradually, then, in addition to using vandalism to illustrate labelling theory (and to analyze such processes as stereotyping, exaggeration and distortion in the mass media), I was drawn towards the complementary enterprise in the 'new sociologies of deviance' of trying to render previously unintelligible behaviour as intelligible and even reasonable. In my writings about the subject (summarized in Cohen, 1973a) I tried to reflect these dual interests in definition and behaviour.

One curious problem was the gap between public and professional interest in the subject. On the one hand, public awareness and anxiety was high and has remained so. In Britain and the United States, from the early 1960s onwards, vandalism has been the object of successive "moral panics" (Cohen, 1980). It was presented periodically not just as ugly, damaging, dangerous or threatening in itself, but also as symptomatic of a wider moral disintegration and decay (lawlessness among the young, lack of respect for property, etc.). But despite this public and media interest – which, in Britain at least, often reached the level of hysteria – there was a profound lack of interest in professional and academic circles. Criminologists had virtually ignored vandalism as a research subject, and despite its often cited prevalence, it seldom figured in typologies or causal theories of crime and delinquency.

After I contributed my bits – mainly, as I said, on questions of definition, a rough typology in terms of motivation, a brief discussion of strategies of prevention and control – I moved on to other interests. Throughout the next decade though, I regularly found myself (together with other interested colleagues in Britain) being invited to talk about the subject to audiences such as magistrates, town planners and social workers. Each time I was in the faintly embarrassing position of having to apologize for the continued absence of solid social scientific work in the area.

Now, on the occasion of what is probably the first international conference specifically about the subject, the picture looks only marginally different. No doubt there has been an increase in the references to vandalism in the appropriate bibliographical citation indices, [1] but it is difficult to know just what of sociological substance has been added by this literature. There have been more studies of specific sub-types of vandalism, organized for the most part in terms of the simple variable of the *physical setting* in which the action occurs (parks, playgrounds, schools, transport facilities, public telephones). There have been more reviews of the existing literature, particularly on prevention and control (e.g. Clarke et al., 1978; Stace, 1978; Central Policy Review Staff, 1978) and there has been a significant increase of interest among architects, town planners and environmental psychologists (Sykes, 1980). In both the United States (Baker and Rubel, 1980) and Britain (Tattum, 1982) there has been a particular concentration on violence, vandalism and 'disruptive behaviour' in schools.

All these various interests are represented in this volume. But we still are left with the curious 'sociology of knowledge' problem which my personal experience illustrates – that is, the disjunction between various indices of high public awareness (in the media, in victim organizations and in day-to-day public perceptions) and low academic/professional interest. I will return later to this

---

[1]   See Van Vliet's paper in this volume (ch. 1) for a review.

important question of how certain social phenomena acquire the full status of social problems.

What follows, anyway, is simply a classification of the five main sociological questions which still seem to me worth posing about vandalism. The presentation is high on abstraction and low on empirical substance.

1. Deviance and labels

The sociological problem here remains how to explain what Schur (1980) calls (rather awkwardly) the "deviantizing process". Deviance is not some fixed entity, a 'thing' *to* which people respond and *about* which social control policy is planned. Rather, "it is through social definitions, responses, and policies that particular behaviours, conditions and individuals acquire there 'deviantness' " (Schur, 1980: 9). This 'deviantness' is attributed to behaviour. It is a matter of degree and is subject to considerable social variability. And the process of attribution is political.

What this means in the case of vandalism, is that the construction of a 'pure' or 'objective' behavioural definition (something like 'the illegal and deliberate destruction or defacement of property belonging to someone else') is only the beginning of the story. It is quite evident that: (i) not all such forms of rule breaking are regarded as deviant, problematic, criminal or even are called vandalism; (ii) not all the rules which forbid illegal property destruction are enforced; (iii) not all the rule breakers find themselves labelled and processed as deviant.

The problem, then, is to explain the conditions under which a society transforms the raw material of rule breaking into fully identified deviance. I suggested constructing something like a series of continua. At the one end would be those particular *forms, contexts* or *people* where property destruction can be accommodated to or absorbed by society without being labelled as vandalism. At the other end would be those forms, contexts or people which are fully 'deviantized' – that is, invariably labelled as vandalism, processed as criminal and regarded as socially problematic. This continuum refers not to invariable categories of behaviour, but to the conditions under which rule breaking is tolerable or tolerated, acceptable or accepted, institutionalized and 'normalized'. Examples of such conditions are:

(i) *ritualism*: fixed, sometimes ceremonial occasions and settings in which property destruction is somehow accepted, condoned or even encouraged;

(ii) *protection*: the existence of certain groups which are given something like a collective licence to engage in vandalism;

(iii) *play*: property destruction is seen as part of play activity. Terms such as 'play', 'fun', 'adventure', 'high spirits' serve to rationalize and neutralize any negative attribution;

(iv) *writing off*: minor acts of damage or defacement are regarded as normal, predictable and routine features of certain settings and organizations. The very predictability and pervasiveness of the behaviour renders it immune to the deviantizing process.

(v) *walling in*: property destruction within the confines of certain semi-closed (school, factories) or totally closed (prison, mental hospital) institutions is rendered invisible to outside awareness and scrutiny. It is either institutionalized or ritually sanctioned only within the walls of the organization.

These, and similar, conditions determine whether and how the vandalism label is applied. It is usually alleged that this sort of approach is too relativistic or is suitable only for those forms of deviance (such as 'crimes without victims') that are subject to widespread normative dissent. The case for fitting vandalism into this framework lies, though, not in the absence of normative consensus in the abstract sense – it is obviously difficult to find *widespread* approval and support for most forms of publicly recognized vandalism – but rather in the extreme variability of the conditions under which the rule breaking is fully 'deviantized'. This is somewhat analogous to the standard philosophical distinction between agreement on the definition of a category as opposed to agreement about what cases to include in the category.

We have to go beyond conventional labelling theory not in the direction of absolutism, but rather by taking relativism seriously. This means not seeing 'conditions' like those I listed as stemming from random or situational variations, but plotting them onto the wider maps of power and conflict in particular societies. This leads us to a more explicitly political question.

2. Politics and ideology

The problem of defining vandalism is political in the broad sense of referring to the contexts of power in which constructions of deviance are made and made to stick. But in the narrower and more conventional sense, vandalism can be political or 'convictional' if the rule is broken as a means towards some explicit and conscious ideological end and/or if there is no consensus about the context of the rule being broken. Both the broader and the narrower usage of the term 'political' pose legitimate problems in studying phenomena such as vandalism (Cohen, 1973b). Much recent controversy in criminology and the sociology of deviance, however, has been somewhat pointless because of its confusion of these two questions. General claims about the class nature of criminal law, for example, are not quite the same as specific imputations of conscious or unconscious political intent on behalf of those who infringe these laws.

There seems to me, however, to be one clear empirical connection between these two questions and that is via the use of <u>motivational accounts theory</u>. [2] The argument is that any form of deviance is accompanied by typical 'vocabularies of motive' – that is, verbal constructions which serve (variously) to justify, excuse, rationalize, neutralize or normalize the action. These accounts may or may not be explicitly political in nature (e.g. appealing to higher loyalties, to clear ideological belief systems) and – crucially – they may or may not be accepted or honoured by the social control system and the powerful. In every instance, what we observe is a struggle to define – a "stigma context" (Schur) or a "negotiation of reality" (Scheff) – the outcome of which is crucial in determining the way images and public policy are shaped. "In the animal kingdom", as Szasz writes, "the rule is eat or be eaten, in the human kingdom, define or be defined".

No act or type of vandalism is immune from being involved in this struggle. Some examples: breaking machines at work might be a way of making 'dead' time pass, an inchoate response to alienating work conditions or a conscious political tactic (Taylor and Walton, 1970); school vandalism may be a way of relieving boredom, an act of revenge in response to a grievance or a protest against authority and rules. In each case, the positions taken by both sides in this definitional contest – and its eventual outcome – are crucial in determining what we eventually come to see as the 'essence' of vandalism. Here, very schematically, are the four logical possibilities in this type of reality negotiation:

Case A: the actor offers an ostensibly non-political account (e.g. 'I only did it for fun', 'I didn't mean to do it') and the audience (crucially, the control system) honours this and does not offer an alternative story.

Case B: the actor offers a clear political account (e.g. daubing slogans in order to campaign for or publicize a cause) and the audience honours this (not necessarily in the sense of agreeing with it, but in regarding it as plausible).

Case C: the actor offers an ostensibly non-political account but the audience (e.g. the sociologists, the political commentator) refuses to accept this (e.g. on grounds of 'false consciousness' or 'unconscious motivation') and instead attributes a political meaning to the action.

Case D: the actor offers a standard political account, but this is discounted or discredited by the observers (e.g. by labelling the behaviour as 'senseless' or 'motiveless').

These possibilities deal only with the political dimension of accounts.

---

[2] The original statement of what is variously called 'motivational accounts' or 'vocabulary of motives' theory is Mills' (1940). The best known application in criminology is Sykes and Matza (1957). A useful, recent summary of some conceptual problems in the theory is Marshall (1981). For an explicit empirical attempt to apply the theory to disruptive behaviour in schools, see Tattum (1982: ch. 4).

Another dimension would be intentionality and responsibility: does the actor claim non-responsibility ('I didn't mean to do it') while the audience refuses to honour this claim (Case C)? Abstract as this exercise might seem at first sight, it might be useful to see to what extent various forms of vandalism might fit these logical cases.

3. Behaviour and motivation

Dominant articles of the sociological faith are that all social phenomena are socially patterned rather than random and are socially determined rather than the product of free choice. In studying deviant phenomena such as vandalism, these articles have been translated into a number of overlapping research and theoretical strategies, notably:

(a) the delineation of typologies based on more or less common-sense observations of the visible features of the behaviour;

(b) the more systematic mapping of the social patterns behind these types, particularly the distribution of rates according to standard variables such as the social class, gender and age of the offender, or the physical and social characteristics of the vandalized property;

(c) the re-construction of stories which explain in biographical or social psychological terms the prototypical causal sequence (or sequences) which leads to acts of vandalism.

As in other areas of crime and deviance, these three types of strategy have left us with some more or less convincing accounts – convincing enough anyway, to dispel simple-minded notions about vandalism being a homogeneous phenomenon explicable in terms of a single cause (such as 'breakdown in morals, 'boredom' or 'meaninglessness'). The credibility of this type of general sociological enterprise in the case of vandalism, is, however, considerably undermined by some rather special difficulties, namely: the widespread normalization of the behaviour; the very low detection rate of official vandalism and the singular lack of many 'good' stories. Most theories of vandalism are based on a mixture of common-sense induction and extrapolation from media reports rather than on immediate data from observation or interviewing.

Nonetheless, my own preference would still be to pursue a theory something like that of motivational accounts which attempts to do justice both to individual consciousness and social structure. The starting strategy would be to collect the full range of typical vocabularies of motive and techniques of neutralization for any particular form of vandalism. We can then compare the acceptability of these accounts to the control system, trace the way they are diffused and learnt through subcultures and the mass media, compare their variations within and between societies, etc.

This type of approach would improve considerably the type of common-sense typology of vandalism which I suggested earlier:

(a) *acquisitive*: damage in order to acquire money or property (or in the course of such acts of theft);
(b) *tactical*: the damage is a conscious tactic, a means to achieve some other end such as publicity for a political cause;
(c) *vindictive*: damage in order to obtain revenge, to settle some real or imagined grievance;
(d) *play*: damage in the course of a game or play in which such motivations as curiosity, fun or competition are dominant;
(e) *malicious*: in which the elements of anger, malice, aggression are not as target-specific as in revenge vandalism, but are nevertheless directed (to particular categories of property) and responsive (as solutions to particular sets of biographical and structural problems).

It is, of course, this last residual category of malicious vandalism which presents the most intractable problems of investigation and explanation. And here we have to turn away from the specific literature on vandalism and towards the general sociological literature on the major group at risk – the urban male working-class adolescent and the type of misbehaviour with which this group is associated: 'expressive fringe delinquency', usually in large groups, often in public settings. [3] The argument – along the lines of traditional subcultural delinquency and its recent revisionist versions – is that vandalism as a solution to this group's problem is just 'right', both in symbolic, expressive (or emotional) and instrumental terms. That is, in its very senselessness, it makes sense – both in terms of what if offers to this group (excitement, trouble, toughness, action, control, taking risks) and in terms of what this group is offered by 'growing up in a working-class city'.

Again though, we must be alert to the possible differences between this type of external explanation and the actors' own, more personal explanation. This is the epistemological distinction between 'the' reasons and 'his' reasons. Precisely because vandalism is such a common, everyday, normalized occurrence, the strategy of examining personal motivational accounts recommends itself. These stories, remember, are the pragmatic statements which people make about themselves to themselves or to others (whether these are demanding control agents or curious social scientists) in order to explain why they have done something. Following Mills, the function of these statements is seen as repairing social bonds: bringing the actor back into line with a group whose norms have been violated. These statements are not simple *ex post facto*

---

[3]   For reviews of recent British literature on the subject see 'Symbols of trouble' (introduction to Cohen, 1980) and Downes and Rock (1982). Key works reviewed are: Hall and Jefferson (1976); Robins and Cohen (1978); Corrigan (1979).

'rationalizations', i.e. fabrications, after the event. They neutralize *in advance* the bind of the rule by protecting the individual from too much self-blame and blame by others. And far from being 'individualistic' or 'subjectivist' this theory is radically sociological in showing how pools of motivational accounts and their accessibility are limited, structured and stratified. The repertoire of accounts, that is, is finite and structurally determined.

It does not seem to me that vandalism is very special or any different from delinquency as a whole in terms of the relevance of either of these two frameworks – that is, revisionist subcultural theory and vocabulary of motives theory. What is likely, though, is that vandalism is somewhat more responsive to situational variations than delinquency as a whole. There are a number of both physical and social conditions (deficient design, brutal architecture, bureaucratic anonymity, demoralized schools, urban decay, etc.) which in common-sense terms would seem to 'produce' vandalism. By 'common sense' I mean here that this sort of associations can be readily articulated by both the actor and the observer.

It may well be, then, that vandalism (in comparison with 'ordinary' routine delinquency, namely theft) is an especially sensitive and visible indicator of various social changes and deficiencies. Take the well-known example of graffiti. Whether or not the daubing of graffiti is indeed an urban folk art, an "act of faith" (Mailer, 1975) the point is that it is both *sensitive* (in the sense of immediately registering urban decay, impersonality, neighbourhood disintegration, etc.) and at the same time *visible* (as evidence of these very causal conditions or stimuli).

Far from being complicated – and social scientists have a vested professional interest in making the world look very complicated – much vandalism might then be a rather simple business. It responds in a more direct fashion than most other forms of delinquency to environmental triggers, and its consequences are also more physically obvious. We 'see' the results of vandalism in a way in which we seldom see the results of theft. This means that the phenomenon has a high potential for being defined as a social problem – my next subject.

4. Problems and claims

I return now to the status of vandalism as a publicly defined social problem. Parallel to the distinction between deviance as 'behaviour' and as 'definition', there lies the distinction between 'objective' and 'subjective' ways of defining what is a social problem. The objective route concentrates on identifying conditions such as value conflict, norm violation, disorganization, damage, dysfunction or threat to cherished values which are thought (variously) to constitute the essence of a social problem. The subjective route concentrates on the definitional process itself: how and why such conditions become labelled as social problems. At its extreme, this route arrives at the conclusion that social problems are what people (or significantly powerful people) think are social problems. Crudely, the difference is between social problems as things or situations and social problems as activities or processes, between the 'objectively given' and the 'subjectively defined'.

In terms of its relevance to vandalism, one of the more useful of recent contributions in the second tradition is Spector and Kitsuse's (1977) concept of social problems as "claims making activities". The focus is on the activities of certain powerful groups as they assert claims or grievances about the existence of some putative condition seen as harmful or threatening. These groups may be more or less successful in publicizing and pressing their claims, in stimulating public controversy or creating an 'issue' and then in setting up agencies and policies designed to eradicate, ameliorate or otherwise change the conditions.

I have suggested elsewhere (Cohen, 1973a) the conditions under which such claims making activities may succeed in the case of vandalism: the exact nature of the imputed harm or threat; the degree of awareness and visibility; the presence of enterprise and publicity; the wider belief systems favourable to complete social problem definition. We might want to speculate again about vandalism's ambiguous and shifting position in the 'social problem league'. It is apparent, for example, that despite periodic claims and campaigns (particularly by victim organizations directly affected rather than by 'disinterested' moral entrepreneurs) that vandalism seldom achieves full 'headline' social problem status. This failure, I suspect, is connected with the perception that methods of control and prevention (whether through criminal law, urban planning or technical innovation) are ritualistic and ineffective. Although cumulative damage might be high, each individual act is perceived (correctly) as insignificant and one does not have to be a criminologist to know that most offenders will not be 'brought to justice'.

Vandalism, then, occupies a somewhat anomalous status as a social problem. The very same factors which make for public awareness (pervasiveness, visibility) also facilitate the widespread belief that 'nothing can be done about it'.

5. Prevention and control

The task of classifying and evaluating the major strategies of prevention and control is not very different for vandalism than it is for other forms of crime and delinquency. And, as with social intervention programmes in general, it is extremely difficult to reach any positive conclusions about 'effectiveness'. For none of the three major preventive strategies – *physical* (building and design

improvements, etc.); *social* (participatory management, community involvement, education, etc.); *deterrent* (block watches, tenant patrols, surveillance,
etc.) – is there conclusive and generalizable evidence that something 'works' at
an acceptable cost.

I would only like to express one personal opinion here about the type of
primary programmes aimed at reducing vandalism through such methods as
improving the quality of the environment, better housing and urban design,
providing more control of public property, increasing play facilities, improving
educational opportunities, etc. Too often, such programmes are evaluated –
and then accepted or (much more frequently) rejected – in terms of their
supposed success in reducing rates of vandalism (in comparison, say, to some
mythical or real 'control group'). This has always seemed to me a false
criterion. These programmes embody values which (presumably) are thought to
be desirable in their own terms. To take a concrete example which has raised
controversy in the vandalism literature: whether or not the construction of a
needed playground for children on a public housing estate actually reduces
rates of vandalism should never determine whether or not to support such
programmes. Such reforms are to be justified for their own sake or not at all.
We are in favour of adequate play facilities, decent housing, creative education
or whatever because we are in favour of them – not because they are alleged to
reduce vandalism.

And there is another, related problem with standard evaluation research in
public policy. The preoccupation with measurable *results* (vandalism rates,
recidivism, costs, etc.) often blinds us to the *effects* of the programme. Often
'nothing works' but 'something happens'.

Paradoxically the best way of dealing with vandalism (and, I believe, with
other forms of crime and delinquency) might be to place it lower rather than
higher on the public agenda (Cohen, 1979; Christie, 1982). Vandalism, no
doubt, is important and interesting enough to be the subject at an international
colloquium but whether it is important enough to justify programmes of social
intervention not otherwise justifiable in themselves, is a question worth con-
templating.

References

Baker, K., R. Rubel, eds., 1980. Violence and crime in schools. Toronto: Lexington.
Central Policy Review Staff, 1978. Vandalism. London: HMSO.
Christie, N., 1982. Limits to pain. Oxford: Martin Robertson.
Clarke, R. et al., 1978. Tackling vandalism. Home Office Research Study no. 47. London: HMSO.
Cohen, S., 1973a. Property destruction: motives and meanings *and* Campaigning against vanda-
    lism. In: C. Ward, ed., Vandalism, pp. 23–54 and 215–258. London: Architectural Press.
Cohen, S., 1973b. Protest, unrest and delinquency: convergences in labels and behavior. Interna-
    tional Journal of Criminology 1, 117–128.

Cohen, S., 1979. Crime and punishment: thoughts on theories and policies. New Society 1, 15 and 29 March.

Cohen, S., 1980. Folk devils and moral panics. New ed. Oxford: Martin Robertson.

Corrigan, P., 1979. Schooling the smash street kids. London: Macmillan.

Downes, D., P. Rock, 1982. Understanding deviance. Oxford: Oxford University Press.

Hall, S., J. Jefferson, eds., 1976. Resistance through ritual. London: Hutchinson.

Mailer, N., 1975. The faith of graffiti. New York: Wiley.

Marshall, G., 1981. Accounting for deviance. International Journal of Sociology 1, 17–45.

Mills, C.W., 1940. Situated actions and vocabularies of motive. American Sociological Review 6, 904–913.

Robins, D., P. Cohen, 1978. Knuckle sandwich growing up in the working class city. Harmondsworth: Penguin.

Scheff, Thomas J.H., 1968. Negotiating reality: Notes on power in the assessment of responsibility. Social Problems 16, 3–17.

Schur, E., 1980. The politics of deviance: Stigma contests and the uses of power. Englewood Cliffs (N.J.): Prentice Hall.

Spector, M., J. Kitsuse, 1977. Constructing social problems. California: Cummings.

Stace, M., 1978. Vandalism and self reported studies. Occasional Papers in Criminology. Wellington: Victoria University.

Sykes, J., ed., 1980. Designing against vandalism. New York: Van Nostrand.

Sykes, G., D. Matza, 1957. Techniques of neutralization. American Sociological Review 22, 664–670.

Tattum, D., 1982. Disruptive pupils in schools and units. Chichester: John Wiley.

Taylor, C., P. Walton, 1970. Industrial sabotage. In: S. Cohen, ed., Images of deviance. Harmondsworth: Penguin.

Abstract: S. Cohen, Sociological approaches to vandalism

This paper classifies and reviews five main sociological points of interest in the study of vandalism: (1) how the label of vandalism as deviance is created and applied; (2) the significance of the political and ideological dimensions of vandalism; (3) the question of constructing causal theories, particularly in terms of motivation; (4) the status of vandalism as a publicly recognized social problem; and (5) the nature of preventive and control strategies.

CHAPTER 3

The equity-control model of vandalism: a refinement

R.M. BARON and J.D. FISHER

Understanding the phenomenon of vandalism, defined as "the willful or malicious destruction, injury, disfigurement, or defacement of any public or private property" (Uniform Crime Reporting Handbook, 1978), represents an important scientific challenge. There are obviously many types of vandalistic acts, and several taxonomies have been developed to differentiate between them. For example, Cohen (1973) enumerates the following categories: *acquisitive* vandalism (looting, petty theft), *tactical/ideological* vandalism (to draw attention to oneself or to an issue), *vindictive* vandalism (for revenge), *play* vandalism (to combat boredom), and *malicious* vandalism (to diffuse frustration and rage; often occurring in public settings wherein the target is depersonalized).

Vandalism has proven equally intractable to theoretical and social solutions. There is at this time neither a good general theory of the roots of vandalism nor anything like a successful societal program of prevention or remediation. Moreover, despite its widespread occurrence as a mode of human aggression and its staggering cost, there has been almost a total neglect of vandalism in recent 'in depth' reviews of human aggression (cf. Bandura, 1973; Baron, 1977).

This discouraging state of affairs led Fisher and Baron (1982) to propose an explanation of vandalism which is unique in its systematic use of constructs derived from current theory and research in both social and environmental psychology. The present exposition represents a refinement and an extension of our equity-control model.

1. The equity-control model

Our original analysis of vandalism began with certain meta-assumptions which we still espouse. These may be enumerated as follows:

(1) Vandalism in most of its forms is *not* a senseless or motiveless act of aggression. We share the view of the sociologist Stanley Cohen (1973) that vandalism is an act which both provides meaning or coherence to the world of vandals *and* is a message to society that 'the system is rotten'.

(2) We assume that because vandalism is rooted in a complex set of

circumstances, any relatively complete explanatory model must allow for the operation of *individual* and *social-group* level factors which address *both* psychological and societal problems.

(3) Since vandalism involves specific forms of property destruction, violation or disfigurement, its likelihood and form is also influenced by properties of the architectural-physical environment ranging from site hardening to the civility of its maintenance.

(4) Fisher and Baron (1982) assumed that by taking into account relevant individual differences and social-contextural factors, one could predict more than the general likelihood of nonplay vandalism – but also whether it would take a more expressive-cathartic form (i.e., malicious or vindictive acts), or a more instrumental form (i.e., ideological or acquisitive acts). [1]

(5) Excluding play vandalism, it was posited that the remaining types can be ordered along an instrumental-expressive dimension. In general, the instrumental forms represent more planned, consequence-sensitive acts whereas the expressive forms typically involve more spontaneous and violent actions regulated less by consequences than by transitory but intense emotional states such as rage.

1.1. Equity as a meta-motive

Given the above presuppositions about the nature of vandalism, our first problem was to see whether we could identify a common motive for the various forms of vandalism. A possible source for such theorizing was Cohen's (1973) conceptualization of vandalism as a form of rule-breaking. Might it not be possible, we asked, to view vandalism as an *exchange* of rule-breaking (Fisher and Baron, 1982)? According to such a view the vandal is, in effect, saying to society 'If I don't get any respect from you (i.e., fair treatment for my needs, concerns, etc.), I won't respect your rules (e.g., regarding the sanctity of property rights)'.

We proposed, then, that what the various forms of vandalism have in common as an underlying motive is a *sense of injustice* – a perception of unfair treatment. In more formal terms, we argued that *perceived inequity* provides much of the motive power behind all forms of nonplay vandalism. A recent field experiment by Moser (this volume, ch. 10) is illustrative. Here, inequality was manipulated by having Parisians who were unable to complete a call from a phone booth either receive their money back, or not. Two striking findings were obtained: (1) across sex and a wide range of social class variations, more than 50% of those in the inequitable (no coin returned) condition engaged in vandalistic acts (e.g., pulling the phone off its cord or kicking the booth), and

---

[1] We omitted Cohen's category of play vandalism from our model because damage in such a context is an unintended by-product rather than an explicit goal of the action.

(2) three times as many violent, vandalistic acts occurred when no coin was returned as when equity was restored.

At a broader level, the inequity motive has been implicated in the report of the U.S. National Advisory Commission on Civil Disorders (Kerner et al., 1968), which noted that "in at least nine cities studied, the damage seems to have been, at least in part, the result of deliberate attacks on white-owned businesses, characterized in the Negro community as unfair or disrespectful to Negroes". Similarly, damage to machinery in factories as far back as the Luddite Riots in 19th-century England and continuing to current industrial sabotage appears largely motivated by perceptions of unfair treatment – be it the fear of unfair competition from machines or inequitable wages (Bass and Ryterband, 1979).

In sum, we propose that perceived inequity, defined formally as a perceived imbalance between one's own inputs and outcomes and those of some comparison other, can subsume the broad array of vandalistic acts captured by Cohen's categories of nonplay vandalism. Perceived inequity sets up a motivation either to achieve *actual* equity through objective action-induced changes (e.g., changes in one's own actual inputs/outcomes or those of others), or to restore *psychological* equity via changes in one's perceptions (e.g., restructured beliefs about one's contributions or other's outcomes) (Walster et al., 1973, 1978). Viewed in this way, vandalism becomes a means of restoring equity by modifying one's own inputs (e.g., making them negative rather than positive), changing another's outcomes (e.g., by lowering the value of his or her property through damage), and/or by augmenting one's own outcomes (e.g., by looting).

1.2. Perceived control as the primary moderator

Fisher and Baron (1982) treat equity restoration as providing the motivation for vandalism, with *perceived control* viewed as a separate continuum which moderates (or guides) how inequity will be coped with. Control is defined in terms of the strength of a person's belief that he or she can effectively modify outcomes and arrangements. As such, it is likely to influence how equity will be restored. We view it as important to separate the sources of frustration from how frustration will be coped with: our argument is that control is more important in relation to vandalism as a predictor of coping mode than as a determinant of the instigation to vandalize (Allen and Greenberger, 1980). It will be argued shortly that control, because it implies a psychological representation of the degrees of freedom available in the environment for coping, can affect the perceived functionality of coping options differing in selectivity, utilitarianism, intensity, etc. That is, certain modes of equity restoration which are possible when the person or group has high control are not likely to be selected when they perceive low control.

Perceived control is determined by a number of factors: (1) actual opportunities for effecting control which are available within the system; (2) one's own abilities to use these, which depend on his or her verbal skills, social skills, power to influence others, etc.; (3) ability to identify the source of the inequity; and (4) one's learned expectations for control in similar situations. Under conditions of *high inequity* and *high control*, one is disposed toward socially legitimate means of equity restoration. One might confront the perpetrator through existing channels 'within the system', organize a legitimate means of protest, or pursue a higher status to insure more equitable treatment in the future. When one experiences high inequity and his or her level of control is *relatively lower* (i.e., when control is low or moderate), more legitimate means of equity restoration are less accessible. Here, non-socially desirable, more immediate, less easily thwarted means of paying the perpetrator back which also have a lower initial cost (e.g., vandalism, personal assault) become more likely. In this situation, the individual believes he or she is being unfairly treated and, for either structural or personal reasons, has few other means of restoring equity. This leads to an immediate, low initial effort, but relatively certain means of seeking remediation with the perpetrator, such as vandalism or personal assault.

For the present purposes, we would like simply to sketch out some preliminary criteria which may distinguish when vandalism will occur, from when the response to inequity will consist of personal assault. In general, we predict that given high inequity and moderate to low perceived control, vandalism will occur when characteristics of the perpetrator of the inequity, the context (including the physical and social environments), and the victim afford a greater probability of re-establishing equity when engaging in vandalism than when engaging in personal assault on the agent who is perceived to be the source of inequity. For example, the probability of restoring equity vis-à-vis personal assault is lower than the probability of restoring it through vandalism when the perpetrator of inequity is an institution, thereby making vandalism the equity restoration mode of choice when institutions are blamed.

Given that conditions suggest that vandalism is likely, one's level of perceived control may predispose them to a particular *type* of vandalism. In terms of Cohen's (1973) typology, we assume that the expressive acts of *malicious* and *vindictive* vandalism predominate for persons high in perceived inequity and relatively low in perceived control. In effect, when one is high in inequity and perceives the likelihood of effecting changes to remedy the situation to be relatively low, diffuse forms of vandalism with a psychological rather than actual equity restoring function (cf. Walster et al., 1973) tend to occur. (People *high* in perceived inequity with *extremely low* perceived control are assumed to be prone to the passivity or apathy of learned helplessness – Seligman, 1975).

On the other hand, more constructive (i.e., instrumentally effective) means of dealing with high perceived inequity are postulated to characterize people with relatively higher perceived levels of control. It is predicted that with relatively higher degrees of control (but not sufficiently high to allow for a socially acceptable response within the system), the type of vandalism chosen becomes more objectively instrumental in restoring *actual* (as opposed to psychological) equity. This is because with relatively higher control one can be more selective in the targets of vandalism. Thus, *acquisitive* or *tactical/ideological* vandalism are predicted for such persons.

1.3. Going from vandalistic intentions to behavior

One can partition the issue of predicting vandalism into two stages. From this perspective, we view the postulated interaction between equity motivation and perceived control as predicting *behavioral intentions* toward vandalism (cf. Fishbein and Ajzen, 1975). Our reasoning can be summarized as follows: (1) perceived inequity constitutes the basic motive for vandalism, and (2) with the consideration of perceived control, we are able to separate the general predisposition toward vandalism into different forms of vandalism varying in expressiveness-instrumentality. These predispositions may be more formally treated as behavioral intentions toward different types of vandalism. Specifically, it is proposed that $BI_v = EM \times PC$. That is, perceived control (PC) is assumed to moderate or interact with the inequity motive (EM) to affect behavioral intentions toward different types of vandalism.

What is the relationship between intentions to commit vandalism and the factors which determine whether such intentions will be translated into behavior? Phrasing the problem in these terms suggests the relevance of the two-stage model of reasoned action proposed by Fishbein and Ajzen (1975), to deal with what is essentially a problem of predicting behavior from attitudes. In order to move from behavioral intentions to predict actual *behavior* we propose that one must consider a second order moderator stage involving specific properties of the physical environment (PE), as well as the social environment (SE). Speaking generally, then, we propose that: $B_v = BI(PE + SE)$.

In effect, behavioral intentions toward vandalism are assumed to interact with an additive combination of barriers and/or supports in the physical and social environments to moderate the actual occurrence of specific forms of vandalistic behavior. Moreover, with the help of these moderators we can sharpen the predictions somewhat to go from expressive-instrumental to specific expressive-instrumental types of vandalism.

1.4. The physical environment as a secondary moderator

In general, *physical* aspects of the environment can make it invulnerable (or at least appear invulnerable) to equity restoration through the form of vandalism the individual is predisposed to enact (e.g., acquisitive, malicious) and/or through the means he or she has available (e.g., rocks, cherry bombs). To the extent that this is the case, such attack may be less apt to occur. For example, vandalism damage is often lower when targets have been 'hardened' (e.g., when window substitutes are used) (Lavrakas et al., 1978), although in some cases such physical properties seem to challenge vandals to destroy them (Allen and Greenberger, 1978; Fisher et al., to appear). Thus, site hardening may sometimes serve to promote vandalism, especially of the malicious and vindictive types.

The extent to which physical properties promote surveillance also serves to moderate vandalism. When surveillance opportunities are minimal vandalism appears to increase, while environments which afford surveillance suffer less damage (Mawby, 1977; Brown 1977). In addition to surveillance by humans, research has found that surveillance through technological means (e.g., radar, alarms, electric eyes) can be quite effective (Pablant and Baxter, 1975). We propose that the amount of acquisitive vandalism may be especially apt to be influenced by the degree of surveillance available (Brown, 1977).

A second class of physical elements which moderate vandalism are signs of *incivility* and signs of appropriation (or demarcation) (Taylor et al., 1980). The former (e.g., a run down, damaged environment which nobody seems to care about) appears to promote vandalism (Pablant and Baxter, 1975). We would predict that 'run down' environments would especially facilitate *malicious* acts; perhaps because such settings are perceived to be highly vulnerable. Under these conditions, targets which break in the most aesthetic way may be most apt to be chosen (Allen and Greenberger, 1978). While attractive, 'cared for' settings generally sustain less damage (Pablant and Baxter, 1975) they should be more common targets for *acquisitive* vandalism than 'run down' ones.

In contrast to signs of incivility, signs of appropriation (e.g., fences, territorial markers, other indications of ownership) tend to *inhibit* vandalism. (See Taylor et al., 1980 for a complete discussion of why this seems to be the case.) We would predict that the moderating effect of signs of appropriation should be greatest for *acquisitive* vandalism (Brown, 1977).

The symbolic value of the environment may also be a potent moderator of vandalism as an equity restoration response. For certain types of vandalism (e.g., *vindictive, ideological*), the closer an environmental setting is in a symbolic sense to the agent which created the inequity, the more apt it may be to be chosen as a target. Equity restoration with the original perpetrator of inequity is generally most satisfying (and such parties are preferable as targets), but restoring equity with third parties who are close to the cause of inequity at a symbolic level has also been shown to reduce distress (cf. Greenberg, 1980). However, for ideological vandalism, a more public target (e.g., writing a slogan in a highly visible place) may sometimes be preferred to a site which is close in symbolic value. Finally, environmental settings belonging to stigmatized parties may be more apt to sustain damage than those belonging to others.

In sum, all types of vandalism are likely to be affected by the properties of the physical environment, although not in the same way. For example, whereas making a run-down building more attractive will diminish the probability of malicious vandalism, the use of territorial markers such as fences and surveillance should be most effective for reducing acquisitive vandalism. However, whereas surveillance may suffice to reduce acquisitive or malicious vandalism it is likely to be inadequate to stop ideological or vindictive vandalism. Here, site hardening may be necessary.

1.5. The secondary moderating effect of group variables

In addition to the physical environment, *group variables* may moderate vandalism. While such variables associated with both the target group and the vandal group importantly influence the likelihood of vandalism (see Fisher and Baron, 1982), the present analysis will focus mainly on the latter. It should be noted, however, that a strong, cohesive neighborhood (target) group is less apt to be victimized by vandals than one which is not perceived as cohesive. This may be because such groups develop stronger territorial behaviors (e.g., engage in more surveillance, both for themselves and their neighbors) (Taylor et al., 1978, 1980). Vandals may realize they are more apt to be caught and that their act will not go 'unanswered'. Also, highly cohesive groups will probably maintain the physical environment better (e.g., it will show caring and concern; contain fewer signs of incivility) which, as we have noted, may lead to lower vandalism. We predict that a highly cohesive target group should have a dampening effect on all types of vandalism.

Characteristics of the vandal's own group moderate vandalism as well. As a facilitator of vandalism groups are at the most basic level apt to affect the likelihood of vandalism by members through modeling, social comparison and conformity-type pressures. Moreover, in highly cohesive groups 'groupthink' types of processes are likely to be unleashed (including risky shifts – Clark, 1971), particularly in regard to ideological types of vandalism (Janis, 1972). Groups may also elicit feelings of diffusion of responsibility and de-individuation, creating the perception that one is anonymous, cannot be identified, and is released from normative constraints (Zimbardo, 1969). Their actions may further suggest that to destroy is normative behavior, while to restrain oneself is deviant. And, in such groups, one's status may be improved by vandalism and decreased by restraint (Richards, 1979). Further, groups elicit arousal (e.g., through the mere presence of others or because frustration with the status quo can be magnified through social comparison), which promotes performance of the dominant response to deal with a threat (Zajonc, 1968). In some cases the dominant response may be vandalism.

In general, it is assumed that the influence of a group on a potential vandal's actions differs with the various types of vandalism. Some acts of vandalism (e.g., acts of the '*malicious*' variety) are likely to require greater diffusion of responsibility, de-individuation, and possibly also evidence 'risky shift' types of social comparison processes. Whereas *malicious* vandalism is likely to thrive on the de-individuation provided by certain groups, *vindictive* vandalism may with equal probability be carried out by individuals *or* in group contexts. Similarly, ideological vandalism is more likely to entail groups than acquisitive vandalism.

In sum, the presence of an antisocial group may be critical for the translation of intentions into certain types of behavioral vandalism; albeit for somewhat different reasons for different types of vandalism. For example, for malicious and ideological vandalism, the group is likely to serve different functions. Specifically, ideological vandalism is likely to be facilitated by the *groupthink* aspects of group processes whereas malicious vandalism will be facilitated by *de-individuation* type processes.

Even more precise predictions can be made if combinations of properties of the physical and social environments are considered. For example, malicious vandalism will be facilitated by the presence of a group and the proximity of a deteriorated setting low in surveillance. At the other extreme the presence of a group is less relevant for acquisitive vandalism. Moreover, such vandalism will be increased as a site is physically improved and as signs of incivility are lessened.

The above type of formulation is designed to predict the occurrence of different forms of vandalism. There is, however, another major issue which needs to be addressed. This concerns the ability of the present model to predict the *re-occurrence* of vandalism. In order to move from predicting the likelihood of occurrence to predicting re-occurrence requires an examination of the short- and long-term effects of different forms of vandalism.

2. The effects of vandalism and the problem of chronicity

The problem of chronicity of different forms of vandalism or the likelihood of re-occurrence over time requires that we move beyond the type of static variable approach we have adopted until now, to a type of sequential flow diagram which allows for the effects of different stages to feedback to earlier steps in the model. This type of model is offered in fig. 1.

One of the advantages of casting our model in a flow chart, systems format is that it allows us to deal with the feedback-dynamic aspects of vandalism. That is, we can ask questions about the likely short- and long-term consequences of different vandalistic behaviors. First, at the most general level, all forms of vandalism are likely to continue so long as:

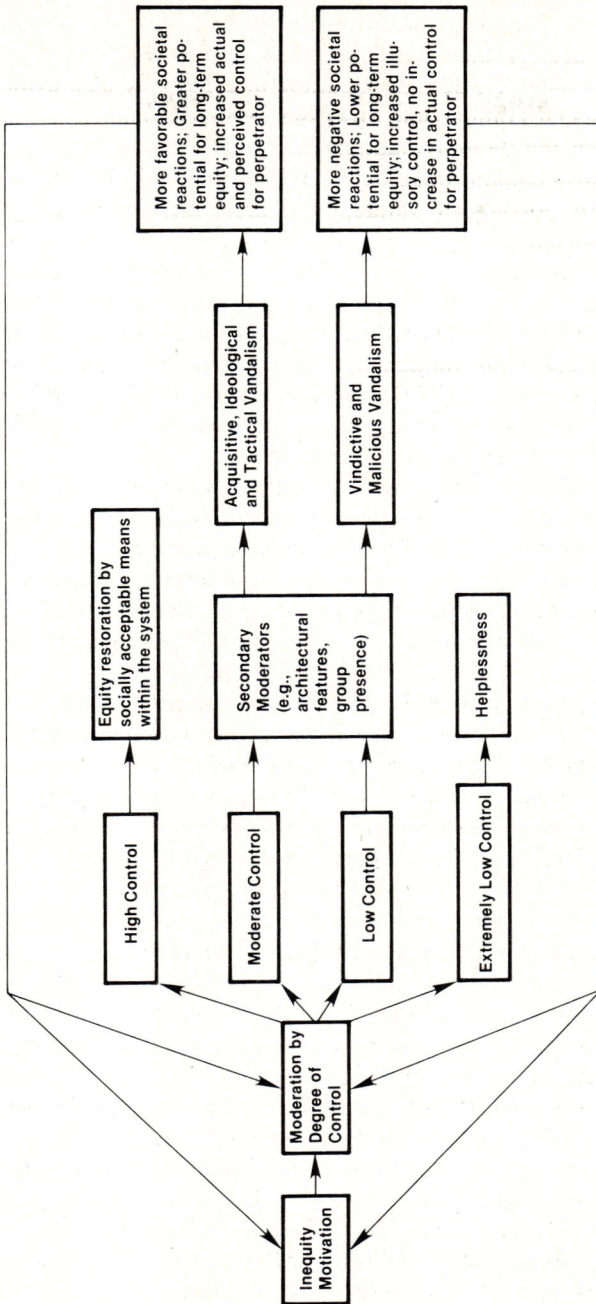

Figure 1. A flow diagram of the process implicated in an equity-based model. (*Note:* the diagram should be read as a temporal flow of events, not as a causal model.)

(1) the sources of instigation remain the same (e.g., perceived inequity remains high and the context continues to be seen as non-responsive);
(2) the barrier properties of the environment are permeable to vandalistic acts. That is, vandalism does not become too risky or effortful.

In this regard, let us compare several different forms of vandalism, in terms of likelihood of *re-occurrence*. First we have to distinguish between short- and long-term effects; and between psychological and objective consequences. With regard to malicious vandalism, there is likely to be a short-term feeling of success due to a venting of anger (catharsis), increased feelings of equity from reducing the other's outcomes, and perhaps a short-term increment in perceived efficacy. While the person may be satisfied in the *short-run* with such actions, in the long run his or her underlying problems have not been resolved. The real issues of inequity have not been addressed, be they improved jobs for blacks, more respect, or a better recreation center. Similarly, the type of control achieved is irrelevant to real environmental control – the larger environment remains unresponsive.

However, although long-term, objective control has not been gained, the destruction of property may provide feeling of 'illusory control' at least in the short-run. Moreover, there may be a certain aesthetic enjoyment in the act of destruction which is reinforcing (Greenberger and Allen, 1980). Further, because there has been little risk or effort since most malicious vandalism focuses on public territories, re-occurrence is highly likely.

The reactions of society to such actions are also likely to facilitate the re-occurrence of malicious vandalism. Specifically, of all the kinds of vandalism, malicious acts are most likely to be misinterpreted at a number of levels. First, the message will be missed. Instead of seeing the act as a response to a possible state of inequity, malicious vandalism will be seen as a random, motiveless act whose cause is *not social injustice* but the distorted psyche of a deviant individual. That is, a dispositional as opposed to an environmental attribution is made. Further, the violence and intensity of the act takes away from its message. People focus on the damage, not the motivation. A 'just world' type of rationalization is also likely – terrible acts come from terrible people, not people with legitimate gripes.

A similar pattern may occur for vindictive vandalism, although here re-occurrence is less likely. This is because while it may resemble malicious vandalism with regard to the expressive dividends of the acts, vindictive vandalism is apt to become increasingly more difficult and costly. Specifically, the risk of identification is greater and the likelihood of retaliation vis-à-vis arrest is much higher since: (1) primary territories may be involved, and (2) a threat to the feelings of control and/or esteem of the target may occur if the vandal is allowed to 'get away with it'.

A different pattern holds for ideological vandalism. Because the message is clear regarding the cause of the action, there is a greater possibility that the target will respond to re-establish actual inequity. Also, more accurate attributions are probable because the level of fear induced is likely to be lower. The possibility for real structural change which will lower actual inequity and raise environmental control is greater. In general, ideological vandalism is likely to persist until innovation occurs; as with the Viet Nam protest movement.

2.1. Remediation

Remediation strategies can be focused either on the barrier-support system or on the motives underlying vandalism (equity and control). If one focuses on the environment, the likely effect with increased surveillance and/or environmental modification is simply a shift to safer, more accessible targets.

Given a particular level of inequity, one way to make the more destructive forms of vandalism less so is to increase perceived control. Increasing control among those with relatively low perceived control will shift vandalism from general to restricted targets (e.g., the PLO focusing on military as opposed to civilian targets). For those with relatively greater perceived control, it could lead to a shift from ideological vandalism to working within the legal-social system (e.g., the PLO working through the UN). This strategy is a bit dangerous at the low end of the perceived control scale, since it can shift people from the passivity of learned helplessness to malicious vandalism.

2.2. Summary

We have proposed a refined equity-control model of vandalism which we feel has a number of advantages:

(1) It moves conceptualizations of vandalism from typology to theory, and advances theory from focusing on a single cause to an appreciation of multiple levels of causation.
(2) It addresses a gap in the human aggression literature with regard to a major type of human aggression.
(3) It extends and clarifies both social-psychological constructs and the phenomena of vandalism (e.g., control, equity, behavioral intentions, etc.).
(4) It is true for the phenomena at issue in the sense that (a) it addresses the meaning of vandalism at the level of the individual, the group and society, and (b) it incorporates properties of the physical and the social environments.
(5) It points to conceptually-driven strategies for remediation rather than to shot-gun approaches.

References

Allen, V.L., D.B. Greenberger, 1978. An aesthetic theory of vandalism. Crime and Delinquency 24, 309–321.

Allen, V.L., D.B. Greenberger, 1980. Destruction and perceived control. In: A. Baum, J. Singer, eds., Advances in environmental psychology, vol. II. Hillside (N.J.): Erlbaum.

Bandura, A., 1973. Aggression: a social learning analysis. Englewood Cliffs (N.J.): Prentice-Hall.

Baron, R.A., 1977. Human aggression. New York: Plenum.

Bass, B.M., E.C. Ryterband, 1979. Organizational psychology. 2nd ed. Boston: Allyn and Bacon.

Brown, B.B., 1977. Territoriality and residential burglary. Paper presented at the Meeting of the American Psychological Association, New York City, May.

Clark, R.D., III, 1971. Group induced shift toward risk: A critical appraisal. Psychological Bulletin 76, 251–270.

Cohen, S., 1973. Property destruction: motive and meanings. In: C. Ward, ed., Vandalism. London: The Architectural Press.

Fishbein, M., I. Ajzen, 1975. Belief, attitude, intention, and behavior: An introduction to theory and research. Reading (Mass.): Addison-Wesley.

Fisher, J.D., R.M. Baron, 1982. An equity-based model of vandalism. Population and Environment 5, 182–200.

Fisher, J.D., P.A. Bell, A. Baum, to appear. Environmental psychology. 2nd ed. New York: Holt, Rinehart and Winston.

Greenberg, M.S., 1980. A theory of indebtedness. In: K.J. Gergen, M.S. Greenberg, R.H. Wills, eds., Social exchange: Advances in theory and research. New York: Plenum.

Greenberger, D.B., V.C. Allen, 1980. Destruction and complexity: An application of aesthetic theory. Personality and Social Psychology Bulletin 6, 479–483.

Janis, I., 1972. Victims of groupthink. Boston: Houghton Mifflin.

Kerner, O., et al., 1968. Report of the National Advisory Commission of Civil Disorders. New York: Bantam Books.

Lavrakas, P.J., J. Normoyle, R. Szoc, 1978. Commercial security systems and burglary reduction. Paper presented at the Second National Workshop on Criminal Justice Evaluation, Washington, November.

Mawby, R.K., 1977. Defensible space: A theoretical and empirical appraisal. Urban Studies 14, 169–179.

Pablant, P., J.C. Baxter, 1975. Environmental correlates of school vandalism. Journal of the American Institute of Planners 41, 270–277.

Richards, P., 1979. Middle class vandalism and the age-status conflict. Social Problems 26, 482–497.

Seligmann, M.E.P., 1975. Helplessness. San Francisco: Freeman.

Taylor, R.B., S.D. Gottfredson, S. Brower, 1978. Urban territoriality and crime in residential settings. Environmental Psychology and Nonverbal Behavior 3, 121–122.

Taylor, R.B., S.D. Gottfredson, S. Brower, W. Drain, K. Dockett, 1980. Toward a resident-based model of community crime intervention: Urban territoriality, social networks, and design. JSAS Catalog of Selected Documents in Psychology 10, MS. 2044.

Uniform Crime Reporting Handbook, 1978. Federal Bureau of Investigation. Washington, D.C.: U.S. Government Printing Office.

Walster, E., E. Berscheid, G.W. Walster, 1973. New directions in equity theory. Journal of Personality and Social Psychology 25, 151–176.

Walster, E., G.W. Walster, E. Berscheid, 1978. Equity: Theory and research. Boston: Allyn and Bacon.

Zajonc, R., 1968. Attitudinal effects of mere exposure. Journal of Personality and Social Psychology Monograph Supplement 9, 1–27.

Zimbardo, P., 1969. The human choice: Individuation, reason, and order versus deindividuation, impulse, and chaos. In: W. Arnold, D. Levine, eds., Nebraska symposium on motivation 17, 237–307.

Abstract: R.M. Baron and J.D. Fisher, The equity-control model of vandalism: a refinement

A revised version of the equity-control model of vandalism is described. In the original model it was postulated that interaction between perceived inequity and perceived control could be construed as providing the essential generative mechanism underlying most forms of nonplay vandalism. Using this model along with properties of the social and physical environment as secondary moderators, it was possible to predict variations in the likelihood of the occurrence of instrumental as opposed to expressive forms of vandalism. In the refined model it is assumed that the equity-control interaction predicts behavioral intentions toward various forms of vandalism which may or may not be actualized into specific forms of vandalistic behavior. In order to go from intentions to behavior it is proposed that one has to multiply one's behavioral intentions by an additive combination of barriers and/or supports in the physical and social environment. This revised model can make more fine-grain predictions such as the relative likelihood of specific types of expressive or instrumental vandalism (e.g., malicious vs. acquisitive or vindictive vs. ideological). The present model also focuses on the factors likely to affect the likelihood of personal assault as opposed to vandalism and on the problem of the differential likelihood of reoccurrence of different forms of vandalism.

CHAPTER 4

Toward an understanding of the hedonic component of vandalism

V.L. ALLEN

The term 'vandalism' ('vandalisme' in French) was first used by the Abbé Grégoire in Paris in 1794 in connection with a report presented to the convention of the *Etats généraux* (Réau, 1959). He was pleading for the protection of ancient inscriptions from being defaced and destroyed by the citizens in the years following the revolution of 1789. Discussing his invention of this word in his memoires, Grégoire stated: "Je créai le mot pour tuer la chose". At the present time – almost 200 years later – we find that the good Abbé's word is still being widely and actively used not only by researchers, but by the mass media and the public in general. The continued wide currency of this term attests to the fact that, unfortunately, "le mot" did not successfully "tuer la chose".

Vandalism has remained for a long time as a stubborn and seemingly unsolvable practical problem for society at large; and neither has it been amenable to the theoretical explanations offered by social scientists. Over the years many attempts have been made to explain vandalism, though most efforts have consisted of descriptive accounts or have suggested typologies designed to reduce a wide diversity of acts to a small number of categories (Cohen, 1973; Madison, 1970; Wade, 1967). Many theories have attempted to be all-encompassing, to explain everything by resorting to a master motive which promises to hold the key to the mystery of vandalism. Such theories have usually been disappointing. As a consequence of trying to explain everything at a very general level, they run the risk of explaining nothing at a specific level with any degree of satisfaction.

Elsewhere I have suggested that at the individual psychological level of explanation a satisfactory theory of vandalism must incorporate at least three major components: affective, cognitive, and social (Allen and Greenberger, 1980b). The first component refers to the positive or hedonic reaction that often accompanies an act of destruction. The second component (cognitive) deals with the consequences of destruction for an individual's perception of personal control or efficacy (Allen and Greenberger, 1980a). The third component (social identity) plays an important theoretical role in unifying the affective and control factors and, in addition, provides a link between psychological processes and higher-level conceptual units in the external social environment. I have discussed each of these three factors in detail, along with relevant supporting research, in previous publications (Allen, 1983; Allen and Greenberger, 1980b).

1. Pleasure in destruction: theory

At the present time, however, I would like to restrict my goal severely and focus only on the affective (i.e., the hedonic) component of vandalism. Abundant anecdotal evidence points to the importance of a factor in vandalism that has been ignored or given only slight attention by previous theories: the sheer enjoyment experienced by an individual during the destruction of an object. That is, the act of destruction is often very pleasurable as an end in itself. It is only too easy to overlook this obvious but critical aspect of vandalism: that there is pleasure in destruction. Not always, by any means; not always to the same degree, by any means; but pleasure is there, as all of us know from everyday experience.

A perusal of data from case reports reveals many instances in which youngsters who discuss their own acts of vandalism make unsolicited comments indicating that the episode was simply enjoyable in itself – or to use their own words, 'It was fun'. For example, a member of a boys' gang studied by Thrasher (1936) stated "We would always tear things down. That would make us laugh and feel good" (p. 95). And a boy explaining the reason for an incident of school vandalism said: "To have fun. They thought it was a big joke breakin' things. Somebody said, 'Let's break the winders' " (Martin, 1961: 103). In a study reported by Farrington and West (1978), delinquent youths were asked to give their motives for committing offenses. Enjoyment was most often given for damaging property, although rational or purposive reasons were most common for other types of offenses. The pervasiveness of enjoyment in connection with destruction is evident in reactions of both children and adults. Piaget (1952) has pointed out that children often engage in destruction as one type of play. In our own research, we have been impressed by the relish with which persons relate incidents of breaking an object (Allen and Greenberger, 1978). In short, destruction does seem often to be an enjoyable experience.

Let us take a deeper look at this hedonic component of destruction and see where it may lead, without any preconceptions or pretentions, without worrying about ultimate explanations or causes, and without constructing complicated and formalistic models that are distant from the psychological experience of individuals involved.

First, though, what are the psychological processes that are responsible for producing an emotional experience of pleasure? A great deal of psychological research supports the well-known curvilinear relation between level of arousal (relative to adaptation level) and positive affect or pleasure. An increase in arousal will be experienced as pleasurable up to a point of high arousal. Any further increase in arousal beyond this point will be perceived as unpleasant. Thus, the positive hedonic value of a stimulus depends upon its potential for producing arousal (at moderate levels) or for de-arousal (at very high levels). Research has revealed that both these mechanisms (arousal and de-arousal) can produce positive affect under specific conditions. The relation between hedonic value and activation can be represented by the familiar inverted U-shaped curve found so often in research on motivation. Several variables produce an increase in arousal, and others produce a decrease in arousal. (These variables will be described in a later section.) The arousal theory can account for hedonic responses across a wide variety of behavioral contexts, as Berlyne (1971) and others have demonstrated in numerous empirical studies.

Applied to vandalism, the hedonic component comes into play in two sets of factors: those extrinsic and those intrinsic to the act of destruction itself. I will allude only briefly to the extrinsic factors for the sake of completeness, and then go on quickly to the intrinsic factors which have been the focus of my own research.

People spend a great deal of time and effort in order to participate in activities that are dangerous, frightening, risky, and physiologically arousing. Such occasions are deemed to be enjoyable and fun by participants. Vandalism fits this description. In interviews, youngsters have said, in connection with their vandalism, that is was great fun trying to avoid getting caught and running away from the police or other adults. The risk and danger, the uncertainty, the thrill of evasive action, are all arousing and hence enjoyable. Research has shown that sensation-seeking is correlated with juvenile delinquency (Farley and Sewell, 1976).

Another extrinsic aspect of vandalism is due to its association with other arousing and enjoyable activities: it is part of a social drama, a sequence of social acts directed toward the goal of sheer enjoyment. For example, a youngster in The Netherlands stated to an interviewer that on the weekends he and his friends were looking for a good time and that a routine was followed. First, he said, we go to the disco; and, after that, we go break a shop window. A prodigious quantity of alcohol consumption is usually involved in this social activity, it should be noted. All of these elements constitute a social drama, having actors, stage, and script, and entitled, 'a good time'. The hedonic components existing within each of these elements reinforce each other during the sequence of events constituting the performance.

To be sure, the importance of extrinsic sources of the hedonic component of vandalism should not be underestimated, but I would prefer in the limited space available to concentrate on intrinsic sources instead of pursuing this line of inquiry further.

1.1. Art and destruction

The act of destruction can be intrinsically enjoyable in itself. Why so? I would say, in a word, that destruction can be an aesthetic experience: breaking can be beautiful. That is, the same variables that account for the pleasure of socially acceptable aesthetic experiences in art, music, and literature also are responsible for the enjoyment of an act of destruction. The degree of enjoyment of destruction will depend upon the presence and strength of the variables that underlie any aesthetic response. Artists as well as psychologists have noted that a close affinity exists between art and destruction – or more generally between creative and destructive acts. This apparent paradox is explicable in terms of the present theory, because the novel transformation of material into a new structure activates the same basic set of psychological processes in both creative and destructive acts. These factors will be discussed below; but first, a few examples will be given of the commonality between creative and destructive acts.

Presenting destruction as art is not particularly new or novel in the artistic world. Typewriter-smashing is the speciality of the artist Jean Toche. Another artist, John Latham, builds and destroys 'skoob' towers ('books' spelled backwards) (Walker, 1973). Arman, a French artist and co-founder of the

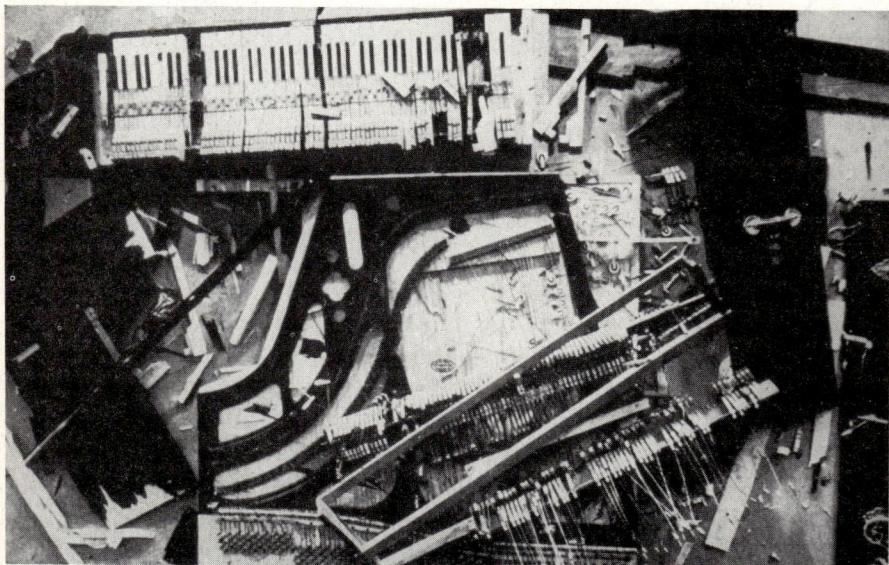

Figure 1. Assemblage by Arman of parts of a grand piano, presently on exhibit at the Pompidou Center, Paris.

group of New Realists and the School of Nice, is known for his 'diverse sculptures'. Among his masterpieces are assemblages of pieces from a clock and a piano (fig. 1). Another example of destruction as art is César's compressed bodies of automobiles and motorcycles. An art critic and follower of César, Paul Restany (1975), wrote as follows about César's exhibit in Paris: "On May 8, 1960, there was a scandal at the opening of the 10th Salon de Mai. César presented his new sculptures: compressed bodies of automobiles, chosen from among the most 'beautiful' – three bales of vividly colored metal, magnificent, compact, monumental, forceful...". These objects caused a scandal at the Salon de Mai in Paris in 1960, but are now in the permanent collections of the Modern Art Museums in New York and Paris (see fig. 2).

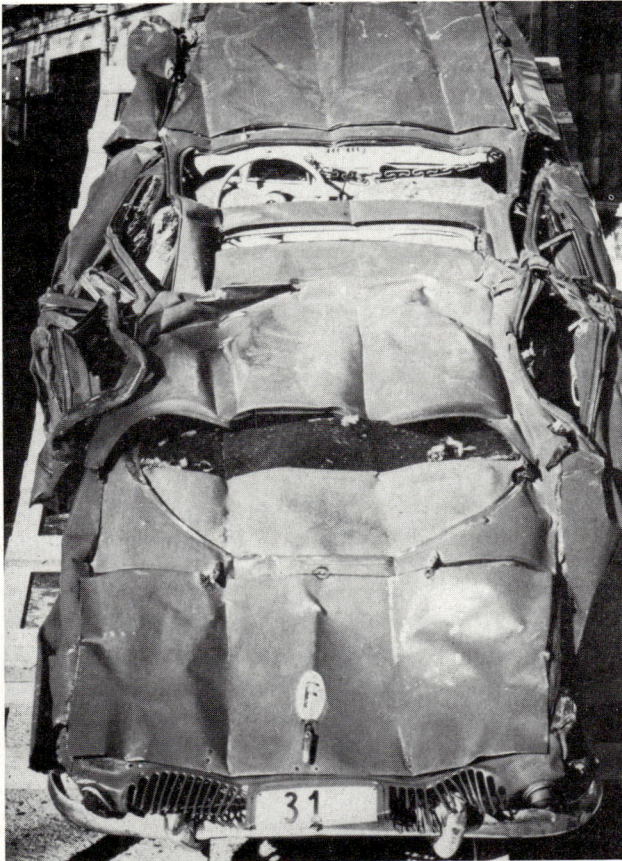

Figure 2. A 'compression' sculpture by César exhibited at the Salon de Mai in Paris, 1960.

Another form of destruction, graffiti, can be viewed as art – and as an improvement over the original environment in many cases (Kurlansky and Noor, 1974). A sociology student from the City College of New York searched out some of the prolific graffitists who had adorned the streets, walls, and subway trains of New York City, and convinced them to exhibit their works as art. Each graffitist sold his 'works' for between $200–300, and they were commissioned to do the backdrops for the Twyla Tharp Dance company's production of 'Duece Couple' and murals for office buildings.

The use of destruction in architecture has been pioneered by James Wines and his associates in New York (SITE, Inc.). Many of their buildings seem to have been 'prevandalized', as it were, by the architects themselves. A building designed for the Best company, a department store, is a case in point. On the front roof it appears that a cascade of loose bricks is flowing down the façade. The building seems to be suspended between the process of construction and demolition (see fig. 3). A state building inspector would not believe that the architect had intentionally designed this 'damage', and officially recorded the flowing bricks as due to 'hurricane damage'. In another building, the corner of one base seems to have broken off. Actually, this large crack conceals the main entrance to the building – apparent when the wedge-shaped section is moved outward by a distance of 40 feet. The work of Wines and the 'SITE' group has been exhibited at the Museum of Modern Art, the Venice Biennale, and has been discussed in art and architectural journals all over the world.

Figure 3. The use of destruction in architecture: a building designed by James Wines for a department store company in Houston, Texas, U.S.A.

1.2. Aesthetic variables

What determines the degree of pleasure a person will experience during an act of destruction? A more specific answer to this question can be found in psychological theories of aesthetics (Berlyne, 1971). The most important

Figure 4. A large broken window which many persons would not hesitate to call 'beautiful'.

stimulus factors which increase the level of arousal (and thus a positive hedonic experience) are a few structural or formal qualities such as complexity, expectation, uncertainty, and novelty. (Variables such as complexity, expectation, and novelty are called 'collective' stimulus properties by Berlyne, since to respond the person must compare the existing stimulus elements with others present in the background or with the preceding stimulus.) In addition, organization (symmetry) and psychological characteristics of the stimulus are important.

Applying aesthetic theory of destruction leads to the prediction that breaking an object will be experienced as being more or less enjoyable depending on the process of the destruction (i.e., the extent to which it is complex, novel, unexpected, etc.). Note that destruction will not necessarily always be enjoyable and pleasurable; the extent to which a hedonic response is produced will vary depending upon the nature of the process of destruction.

In terms of the stimulus characteristics relevant to aesthetic theory, the destruction of an object constitutes a very complicated situation. Aesthetic variables are involved in three phases of the destructive act: before, during, and afterwards. Before any destruction occurs, there are differences among objects in their appearance in terms of structural variables (e.g., complexity, novelty, and expectedness), psychophysical properties (size or intensity), and organization of the stimulus elements (pattern or symmetry). If an individual expects that changing the appearance of an object will make it more interesting or pleasing, an effort may be made to do so even if socially disapproved methods such as vandalism are necessary. During the process of destruction itself, the enjoyment is derived primarily from the visual and auditory cues that occur as part of the rapid structural transformation of the object. Thus, greater enjoyment should be derived from destroying an object if the process of breaking is more complex, unexpected, novel, etc. The appearance of the stimulus object after destruction has been accomplished will also vary on the dimensions specified by aesthetic theory. At this phase the pattern and organization of the component parts of the object are important determinants of its appearance. For example, breaking a particular pane of glass in a large window could create a more or less interesting and pleasing pattern which could be observed afterwards. Fig. 4 shows an aesthetically pleasing result of the breakage of a large window in the student union of the University of Wisconsin.

2. Pleasure in destruction: research

To investigate the role of aesthetic variables in destruction, a series of studies was undertaken using both experiments and interviews (Allen and Greenberger, 1978). Space permits only a brief summary of some of the relevant results from our research. An experiment was designed to test the hypothesis that the desire to break an object is related to the complexity manifested during its destruction. Subjects observed films and then indicated how much they wanted to break each one of 26 panes of glass that had been shown breaking under standardized conditions. Results showed a significant relation between a person's commitment to break a pane of glass and subjective complexity: that is, subjects preferred to break those objects that break in a more complex way. In a related study, both pleasingness and interestingness of destruction were found to be directly related to stimulus complexity.

The initial objective complexity of a structure prior to its destruction was examined in a study directed toward understanding the determinants of selection of targets to be destroyed (Allen and Spencer, 1977). It was assumed that subjects would anticipate that the process of destruction would be more pleasing in the case of complex as opposed to simple structures. Results revealed that the subjects consistently chose to break a complex (rather than a simple) structure; moreover, they expected that the outcome of the destruction would be more interesting and pleasing for a complex than for a simple structure. Overall, 82% of the subjects chose to destroy the more complex structure.

The role of the pattern or symmetry produced by a specific type of breaking has been explored in one experiment. It was hypothesized that a person will choose to destroy the particular elements of an object that will have the result of producing the most pleasing of all possible patterns. As we predicted, it was found that subjects chose to break the one pane of glass (from among several in a window) that resulted in the most pleasing configuration remaining after the break.

We have also examined the effect of expectation or uncertainty on the enjoyment of destruction (Allen and Greenberger, 1979). According to aesthetic theory, destruction should be most enjoyable when it disconfirms one's expectation. Films were constructed which showed a series of episodes in which a pane of glass broke in the way the subject expected it to do on the basis of previous trials – with the exception of one instance. Thus, in one experimental condition the person's expectations about the success of attempted destruction was either confirmed or disconfirmed. Note that the objective characteristics of the destruction were held constant in all cases. Results indicated that the destruction was reported as being more enjoyable when the expectation about when the object would break was disconfirmed. Similarly, in an interview study we found positive correlations between the degree of enjoyment reported during destruction and the nature of the aesthetic variables present during the destruction, such as complexity, expectedness, and excitingness.

The psychophysical variable of size of stimulus in relation to enjoyment of destruction has been investigated (Allen and Sobel, 1978). It was predicted that subjects would prefer to break larger (as opposed to smaller) windows, since the destruction of large objects would be more likely to provide a more interesting and pleasing pattern of breaking. Results revealed that subjects clearly preferred to break large rather than small windows. Data were also obtained concerning the subjects' expectations about the way the windows would break as a function of their size. As expected, results showed that individuals believed that the larger windows (compared to smaller) would break in a way that would be more complex, interesting, pleasing, novel, beautiful, exciting, and loud. The anticipation about the process of breaking can help account for the choice made among potential targets which vary in size.

In a more practical vein, we looked at the degree of enjoyment produced by the destruction of common building material used in construction (Chao and Allen, 1978). Subjects rated their degree of enjoyment in observing the breaking of each of 20 filmed segments of different types of material. Results indicated that several factors, such as complexity and unexpectedness of the breaking, were correlated with level of enjoyment of the destruction of the material. Categorizing all the material into five different clusters yielded the following ratings of enjoyment of the breaking (from most to least): glass, tile, wood, and metal. The importance of the aesthetics of destruction is emphasized by the strong correlation found between enjoyment of the breaking and the subject's reported desire to be allowed to destroy a particular type of material.

Although I have discussed several aesthetic variables separately, it is obvious that in everyday life many of them are actively involved in any specific instance of destruction or vandalism, and that they all contribute to the total hedonic experience. In another of our studies, male respondents recalled all incidents within the past five years in which they had engaged in destruction (Allen and Greenberger, 1978). Detailed questions were asked in a personal interview concerning the three most serious incidents. Many respondents stated that they had selected a particular object to destroy because of the way they expected that it would break in terms of the presence of variables specified by aesthetic theory. For example, one person broke a particular light because the glass was very thick and he expected that it would break in an interesting way. After completing the open-ended questions about an incident of destruction, respondents assessed it on a number of bipolar scales. Significant positive correlations were found between hedonic experience (degree of enjoyment) during the destruction and characteristics of the process of destruction, such as complexity, interestingness, expectedness, and level of excitement. The relation of complexity and interestingness with enjoyment was consistent with our predictions and with previous results. In addition, interestingness of the breaking was also correlated with the level of excitement reported by respondents.

The studies I have mentioned concentrated primarily on the visual sense modality. Of course, in many cases of vandalism auditory cues may be even more important than visual cues. (This is certainly likely to be true at night!) I have been told by Dutch colleagues that in former times a student in a university student club in The Netherlands could order a 'meter of noise'. This consisted of a meter of plates which were brought to the student, who proceeded to throw them all on the floor in order to produce the desired sound from the breaking. In two studies we have investigated enjoyment of the sounds that accompany a wide variety of types of destruction (Lewis and Allen, 1982). It was clear from the results that sounds associated with destruction are often quite pleasant and enjoyable. Results disclosed several aesthetic variables that were correlated with the degree of enjoyment of the sounds produced by destruction.

In addition to visual and auditory cues, tactile-kinesthetic information is often particularly relevant when destruction involves direct contact between the person and the object (e.g., kicking or striking with a stick), rather than being accomplished from a distance (e.g., throwing a stone). The feedback and resistance accompanying the act of destruction (the 'feel' of it) may influence the degree of enjoyment experienced by individuals. Further, the nature of the relationship between the cues from different sense modalities introduces further complications. Additional research is needed on the relative contribution of visual, auditory, and tactual-kinesthetic cues to the hedonic response produced by different types of vandalism.

3. Conclusions

The aesthetic or hedonic theory can be stated in either a strong or weak form with respect to its causal role in vandalism. A strong version of the present theory would predict that: (a) the appearance of objects in the environment; or (b) a person's anticipation of the forthcoming hedonic experience during the destruction; or (c) the anticipation of the post-destruction appearance of the object – will all serve as cues evoking vandalism. A less strong version of the theory would predict that aesthetic variables serve as discriminative cues which influence selection among potential targets. Furthermore, even if vandalism were produced by motives that are totally extraneous to this theory (e.g., imitation or revenge) the hedonic experience would still reinforce destructive behavior and thus increase the likelihood of vandalism occurring again. Since degree of enjoyment in destruction varies across different acts, intermittent reinforcement is produced; and as we know, such a pattern produces strong resistance to extinction.

It is important to emphasize two distinctive characteristics of the aesthetic theory of vandalism. First, it focusses on distal factors that are intrinsic to the stimulus itself, rather than on personality traits within the individual. Second, the present point of view emphasizes the continuity rather than discontinuity between psychological processes in vandalism and in more socially acceptable behavior. Stated another way, stress is placed on the normality and universality of the underlying processes that determine the hedonic component of vandalism. One straightforward implication from this position is that vandalism might be reduced by using architectural designs and building materials that minimize the enjoyment of destruction. According to the present view, the appearance of an object before and after destruction is important in vandalism. If an object looks as if it would break in an interesting and pleasurable way, then destruction would be more likely to occur. Similarly, any object is a candidate for vandalism if it can be made to be more aesthetically pleasing by destruction. Vandalism should be reduced, therefore, by the use of architectural designs and type of materials that would minimize those processes which contribute to enjoyment during destruction.

Acknowledging the important role played in the hedonic component of vandalism may also suggest types of preventive programs. Perhaps socially approved activities could be found which would produce the same hedonic outcomes that are produced by destruction. A first step in this direction would be for all of us to become more aware of the psychological benefits that individuals derive from the hedonic reactions that are often found as intrinsic elements in the act of destruction.

In closing, I want to reiterate the thesis advanced at the beginning: hedonic experience is often a strong component (extrinsic and intrinsic) of the act of destruction. We should think seriously about the implications of this fact when constructing theories and when designing programs to prevent vandalism.

References

Allen, V.L., 1983. Arousal, affect, and control: The role of the physical environment. In: C. Spielberger, I. Sarason, P. Defaris, eds., Stress and anxiety, vol. 9. New York: Wiley.

Allen, V.L., D.B. Greenberger, 1978. An aesthetic theory of vandalism. Crime and Delinquency 24, 309–332.

Allen, V.L., D.B. Greenberger, 1979. Enjoyment of destruction: The role of uncertainty. Journal of Nonverbal Behavior 4, 87–96.

Allen, V.L., D.B. Greenberger, 1980a. Destruction and perceived control. In: A. Baum, J. Singer, eds., Advances in environmental psychology, vol. 2, pp. 85–109 New York: Erlbaum.

Allen, V.L., D.B. Greenberger, 1980b. Aesthetic theory, perceived control, and social identity: Toward an understanding of vandalism. In: K. Baker, R.J. Rubel, eds., Violence and crime in the schools, pp. 193–207, Lexington (Mass.): D.C. Heath.

Allen, V.L., S. Sobel, 1978. Preference for destruction and size of stimulus object. Madison (Wisc.) (unpubl. MS).

Allen, V.L., D.R. Spencer, 1977. Initial complexity and preference for destruction. Madison (Wisc.) (unpubl. MS).

Berlyne, D.E., 1971. Aesthetics and psychobiology. New York: Appleton-Century-Crofts.

Chao, T., V.L. Allen, 1978. Characteristics of building materials as a factor in vandalism. Madison (Wisc.) (unpubl. MS).

Cohen, S., 1973. Property destruction: Motives and meanings. In: C. Ward, ed., Vandalism, pp. 23–53. New York: Van Nostrand Reinhard.

Farley, F.H., T. Sewell, 1976. Test of an arousal theory of delinquence: Stimulation-seeking in delinquent and non-delinquent black adolescents. Criminal Justice and Behavior 3, 314–320.

Farrington, D.P., D.J. West, 1978. The Cambridge study in delinquent development. In: S.A. Mednick, A.E. Baert, eds., A survey of prospective longitudinal research in Europe. Copenhagen: World Health Organization.

Kurlansky, M., J. Noor, 1974. The faith of graffiti. New York: Praeger.

Lewis, S., V.L. Allen, 1982. Sounds of destruction. Madison (Wisc.) (unpubl. MS).

Madison, A., 1970. Vandalism: The not-so-senseless crime. New York: Seapury Press.

Martin, J.M., 1961. Juvenile vandalism: A study of its nature and prevention. Springfield (Ill.): C.G. Thomas.

Piaget, J., 1952. The origins of intelligence in children. Transl. M. Cook. New York: International Universities Press.

Réau, L., 1959. Les monuments détruits de l'art français. Paris: Hachette.

Restany, P., 1975. César. Transl. J. Shepley. New York: Harry N. Abram.

Thrasher, F.M., 1936. The gang. Chicago: University of Chicago Press.

Wade, A.W., 1967. Social processes in the act of juvenile vandalism. In: M. Clinard, A.W. Wade, eds., Criminal behavior systems, pp. 94–109. New York: Holt, Rinehart and Winston.

Walker, J.A., 1973. Glossary of art, architecture and design since 1945. London: Clive Bingley.

Abstract: V.L. Allen, Toward an understanding of the hedonic component of vandalism

A theory is presented which attempts to provide a better understanding of the contribution of the physical environment or stimulus characteristics in vandalism. Destruction often seems to be an enjoyable experience. It is hypothesized that destruction is pleasurable because it has the characteristics of an aesthetic experience. That is to say, the variables that account for pleasure and enjoyment in socially acceptable experiences such as art, music, and literature are also responsible for the positive hedonic responses often associated with acts of destruction. Applying aesthetic theory to vandalism leads to the prediction that the breaking of an object will be experienced as more enjoyable if the process is more complex, novel, unexpected, symmetrical, etc. In several empirical studies evidence has been obtained which supports the theory. Implications of the theory are discussed for reducing vandalism both through changes in architecture or design and through preventive programs directed toward individuals.

CHAPTER 5

Countries without vandalism?

An interpretive frame for the Swiss case

K. NOSCHIS

This paper addresses itself to a multifaceted question that calls for a broad ranging and, of necessity, an intricate response. [1] Why are some countries less vandalised than others? Such a question admits of a relationship between measures of vandalism and identifiable cultural and geographical entities. Thus, the question is multifaceted because it opens up many issues and lines of argument about what is vandalism and about how countries should be considered, and the answer is complex because it must be seen from a cultural and a historical as well as from a geographical perspective.

As it would be far beyond the scope of this paper to develop such a comprehensive thesis, the theme of negligible vandalism in some countries is here addressed by discussing the case of a single country, within a specific perspective and bearing in mind the following two assumptions:

(i) countries are cultural and geographical entities that may be considered *in toto* and *autonomously* when discussing the collective identity of their inhabitants;

(ii) the image of a less-vandalised country is one where public areas, as well as the public transportation and communication network, appear to be undamaged and clean.

The case that will be discussed is that of Switzerland. This country has the image and renown of a country with little or no vandalism. At the same time it is recognised as fostering a collective identity quite distinct from that of its neighbouring countries, Germany, France, Italy and Austria. Thus, the purpose of the paper is to explore how vandalism might be approached in the Swiss context.

The paper is divided into three parts. Firstly, a number of conjectures will be formulated about why there is only negligible vandalism in Switzerland, with evidence to support this claim; secondly, it will be shown that, notwiths-

[1] The author is grateful to several persons, in particular A. Noschis and F. Rochat, who have contributed to this paper in various ways. M. Jaccard, of the PTT in Bern provided the data about the telephone booths. M. Martin, from the Town Council of Lausanne, volunteered data about restoring vandalised public buildings. Prof. C. Lévy-Leboyer first invited the author to reflect on the problem of vandalism in Switzerland.

tanding this claim, there is increasing vandalism in that country and, thirdly, some conclusions will be suggested on the basis of the to some extent contradictory evidence discussed in the first two sections.

The definition of vandalism to which this paper addresses itself limits the phenomenon to 'the destruction or disfigurement of communal property'. This definition is quite unsatisfactory for many purposes. For instance, it does not comprise as vandalistic a hammer blow dealt to a private car – but, in terms of the above assumption of what is the image of a less-vandalised country, it would appear to be sufficient and at the same time it is the most adequate for the argument developed herein. In other words, the core of the paper is based on a perspective of vandalism wherein the most important opposition is that between an object, a site or a construction that a group of people is concerned about, be it only as users, and vandals, that is those who destroy or disfigure such objects. Evidently the term 'vandal' could refer to a municipal authority that destroys a building valued by local residents just as well as to a group of unoccupied youngsters.

1. Negligible vandalism

As evidence for the negligible amount of vandalism in Switzerland, it is useful to consider some data with respect to vandalism in telephone booths and graffiti on the walls of public buildings. In Switzerland as a whole there are about 10,000 public telephone booths. In 1975, the PTT (GPO) were called out about 5,600 times in order to repair damage caused by acts of vandalism – that is, voluntary acts of destruction or disfigurement of public telephones or booths. Total expenditure on these repairs was 316,000 Swiss francs. In 1980 the corresponding figures were 4,900 calls and 406,000 Swiss francs for repairs.

Thus, the figures are fairly stable, taking into account the rising costs, and may be summarised in the following way: about *one* telephone booth out of two receives *once* a year the visit of *one* vandal, while the damage, spread over all the telephone booths, amounts to about 40 Swiss francs per year and per telephone booth. These figures do not cause undue concern to the authorities, particularly not when compared with data from countries that share a border with Switzerland. For instance, according to evidence from the work of Moser (See ch. 10 in this volume), it is possible to estimate that both the number of vandalised phone boxes and the ensuing damage in France are double those in Switzerland, while earnings are no greater.

Some further data may also be of interest. The Swiss GPO considers that the fundamental condition to be met for telephone booths to be a source of income is their uninterrupted operation. Thus, in large towns, the procedure is to carry out repair work within one hour of the report that a booth has been damaged – be it by an act of vandalism or for another reason – while in other countries the rule is to take action within four hours.

Furthermore, a survey carried out by the GPO itself established that, among 623 cases of out-of-order telephone booth reports during a two-month period in 1978, 402 came from the public itself, while about 120 came from the cleaning or service staff. In other words, in about 65% of the cases a Swiss citizen was responsible for reporting the existence of a damaged phone from another telephone booth.

It is worthwhile now to look briefly at some other data on graffiti on the walls of public buildings in a medium size Swiss town such as Lausanne which has a population of about 120,000. The average cost of renovating façades is about 5–6,000 Swiss francs per year, which is negligible, according to the local authorities themselves. Inscriptions or drawings on walls are immediately removed when they are offensive to local authorities, while less personalised graffiti can be left untouched for longer – even up to a month when 'frankly speaking they are not unpleasant'.

That vandalism is a minor problem in Switzerland is further confirmed by several survey studies. Thus, Casparis and Vaz (1979), following an anonymous self-report survey of 707 males of varied origin aged 15 to 19, carried out in Zurich in 1973, noted that 26% stated that they had never perpetrated any vandalism on public or private property, 36% admitted to this having been the case once or twice, and only 23% said that they had engaged in such acts more than five times. The definition of vandalism in this survey included "breaking windows or street lights, destroying gardens or flower beds, slashing automobile tyres, etc.". These percentages are strikingly modest when compared with those from other countries.

In his extensive study of criminality in Switzerland, Clinard (1978) also insists on the limited amount of vandalism in the country. Thus he notes that in the canton and city of Bern "only 4% of the approximately 4,000 cases coming before the juvenile prosecutor in 1971 involved vandalism. In Basel-Stadt, only 5.4% of the 1,643 juvenile and youth cases handled by youth officials were vandalism cases" (1978: 126). Clinard compares these data with figures from the United States where "the malicious destruction of public property by juveniles and youth groups constitutes a major problem" (*id.*: 126).

These few figures, then, do confirm that in Switzerland the problem of vandalism to public property is of modest dimensions. Consequently, it is appropriate to suggest some ideas which may help us to understand why vandalism is of such negligible importance in that country.

For this purpose, I will suggest a specific perspective with reference to an extensive study by Heller (1979), wherein the author sought to understand the proverbial phenomenon of Swiss cleanliness, which today is almost the trademark of the country. Heller analyses the advent of cleanliness between 1850 and 1930. One interesting aspect, among others, is the growth of tourism for health purposes. The purity of the Alpine air as well as of the water in the mountain lakes was already a feature of the country, but the infrastructure and hotels had to be adapted to it. In other words, the cleanliness of habitats and inhabitants had to reflect that of nature. Only in this manner could the country measure up to the expectations of the tourists. And that is what happened. But obviously the success of such an operation has many reasons. Two of these warrant attention for our purpose. On the one hand, the public hygiene campaigns conducted in Switzerland were closely linked to educational campaigns in the schools, and naturally were orchestrated with particular care in a country well known to constitute a propitious environment for pedagogical experiment. The necessity, supported by scientific evidence, of promoting cleanliness for health reasons was particularly emphasised.

On the other hand, the religious movement, the 'Reveil' (awakening), – the revitalised protestantism of the 19th century – also contributed to the equation, physical health = moral health. The simultaneous insistence of the 'duty' of working stressed the value of working and, even more so, of working on increasing cleanliness.

The above observations are sufficient to postulate a hypothesis about the internalisation of the idea of order and cleanliness by the Swiss: it pays off from a moral standpoint, i.e. some existential problems are done away with, as well as in terms of health, i.e. less problems and medical expenses, and with respect to job opportunities in tourism, i.e. more money in people's pockets. From then on, cleanliness and order no longer were private matters but rather issues of public concern.

Today, cleanliness and order are recognised attributes of the Swiss and – more importantly for our purposes – give them the opportunity to assert their specificity when, for example, they go to a foreign country and judge it to be 'dirty' or 'disorganised'. Thus, Swiss citizens have gradually identified themselves with this image of cleanliness and order as values to be pursued and to be practised – to the point that today they are considered as perennial values of the national heritage.

Let us now connect the above considerations with vandalism in Switzerland. To put it briefly, every act of vandalism is directed explicitly against the order and cleanliness of the public domain, thus against the identity of the Swiss. If order and cleanliness are interiorised values that correspond to ourselves it is desirable that the environment fit these values or, to put it differently, that there be congruence. In other words, we see here an extension of the private domain into the public environment. That is, not only the single individual is characterised by cleanliness and order, and therefore not only the personal environment or private property that corresponds to it, but the entire community and thus also communal property and the environment. To create disorder or 'dirtiness', be it by breaking up a telephone booth or by painting slogans on walls, is to do violence to this relation of identification with the environment. Let us note in passing that, when a municipality orders a building to be destroyed, it is not acting in quite the same way as other vandals, although such an intention could be blocked by a referendum (a form of expression of the electorate's desires that is quite popular in Switzerland), since such destruction is usually subject to a logic of 'clean = modern' that in turn is part of the identity under consideration.

To sum up, everyone tries to ensure that non-congruence between person and environment will not occur, as this would be an obstacle not only to the pursuit of practical aims, but also, and this seems more deep-rooted, to the survival of the very identity of the Swiss.

2. Yet, there is vandalism

Yet, in Switzerland, there is vandalism. In 1972, the GPO had to take action 1,673 times, repairing damage caused by vandals, while in 1975 these calls had trebled in number. However, since then, the amount of repair work has increased only slightly, though it must be remembered that in the meantime new, more resistant telephones have replaced the former models. Thus, today, when a telephone booth is vandalised the damage is greater. Ten years ago a few hasty turns of the hand were enough to stop a public telephone working, whereas today it is necessary to use tools.

Let me present some more data. Clinard (1978: 125) in his study of criminality notes that "an analysis of vandalism cases in the canton of Bern from 1963 to 1972 indicated an increase in rates", although he stresses that "the annual increases, as measured by correlation and regression coefficients, were unusually small". Clinard makes two points in order to explain this "low profile of vandalism". "Under Swiss criminal law a person can be convicted for vandalism only if the person affected by the action requests it. In other words, there must be a plaintiff. Furthermore, any vandalism in connection with an offence such as burglary is generally recorded only as burglary" (Clinard, 1978: 197).

Thus, vandalistic acts occur more and more frequently, although several initiatives – be these preventive or statistical – have been taken in Switzerland in order to maintain the 'low profile'.

It is worth noting, however, that, in spite of such measures, ten days of youth fury in Lausanne in 1981 were enough to cause 110,000 Swiss francs worth of damage to public buildings – that is 20 times the usual amount. In Zurich, the same year a youth demonstration was the cause of incalculable damage – smashed shop windows, defaced traffic and road signs, barricades, widespread slogans and drawings on walls – changing the public appearance of the whole town to that of a battle ground for several weeks. [2]

Thus, there is vandalism in Switzerland, slowly increasing and for the time being more in fits and starts, but which nevertheless merits the label of a societal phenomenon.

Now, if one looks at the vandals, who, in Switzerland perhaps more than elsewhere, find themselves fairly frequently in the hands of the police, with whom the population collaborates willingly, they will talk like their counterparts in other countries. At least, one may suppose this to be true. They will talk about rejection by the system, about rebellion against society, about disgust for the materialism of the welfare society, about the sadness around them. In opposition to this viewpoint, the vandalised municipality will invoke the absolute necessity of efficiency, order and cleanliness.

In both cases we have to attempt to understand what underlies these observations. But it would be beside the point of this speculative paper to do that directly. In fact, most empirical studies of vandalism deal with precisely this question and there is no *a priori* reason for supposing that what contributes to a scientifically oriented explanation of specific forms of vandalism in France or in the United States should not apply to Switzerland. On the other hand, this obviously does not exclude the appropriateness or usefulness of comparative research in various countries.

3. Interpretative frame

In this section, an attempt will be made to propose an interpretative frame for the forms of vandalism mentioned, with the intention of relating it specifically to the themes that were developed in the first section above. For this purpose reference is made to the views, not about vandalism, but about animism and projection as propounded by two eminent Swiss psychologists, Jean Piaget and Carl Gustav Jung, respectively.

Piaget – whose studies deal mainly, as is well known, with the development of intelligence – speaks of a child's initial lack of differentiation between himself and the world that surrounds him. Consciousness arises precisely from a process of progressive differentiation, a phase of this development being the types of behaviour that Piaget (1929, 1973) groups under the name of animism. We can speak of animism when the child attributes life, intentions and forces to objects as such.

---

[2]   De Martino (1962) discusses such collective outbursts of rage by developing the theme (complementary to the argument proposed herein) of the importance – from a collective standpoint – to members of a society of feeling part of an order of moral values that offers a level of control and cultural resolution of instinctive life. Otherwise these forms will become hazardous.

We will now explore the hypothesis that this is also what happens to an adult when he uses violent gestures with respect to parking meters or public telephones that are out of order, while at the same time threatening these objects aloud. This is the type of vandal that is specifically considered in the following section.

According to Piaget there are causes of both a personal and a social nature that converge in the phenomenon of animism. As to the causes of a personal nature, Piaget notes that a child does not dissociate what pertains to the physical world from what pertains to the psychic world and, as a second factor, mentions what he rather curiously calls introjection, the attribution to objects of feelings similar to those experienced by the child himself. Generally speaking, these are characteristics of a developmental phase that Piaget qualifies as being egocentric.

As to the causes of a social nature, which are related to the fact that the child is a member of a group, Piaget talks about a feeling of participation, as when for instance, a child judges without further ado that his or her teddybear is aware of the difficulties that the child experiences in his or her relations with the father. Again, and this example is probably more familiar, when the child asserts that the moon is watching us, or that the sun moves in order to hear us, this means that they take part in the everyday vicissitudes of our lives.

The second social factor discussed by Piaget is what he calls moral obligation. In the young child, physical and moral necessity are confounded. The laws of nature have a moral origin: there is someone (e.g. an adult) who tells the objects (e.g. a child) what they have to do. Piaget (1973: 277–8) says: "It is not because the child believes things to be alive that he regards them as obedient, but it is because he believes them to be obedient, that he regards them as alive".

These four factors, that Piaget considers to be at the root of animism, viz. absence of dissociation between the physical and psychic worlds, introjection, participation and obedience or morality, can now be related specifically to acts of vandalism. In fact, the above causes are intimately linked, but it may also be profitable to separate them. Thus, the vandalistic behaviour of an adult in a telephone booth or with a parking meter – and further in other cases of vandalism to be mentioned – could well be related to the above causal model of animism.

The user who is dissatisfied with a telephone booth or with the response he receives or does not receive from the phone considers the telephone itself part of this non-congruence between him or herself and someone or the community: the object is at fault and has to be punished. Moreover, it is precisely because the phone is supposed to obey the frustrated user's commands that he or she attributes to the machine a life of its own and strikes it.

As to the causes of an individual nature – the absence of dissociation between the physical and psychic world on the one hand and the attribution to an object of feelings similar to those experienced by oneself, on the other – it is probable that even here one might propose a parallel between animistic and vandalistic behaviour. This would be characterised by an unjustified extension of the psychic to the physical – for example, by the intention to 'harm' the object in order that it might 'suffer'.

In spite of possible similarities between animist behaviour and its causes and vandalistic behaviour and its causes, a difficulty arises from taking vandals to be children. Another study by Piaget shows clearly the problems that such a procedure can give rise to. Piaget, in *Language and thought of the child* (1926), stresses the distinction between directed, or intelligent, thought and non-directed, or autistic, thought.

Intelligent thought is controlled by the laws of experience and logic, autistic thought by those of symbolism and immediate satisfaction. Here, implicitly at least, if one pays attention to the terminology, is a devaluation of non-directed thought. An example will make this point clear. According to Piaget, in the case of non-directed thought water is primarily to be considered as satisfying organic needs. It is by extension of this view that water becomes a symbol of the amniotic liquid, of birth, of rebirth and of baptism. Intelligent or directed thought, on the contrary, views water as a natural substance, the origins of which can be observed, at least partially, and whose movements and regularities can be studied and experimented with in chemical terms.

To sum up, Piaget, the psychologist of intelligence, is intolerant with respect to non-directed thought, that which proceeds by associations and symbolism. Now, if we reconsider the example of the potential vandal in front of the parking meter, his or her thought when he/she ends up smashing it calls for a 'logic' of immediate satisfaction and of symbolism, wherein the object is used as a scapegoat making amends for its supposed wrongdoing.

If we adopt Piaget's viewpoint the vandal is to be viewed as a child. Nevertheless, as the example of water helps to show, despite itself, both forms of thought are equally present in the world of the adult. [3] Thus, one could speak here of a rationalist bias of Piaget and of its corollary, a dismissal of non-directed thought, or its relegation to early developmental stages, primitive peoples or pathology. By seeking to analyse vandalism in purely rationalistic terms one can end up with views such as the above which, it should be noted, are in harmony with the stereotypes that are attached to vandalism.

Before proposing another perspective it is appropriate to stress that Piaget has never explicitly spoken about vandalism and that, by referring to his analysis of child animism and different forms of thought, my aim was to point at what might be labelled as the limit of an exclusively rational paradigm for

---

[3]   This might be formulated wittily by noting that technicians to be are still baptised.

analysing the phenomenon, once the existence of a parallel between animism and vandalism is granted. Cases, such as graffiti on walls, where this parallel between vandalism and animism does not seem to hold will be mentioned later.

A different perspective comes from the psychology of the unconscious. According to Jung, projection, i.e. the transposition of psychic content to objects or people in the real world, is a common adult psychological device. Here, it is suggested that by considering projection as being at the forefront of acts of vandalism one avoids the rationalist perspective which considers associative non-directed thought as infantile or pathological.

Jung (1921, ed. 1971: par. 783) develops an original viewpoint on projection that is relevant to our purposes. Projection is seen as resulting from the dissociation of the archaic identity (a most Jungian term) between subject and object. This can be understood in the following terms. To start with, the world and the subject are identical. When there is differentiation of one aspect of personality this is projected outside on someone or something else.

In other words, as a psychological process the animism of Piaget and the projection of Jung overlap. However, for Jung it is not a question of a child's psychological mechanism during the egocentric phase, but primarily of an original identity between subject and object that is *lost* with projection, whereas, for Piaget, animism is but a stage in the gradual and progressive differentiation toward intelligent thought.

Fury with a parking meter might serve as an example of projection: the individual projects onto the parking meter an aspect of himself or herself that in this manner has become dissociated; an aspect that the parking meter allows him/her to recall symbolically, for instance his or her relation to order, discipline, or to the inhuman time of watches and clocks.

According to Jung, depending on the context, an individual may later recall his other projections and introject them, but this time consciously. Projections may be momentary or lasting and quite variable.

4. Conclusion

With these elements in mind it is now appropriate to conclude by connecting this theoretical framework for the interpretation of vandalism with what was previously said about Swiss identity.

I have suggested that the vandal in Switzerland harms his or her own identity as a Swiss and thus somehow harms himself or herself. To put it briefly, this view of the negligible amount of vandalism in Switzerland strengthens and is strengthened by Jung's conception of projection. In fact, order and cleanliness would today be part of the constitutive – not to say archaic – identity of the Swiss.

As act of vandalism in terms of the individual would then be a projection, that could be considered either positively as a dissociation anticipating a future consciousness, or negatively as a dissociation *per se*. Inversely, the lack of Swiss vandalism could be regarded negatively as a complacent original absence of dissociation, at least for the present generation, or positively as the outcome of a long-standing relationship with order and cleanliness.

From this it becomes apparent how a symbolic view of vandalism – here to be understood according to our initial definition – opens up the range of possible interpretations and does not reduce its causes to infantility or primitiveness.

Nevertheless, while causal perspectives do involve – at least in the case of some specific manifestations – kinship between the relation of the child to the world and that of the vandal, might there not also be the possibility of considering vandal-animistic behaviour either as a reversion (regression) to egocentrism, or as a paradoxical attempt to be re-connected with the group, to assert that one is a member of the group but under different conditions? Thus, although writing on walls at first appears to be the same as animistic behaviour, it could also be interpreted precisely as a desire to re-affirm the priority of participation and moral obligation – in other words, of a desire for unconditional unity with the group.

To sum up, although Switzerland has its reasons for being but little vandalised while, notwithstanding this, vandals who are active in Switzerland respond to the same motivations as vandals elsewhere, the question is, for how long will Swiss identity remain anchored in the values of order and cleanliness whose advent was evoked earlier. The study by Heller (1979) ends with a question: what if uncleanliness should come back? This question is suggestive of the following conjecture: the return of uncleanliness would mean that vandalism had become banal in Switzerland.

It might be appropriate to add that one of the purposes of this paper was to show that the contrary may not be inferred: cleanliness and order *per se* do not ensure an absence or reduction of vandalism. Thus, there may be, for better or worse, a Swiss recipe, but there is every reason to believe that it is intimately linked to the history of the country. In other words, one cannot infer general rules from the Swiss case.

References

Casparis, J., E. Vaz, 1979. Swiss family, society and youth culture. Leiden: E.J. Brill.
Clinard, M., 1978. Cities with little crime. The case of Switzerland. London: Cambridge University Press.
De Martino, E., 1962. Furore, simbolo, valore. Milano: Feltrinelli.
Heller, G., 1979. Propre en ordre. Lausanne: Editions d'en Bas.
Jung, C.G., 1921. Psychological types. In: Collected works, vol. 6. Princeton: Princeton University Press, 1971.
Piaget, J., 1926. The language and thought of the child. London: Kegan Paul.
Piaget, J., 1973. The child's conception of the world. London: Paladin. (Originally publ. London: Kegan Paul, 1929.)

Abstract: K. Noschis: Countries without vandalism?
In this paper, vandalism is addressed as the destruction or disfigurement of collective property. Although Switzerland is subject to vandalism, there is evidence to support the claim that the frequency and extent of such behavior is minor when compared with that in other countries. In the course of the last century, cleanliness and order may be considered to have become part of the Swiss identity. Thus, when they act as vandals, the Swiss are violating not only public property but also their own identity. This, it is suggested, is one reason for the relatively small amount of the vandalism in the country. From the individual's standpoint, the phenomenon may also be analysed by reference to Piaget's concept of animism – where objects are considered as animated – and Jung's concept of projection – where part of the individual's psyche is projected upon an object. The non-vandalism of the Swiss can accordingly be defined either negatively as a stage where the object (to be vandalised) and the subject (the potential vandal) are not yet dissociated, or positively, as a stage resulting from a long-standing relation with cleanliness and order – a time when the projection is withdrawn.

PART TWO

Vandalism as a social fact

Vandalism as a fact of life in society

J.Cl. SPERANDIO

As one reads through the specialised literature it becomes clear that vandalism is still thought of as a highly diversified phenomenon. This is so with respect to the forms it takes, its targets, the causes and determining factors involved, its actual or presumed perpetrators and the theories and models seeking to account for it. At the present time it is probably premature to seek a single explanatory system and it may be expected that workers in the field will have every opportunity to examine the problem from new and varied angles over the next few years. Although the data currently available are sufficiently plentiful and coherent to have justified the organisation of an international colloquium, they are still so fragmentary that they tend to lead to questions rather than solutions. Notwithstanding this, there is general agreement on at least one point: vandalism is a fact of life in society.

First and foremost, it is clear that society reacts to vandalism. It is by no means the least important manifestation of this reaction that vandalism is viewed as an abnormal occurrence, i.e. deviant behaviour with respect to social norms and the behaviour of the majority: in this respect it resembles other more or less prohibited behaviour such as theft, aggression and drug addiction, the relationships of which to vandalism are often compared.

Society also reacts passively to vandalism by accepting responsibility for its consequences, notably the costs of refurbishment or modification or the inconvenience of a deteriorated or malfunctioning environment. It is probably the financial burden of refurbishment which constitutes the main motivation for institutions to take action in the form of encouraging research on vandalism, or, more precisely, 'their' vandalism, identifying and punishing vandals or designing more resistant and better guarded models of choice vandal targets.

That vandalism is a social phenomenon becomes particularly apparent when one looks at the approaches which have been adopted to its investigation. Research into vandalism has tended as a rule to rely on the methodology of sociology and social psychology, despite the fact that the main actors of interest, i.e. the vandals themselves, are difficult to identify. Above all, however, the use of a general framework of social variables corresponding to targets, vandals or the relationship between the two, highlights the social nature of vandalism. It is a fact that some targets are more prone to attack than others and this may be ascribed to two overlapping types of causes. Some acts doubtless result partly from functional causes, e.g. vengeful reactions to unbearable or unjust malfunctions such as out of order pay phones or parking meters which fail to work but which withhold the money inserted or, again, aggressive reactions to deteriorated or hostile environments. Others are perpetrated partly for symbolic reasons, i.e. targets are selected for what they represent (e.g. public buildings standing for the State, Law and Order, Repression, Money or a particular social class). It is consequently of value to decipher the messages which are being consciously or subconsciously addressed to a society called into question. If acts of vandalism do constitute messages, it is important to find out to whom they are directed and the motives behind their transmission.

While the targets of vandals are at risk to varying extents it would appear that vandalism is common to all countries (even Switzerland?), although amounts and targets differ. Is vandalism then a fact of social life, a response to a certain type of society? International comparisons are very enlightening in this respect, especially when it is possible to adopt semi-epidemiological methods at different time periods, keeping some factors constant and monitoring those which vary, e.g. level of civilisation, standards of living, political orientations of governments and social stratification. None of these factors would appear to be fundamental or all embracing, but it must be remembered that only a small number of large scale studies have as yet been carried out. Some international comparisons have been made, but these deal only with a few specific targets such as undergrounds or public telephones. Comparative studies of the location of the most frequently vandalised targets have generally tended to look at environmental types (e.g. urban vs rural habitats, suburbs vs town centres, single family dwellings vs blocks of flats). Most of these studies have in fact highlighted the existence of significant differences, but it is not always easy to single out the social factors as such characterising vandals, their targets and the relationships between them from confounding influences such as population distribution or inadequate protection, which can themselves account for the inhomogeneous spatial distribution of the phenomenon.

Lastly, it is clear that the framework of social or sociological variables is most systematically applied as a method of analysis to those who perpetrate acts of vandalism. These variables add to and go far beyond those characterising individuals as such which are studied by clinical psychologists. The most commonly used variables in this case are age, sex, institutional affiliation (e.g. school, army, hospital, sporting association), integration into social groups (e.g. family, religion, ethnic groups, immigrant group, neighbourhood, gang, etc.), unemployment and social life style which is closely linked to or viewed as synonymous with environmental types. The insertion of these social variables into a descriptive model of vandalism, however, suggests further research with a view to obtaining some degree of explanation. For instance, knowing that most acts of vandalism are perpetrated by juveniles with little or nothing to do and who live in the suburbs rather than the rich areas, etc., does not explain why this is so. It is time that theory took over from case studies and it is this desire for theoretical development which constitutes the theme of the first part of this book.

The second part introduces four complementary points of view. Nilsson starts off by presenting some figures exemplifying the growth of vandalism in Sweden over the last 30 years before going on to her own research on vandalism on new Malmö housing estates. She uses one set of variables corresponding to voluntary social monitoring by those residents who own their home and another corresponding to the identified vandals, whose motives the author analyses.

Reade's main contribution, in addition to his field study of vandalism in Oldham, England, lies in his critical analysis of what he terms the 'conventional' explanations of vandalism. He replaces these with a 'situational' theory, the fundamental variable of which is the degree of social control. In Reade's view, vandalism arises from inadequate amounts of this social control rather than from an unequal share of material and cultural goods for the least privileged element of a class society.

Phillips and Donnermeyer adopt a different standpoint on the basis of two studies carried out in Ohio and Indiana, U.S.A. They stress the facts that the acts of vandalism studied by them are not 'harmless pranks', judging by their financial consequences, and that vandalism is perceived by its perpetrators as 'normatively' acceptable behaviour (cf. Corrigan and Reade), associated, nevertheless, with the use of drugs or alcohol and inversely correlated with religious affiliation.

To sum up, each of the contributions to this second part of the book throws new light on the social definition of vandalism. The phenomenon is seen alternatively as deviant behaviour with respect to current norms, as coherent behaviour in the framework of the daily activities of vandals and finally as a level – tolerated, more or less – in the range and hierarchy of small time crime.

CHAPTER 6

Vandalism in Sweden

C. NILSSON

Since the 1960s, and especially during the 1970s, the crime of vandalism in Sweden has been the subject of considerable attention due to the mass media, different studies, conferences, and various prevention programmes which have been tested. The debate and prevention programmes were, in general, first tested at the end of the 1970s. The consideration of vandalism in Sweden came later than for instance in the United States and in Great Britain, where the problems of vandalism were obvious already during the 1950s. The youth culture and other trends have, in many respects, come from these countries and have influenced the youths in Sweden.

The costs of vandalism in Sweden were first realized during the middle and late 1970s. Even if only a small part of the real number of acts of vandalism is known, the cost of the known cases reaches several million Swedish crowns per year. In addition, vandalism has come to be viewed as a serious offence since it is seen as primarily a juvenile offence possibly leading to further criminality.

The crime of vandalism is included in Chapter 12 of the Swedish Criminal Code. In the Criminal Code, the word vandalism itself is not used, although the word damage is. The percent of police-reported cases of vandalism in relation to the total amount of reported crimes in Sweden between 1950 and 1980 is represented in fig. 1, showing a noticeable increase of cases of vandalism between 1970 and 1975. The rate went up from 5.2% to 7.2%. After this period of increase, there was a small decrease in 1976, when the reported cases of vandalism were 6.9% of the total number of reported crimes. In 1979, there was again a decrease in the rate of vandalism and this decrease has continued for the year 1980. The percent of police-reported cases of vandalism in relation to the total number of reported crimes for 1980 was 6.4 %.

The real number of cases of police-reported vandalism for the period 1950–1980 is shown in fig. 2. There was a continuous increase in the number of cases up to 1977. This period of increase was followed by a period of decrease in the number of cases for the years 1978–1980. Between 1950 and 1977, the number of cases of vandalism rose from about 5,000 to about 62,000 reported cases. For the total number of reported cases of crime, the increase during the same period was from about 195,000 cases to about 844,000 cases, so that there were 12 times as many cases of vandalism, while the total number

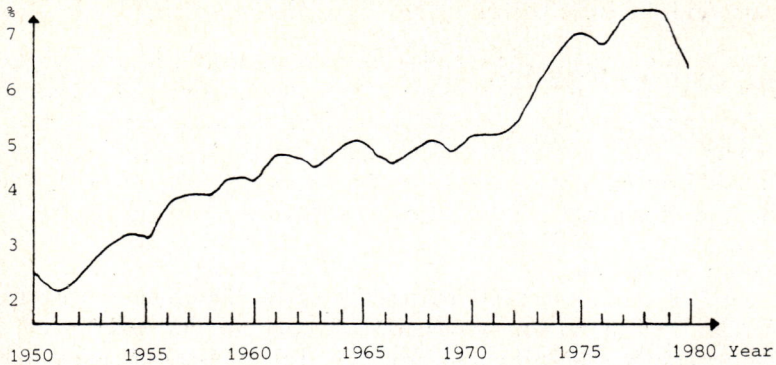

Fig. 1. Police-reported cases of vandalism in relation to the total number of reported crimes in Sweden 1950–1980 (in %) (Yearbook of legal statistics 1981).

of cases of crime was four times as high. In the Criminal Code, the crime of vandalism is divided into four subgroups: damage to motor vehicles, damage by fire, damage to public property and, finally, 'other' damage. The subgroup 'other damage' includes destruction of windows, doors, lights, cycles, different equipment in houses, telephone boxes, etc. More than half of all the reported cases of vandalism for the year 1980 are referred to this group.

The second largest group is damage to motor vehicles. About one-fourth of all the cases of vandalism reported in 1976 falls into this category. The third group in frequency of acts of vandalism is damage to public property, which covers about 16% of the cases, followed by damage by fire which covers only 3% of all the cases of vandalism.

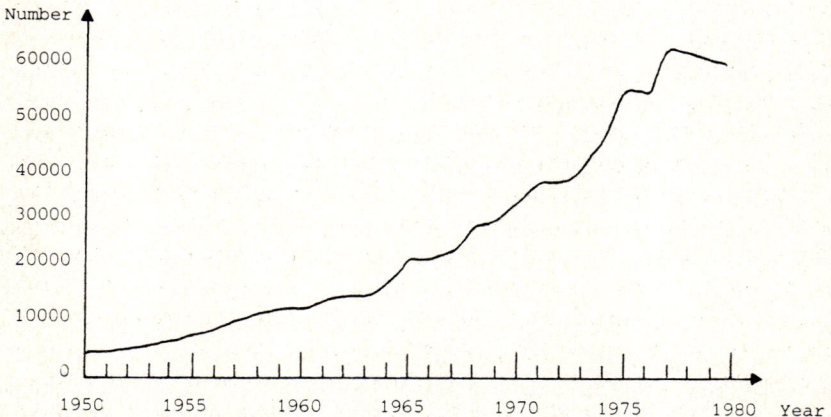

Fig. 2. The real number of cases of vandalism 1950–1980 (Yearbook of legal statistics 1981).

1. Vandalism in residential areas

The study of vandalism in residential areas in the city of Malmö was carried out with the purpose of elucidating the differences in level of vandalism among the various residential and commercial areas within the city and to analyze the environmental factors and mechanisms that might reinforce or restrict an individuals' proneness to commit acts of vandalism. In the following, some of the results of this research project will be presented.

1.1. The empirical data

The empirical data of the research project 'Vandalism in residential areas' concern the third biggest city in Sweden, Malmö, which is situated in the south-west of the country. In 1976, the number of inhabitants of the whole city was about 240,000 and in the research district there lived about 230,000 people. A few residential areas further south of the city were excluded from the research district because some of them were still under construction during the research year.

The empirical data include information about the environment and the crime of vandalism. The environmental data are based on public statistics documented by the municipality. These statistics give information about the physical and social environment and about the population down to the block level. The crime of vandalism is studied through police-reported cases of vandalism. These reports describe the crime, where and how it was committed, and, if the suspect was known, also information about the vandal's character, motives, etc. for the crime.

Within the research district, 2,067 cases of vandalism were reported during the research year. The rate of vandalism is about 7% of all the reported cases of criminality in Malmö that year. In 33% of the cases, a suspect was reported to the police and a total of 661 persons were reported for acts of vandalism. About 22% of the reported individuals committed more than one reported act of vandalism in the research year.

The choice of police-reported cases of vandalism as an indicator for the real figure of cases of vandalism needs perhaps some explanation. I have made the assumption that residential areas with a high frequency of reported cases of vandalism in relation to the number of tenants, will also have a high frequency of unreported cases of vandalism and vice versa. In a minor pilot study I have, through direct observation, studied the level of vandalism in nine housing areas – chosen from among those in the research district. My classification of the nine areas, according to these observations, corresponded with the areas' classification with respect to the police-reported cases of vandalism. Other studies, in which official statistics were used as an indicator of the crime's real figure, have shown that in regard to traditional criminality the official rates of the crime can very well be used as an indicator of the crime's real figure. The implication is that persons frequently engaging in traditional criminality such as theft, burglary and vandalism will sooner or later be known to the police and reported for their crimes (Persson, 1980).

1.2. Some results of the research project

The study of police-reported cases of vandalism has indicated two main city areas with a high frequency of vandalism: the new multi-storey housing projects in the outer districts and the commercial areas in the centre.

In Malmö, the major part of the multi-storey housing projects was built between 1961 and 1975. These housing projects were built in non-traditional residential areas. The density of population is high and the houses and dwellings all have almost the same exterior and interior. Contrary to the new large housing projects, the buildings in the centre of the city stem mainly from the period before 1950. These dwellings are of varying quality, from dwellings without modern conveniences to exclusive, modern dwellings.

The new housing projects were built for the purpose of giving young people and people with low incomes a modern dwelling at a low cost. These housing developments came to be occupied mainly by young families with small children and by other adults who could not afford a more expensive dwelling in the centre of the city. The social problems which emerged out of this high concentration of people with different traditions, needs and aims of life into a limited physical area where individual creativity could not be fully expressed, gave rise to feelings of tension and frustration among the tenants.

These housing areas soon acquired a negative reputation; anyone who could choose his dwelling-place avoided these large new multi-storey developments, which gave them a low status profile. Some of these residential areas still have, 15 years after they were built, many social problems, to a large extent because of their persistent low status profile, high geographical mobility and unstimulating physical environment.

A factor, probably essential when discussing vandalism in housing areas, is the ownership of the dwellings. My study of vandalism has shown that residential areas with a large percentage of owner-occupied dwellings have few reported cases of vandalism. The ownership can be either in the form of private one-family houses or of a dwelling in a multi-storey block which is managed as a tenant-owners' association. The highest level of vandalism was found in the areas where a major share of the dwellings were rented in storey blocks. In these high vandalism residential areas, more than half of the dwellings are council houses situated in the outer districts of the city. The storey housing areas with a high level of vandalism, situated in the older, central parts of the city, have houses owned mostly by private house owners or by company house owners.

One explanation for the differences between rented and owned dwellings can be that the tenants who choose and have the means to own the dwelling, also are conscious of the implied responsibility for the dwellings and they have also an interest in keeping their property valuable and free from damage. The difference between residential areas with mainly rented and those with mainly owned dwellings remains even after controlling for other variables such as, for instance, socio-economic status. In residential areas with mainly owned dwellings, different systems of social control will probably be developed more frequently than in residential areas with only rented dwellings. Informal control, like social control, will very likely be developed and used in these areas with owned dwellings. For many children, the adult's use of social control will be enough to prevent them from law-breaking behaviour. A further explanation for these areas' lower level of vandalism is that it is easier for the tenants to control the surrounding areas because fewer strangers will have errands bringing them to these residential areas, the geographical mobility is low and the anonymity among the tenants will be less than in the large multi-storey housing projects.

The crime of vandalism is mostly viewed and explained as a juvenile crime and a possible explanation for the high frequency of vandalism in housing areas could be their high density of young people. But in my study of vandalism the share of young people was high both in the high and low vandalism areas, i.e. both in the storey housing developments and in the one-family housing projects. I have not found the variable 'amount of young people' to be a sufficient factor for differentiating between housing areas with various levels of vandalism (cf. Wilson, 1978).

An essential factor when explaining the relation between vandalism and child density is probably the children's access to stimulating and exciting activities. One explanation might be that children in the high status sections have a better chance of receiving stimulation within the home and the surroundings than children from low status projects. It might also be easier for the parents in the high status areas to help the children with school work and with various problems in school because of their own educational and occupational level.

Further, these parents might be more apt to encourage their children to participate in organized activities within or outside the housing areas and they have also the economic resources to permit this. With these opportunities, the children have less reason to seek excitement in acts of vandalism as a compensation for a lack of stimulation.

Other studies of vandalism have shown that the traditional delinquent class structure of vandalism has changed from almost exclusively lower-class offenders to both lower-class and middle-class offenders (cf. Cohen, 1957; Fannin and Clinard, 1965; Scott and Vaz, 1963, Richards, 1979). Of the reported offenders in my study, nearly all were classified as belonging to the lower class. An explanation for this can be that, even if middle-class and upper-class young people commit acts of vandalism, the number of their destructive actions is lower and their vandalism-prone period shorter than is the case with the lower-class children and adolescents, because other interests will take over. This explanation of the lack of middle-class children and adolescents among the reported vandals can verify the stated assumption that it is the most active vandals that will be discovered and reported to the police.

The reported cases of vandalism are, as already mentioned, mainly located in the centre of the city and in the new multi-storey housing projects. In the study of vandalism in residential areas, I have also studied the vandals' home address and the address of the place where they committed the acts of vandalism.

The results of the study show that in 23% of the cases, the vandals lived in the areas where they committed the acts of vandalism. In a further 25% of the cases, the vandals chose to vandalize a housing development directly adjacent or very near to their own. In other words, in nearly half of all the cases of reported vandalism, the vandals chose their objects of vandalism in their immediate surroundings. In still another 29% of the cases, the distance between the vandals' home address and the area where they committed the acts of vandalism was just a short walk.

In only 15% of the cases of vandalism did the vandals live at any distance from the place where they vandalized but still within the research district. A further 8% of the vandals who committed vandalism in the research district lived outside the city.

To summarize the results, one can say that in 77% of the cases of reported vandalism, the vandals chose to vandalize in their home areas or within short walking distance from them. In only 23% of the cases did the vandals live a greater distance away from the vandalized areas or outside the city.

1.3. The vandals

If the offender is known, the reports on the crime of vandalism give some information about, for instance, the offenders' individual characteristics, motives for the acts of vandalism, and also some information about the circumstances of the crime. In the following, I will give some explanation of why a person takes part in acts of vandalism from the point of view of the offenders' reported motives for committing acts of vandalism.

To study the offenders, it is fruitful to divide them into age groups. I have used the groups 'children of 11 or under', 'adolescents aged between 12 and 20', and finally 'adults of 21 and over'. Of the reported individuals during the research year 3% were children, 63% adolescents and 34% adults.

Children form the group of vandals who commit acts of vandalism most frequently in the home areas or in their immediate surroundings. This is, however, partially a consequence of the practical restrictions on the children's leaving the home areas. The children's day is full of different play situations and they are constantly looking for new exciting situations and play. Their cases of vandalism can mostly be explained as a way of searching for excitement and enjoyment. The children most likely do not intend to destroy things, but may do so as a consequence of their play and this is often not overlooked by the children themselves.

One typical kind of vandalism among children and younger adolescents is damage by fire. The small fires frequently occurring in the cellars of buildings and in lumber-rooms, empty houses and dwellings, are very often caused by children playing with fire.

Adolescents are the most frequent vandals and their acts of vandalism are mainly committed in the centre of the city and in other commercial meeting-places in the residential areas. Their objects of vandalism can be nearly everything, cars, street lamps, windows, telephone boxes, lifts in multi-storey blocks, graffiti, etc.

For the adolescents, the committing of vandalism can have many reasons. It can be a way for the individual to create a position in the peer group as well as a way for the peer group or the gang to show its independence of the norms and values of society.

The adolescents' reported motives for acts of vandalism arise from general boredom, frustration about the social situation, and enjoyment. Vandalism can also be a way of taking revenge on, for instance, school authorities.

The last group, the adult vandals, commits acts of vandalism as a way of getting revenge for a wish not granted by someone in the circle of acquaintances or by the authorities, often the social welfare staff. The revenge is very often directed at an ex-wife or ex-husband, friends or parents.

Within this adult group of vandals we also find those who are deviant in other respects: they have different social problems, they commit other forms of law-breaking and some of them are habitual drunkards. From the age of sixteen the use of alcohol was, for the reported vandals, the rule when committing acts of vandalism.

In summarizing the explanations of some of the results of the study of the vandals' motives for taking part in vandalism, one could say that the children's acts of vandalism can be explained as a result of a play situation. The adolescents, by their vandalism, wish to express their independence from the norms and values of society, but the adolescents will also commit acts of vandalism for the enjoyment of destroying things. The adults' vandalism can be characterized as revenge for their social situation. Their lives are full of social and economic problems and they have been deeply disappointed by persons in their circle of acquaintances and by the authorities.

2. Conclusions

This short report has touched briefly upon vandalism and attendant issues and problems. It was seen, for example, that vandalism has increased considerably since the 1950s. Further, this crime is concentrated mainly in the commerical sections of urban environments and to the housing areas composed of multi-storey houses built during the 1960s and 1970s, situated mainly on the outskirts of cities.

Even if young people commit the majority of the cases of vandalism, a high percentage of young people in residential areas does not imply a high level of vandalism. What might be of more significance regarding the level of vandalism in any area are its physical design (is it unstimulating, are there areas concealed from public view) and its residents (are they indifferent to prevention of vandalism and other crimes). The low socio-economic status of the residents in a residential area with mainly rented dwellings as well as a high geographic mobility, perhaps as a consequence of the physical and social environment, raise the level of vandalism of the area. The complexity of the factors causing vandalism also contributes to a low status segregation of certain residential areas and makes it difficult to effect changes. This is also documented by the fact that, after 15 years, some residential areas still suffer from the same problems.

The reported vandal is in many respects similar to the traditional offender who belongs to the working class, often has problems at school and has become a truant. The most intensive period of vandalism for the individuals is between the ages of 16 and 20; after the age of 21, the major percentage of vandals stop vandalizing as their interests turn to work and family. Those who remain vandals often commit other crimes and also have some form of social problem, as for instance problems with alcohol. The use of alcohol was found to be closely connected with vandalism, at least for the vandals of 16 years and older.

The crime of vandalism is a crime which might also appear to middle- and upper-class youths, because it is often viewed as less serious, the punishment is often none or low, the crime is easy to carry out and the risk of being reported is very low. In the official statistics of suspected offenders, only few are from the middle- or upper classes but in studies of self-reports on acts of vandalism, it is indicated that the youths from these social classes as well are frequent vandals at some time during their adolescence.

References

Cohen, A., 1957. Middle-class delinquency and the social structure. In: E. Vaz, ed., Middle-class juvenile delinquency. New York: Harper and Row, 1967.
Fannin, L., M. Clinard, 1965. Differences in the conception of self as a male among lower and

middle class delinquents. In: E. Vaz, ed., Middle-class juvenile delinquency. New York: Harper and Row, 1967.

Nilsson, C., 1980. Vandalism in urban environments. Lund: Department of Sociology (mimeo).

Persson, L., 1980. Hidden criminality. Deparment of Sociology, University of Stockholm.

Richards, P., 1979. Middle-class vandalism and age-status conflict. Social Problems 26 (4), 482–497.

Scott, J., E. Vaz, 1963. A perspective on middle-class delinquency. In: E. Vaz, ed., Middle-class juvenile delinquency. New York: Harper and Row, 1967.

Wilson, S., 1978. Vandalism and 'defensible space' on London housing estates. In: R.V.G. Clarke, ed., Tackling vandalism. Home Office Research Study no. 47 London: HMSO.

Statistical abstract of Sweden 1981.

Yearbook of legal statistics 1981.

Abstract: C. Nilsson, Vandalism in Sweden

In this short report some of the issues concerning vandalism in Sweden are indicated and some results of a research project on Vandalism in Residential Areas in a Swedish city are given. The research project is supported by The Swedish National Council for Crime Prevention.

From the 1950s up to 1977 vandalism was increasing but during the last few years, there has been a decrease in reported cases. The majority of the cases of vandalism are concentrated within urban environments and, within this environment, most cases are to be found in the commercial centre of cities and in the new multi-storey housing projects on the outskirts of the cities.

In this study of vandalism in residential areas, it is indicated that the percentage of children and adolescents is not a determining factor for the level of vandalism in a residential area. The residential areas with no reported cases of vandalism and those with the highest percentage of reported cases had proportionally the highest density of young people. Factors influencing the residential areas' level of vandalism might rather be sought in the social and physical environment of the areas; a further important factor is the level of geographical mobility in the areas.

CHAPTER 7

Vandalism as a social problem

H.E. ROOS

1. Big-city and rural vandalism

1.1. Aim of the project

The aim of the 'Big City and Rural Vandalism' project is to study the origins and growth of vandalism in both a large city and a rural area of Sweden. We are also studying the impact of vandalism on five different social milieus within these two areas. In addition to comparative analysis, special emphasis is placed on the problem of rural vandalism with respect to the local municipality and its authorities. Vandalism in our research is treated both as a cause and as an effect. A multitude of methods are used to highlight the relationships obtaining between population, settlement and society as a whole.

1.2. Earlier research undertaken for the project

In an earlier study, where the incidence of mobbing was also examined, we sought to measure the extent of vandalism. For this purpose we measured the costs of vandalism to schools incurred by five Swedish municipalities (about 350 schools in all). Although it is impossible to ascertain the exact amount, vandalism in Sweden is estimated to have caused damage totalling 500 million Swedish crowns.

Vandalism in schools was evaluated at about 25% of this amount. Our studies of vandalism in schools showed a high degree of vandalism in schools which were (a) located in big city areas, (b) located in negatively segregated apartment housing developments, (c) situated in such a way as to render them susceptible to attacks and raids, i.e. isolated and along heavily used roads, and (d) built in the 1960s and 1970s. The highest degree of vandalism was found in schools where two or more of these factors were simultaneously present. This study, in common with our later reports, also includes a theoretical approach to the destructive behaviour of vandalism as a social problem and a discussion relating this to sociological and urban sociological theory.

In a later study, concerning the city of Malmö, we found milieus most affected by vandalism to be public places and unguarded objects in the city and areas with high-rise apartment buildings which had been hastily built during the sixties and the beginning of the seventies. A more surprising discovery was the spread of vandalism to some residential, single-family dwelling areas as well as smaller suburban communities outside the municipality of Malmö, which had previously been spared this kind of social problem.

Whilst carrying out this study in Malmö we received alarming reports that even a small town had been hit by an explosive increase in vandalism. A few brave decision makers in this town, the municipality of Arvika, gave the problem publicity and asked us to undertake an investigation. Arvika is a regional centre, about 27,000 strong, located in an extensive rural area not far from the Norwegian border.

In a preliminary study we found that vandalism in Arvika was perpetrated to a greater extent by individuals from outside Arvika than by residents of the town itself. We also found acts of vandalism to be carried out more and more frequently outside that part of the city or community where the vandals themselves were living. Our results suggest that the explanation of this phenomenon cannot be restricted to discussions of resource distribution, implying a lack of resources such as education, income, employment, services, etc. as a causal factor. The problem seems to be basically one of life style. Ways of life in Arvika became riddled with conflict situations when a new urban and commercial life style came up against an old-fashioned rural structure characterised to a high degree by the existence of informal and familial social networks. There were no public and formally organised leisure time activities in Arvika. At the same time, this municipality in many ways played the role of 'relief community' for the whole population living in the surrounding rural area. In other respects, for instance that of intra-urban migration, it was found that big city vandalism differed from that occuring in rural areas.

In our ongoing research we intend to study attitudes towards vandalism whilst simultaneously continuing with our community work project.

2. The problem of social problems and the phenomenon of vandalism

The social problem concept has been defined in many different ways. Firstly, three different areas may be distinguished in which social problems arise; production and class, market and welfare, and consumption and lifestyle. In the case of production, social problems occur when the physical and psychological conditions of the labour force cannot be maintained. A rapidly growing middle class and a diminishing petty bourgeoisie have meant that a greater part of the population have become employees. The State has shouldered greater responsibility for the provision of healthy, well-educated and fit individuals for the work force from an increasing portion of the population. In the case of the market, defective and unequal distribution of wealth, welfare and other living standard components bring about social problems. Under these circumstances, the individual does not have access to or is not able to enjoy collective assets and is therefore not in a position to modify and control his living conditions. We are not concerned here with how these activities may or may not lead to satisfaction. In the case of consumption, social problems appear when individual aspirations or needs are not satisfied. Attention is not directed toward the possibility which the individual has of consuming, but rather toward the result of his or her actions. This may involve both material needs (food, housing, social security) and personal feelings of well-being (happiness, satisfaction). This view of social problems, however, i.e. the inability of the individual to implement his life style options, refers both to the complacency of the poor and to the dissatisfaction of the rich.

As a social problem, vandalism as such can be defined in terms of concepts like class belongingness and class consciousness, concepts such as resource access and social mobility, or concepts like motivation and need satisfaction. Different researchers, therefore, working from different points of view, place differing emphasis on concepts such as power and ideology, deprivation, status and anomy, or frustration and aggression.

One finds that the view adopted with respect to social problems also plays a decisive role with respect to opinions about the steps to be taken against vandalism. Examples of sociological interpretations of social problems are:

(i)   social pathology – which is solved by stressing the role of upbringing and education;
(ii) social disorganisation – which is solved by contract and agreement;
(iii) deviant behaviour – which is solved by re-socialisation and integration and sometimes by repression;
(iv) labelling – where the solution is to change the definition of what is considered deviant and illegimate.

From this classification it is clear that social problems can be seen as a natural illness afflicting certain groups as a consequence of value conflicts or conflicts of interest, as a result of faulty social control, as a minority problem and the result of an individual's frustrations at not attaining certain goals, and as a power problem and a problem of definition. The differences between the theories reflect the different interests with regard to the various types of social problem that exist.

A critical appraisal of the theories on deviance has been put forward by George and Wilding (1979). They feel that these functional and pluralist views are non-political and non-ideological. They consider this to be a typical relationship in the welfare state which is characterised by a broad political consensus and where the most difficult problems are already solved, with only a few technical details remaining to be mopped up. Social problems, in their view, are to be seen as the outcome of conflicts between economic interests, and must be solved through political action. Examples of such problems are poverty and racial conflicts. They also emphasise, however, that certain social problems should be seen as conflicts between different moral values – as is the case with homosexuality. Social problems are seen as a continuum where the end points are composed of economic interests and moral values. Other problems such as theft should, according to George and Wilding, be placed in the middle of the continuum. Theft is not only a conflict between the one who owns and the one who does not, but also a conflict between those who see theft as morally wrong and those who can accept it under certain conditions. From this example it is clear that the definition of social problems is open to discussion and that the way in which different persons define social problems is *not* merely a matter of chance.

3. The increase in Swedish vandalism

The increase, in absolute terms, in the number of registered incidents of vandalism has been quite dramatic, especially during the 1970s. The increase has been very regular and continuous and one does not find the irregularity and fluctuations characteristic of, say, burglary in Sweden. If we look at the percentage increase in vandalism, a number of trends may be picked out (see table 1).

The percentage increase was greatest during the fifties. Our first thought was that this increase may have had something to do with public opinion at the time. This, however, was not the case. The perception of vandalism as a social problem did not become established until the seventies, when a high level of vandalism had already been reached. It was then that the first public debate and discussion took place, measures were taken and so on. This implies that, during a period with a lesser percentage increase in vandalism, more attention was given to the problem than previously. There could be many reasons for this, but I would like to point to at least three possible causal factors.

Firstly, it may have been related to the great expansion, throughout the country, of the public sector and its personnel, whose work was to locate and take measures to prevent social problems. If a teacher is asked whether his pupils have problems, he will answer that one or two have difficulties. If the school counsellor is then asked the same question, practically all the children will be perceived as suffering from problems of various kinds. A further example is afforded by quarrels, fights and drunkenness which were formerly

Table 1. Vandalism in Sweden.

Period	Increase	Population increase
1950–59	166% (5,000–13,300)	6%
1960–69	129% (13,200–30,000)	7%
1970–79	79% (34,000–61,000)	3%

accepted parts of everyday life but which today are immediately defined as problems to be taken care of.

Secondly, Sweden's declining economic growth and the business slump meant a decrease in Sweden's ability to attack social problems with the traditional, extensive panoply of resources and services. Traditional measures and solutions in the social field seem, in many cases, inadequate to cope with the social problems of the eighties. The growth of old problems, the appearance of new ones and the feeling of insufficiency with respect to old solutions has, in many respects, left public planning in a state of turmoil.

Thirdly, the rising level of destructiveness has resulted from the spread of vandalism to places and residential areas which had previously been more or less spared this kind of problem. Up until the end of the 1950s, social criticism was directed towards the old society and the remaining defects which social welfare had not yet put to rights, like poverty and lack of basic resources (housing, food, money). From the beginning of the sixties, criticism began instead to be directed towards the effects of an expanding industrial society upon people and to how the past had become a lost horizon. This meant that many of today's social problems were to a great extent defined as involuntary consequences of essentially well-meaning intentions rather than as the outcomes of deficit or need situations.

4. Mass consumer society

The discussions about vandalism took place at the same time as those about the depopulation of the countryside, the growth of suburbs, slums, commercialisation, segregation, neo-poverty, etc., i.e. the social consequences of an expanding industrial society. It was maintained that, in a society where the fundamentals of the economy are a continual accumulation of consumer products and where welfare is associated with a rapid turnover of goods used in an increasing number of ways in the life of an individual, property is seen more as something easily replaceable and less as something difficult to acquire. A broken window in a telephone booth or a broken street light leads to no great involvement of the population in general and no-one in particular is affected. This relationship of absent ownership means that no-one feels personally harmed if the object is damaged. In this respect, vandalism can be said to be 'prosperity based', i.e. the consumer industry has reached full scale production at the same time that the distribution apparatus has changed in such a way as to facilitate the opportunities and possibilities for theft and destruction.

Cohen and Felsen (1979) perceive 'welfare' and 'freedom' and their expression in daily life, ironically enough, as the cause of a great deal of crime rather than social destitution. They feel that an increase in the number of objects susceptible to criminal activity and the absence of surveillance can result in great increases in crime rates which do not correspond to changes in the structural relationships which would motivate the involvement of more individuals in crime. They maintain that a convergence in time and space of potential offenders, suitable objects for criminal offences and the absence of social supervision explain the modern development of crime. The authors see theories of criminology as useful in explaining criminality during certain periods, within certain environments, or for certain groups, but they point out that conventional criminological studies have trouble explaining the yearly changes in the development of crime during the postwar period. They feel, therefore, that an ecological approach would facilitate an analysis of how the social structure creates this convergence, where illegal activities become a direct result of the legal activities of daily life. They also believe that it is difficult to approach the occurrence of crime without a great deal of modification of our lifestyle, which manifests itself in the daily routines of life.

'Prosperity based' explanations of the phenomena of vandalism are necessary but not sufficient. They do give a good understanding of the daily and continual destruction which arises from carelessness, nonchalance and disinterested behaviour. Tolerance levels of what may be accepted as 'normal' consumption and wear and tear of material goods have risen considerably during the sixties and seventies. The question is whether this type of damage is seen as a problem to any great extent.

The concept of vandalism is often associated with illegitimate destructive actions where the damage to property is easily observed, obviously of criminal intent, causing strong feelings of annoyance in the public. This criminality is also seen by the authorities as an important indicator of problems among youths, and vandalism is, in this perspective, a public crime which it is important to deal with and control. What one would call 'poverty based' vandalism is, on the other hand, most often seen as a social problem, i.e. damage to property inflicted by the underprivileged groups where different types of resource deficiencies are seen as giving rise to deviant behaviour and reactions against unsatisfactory circumstances.

5. Power and definition

All rule breaking is not labelled as deviant, and it is questionable under what circumstances an action is defined as a social problem and, in fact, as deviant. These circumstances should be seen in terms of power and conflict relations in a society: to what extent can a group limit the possibilities for such deviant behaviour and to what degree do those labelled as deviants accept this interpretation of their actions? Much property destruction is tolerated and legal; much more is not. Compare, for example, the expressions 'use of alcohol' and 'abuse of alcohol'.

6. Regional and local factors

Consumer culture, structure of availability and defective social control can partially explain the generally high level of destruction during the sixties and seventies, but can hardly account for the periodic increases in, for instance, 1970–73 and 1974–77. Although crimes of property damage increased by 79% during the seventies, the effects of the consumer culture did not undergo a comparable spurt in growth. Indeed, they declined owing to the successive economic crises of the period. It is, instead, essential to distinguish certain specific characteristics of Swedish social development which have had a decisive influence upon the incidence of vandalism in the country over recent years. It may therefore be meaningful to examine certain regional, as well as local, differences within city centres and within the centres of sparsely populated areas.

Vandalism constitutes a many-sided problem. Its occurrence is common and widespread and is the sum of many smaller actions which go to make up the phenomenon, while, at the same time, the border between what is normal and what is deviant is a fluctuating one. Van Vliet, in his chapter in this volume, writes that the community level should provide a relevant and acceptable constellation of the factors needed to explain vandalistic behaviour. For example, social, economic and demographic characteristics define ecological relations and the value system of the members of the community helps one to understand socialisation. He points out that vandalism is not of course an exclusive function of community characteristics, but that the individual factors mentioned above increase or reduce the possibilities of vandalism and influence the tendency for these possibilities to materialise.

7. The regional character of vandalism

7.1 Big cities

Our research with respect to large cities indicates that the limitation of the growth of cities and the stagnation of urbanisation during the first half of the 1970s seems to have resulted in an intensification of social problems and vandalism in certain new housing areas. When the expansion of large cities ground to a general halt no new areas appeared to take over the role of the negatively segregated areas known as 'problem areas'. The high-rise apartment buildings hastily built during the sixties and during the early seventies became a terminus, i.e. the end of the line. Social problems in those areas were therefore not 'self-healing' as those of the housing areas of the fifties seemed to be. At that time, people could move out to the housing areas which were to become the new problem areas of the sixties.

Short-distance, intra-urban migrations seem to have been able, by their strong character of social hierarchy, to reinforce segregation and result in reducing the number of households with more resources in those areas which were already at the bottom of the social scale in terms of housing. This tendency may have led to increased depreciation of certain affected housing developments during this period. It is probable that this 'new slum' development process is related to the increase in property damage in the large Swedish cities.

It is not impossible to envisage that the spread of property damage to residential areas which had not previously suffered from this type of problem, for instance certain single family dwelling areas which have since become less attractive, may have been the first step towards a future depreciation of the living environment leading to further vandalism. There is even evidence that this process of segregation has also occurred within the same residential area. We have found that certain neighbourhoods and buildings are characterised by duration of residence, i.e. are resided in by the same family (persons) for more than six months and have several vacant apartments: other buildings in the same area house a large number of recently arrived residents and have few vacant apartments. Those buildings and neighbourhoods with many recently arrived residents and small numbers of vacant apartments are, to a great extent, occupied by persons who have the economic and personal possibility of leaving the area. Those buildings and neighbourhoods with a large number of vacant apartments and many residents of long standing are, on the other hand, occupied by persons who have economic and social problems and little possibility of moving away. This tendency may have given rise to housing depreciation in especially affected areas. It is probable that this process of new slumming is related to the increased destruction in Sweden's larger cities. In conclusion, the reduction in residential building, social segregation and short-term movements between residential areas have led to increased vandalism in Sweden's big cities.

7.2. Rural areas

The regional level factors that lie behind the great increase in vandalism in sparsely populated areas do not seem to be linked to big city problems such as segregation, housing problems, etc. Many of Sweden's sparsely populated areas lay outside the areas of the great geographic expansion in the labour market catchment which took place during the years of economic growth. Consequently, the development of urban values and life styles which occurred in the small towns had no roots in this growth. The important relationship here is the difference between high unemployment and the low level of service on the one hand, and, on the other hand, the degree of dependence upon private consumption, transportation, etc., expectations which can never be fulfilled.

Table 2. Social problems in small towns outside major labour catchment areas.

Resource problems	Lifestyle problems
(1) High unemployment Low income level Low service level Poor communications	(1) Diffusion of urban and commercial values
(2) High dependence upon private consumption, transportation, etc.	(2) 'Familial gemeinschaft' no longer creates safety, social connection and protection for all members
(3) Lack of resources like leisure time activities, entertainment, stimulus, places for social activity	(3) Conflicts between 'integrated' members of the society and 'outsiders' who are not personally affected, i.e., not so anonymous as in big cities
⇓	⇓
The closed and deserted city ←——————→	High expectations among unoccupied and norm-confused youth and individuals

VANDALISM

Young people are drawn to the village centre where they do not find what they are looking for and where there is a lack of activity and of various kinds of stimulus. The large numbers of single senior citizens living in the central areas of small towns like Arvika adds to the deserted atmosphere in the evenings. There is a confrontation here between youth and the 'deserted' town. Vandalism, and even alcohol and drug abuse, can be seen as a protest against this. Young people are furthermore only weakly bound by old moral codes. They do not participate in the traditional network which previously inhibited deviance among the youth. Labelling and mechanisms of rejection become more accentuated. Conflicts and problems take on a more personal nature than in the more anonymous environs. Anonymity is often less in smaller localities and offenders are often known to local residents. Labelling and rejection mechanisms are more accentuated in such areas. To understand this type of criminality, I feel it is important to show how the special life style of the countryside and small towns, over and above the problems of resource distribution, complicates the interpretation of vandalism. The understanding of social problems must take regional considerations into account (Roos, 1980).

8. Destruction by outsiders and by locals

It may be useful to distinguish between the destruction and damage perpetrated by locals, i.e. those who vandalise their own environment, their own school, their own housing area, etc., and that based on raids and attacks on other environments than those in which the vandals themselves live.

In cases where the distribution pattern of crimes of vandalism does not match that of residential segregation, it is reasonable to suspect that such vandalism is perpetrated by persons living outside the area affected. The segregation factor can sometimes be modified by the raids factor in the sense that the occurrence of damage can be spread out over different areas. In a study of vandalism in schools in six Swedish municipalities there were several cases where a correlation was not found between the damage cost per pupil and the size of schools as measured by the number of pupils in attendance. This was explained by attacks on the schools during the evenings and over-night which accounted for a large part of the damage. These raids were made upon the smaller schools with a smaller number of pupils. The lowest degree of damage was found to occur in schools which were centrally located in the inner city and in small schools in the countryside. Other public property in the city centres, however, was subject to a great deal of damage inflicted in the course of raids. Vandalism by locals is most common in negatively segregated areas with social problems, while vandalism by persons living outside the area itself occurs through occasional raids on isolated buildings and the centres of congested areas. There are indications that vandalism by outsiders accounts for a great deal of the increase in the phenomenon.

The level of property damage in schools in the southern parts of Stockholm, i.e. a low status area with relatively new schools, is about 30 Swedish crowns higher per pupil than in the western parts of Stockholm with both old and newer low status schools. Moreover, newer schools in peripheral areas of the city, which are relatively isolated from the original buildings in their respective areas, consistently show a higher level of damage than the older schools in the inner city areas.

Our studies of vandalism in small country towns show that not only were most cases of vandalism that were tried in court found to have been committed by persons residing outside the area where the act took place, but also this type of vandalism is on the increase (see table 3). Our results show that the vandalism committed by outsiders occurs most often during weekends or late in the evening. Vandalism committed by persons living within the area where it

Table 3. Percent of tried cases of vandalism committed by offenders living within and outside the small town of Arvika.

	Committed by locals	Committed by outsiders	Total
1975	40%	60%	100%
1978	25%	75%	100%

Table 4. Factors which lead to different types of school vandalism.

Background factors leading to vandalism	Intermediate factors	Type of vandalism which will increase
Strong negative segregation	Weak system of norms and a poorly developed social network	Vandalism by locals
Raids	Directed toward isolated schools and city centres	Vandalism by outsiders
High number of pupils	High level of passivity in certain sectors of the school	Vandalism by locals
Recently built schools	Often built of 'fragile' material and adapted for flexible use leading to high mobility among teachers and pupils	Vandalism by both locals and outsiders

takes place accounts for a greater spread of its incidence over all of the days of the week (Roos, 1980).

We can summarise our discussion of vandalism caused by people living within and outside the affected area as in table 4. The categories 'prosperity based', 'poverty based', 'locals or outsiders' can help us to understand different patterns of vandalism in terms of spatial distribution and motivation.

9. The motivation behind acts of vandalism

An analysis of the social structure and of the aggregate data in terms of community and residential area is not sufficient for a study of vandalism. The question of motivation is essential, not least to counter the stereotyped opinion that vandalism is meaningless, lacks motivation, is crazy, accidental, etc. – assumptions which sometimes receive support from the fact that the offenders themselves are often incapable of giving reasons for their actions.

Minor acts of vandalism resulting from nonchalant and careless behaviour which, in many cases, could be considered unconscious and unintentional were referred to earlier. 'Serious' vandalism, on the other hand, is an intentional act, even if there is often no motive or purpose behind it. The degree of motivation can also be modified by the 'structure of opportunity', i.e. the character of the vandalised object. The objects most frequently vandalised are often public property, easily breakable, unattended and/or frequently used property. Insofar as buildings are concerned, both building material and design are found to be significant.

There are other kinds of destructive activities besides the destruction of material objects, for example, self-destruction by alcohol and drug abuse or suicide, and there are destructive activities aimed at others such as assault, rape, homicide and murder. When vandalism occurs in connection with any of the other types of behaviour, the motivation immediately becomes more difficult to distinguish. Property damage often occurs in connection with other criminal offences such as burglary, theft or attempted burglary. Property damage can also occur during gang fights. In the rural community of Arvika 65% of those who committed crimes of vandalism had been drinking alcohol. This can be interpreted in a number of ways: we can accept the figure as given or we can conclude that it only tells us about those who were caught by the police. National statistics indicate that, in most of the cases involving property damage that were brought to court, offences had been committed by persons acting alone, the majority of whom were over 21 years of age. When two or more persons were involved those convicted were younger.

10. Vandalism control measures

There are many different ways of approaching the problem of property damage, and several of them have been tested in Sweden and in other countries. In the light of these, I should like to propose two main directives for counteracting the destruction of property.

One of these directives can be said to be a 'socially responsible and constructive perspective'. This involves the view that each person has different potential resources for actively participating in building a society by influencing and changing his or her own living conditions in a rational and purposeful way.

This means that the inhabitants of a residential area, the pupils of a school or the workers in a factory should be given the opportunity to create the environment in which they live to meet their own needs, demands and desires. Through this, people would become conscious both of their own possibilities and of the limitations to change in their conditions and in the mechanisms of society and the social development which have created the conditions under which they live. The researcher's contribution to such work would be directed by the participants in action-oriented community work.

The other directive comes from the perspective of 'defensible space' (Newman, 1973). Measures which emanate from this point of view result in the attempts of schools and residential areas to protect themselves from attacks by outsiders. In the U.S.A. in particular people try to prevent property damage with the help of armed guards, alarm systems, TV surveillance, barred windows, etc. There are even attempts to protect schools and apartment buildings using construction techniques. Entrances, courtyards, etc. are built in such a way that there are no concealed or secluded spaces where someone could hide out of sight of other people in the area. Buildings, driveways and the like are planned so that areas are protected like fortresses. Fences therefore are often put up around schools and housing projects to protect them from attack.

In Sweden, 'defensible space' has not yet taken its place among the panoply of vandalism control measures. This is partly because property damage is, after all, still not as serious a problem in that country as in the U.S.A., and partly because, in Sweden, there are other traditions upon which measures for dealing with social problems are based. There are two current tendencies, however, that increase the likelihood that defensible space will play a greater role in the Sweden of the future.

One tendency is that serious and intentional vandalism involving raids and attack has become more common in the country. The other tendency is that the serious vandalism perpetrated by outsiders has, to a great extent, taken place in residential areas with single family housing units in the large cities and in smaller villages in the countryside. This implies a threat to those residential areas in Sweden where the schism between public and private interests is most pronounced. The demand for seclusion, integrity and individual freedom is certainly greater in suburban areas with single family housing and in country villages. Threats to these values, through an increase in damage for example, would probably increase the demand for protection and for 'defensible space'.

It is important now to approach the problem from a standpoint rooted in the socially constructive perspective. Such a perspective should go hand in hand with everyday life and work if further increases in vandalism are to be prevented.

References

Cohen, L.E., M. Felsen, 1979. Social change and crime rate trends: A routine activity approach. American Sociological Review no. 4.
George, V., P. Wilding, 1979. Ideology and social welfare. London: Routledge and Kegan Paul.
Newman, O., 1973. Defensible space. New York: Anchor Press.
Roos, H.-E., 1980. Vandalism i glesbygd. University of Lund, Department of Sociology.
Simmel, G., 1970. Struggle. Uppsala: Argos Forlag.

Abstract: H.E. Roos, Vandalism as a social problem
The discussions taken up in this paper are based on the findings of the Swedish research project, 'Big city and rural vandalism'. Vandalism is seen to be a social problem with respect to which social definition determines to what extent destruction of property is or is not considered a 'problem'. Not all types of property destruction are considered to be illegitimate. Vandalism has come to be seen as a social problem in Sweden only over the last decade, although the level of vandalism had been rising substantially during an earlier period. Traditional criminological theories cannot adequately explain the increase in vandalism in the post-war period. Factors such as mass consumer culture, general urbanisation, etc. can help to explain the high level of property damage in general, but they can hardly explain the periodic increases in Sweden in the last decade.

It is instead important to direct attention toward regional and specific factors such as the stagnation of urbanisation, intra-urban movements and segregation, with reference to vandalism in Sweden's big cities. To understand the regional character of this type of criminality in the rural areas, it is important to show how distribution policies, combined with changes in life styles in the countryside, complicate the picture of vandalism. A distinction is made between vandalism by persons living within and outside an area. Vandalism by persons from outside an area is shown to be responsible for a great deal of its increase. After presenting two motives for vandalism, excitement and desperation, the paper concludes with a short discussion of views on measures to counteract vandalism.

CHAPTER 8

Vandalism: is household movement a substitute for social control?

E. READE

First, it seems useful to explain how the ideas underlying this paper were developed. We were invited in 1977 to carry out research into vandalism in council housing estates in Oldham, an industrial town with a population of 227,000, 12 km northeast of Manchester. The local authority felt that vandalism was an urgent problem within its area, and had established an 'anti-vandalism committee', consisting of elected members of the local authority, together with co-opted local notables, police, social workers, and so on, to advise it on this problem. This committee had advised that research was necessary, and two research teams were established, one to investigate vandalism in schools, the other (our own team) to look at public housing estates. As regards our own team, three lines of enquiry were suggested. First, the administrative procedures were to be investigated, whereby damage was reported, and repairs arranged. *Inter alia*, this was justified on the grounds, frequently suggested in Britain, that vandalism occurs far less, where public property is seen to be cared for, and immediately repaired when damaged. The second line of enquiry lay in a study of the design and layout of the various housing areas, of the building materials used, and so on. This second line of enquiry was supervised by my colleague Jack Wawrzynski, and is reported in a parallel paper presented in this volume. The third line of enquiry was to be concerned with 'social aspects', and it was this with which I was myself concerned. The official report on our work (Pease et al., 1979) was presented about eighteen months after we started work. A paper setting out the arguments relating vandalism to patterns of household movement, developed in response to the request to investigate 'social aspects', was presented to a meeting of the Urban Sociology Group of the British Sociological Association, and was subsequently published (Reade, 1982).

The present paper is seen as constituting a challenge to the 'conventional wisdom' on vandalism, because the views which it advances are rarely encountered at the present time, and because when they *are* heard, they are often seen as lending support to authoritarian, 'elitist', and generally right-wing attitudes. The paper seeks to show that this latter interpretation is incorrect, and that the arguments which it defends are in a specifically sociological sense more intellectually credible than is much of the 'conventional wisdom' concerning vandalism.

Next, we can look in more detail at what the conventional wisdom says on each of the points listed above. This seems amply documented in a book by Morgan (1978) which, like the present paper, is concerned to question these prevailing assumptions.

First, then, we see that the 'conventional wisdom' stresses *deprivation*. Vandalism, along with a number of other forms of anti-social behaviour among young people, is seen as resulting from their having been deprived of a whole range of possible material or cultural benefits. Frequently, if not usually, the argument seems to be that the things of which they have been deprived are not merely desirable, but are 'needs', apparently in some objective sense. Thus it is common, in liberal, academic and professional circles, to ascribe delinquency to such factors as inadequate playspaces, to a lack of youth clubs, sports and entertainment facilities, to inadequate education, and increasingly at the present time, to unemployment. As a result, it is suggested, the young people in question are 'bored', and become involved in vandalism as a consequence.

An important question posed by this assumption is whether the postulated deprivations are thought to be relative or absolute. Unfortunately, those who put forward this type of explanation are rarely explicit on this point. But as mentioned above, the impression is often given that they are absolute, objective human needs, which, if not met, will cause delinquency. This assumption seems untenable, for we know that various societies have maintained socially acceptable standards of behaviour among their younger members at vastly differing levels of cultural and material development. If what is being suggested, by contrast, is that those concerned are suffering from *relative* deprivation, from the perception that other young people in society are better off than they themselves are, this would be a very much more credible hypothesis. Indeed, there is evidence that the *best* hope of reducing delinquency lies in a reduction of material and educational inequality. But this is a very different theory from that which speaks of 'deprivation' and 'needs'. To postulate inequality as a cause is to hypothesize that delinquency would be at a low level irrespective of whether social opportunities were abundant or meagre, provided they were equally shared.

Morgan, however, shows the extent to which the 'conventional wisdom' hinges on the notions of deprivation, and needs, and that frequently, these needs are assumed to be absolutes:

"In this psychology, concern has not been with how children come to understand and adjust to complex social requirements. It has rather been with what the innate 'needs' of the child are, which the adult world can provide for. The adult looks to the child, and is guided by the child's behaviour, rather than acts as his initiator and instructor into the rule-governed tasks and arrangements of his culture. If the adult can provide for the child's needs, then development is assumed to proceed fairly spontaneously, resulting in a good, mentally healthy person who is favourably disposed towards his fellows and adequate in his dealings with them. With everything child-centred and child-motivated, not only is there no room for adult control but the necessity for it would wither away. Here we short-circuit the cumbersome process of choosing, defending, transmitting and maintaining social rules. Only satisfy 'needs' properly and you can dispense with the imposition of norms and values, and the implicit element of coercion indispensable in securing obedience to them. We now deal in 'facts' about human development and have no further need for value judgments, and an externally imposed social morality" (Morgan, 1978: 51–2).

Many social scientists would question whether this suggestion that human beings have objective needs has any credibility at all. On the contrary, they would suggest, all knowledge concerning human behaviour must be of the 'If...then', type. Only *if* one is prepared to urge particular patterns of behaviour, or particular outcomes, does it become relevant to point out that specific preconditions are essential to the production of these patterns or outcomes; the desired outcomes themselves can be justified only in terms of values, since no social science can tell us how we ought to live. Plant (1974: 79) puts this well:

"Far from deriving society or community from some neutral definition of needs the reverse is the case: what counts as a need, or any other attribute, capacity or power depends upon the kind of social and ideological context involved".

Social science, then, is in principle interested only in causal relationships. If it could be shown that those who commit acts of vandalism are those who lack the material or cultural provisions mentioned above, the problem would be well on the way towards being solved. But this is unfortunately not the case. On the one hand, we know that young people who have been brought up at quite low material and educational standards, whether in absolute terms or relative to other groups in society, often commit no vandalism. On the other hand, we know that quite privileged young people often do commit such acts. And in the case of unemployment, at the moment the form of deprivation causing the greatest concern, there is again little evidence of any causal connection. Morgan mentions that a study of the connection between crime and unemployment in Britain over nearly one hundred years "found little discernible correlation" (Morgan, 1978: 163; for a summary of conflicting evidence, however, see e.g. Mannheim, 1940). What does seem clear, at least, is that there is a connection between delinquency and the quality of social control exerted over those in question. This may seem close to tautology. But it is not. To concentrate on this known connection between delinquency and social control is in fact of crucial importance.

    It is generally accepted that to be effective, formal and informal social control must reinforce each other. The prevention of such problems as vandalism, however, depends to a very considerable extent on informal social control, a point made clear by a wealth of anecdotal evidence in Jane Jacob's *Death and life of great American cities*:

"The first thing to understand is that the public peace – the sidewalk and street peace – of cities is not kept primarily by the police, necessary as police are. It is kept primarily by an intricate, almost unconscious, network of voluntary controls and standards among the people themselves. In some city areas – older public housing projects and streets with very high population turnover are often conspicuous examples – the keeping of public sidewalk law and order is left entirely to the police and special guards. Such places are jungles. No amount of police can enforce civilisation where the normal, casual enforcement of it has broken down" (Jacobs, 1962: 31-2).

A second feature of the 'conventional wisdom' is that in emphasizing 'deprivation', or failure to meet 'needs', it tends to stress the extent to which those concerned have been deprived *in the past*, and especially in their early years. To emphasize this is not of necessity to deny that past experience can be overcome, or counteracted. Nevertheless, it is at the very least to imply that these previous experiences continue to be an important influence in the lives of those concerned, and are not *easily* overcome. Morgan shows that this pessimistic tendency is highly characteristic of what in this present paper is termed the 'conventional wisdom':

"Those with a bad start are invariably spoken of as 'damaged' – like chipped china – implying some handicap or malformation of mentality, rather than inexperience or undesirable (but alterable) behaviour and attitudes ... The pervasive talk of emotional or other 'damage', with all its connotations of ruin and irreversibility, leads easily to a wringing-of-hands, a 'nothing can be done' attitude, because intervention was not early or thorough enough ... This contrasts oddly with the ostensibly harder, more 'cynical' traditional approach, which sees people (and children!) as altogether more resilient, capable of 'getting over it' and changing over time" (Morgan, 1978: 53).

Further, Morgan notes that the 'conventional wisdom' assumes that the average human being is

"... a creature of extraordinary rigidity ... so unadaptable, so unopportunist, he seems incapable of altering and adjusting his behaviour to suit his contemporary surroundings. No concession is made to any sensitivity to perceived opportunities, incentives and disincentives" (Morgan, 1978: 56).

Wheeler (1968: 83) contrasts this assumption that behaviour reflects fixed propensities with what he terms the *situational* approach, which assumes that "delinquency is not deeply rooted", and that the motives for it "are often relatively simple". The distinction between these two approaches might be considered similar to, though it is not the same as, that between 'crime as predisposition' and 'crime as opportunity' (Cloward and Ohlin, 1961; Himmelhoch, 1965). It is not the same distinction, because those, like the present author, who tend to find the 'situational' model of man the more convincing, need not necessarily also adopt the view that crime or delinquency is mainly the outcome of opportunity. After all, one could take the 'situational' stance, and yet also take the view that *what* are being constantly shaped, in each ongoing situation, are predispositions, or moral attitudes.

In contrasting the 'fixed propensities' and the 'situational' models, we find a strange paradox. A tendency to assume the validity of the 'fixed propensities' model is, as we have seen, a feature of the 'conventional wisdom'. And the 'conventional wisdom' on vandalism is that view of the matter which is characteristic of the broadly Left-orientated 'caring professions', of academic social scientists, and of the 'enlightened' 'Guardian'-reading professional middle classes. Its appeal to such Left-oriented groups, it seems, lies broadly in its blaming vandalism not on the vandal, but on 'society'. Yet when we examine the assumptions of this 'fixed propensities' model of man more closely, we see that it ought more logically to make its appeal to the Right. In its strong emphasis on past experience rather than present experience, and in its assumption that the harmful effects of faulty patterns of early socialisation can hardly be corrected, it is anti-environmentalist, and deeply pessimistic. In its implicit assumption that the culture and values of the various classes in society are utterly different, and that there is little hope of developing a set of shared norms in society as to how young people should behave, it is profoundly passive. In its assumption that nothing short of a cataclysmic redeployment of wealth in society, an obviously unlikely event, could remedy the deprivations which it stresses, it provides, in effect, virtually a legitimation of the status quo. The basic message of the 'conventional wisdom' would seem to be that we must not condemn, but must exercise all-embracing tolerance. The deprived, it seems to suggest, are not as we are, and it would be wrong to expect them to be. Above all, we must not presume to impose our middle class values upon them. In one, limited sense, this 'conventional wisdom' is democratic; it assumes the desirability of a plurality of value systems. But from another point of view it is profoundly anti-democratic; its conception of the values and of the culture of the underprivileged classes in society, from which it assumes the majority of delinquents are drawn, is condescending, and patronizing, and it denies the common humanity of man.

The opposed, 'situational' model, which assumes that it is perfectly possible, and indeed necessary, for society to impose a shared set of norms as to what is and what is not acceptable behaviour, and that by constantly shaping behaviour in this way we can in effect shape moral attitudes, is widely regarded as authoritarian, and 'elitist', and as having its natural appeal to the Right. After all, its basic message is that we *do* have the right to impose our values upon those whose behaviour we judge to be anti-social. It is assumed, probably correctly, to be the view generally held by the police. It is also, interestingly, highly characteristic of the working class itself, a point brought out well by an

anecdote recounted by Morgan (1978: 57). Morgan describes a working class
mother, visiting her child's school, who saw another child who "appeared to be
in the process of dismantling the classroom while the teacher stood passively
by". The teacher's attitude was that she would do little, since the child came
from a 'broken home'. The attitude of the working class mother, by contrast,
was that the child could 'bloody well learn'.

The argument of this paper is that the association of the 'situational'
approach with Right-wing political thought is profoundly mistaken. On the
contrary, the assumptions underlying this view ought more logically to make
their appeal to the Left. The 'situational' view assumes, optimistically, that a
common culture *is* possible, and can be shaped by common consent. It places
the interests of society before those of the individual. It is optimistic, and
environmentalist, in assuming that we *can* learn from each other, throughout
our lives, becoming increasingly considerate, and more concerned for the
welfare of others. But the 'situational' approach is also *sociologically* sounder
than is the 'conventional wisdom'. As well as reflecting the fact that without
social control, civilized life is in fact impossible, it also provides us with an
intellectually credible explanation as to exactly how this social control can be
exerted. Whereas the 'conventional wisdom' provides only explanations, the
'situational' view suggests remedies; it unites theory with practice.

The third point to be challenged concerns the 'conventional wisdom's' seeing
vandalism as a rather special type of deviant behaviour, requiring considerable
explanation. The present paper, by contrast, sees it not as a type of deviant
behaviour at all, but as merely a by-product of another, perfectly normal type
of behaviour, play (or horse-play) *when that normal type of behaviour is not
subjected to adequate social control*. The 'conventional wisdom' associates
vandalism with working class values and subculture, and more especially with
the way of life of a very underprivileged substratum within the working class.
This renders it very mysterious, for this way of life is unlikely to be within the
personal experience of those who embrace this 'conventional wisdom'. Thus,
they suggest, research is needed. Only when we discover exactly how and why
this particular type of deviant personality, the 'vandal', is produced, shall we
be in a position to use social science in order to reduce his proclivities to
engage in 'senseless destruction'.

This present paper, by contrast, suggests that vandalism needs little, if any,
explanation. It is merely the physical outcome of what could result whenever
any young people get together in groups, and engage in an activity which is
absolutely normal, that is, play, or horse-play. One says 'could' result, because
usually in such situations, social norms operate in such a way as to ensure that
things do not escalate, and get out of hand, and that property is therefore not
destroyed. To impose such norms, however, is to practice restraint, which

implies the expenditure of some kind of effort, or cost. This may be self-restraint, if exercised by the young people themselves. If by contrast it is imposed by adults, it is likely to involve judgment, tact, diplomacy and other social skills. We can only reasonably expect those concerned to make this investment of effort where they have some incentive to do so, which probably means, in general, where they perceive some advantage in *not* allowing their physical surroundings to be damaged or destroyed. This will be taken up in the final section of the paper.

For the moment, the point to be made is simply that vandalism is a possible consequence of perfectly normal behaviour, and that there is therefore no great problem involved in explaining it. Writing of juvenile delinquency in general, and not specifically of vandalism, Sykes and Matza make the point that the delinquent is far less deviant than he is thought to be. It is normal, they say, for children to seek thrills. And it is the failure to realize this which has led to what are in fact unnecessary theories, attributing delinquency to such abnormal factors as personality disturbance or emotional disorders, the involvement of the delinquents in deviant subcultures, and so on (Sykes and Matza, 1961).

If this is true of delinquency in general, it must be even more true of vandalism in particular. For vandalism, of all forms of juvenile delinquency, would seem to be the one in which we have least need to search into the personal attitudes, motives, or predispositions of those concerned. It is an almost perfect example of unpremeditated or unintended behaviour, usually or very largely the outcome of the fortuitous juxtaposition of a specific social process in a particular physical milieu. It seems best understood as an example of what McCord (1968) terms 'socialized delinquency':

"The socialized delinquent does not suffer from any particular psychological disorders, other than those which characterize the typical adolescent. His crimes are not motivated by deep-seated anxieties or unresolved conflicts, but rather by a simple desire to conform to the norms of his gang" (McCord, 1968: 88; see also Wilson and Herbert, 1978).

Nor does it follow that such young people have any particular attitude to property, private or public, or are expressing any conscious or even unconscious social or political attitudes. On the contrary, this damage to property is usually a by-product of behaviour which has quite other motives, based, for example, on a desire to 'show off' in front of girls, to go one better than everyone else, or merely to demonstrate that one is a 'good sport' and a member of the group.

The fourth point on which the 'conventional wisdom' is questioned concerns the class basis of the concern about vandalism. As pointed out above, it has become common to regard vandalism as a phenomenon very much associated with the least privileged classes in society, and with the areas in which they live. It has also become common to focus on 'values'. It is assumed that the values of the most deprived groups in society, within which most vandalism is assumed to occur, are simply totally different from middle class values, and that it is this gulf between these two value systems which, in a very real sense, lies at the root of the problem of vandalism. By an extension of this argument, and reflecting a kind of misplaced cultural modesty, it has become common to assume that it would be morally wrong, and in any case impossible, for those middle class professionals who are most concerned, such as teachers and social workers, to impose middle class values upon those who have their own supposedly quite different, but equally valid, value system. Such assumptions are often reinforced by suggesting that those living in relative poverty have far more important things to worry about than the upkeep, and especially the visual appearance, of their physical environment, and that such aesthetic sensibility is merely a middle class luxury. They are further reinforced by the suggestion that what lies behind this middle class concern for physical surroundings is really no more than a concern for property, and the financial value of property, and even that the poor, in showing their disregard for such matters, show themselves in fact to have a set of values *more* worthy of respect than those of the middle classes. Such attitudes have been strengthened by prevailing fashions in social science. Among groups as disparate as phenomenologists and neo-Marxists, and indeed, among sociologists of virtually *all* theoretical persuasions, it has become *de rigueur* to argue that much so-called crime and delinquency is merely a matter of 'labelling', that it is far less of a problem to those concerned than we had supposed it to be, and that such labelling is of interest more for what it tells us concerning the social attitudes of the labellers, than for what it tells us about the behaviour thus labelled. Finally, all this syndrome of attitudes and assumptions has been further strengthened by the increasing tendency among self-styled neo-Marxist sociologists, usually themselves of middle class origin, to romanticize what they see as working class culture, and thus to condone behaviour which by any objective standards is simply selfish, and anti-social.

This whole syndrome of liberal attitudes and assumptions seems highly questionable. It appears to rest *first*, on a tendency to grossly exaggerate the differences between middle class and working class values (at least insofar as they relate to the subject of this paper, vandalism), and *second*, on a tendency to exaggerate the importance of values themselves, as explanatory variables in sociology. The present paper, by contrast, suggests that it would be more useful to focus our attention instead on physical, material considerations, and on behaviour itself, rather than on the values said to be implicit in that behaviour.

This alternative, 'materialist' approach, rests on such facts as the following: the poor are harmed quite as much by vandalism as are the middle classes.

Arguably, they are harmed more by it, since on average they experience more of it. They pay the cost of it, in the form of increased rates and rents. To be intimidated by gangs of youths, to have one's garden fence broken down, one's windows broken, and so on, is just as damaging to those who live on council estates as it is to those living in exclusive suburbs. The residents of those council estates which acquire a reputation for vandalism suffer social stigma, even though their own patterns of behaviour are perfectly responsible. That many of the least privileged members of society have more pressing problems, and therefore appear to be less outraged than are the middle classes by, for example, graffiti, or the general air of neglect which pervades their surroundings, is no evidence that they have different 'values'. On the contrary, that within the council sector there is a constant 'internal migration' of households continually trying to move away from the worst estates, and into better ones, or into areas of owner-occupation, suggests that these working class people have *the same* values as do middle class people. Or, in the more 'materialist' terms preferred in this present paper, it suggests that working class people are harmed by the same things, and benefitted by the same things, as are middle class people (Morgan 1978: 214).

Morris, too, had made the same point many years previously:

"Those delinquencies which are not illegal, and which would be kept in check by the informal pressure of public opinion in a middle-class neighbourhood are integrated within a normative cultural pattern, (in which) the only control being exerted is by an adaptation of the *lex talionis* ... the principle of 'giving as good as you take' operates, so that abuse over the garden fence must be met by further abuse, slanders by counter slanders and so on. Such a way of life is essentially unsatisfying and frequently mentally unhealthy. It is not surprising that almost all those individuals who can, seek to abandon it and adopt the norms of the middle class" (Morris, 1957: ch. 10).

It would seem fundamentally mistaken, given the objective of reducing the incidence of vandalism, to underestimate the extent to which working class people themselves appreciate high standards of behaviour on the part of their neighbours. That they so often see themselves as able to achieve such standards only by moving house, is itself a major social problem. Indeed, it could be argued that it is a far greater problem than is vandalism, for as will be argued below, it is in a sense the *cause* of vandalism (see e.g., Tucker, 1966; Heraud, 1968; Kirby, 1973; Ravetz, 1974: esp. 179-81; Marsden, 1976).

This fact, that much household movement reflects a desire to get away from areas in which there is an inadequate standard of social control, brings us to the fifth of the points on which the 'conventional wisdom' is questioned in this paper. Whereas the 'conventional wisdom' sees vandalism as a problem *sui generis*, this paper sees it as merely one element in a wider syndrome of attitudes and patterns of behaviour. This wider syndrome can be summarized as *neglect*. Indeed, it seems useful to regard vandalism not as actions committed by young people, but as the result of *failure* to act, on the part of *adults*. Failure to act to prevent play escalating into vandalism is very similar to failure to act when litter needs to be picked up, failure to keep one's garden tidy, failure to attend to necessary repairs, and so on, even including failure to take the trouble, oneself, to avoid dropping litter. Those living in any given area *can only be expected* to take trouble in such ways, in order to maintain the physical standard of that area, as long as it appears to them that such trouble will repay itself. To maintain adequate standards of social control within a neighbourhood, such that children's play does not escalate into vandalism, demands considerable investments of time, tact, patience, and even courage. The adults must devote much attention to the task of developing a shared set of perceptions and norms, such that they come to agree on such matters as when it is permissible for an adult to control the behaviour of other people's children. It is only reasonable to expect people to take this trouble where they have some material interest in the matter, and clearly perceive this interest.

In an area of owner occupation for example, residents have a shared interest in ensuring that the physical milieu of their homes is well maintained, in order to protect their property values. But even tenants normally have an interest in enforcing considerate patterns of behaviour, such that their enjoyment of their homes and gardens is not impaired. Once any of those living in the area in question seem not to understand the need for such norms, however, or seem to their neighbours for whatever reason unwilling to play their part in enforcing them, there is a risk that, for example, children's play could develop into vandalism at any time. In this situation, any particular household must weigh up whether it seems worthwhile to try to reimpose the norms which were previously obtained, or whether it would be easier simply to move away. Once households begin to think it would be less trouble to move away, the neighbourhood is in decline. And once a neighbourhood becomes thus stigmatized, we cannot expect any of those who live in it to take the trouble to ensure that it is well cared for. It is, after all, hardly reasonable to expect human beings to take trouble to safeguard a neighbourhood which has become a social symbol of their own low status.

It was on the basis of such arguments that we decided, in the research in Oldham, to pay particular attention to patterns of household movement (Pease et al., 1979: 39-56, further developed in Reade, 1982).

It would be wrong, however, to assume that in a situation where a neighbourhood has begun to decline in this way, *all* those who can, will move away. For all kinds of reasons, ranging from family or neighbourly ties to sheer inability to face up to the task of moving itself, many will remain whose enjoyment of their homes, and of their neighbourhood, is seriously reduced by the air of neglect, and the reduced standards of behaviour, which increasingly prevail. Indeed, it seems likely that in many such declining neighbourhoods, even a majority of the population still continues to attempt to maintain those standards of behaviour which, if practiced by all, would prevent decline. Most people probably prefer to live in neighbourhoods in which people do behave with consideration, both for other people, and for the physical artefacts on which their sense of well-being and of security so often depend.

If this can be accepted, it throws doubt on the suggestion that where vandalism is concerned, the values of the various classes in society are so different. One might suggest, by contrast, that the difference between the classes lies not in their having different values, but in their having vastly differing abilities to act on the same values. The sheer volume of household movement, within the public housing sector, is testimony to the extent of working class people's desire to live in neighbourhoods in which social control ensures responsible behaviour. Equally, it suggests that many manage only to move to neighbourhoods which have standards little higher than those from which they have escaped. The apparent equanimity with which middle class academics and professionals assure us that the working class have different values, and are therefore relatively little troubled by such things as vandalism, may be due mainly to the fact that these people have never themselves lived in working class neighbourhoods. It is very easy to be tolerant and liberal towards anti-social behaviour, if one runs little risk of coming into contact with it.

One of the most significant ways in which western societies differ from communist ones is that in the West, society can reward 'success' by offering physical isolation from areas of hopelessness and decay. And if some areas are going 'up', it follows, of necessity, that others must be going 'down'. The resulting hierarchy of residential environments of varying standards is quite considerable, such that though many individuals experience movement to higher status areas over their lifetimes, probably very few experience anything approaching the full range. Nevertheless, constant residential movement is a feature of our way of life. One might suggest that to a large extent, such movement, or the promise of it, replaces social control. If we did not have this possibility of movement, we would instead have to devote time and effort to negotiating the often very delicate processes whereby, otherwise, human beings educate each other into habits of considerateness. Thus, it is easy to see why Sennett (1970), for example, sees spatial class segregation as one of the main causes of malaise in Western society. Other incisive accounts of the part it plays in shaping and maintaining the capitalist social structure, and the capitalist economy, are provided by, for example, Williams (1971), Lofland (1973), Lee at al. (1974), Young and Kramer (1978) and Bassett and Short (1980).

It seems difficult to avoid the following conclusion. The creation of 'areas of hopelessness', in which normal standards of social control no longer operate, and in which unnecessarily rapid deterioration of the physical fabric therefore sets in, aided by 'vandalism', and occasionally by riots, is associated with our tendency, at every level of society, to move away from those whom we consider to be our inferiors, or who seem to pose a threat to us. The creation of a common culture, with shared conceptions of what is acceptable behaviour, seems unlikely in a competitive market society. That such shared norms are desirable is all too rarely accepted, even by sociologists in the West; among them, the very concept of social control is unpopular. Practice in the communist countries, by contrast, seems to offer a better hope, since it is based on a sounder theoretical understanding of the necessity of careful socialization of children into patterns of behaviour which do not harm others, and of the need for congruence between formal and informal social control.

Kessen, for example, reports (1975) how by constant example, explanation and encouragement, children in China are socialized into patterns of behaviour which are seen by all members of society as socially responsible. The patterns of behaviour expected in the home, in the school, and in the community generally are congruent, and therefore reinforce each other. Adults generally intervene, whatever the immediate context, and whether the children in question are their own or others', whenever children's play threatens to get out of hand. As Kessen points out, Chinese society is thus in a real sense adult-centred rather than child-centred. This careful socialization is not, however, in any sense repressive. The methods used are based on reason, rather than on coercion, and certainly not on physical coercion. Above all, however, what comes out most strongly from Kessen's account is the sheer power of universally shared expectations:

"The adults know what a child should be like, they behave as though it were certain the child would behave in the expected way; and on his side the child joins a social structure where the definition of his place and the definition of his proper behaviour, are, by and large, without ambiguity and without conflict" (Kessen, 1975: 218-20).

Bronfenbrenner (1971) provides similar evidence from the Soviet Union. What seems often to get forgotten in the prevailing liberal 'conventional wisdom' is that children (and adults too, for that matter) actually *prefer* to live in a well ordered social milieu, in which other people expect them to conform to fairly demanding standards of behaviour.

Braithwaite (1979: ix) reviews the available empirical evidence on what he defines as two 'policy questions'. *First*: 'Will policies to redistribute wealth and power within capitalist societies have effects upon crime?'; *second*: 'Will policies to overcome the residential segregation of social classes have effects upon crime?'. The second question, which reflects a traditional interest among

criminologists in the ecology of lawbreaking, is highly relevant to the arguments advanced in the present paper. On this second question, Braithwaite
concludes that the available evidence lends weight to the suggestion that class
heterogeneity, in residential areas, is indeed associated with lower rates of
crime. He cautiously avoids suggesting, however, that class mix in itself can
bring about reduced crime levels, instead putting forward the more specific
suggestion that lower class people are more likely to engage in crime if they live
in areas which are predominantly lower class in social composition: "Cities
which segregate their poor have higher crime rates ... Therefore, policies which
result in fewer lower-class people living in predominantly lower-class areas
might be granted some efficacy for crime reduction" (Braithwaite, 1979:
171-2).

Though suggesting that it would be premature, on the evidence available, to
embark upon a programme of residential class mixing as a means of reducing
crime, Braithwaite does nevertheless consider this evidence to be sufficiently
strong to justify his devoting an appendix of his book to a consideration of a
number of ways in which public policies in Western societies can and do
counteract residential class segregation.

In this present paper the same question is approached from a different
angle. The hypothesis advanced is that class segregation, from the point of
view of those concerned, is an easier option than social control. Finding it
difficult to maintain those norms of behaviour which would ensure them
peaceful enjoyment of their homes, individual households find it easier to
move house, or to live in the hope of moving house. If this hypothesis has any
validity, it suggests that we might usefully reformulate Braithwaite's second
question. Instead of asking: 'Should government seek to promote social mix?',
we might ask: 'Should government continue actively to promote and encourage
increased residential class segregation?'. For there is ample evidence that, in
fact, housing policy in Britain is having precisely this effect (Pease et al., 1979:
39-56; Reade, 1982). There is also much evidence to suggest that rating
policies, too, have broadly similar consequences.

Reformulating Braithwaite's question in this way seems useful. To ask
whether government should promote social mix is to ask what in Britain at
least has come to be regarded as a utopian question. To ask whether government should continue to promote segregation, by contrast, reminds us that this
tendency to segregation may not in fact be 'natural' (whatever that might
mean), but may in part at least be itself a consequence of public policy.

If it can be accepted that to some extent at least, and from the viewpoint of
the individual household, the maintenance of adequate standards of social
control and removal to a more respectable area are alternative courses of
action, it follows that these two things may also be alternatives so far as public
policy is concerned.

Instead of assuming the inevitability of spatial class segregation, and thus of differential levels of public safety and well-being, public policy could be grounded in a very different principle. It could rest on the assumption that adequate social control should exist in all areas equally. It was argued above that those who live on council estates, and in less privileged areas generally, have just as much desire for the maintenance of social order as do those who live in exclusive suburbs. That they must endure lower standards is not because a majority of them are content with such lower standards, but because, unlike exclusive residential areas, these neighbourhoods contain a minority of anti-social families and individuals. Constant 'sifting and sorting', by removal van, ensures that the size of this minority increases as the social status of the area in question goes down.

Existing policies, since they rest on the assumption of the 'naturalness' of spatial class segregation, imply equally the 'naturalness' of a status hierarchy of residential areas, in which the exact social status of each neighbourhood, among all those which make up any given local housing market, is widely understood. Thus, public policy not only contributes to a system in which large numbers of people are condemned to live in areas in which relatively low standards of public behaviour prevail. It also results in the unnecessarily rapid decay of the physical fabric of these areas of lower status. Their inhabitants cannot be expected to take trouble to prevent the physical decay of artefacts which are symbols of their own supposed social inferiority. Since social control is generally effective only where it observes the same norms in the public sphere as in the private, it follows that the best hope of reducing this unnecessarily rapid decay of the housing stock (in which 'vandalism' plays a part) lies in public authorities using their powers in such a way as to help residents in poorer areas to impose good standards of behaviour upon each other. It is therefore not surprising to find that in Britain, the initiatives most successful in reducing vandalism have not been directed at vandalism as such. Rather, they have had the much wider objective of giving the residents in such areas some 'stake' in maintaining adequate social standards and some help in maintaining these standards. (See, for example, Department of the Environment 1981a, 1981b, 1981c, 1982: Hedges et al., 1980). Often, residents find it difficult to enforce the norms which reflect this interest, unless helped by public authorities:

"One of the major benefits of resident participation can be in bringing residents together and encouraging parental involvement in assisting and supervising children. This was observed on the Cunningham Road Estate where parents, having come to know and cooperate with their neighbours, became confident in intervening in a positive way with their own children and others" (Department of the Environment, 1981c: 6).

In addition to reducing the rate of physical decay of those residential areas previously perceived as less desirable, such policy intitiatives would seem likely to reduce the rate of household movement. But they should not be seen as special initiatives, directed to particular areas. Instead, all citizens should have an equal right to expect social control to be maintained in their neighbourhood, irrespective of where they may happen to live.

Braithwaite's first 'policy question' should not be forgotten, either. The evidence seems to suggest that the reduction of inequality in society offers the best hope of reducing the level of anti-social behaviour. Falkin (1979: 134), for example, concludes that income redistribution would be "the most cost-effective method of reducing delinquency" (see also Braithwaite, 1979: 236).

In this paper, attention has focussed on social control. One might suggest that there is a need, within sociology, to rehabilitate this concept, to demonstrate that acceptance of the necessity of social control need not brand us as authoritarians of the Right. The fashionable assumption that all social countrol of necessity operates to the benefit of the privileged classes is patently false. This assumption often harms precisely those, the less privileged, with whom those who espouse it consider themselves to sympathize.

References

Bassett, K., J. Short, 1980. Housing and residential structure. London: Routledge.

Braithwaite, J., 1979. Inequality. Crime and public policy. London: Routledge.

Bronfenbrenner, U., 1971. Two worlds of childhood: USA and USSR. London: Allen and Unwin. (Also Harmondsworth: Penguin, 1974.)

Cloward, R.A., L.E. Ohlin, 1961. Delinquency and opportunity. London: Routledge.

Department of the Environment, 1981a. Reducing vandalism on public housing estates. London: HMSO.

Department of the Environment, 1981b. Reducing the number of empty dwellings. London: DOE.

Department of the Environment, 1981c. Security on council estates. London: HMSO.

Department of the Environment, 1982. Priority estates project 1982: A summary of ideas and progress. London: DOE.

Falkin, G.P., 1979. Reducing delinquency: A strategic planning approach. Lexington (Mass.): Heath.

Hedges, A., A. Blaber, B. Mostyn, 1980. Community planning project: Cunningham Road improvement scheme. London: Social and Community Planning Research.

Heraud, B.J., 1968. Social class and the new towns. Urban Studies 5, 33–53.

Himmelhoch, J., 1965. Delinquency and opportunity: An end and a beginning of theory. In: A.W. Gouldner, S.M. Miller, eds., Applied sociology: Opportunities and problems. New York: Free Press.

Jacobs, J., 1962. The death and life of great American cities. London: Cape. (Also Harmondsworth: Penguin, 1965.)

Kessen, W., ed., 1975. Childhood in China. New Haven: Yale University Press.

Kirby, D.A., 1973. Residential mobility among local authority tenants. Housing and Planning Review 29, 11–12.

Lee, J.M., B. Wood, B.W. Solomon, P. Walter, 1974. The scope of local initiative: A study of Cheshire Country Council, 1961–1974. London: Martin Robertson.

Lofland, C.H., 1973. A world of strangers: Order and action in urban public space. New York: Basic Books.

McCord, W., 1968. Delinquency: Psychological aspects. In: International encyclopedia of the social sciences. New York: Macmillan/Free Press.

Mannheim, H., 1940. Crime and unemployment. In: W.G. Carson, P. Wiles, eds., The sociology of crime and delinquency in Britain. London: Martin Robertson, 1971.

Marsden, D., 1976. The rough. New Society, 11 November.

Morgan, P., 1978. Delinquent fantasies. London: Temple Smith.

Morris, T., 1957. The criminal area: A study in social ecology. London: Routledge.

Pease, K., E.J. Reade, J. Wawrzynski, 1979. Investigation of vandalism in residential areas of Oldham. Oldham Metropolitan Borough Council.

Plant, R., 1974. Community and ideology: An essay in applied social philosophy. London: Routledge.

Ravetz, A., 1974. Model estate: Planned housing at Quarry Hill, Leeds. London: Croom Helm.

Reade, E.J., 1982. Residential decay, household movement and class structure. Policy and Politics 10 (1), 27–45.

Sennett, R., 1970. The uses of disorder: Personal identity and city life. Harmondsworth: Penguin.

Sykes, G., D. Matza, 1961. Delinquency and subterranean values. American Sociological Review 26, 712–719.

Tucker, J., 1966. Honourable estates. London: Gollancz.

Wheeler, S., 1968. Delinquency: Sociological aspects. In: International encyclopedia of the social sciences. New York: Macmillan/Free Press.

Williams, O.P., 1971. Metropolitan political analysis: A social access approach. Glencoe (Ill.): The Free Press/London: Collier Macmillan.

Wilson, H., G.W. Herbert, 1978. Parents and children in the inner city. London: Routledge.

Young, K., J. Kramer, 1978. Strategy and conflict in metropolitan housing, Suburbia versus the Greater London Council, 1965–1975. London: Heinemann.

Abstract: E. Reade, Vandalism: is household movement a substitute for social control?
This paper questions what the author takes to be the 'conventional wisdom' on vandalism, seen as consisting of five main strands. *First*, this 'conventional wisdom' assumes that the main cause of vandalism lies in material or cultural deprivation, whereas this paper argues that the main cause lies in an inadequate level of informal social control. *Second*, the 'conventional wisdom' tends to assume a 'fixed propensity' to delinquency, whereas this paper suggests that behaviour is more malleable. *Third*, the 'conventional wisdom' sees vandalism as a form of deviant behaviour, whereas the present paper regards it as a byproduct of a form of behaviour which is quite normal, play. *Fourth*, the paper questions the assumption, also characteristic of the 'conventional wisdom', that the middle class and the working class have strongly contrasted value systems, and instead argues for the existence, and the desirability, of a set of attitudes common to all classes and based on shared norms. *Fifth*, the 'conventional wisdom' tends to approach vandalism as a distinct problem, whereas the present paper sees it as merely one outcome of a wider syndrome of attitudes to the physical environment.

The paper suggests that in a stable neighbourhood, informal social control ensures that normal play does not escalate into vandalism. In the kind of competitive society which actually exists, however, neighbourhoods are *not* stable. Even in the public sector, there is constant household movement, motivated by desire to 'trade up' to a more respectable neighbourhood. Those left behind in the less respectable neighbourhoods thus find it increasingly difficult to maintain adequate standards of behaviour, and physical decay, aided by 'vandalism', sets in. Thus, vandalism is seen as resulting from the fact that household movement replaces informal social control.

CHAPTER 9

Vandals and vandalism in the USA: a rural perspective

J.F. DONNERMEYER and G.H. PHILLIPS

The purpose of this chapter is to examine the extent and pattern of vandalism in the rural United States, both from the perspective of the victim and from the perspective of the offender. Information for this chapter was derived from a series of rural vandalism studies conducted by the National Rural Crime Prevention Center. In the first part, the impact of vandalism on the victim will be assessed. In the second part, the results of two self-report studies of participation in vandalistic activity among rural high school sophomores and juniors will be reviewed. In the summary section, differential perspectives on vandalism will be identified, using as a base and then expanding upon Cohen's (1973) typology of vandalistic motivations.

1. Vandalism and its impact on the victim

1.1. Source of data

Victimization research is a data collection procedure using scientific survey methods to examine the crime experiences of the population, regardless of whether or not the incidents are reported to law enforcement officials.

A series of four rural victim studies have been completed by the National Rural Crime Prevention Center. These include: (1) 1974 Ohio Rural Victim Study – this research was a victim survey of 899 open-country households (i.e., households not located within any type of incorporated place, such as a city, town, or village) from nine counties in the state of Ohio. (2) 1980 Ohio Rural Victim Study – this study represented a replication of the 1974 study, in which 891 open-country households were interviewed. The same nine counties from Ohio constituted the study areas. (3) Roadsign Vandalism and Theft – interviews with 48 supervisors of County Engineer Departments in Ohio were completed in order to estimate the frequency of occurrence and cost of roadsign vandalism and theft. County Engineer Departments are responsible for the maintenance and repair of county roads, most of which are located in the rural parts of Ohio. (4) Farm Retail Market Study – the purpose of this study was to examine the extent and cost of crime to a type of predominantly rural business. Farm retail markets are of two types: (a) roadside markets, which sell fresh farm produce; and (b) 'U-Pick' or pick-your-own markets which allow the customer to harvest his own produce. Victim surveys were completed for 361 farm retail markets, most of which were located in the Great Lakes states. [1]

1.2. Extent of vandalism

How extensive is vandalism? The 1974 Ohio Rural Victim Study found that 14.3% of the 889 open-country households had experienced at least one incident of vandalism over the 12-month period covered in the research. Among victimized households, 46% had two or more incidents of vandalism. In the 1980 Ohio Rural Victim Study, the proportion who experienced one or more incidents of vandalism during a similar one year time span had increased to 15.5%. Slightly over 40% of these victimized households had two or more separate vandalism incidents occur.

In both the 1974 and 1980 Ohio Rural Victim Studies, vandalism was the most frequent type of crime experienced by open-country households, exceeding larceny, burglary, motor vehicle theft, and all forms of violent crime.

What were some of the more frequent types of vandalism experienced by rural residents of Ohio? From the 1980 Ohio Rural Victim Study, typical examples included:

(a) destruction or defacement of the mailbox often by smashing with hammer or baseball bat, or running over with an automotive vehicle;
(b) the front lawn driven over by an automotive vehicle, hence, destroying or damaging the turf;
(c) garage, barn, house or car windows broken;
(d) parked car was splattered with paint, or shot by a gun;
(e) corn or wheat fields were driven through, often by an 'off-road' or four-wheel jeep or other type of automotive vehicle;
(f) fencing destroyed or gate left open;
(g) outside lights broken or shot out.

Vandalism is also the leading type of crime affecting farm retail markets. Among these rural businesses over two in every five experienced at least one act of destruction or defacement to property. Of these, 38% had two or more incidents occur. Again, vandalism exceeded in frequency the occurrence of

[1]   The rural victimization studies and self-report studies used in this chapter were funded through the support of the Ohio Agricultural Research and Development Center, College of Agriculture, The Ohio State University (no. OH00476-S). The Indiana self-report study was supported by the Purdue University Agricultural Experiment Station (Hatch Project no. 45068). For additional information on the data collection and research procedures of these studies, write to the National Rural Crime Prevention Center, 2120 Fyffe Road, The Ohio State University, Columbus, Ohio 43210 (614/422-1467).

burglary, larceny, robbery, shoplifting, and employee theft. Typical examples of vandalism to farm retail markets included:

(a) automotive vehicle driven through farm fields;
(b) defacement or destruction of signs along the road which advertise or give directions to the farm retail operation;
(c) tires slashed on farm equipment, such as a tractor;
(d) glass windows were broken or plastic sheeting around greenhouses were ripped;
(e) irrigation equipment, especially the pump, were run over or rammed with an automotive vehicle.

1.3. Economic cost of vandalism

Estimated dollar losses were collected for vandalism in the 1980 Ohio Rural Victim Study. In 51% of the incidents, no direct dollar costs were incurred. However, this does not mean that there were not clean-up or other non-economic costs. It simply means that repairs were made without the purchase of new parts and materials, or that the damaged items were never replaced.

Where a direct dollar cost was involved, estimates provided by the respondents indicated a median cost of about $20. However, there were 15 incidents greater than $100 in cost, of which four involved amounts exceeding $1,000.

Among farm retail market operations, only about 20% of the vandalism incidents did not involve some type of dollar damage. The median cost of vandalism was about $150 per incident.

There are both direct and indirect economic costs to vandalism. Not only private, but public property is likewise subject to malicious destruction. When public property is involved, everyone who pays taxes becomes a victim.

In a study of the cost of roadsign vandalism along county roads in Ohio, an annual rate of $20.69 per mile of roadway was estimated. Considering that Ohio has nearly 30,000 miles of county road, and that township roads (of which there are about 40,000 miles, largely in rural Ohio), Federal and State highways, and city streets were all excluded from the analysis, it can be seen that roadsign vandalism is a multi-million dollar problem nationwide.

1.4. Psychological impact of vandalism victimization

What is the effect of vandalism on its victim? Do the victims of vandalism experience higher levels of fear than non-victims?

Table 1 summarizes five attitudinal measures associated with perceptions of vulnerability, from the 1980 Ohio Rural Victim Study. The exact wording of each question is contained in table 1. Two of the measures show statistically significant differences between vandalism and non-victims, and all five consistently indicate that vandalism victims perceive greater vulnerability.

The first two measures asked the respondents to express their concern about

Table 1. Perceptions of vulnerability to crime and vandalism victimization (1980 Ohio Rural Victim Study).

Perception of vulnerability	Vandalism victimization status			
	Victim		Non-victim	
	Frequency	Percent	Frequency	Percent
A. Some people worry a great deal about having their house broken into or their property damaged. Are you:				
Very concerned	60	44.4	270	37.8
Somewhat concerned	70	51.9	406	56.2
Not concerned at all	5	3.7	43	6.0
Total	135	100.0	722	100.0

Chi-square = 2.7   DF = 2   Significance = 0.26   Phi = 0.09

B. Some people worry a great deal about being attacked or robbed. Are you:				
Very concerned	27	20.0	172	23.8
Somewhat concerned	95	70.4	427	59.1
Not concerned at all	13	9.6	123	17.0
Total	135	100.0	722	100.0

Chi-square = 7.0   DF = 2   Significance = 0.03   Phi = 0.24

C. Compared to other parts of this county, how likely is a home or apartment in this neighborhood to be broken into?				
More likely	46	40.0	215	34.2
Less likely	68	60.0	413	65.8
Total	114	100.0	628	100.0

Chi-square-1.6   DF = 1   Significance = 0.20   Phi = 0.06

D. Compared to other parts of this county is a person walking around this neighborhood likely to be attacked?				
More likely	34	29.3	148	22.9
Less likely	82	70.7	499	77.1
Total	116	100.0	647	100.0

Chi-square = 2.2   DF = 2   Significance = 0.13   Phi = 0.08

E. How fearful are you that someone in this household will be victimized?				
Fearful	22	17.2	54	7.8
Not fearful	106	82.8	634	92.2
Total	128	100.0	688	100.0

Chi-square = 11.1   DF = 1   Significance = 0.0008   Phi = 0.39

property crime. Forty-four per cent of the vandalism victims, compared to 38% of the non-victims were very concerned. There was a larger attitudinal differential expressed between victims and non-victims on concern for violent crime, and the difference was statistically significant.

The third and fourth attitudinal measures asked the respondents to indicate if their neighborhood was more or less likely to experience crime than other parts of the county. Although the difference was not statistically significant, 40% of the vandalism victims versus 34% of the non-victims perceived a greater likelihood of being broken into. In addition, 29% of the vandalism victims compared to 23% of the non-victims perceived a greater likelihood of violent crime in their neighborhood.

The fifth and final measure of perceptions of vulnerability asked the respondent if they were fearful that someone in the household would soon become the victim of a crime. Twice the proportion of vandalism victims than non-victims agreed with this statement.

All five attitudinal measures indicate that vandalism victimization results in increased perception of vulnerability to crime. The greater difference in perceptions of vulnerability between victims and non-victims was with fear of violent crime. This may seem contradictory because vandalism is a property crime. Yet it does make sense because vandalism can be described as 'violence against property'.

2. Rural youth vandalism: participation and motives

2.1. Source of data

This section is based upon two self-report studies of involvement in vandalistic behavior among sophomores and juniors from selected rural high schools in Ohio and Indiana. The Ohio sample consisted of all sophomore level studies from three high schools in various regions of Ohio. The sophomore level was selected because this grade level contains mostly 15 and 16 year olds. Students in this age group become licensed drivers and this phenomenon was hypothesized to be related to a marked increase in vandalistic behavior.

The total number of sophomores from the three high schools was 634. The survey instrument was administered at the high schools in March 1975. The instrument was distributed to 599 sophomores, of whom 572 returned usable responses (average absentee rate the day of administration was 5.5%).

The content of the survey instrument relied upon self-reports by the respondent with respect to committing acts of vandalism. The instrument included questionnaire items on the number of acts of vandalism engaged in by the respondent. In addition, for the most recent act of vandalism, more detailed information surrounding the event was asked, such as when the act was committed, number of persons present, type of property which was damaged or destroyed, how the respondent became involved, and self-perceptions of his own vandalistic behavior. The instrument also included questions pertaining to the social, economic, and family background of the respondent.

The Indiana study was conducted in an effort to replicate the results of the Ohio study. Following some minor changes in working and format, the same survey instrument was employed.

The survey instrument was administered to 354 junior level (eleventh grade) high school students from two school districts in a rural county of southwestern Indiana in March, 1979 (absentee rate was 4%).

Both the Ohio and Indiana samples represented a large segment of youth growing up in rural areas in the Midwest. The purpose of both studies was to examine vandalistic behavior among typical rural young persons. Neither study was designed to measure the vandalistic behavior of high school drop-outs or chronic truants (a small proportion of the total rural youth population).

2.2. Patterns of rural youth vandalism

Fifty-one and six-tenths per cent of the Ohio sample versus 55.3% of the Indiana sample had been involved in at least one act of vandalism. Among those involved, nearly 75% from the Ohio sample, and 60% from the Indiana sample had engaged in three or more acts of vandalism. This suggests that for many rural youth who engage in vandalistic acts, vandalism is a recurring form of behavior.

The Indiana study expanded the analysis of rural vandalism by soliciting a brief narrative description of the most recent act of vandalism in which the respondents had engaged. Each description was classified into one of four categories, according to the severity of the vandalistic act. Severity was defined as the degree of damage or destruction to the vandalized property. Damage or destruction was designated as referring to either the dollar value of the affected object and/or to the amount of work or effort necessary for the victim to repair, clean up, or in some way correct the damage. The four categories included: (1) minor; (2) somewhat serious; (3) serious; and (4) very serious.

Types of vandalism which fell into the minor category included such 'traditional' activities usually associated with the American fall holiday of Halloween. These include: soaping car or house windows and draping toilet paper over trees, shrubs, houses, and other objects. Minor acts of vandalism composed 26.2% of all acts described by respondents to the Indiana study.

The 'somewhat serious' category exhibited more malicious examples of vandalism. Typical of the vandalistic acts at this level included throwing eggs at cars and houses, damaging or attempting to crush trash cans, spray painting road signs, and digging up bushes in yards. What may perhaps be a unique form of rural vandalism was the practice by one respondent of filling the purses of female students at his high school with fresh cow manure. This level of vandalism represented 29.6% of the total acts described by the Indiana sample.

The type of vandalism classified as 'serious' included such acts as breaking street lights or house windows, shooting out road signs, and spray painting automotive vehicles. Two particular types of vandalism included in this category required access to a car or truck. These were 'driving a 4-wheel drive vehicle' through a recreation area in order to rip up the sod on the baseball and other playing fields and driving through a graveyard for the purpose of damaging grave stones. Acts of vandalism within the 'serious' category made up 35.3% of all acts described in the Indiana study.

Within the 'very serious' category were included the most malicious forms of property destruction and defacement. Examples of the type of vandalistic acts at this level of severity were breaking out car windows, ripping out speakers from their stands at outdoor drive-in theaters, and burning bales of hay left in a field. These examples of vandalistic behavior, accounting for 8.9% of the total, generally represented a high dollar cost to the victim.

The most frequently mentioned targets for the rural vandal were primarily a private residence in the countryside or in a nearby town, and secondarily some type of public property. Most of the time, the vandalism occurred in a rural setting (about 40% of the time in an urban location). In nearly three-fourths of the cases, among both the Ohio and Indiana samples, the vandalism incidents occurred in the same county in which the vandal lived.

The commission of vandalism was a year-round phenomenon. Rural youth did not restrict themselves to the autumn season as one popularized image of vandalism would suggest. In both studies, however, weekends and the evening hours were the more popular times for involvement in vandalism.

In a majority of cases, the perpetrators of vandalism arrived at the location via a motor vehicle. In nearly half of the cases, beer, whiskey, or marijuana was being consumed by the participants.

2.3. Perceptions of vandalism by rural vandals

Over 90% of rural vandals committed their deeds in the presence of others. Vandalism indeed is a group activity, and one that is committed by a majority of rural youth.

How did rural youth who committed vandalism perceive their own actions? Was vandalism viewed as a game, joke, or a peer challenge? Or was it viewed as something more serious? The Ohio study found that a majority of those who had committed an act of vandalism became involved because they 'just happened to be there', 'were bored', 'playing around', or 'pressured by others'. Significantly, less than one in ten described their involvement in vandalism as a 'Halloween prank' or 'practical joke'. In essence, involvement was unplanned and, in many cases, spontaneous.

Table 2 summarizes the self-perceptions of respondents in both the Ohio and Indiana studies about their vandalistic behavior. It is readily apparent that a large majority of the respondents viewed their most recent act of vandalism as a game, joke, or contest. In other words, the commission of vandalism was perceived as 'just for fun'. Less than one out of every five acts of vandalism was viewed as 'getting even' or revenge, and fewer than 10% were perceived as the consequences of other reasons, such as seeking to draw attention to a problem or issue, expressing rage, or associated with the commission of some other crime.

The majority of reasons given for vandalism appear to be similar to the motivation for youth shoplifting. A 1980 national poll of teenagers found 25% had shoplifted (Gallup, 1980). The youthful respondents were asked: Why do you shoplift? Nearly three-fourths (72%) said they do it for 'kicks'. Only 21% said they did it for money. Thus it appears that vandalism and shoplifting among youth have a similar motivation pattern in terms of why they engage in these particular acts of deviancy.

The Ohio study expanded the analysis of self-perception of vandalism to include whether or not the respondents viewed their own vandalistic behavior as a criminal act. Nearly 71% did not view their behavior as in any way constituting a crime or as wrong. The consensus among social scientists who have studied vandalistic behavior is, that in general it is motivated by competitive and status-seeking opportunities within the peer group setting (Richards, 1979). As evidenced by the results from the Ohio and Indiana studies, these same social forces appear to be operative among rural youth.

Table 2. Self-perceptions of vandalistic behavior by rural youth.

Behavior	Study area Ohio		Indiana	
	Number	Percent	Number	Percent
A game, fun, contest, etc.	164	64.3	102	67.5
Getting even, revenge	32	12.3	2	19.2
Side effect of committing a more serious offense	20	7.8	1	6.6
An expression of rage	11	4.3	0	0.0
To draw attention to an issue or grievance	10	3.9	5	3.3
Other reasons	18	7.1	5	3.3
Total	255	100.0	151	100.0

2.4. Correlates of participation in vandalism

To gain insight into why rural youth become involved in vandalism, two additional statistical procedures on the Ohio sample only were conducted with life-time vandalism as the dependent variable. These procedures included stepwise regression and discriminant analysis.

The following independent variables were initially utilized in the regression and discriminant analysis: (1) age of respondent; (2) sex (dummy variables); (3) participation level in religious activities (6-point frequency scale); (4) years lived in community; (5) degree of perceived attachment to parents (4-point scale); (6) being with and doing things with family (4-point scale); (7) amount of time spent with family (5-point scale); (8) amount of time spent with friends (5-point scale); (9) number of older brothers; (10) number of older sisters; (11) total number of persons in household; (12) age of household head; (13) education of household head; (14) occupation of household head (5-point scale); and (15) suggestions to young people concerning vandalism (5-point scale).

After the initial computer run, only six independent variables were retained in the regression analysis. As may be seen in table 3, the independent variables of sex, time spent with family, advice to property owners, time spent with friends, advice to younger persons, and attachment to parents were all significantly related to the dependent variable, life-time vandalism. The beta coefficients revealed significant change in each independent variable with a change in the dependent variable with the exception of attachment to parents. The step-wise regression analysis disclosed that whether a person is a male or female is the greatest predictor of whether or not one has committed an act of vandalism. Active involvement with the family offers the second largest amount of explanation to life-time vandalistic behavior.

Results of the discriminant analysis are shown in tables 4 and 5. In table 4, the eigenvalue represents the total variance existing in the discriminating variables (0.16%). The squared canonical correlation represents the proportion of variance in the discriminant function explained by the groups (0.14%). The function discriminates between non-vandals and vandals at a significant level. The independent variables which were significant in explaining this variance, in order of importance were: advice to young people, sex, time spent with family, attachment to parents, active in family affairs, religious participation, and number of persons in the household.

Information in table 5 depicts the ability of the discriminating variables to classify cases into their respective groups. As may be noted, 67.3% of the cases were correctly classified by the discriminating variables. One-third of the student respondents failed to be correctly placed, and therefore more precise variables are needed for this group in future research.

Table 3. Summary statistics of the stepwise regression of life-time vandalism with selected independent variables.

Step	Sex	Time with family	Advice to property owners	Time with friends	Advice to younger persons	Attachment to parents	Multiple R	Multiple R²	Multiple entering variable F-Ratio	Total Regression F-Ratio
1	−0.290 **						0.290	0.084	46.112 **	46.112 **
2	−0.285 **	0.145 **					0.325	0.105	11.758 **	29.430 **
3	−0.279 **	0.155 **	0.130 **				0.349	0.122	9.553 **	23.140 **
4	−0.287 **	0.147 **	0.125 **	0.110 **			0.366	0.134	6.938 **	19.296 **
5	−0.266 **	0.126 **	0.133 **	0.107 *	−0.102 *		0.379	0.144	5.492 **	16.674 **
6	−0.271 **	0.088 *	0.133 **	0.106 *	−0.094 *	0.072	0.384	0.147	2.087	14.273 **

* Significant at the 0.05 level.
** Significant at the 0.01 level.

Table 4. Discriminating power of discriminant functions for vandals and non-vandals (Ohio study).

Discrim- inate function	Eigen- value	Percent of variance	Canonical corre- lation	After func- tion	Welks' lambda	Chi- square	d.f.	P
1	0.162	100.0	0.14	0	0.861	84.881	7	0.000

Table 5. Predicted results: discriminant analysis for vandals and non-vandals (Ohio study).

Group	No. of cases	Predicted percentage group memberships	
		Non-vandals	Vandals
Non-vandals	305	66.9%	33.1%
Vandals	267	32.2%	67.8%
Percent of cases correctly classified = 67.3%			

3. Vandalism: differential perspectives

Cohen (1973) divided vandalism into four major types: play, acquisitive, vindictive and malicious. As experienced by rural people, especially victims, in the United States, vandalism is viewed largely as malicious in nature. The victims' interpretation of the event is that an act of violence has been committed against their property, and hence, a general attitude of vulnerability to crime is developed.

As perceived by the offenders (i.e., rural youth), vandalism takes on a different image. Vandalism is something which takes place in a group setting, and is usually committed for 'kicks'. Vandalism is not viewed as criminal. From a sociological point of view, vandalism is normatively acceptable behavior. The more a young person is oriented away from family activities and toward the peer group as a major source of behavioral standards, the more likely they become involved in vandalism.

Again, referring to Cohen's typology, vandalism in these research studies were seen by rural youth as a form of play. However, it was a specific form of play, one which is not fully explicated in the Cohen typology. For Cohen (1973) play, as a form of motivation, is exactly as the word is generally defined: damage in the process of playing a game or in which the primary motivations are curiosity, fun or competition.

The findings of the Ohio and Indiana self-report studies suggest that it would be useful to divide 'play' as a motive for vandalism into two separate concepts. Play-in-itself, as the first definition, should correspond closely to the original explanation assigned to play from the Cohen quote above. The second, and more applicable to the results of the Ohio and Indiana rural youth studies, is 'playful status-seeking'. Vandalism was found to be a status-seeking enterprise, that is, as a method of achieving prestige or ranking within the peer group setting. This seems analogous to the pecking order established among young male deer as they approach maturity. The playful head butting is an early means of establishing dominance–subordinate relations. Likewise, vandalism in the rural United States has taken on status-establishment characteristics within the rural youth peer group.

In conclusion, the perception of vandalism differs depending upon whether it is the viewpoint of the victim or the offender. The victim sees it as malicious destruction while the offender views it as status-seeking play. These different viewpoints must be constantly 'kept in mind' in terms of society's attempts to address vandalism.

References

Cohen, S., 1973. Property destruction: Motives and meanings. In: C. Ward, ed., Vandalism, pp. 41–51. New York: Van Nostrand Reinhold.
Gallup, G., 1980. Teen thievery is major trend. Columbus Dispatch, Febr. 6. Columbus (Ohio).
Phillips, G.H., 1976. Rural crime and rural offenders. Columbus, (Ohio): Ohio Cooperative Extension Service and The Ohio State University, Department of Agricultural Economics and Rural Sociology. Extension Bulletin 613.
Richards, P., 1979. Middle class vandalism and the age-status conflict. Social Problems 26, 482–497.

Abstract: J.F. Donnermeyer and G.H. Phillips, Vandals and vandalism in the USA: a rural perspective
This chapter reviews a series of rural victim and rural youth self-report studies of vandalism conducted by the National Rural Crime Prevention Center. The differing perspectives of vandalism are examined, from the point of view of the victim and that of the offender. From the victim's perspective, vandalism is a form of malicious property destruction. Vandalism is the most frequently occurring crime, and one that often incurs a monetary loss on the victim. Vandalism is also fear provoking to victims. Among rural youth, a majority are involved in at least one act of vandalism, two-thirds of whom repeat the behavior three or more times. Vandalism is a group activity, and one that is perceived by the perpetrator as a 'game, fun, or contest' (i.e., 'for kicks'). Additional statistical analysis reveals that vandals are more likely to orient to the peer group for behavioral standards, and not as likely to be involved in family or religious activities. The chapter concludes by reviewing Cohen's typology of motives of vandalism. It is suggested that Cohen's definition of 'play' as a vandalism motive be subdivided into: (1) 'play-in itself', that is, primarily as a game; and (2) 'play as status-seeking', that is, primarily as a means to achieve prestige. The latter more aptly describes the motivation of rural youth involvement in vandalism.

PART THREE

Vandals' behaviour

INTRODUCTION

Some approaches to vandals' behaviour

J. LAWRENCE

In Part Three, a series of papers are brought together whose two basic concerns are to consider the observed or reported behaviour of vandals, and to attempt to explain this behaviour.

The settings in which the acts of vandalism occur vary from paper to paper. Thus for Moser it is the restricted area of the telephone kiosk, for others it is wider: areas of council housing in a town in Surrey, England for Webb, secondary schools in England for Lawrence. The location changes in Dunning's paper to football grounds, and to the beautiful city of Racine, Wisconsin, U.S.A., in Shannon's study. The section thus illustrates the diversity of contexts within which vandalism occurs, each with specifics which make it essential to be cautious before making overgeneral statements about its control. At the same time, however, it illustrates the widespread nature of the phenomenon, which makes it one on which it is important to make efforts at analysis and control, even though the success rate, in relation to the latter, may not always, as Cohen realistically warns in his paper, be high.

The papers' theoretical concerns arise from the study or direct observation of vandals' behaviour. Thus for Moser, the specific situation studied is that in which a member of the public, using a phone booth, finds that the phone will not work and reacts physically, verbally, emotionally to this situation. The vandals' reactions to two differing circumstances (money withheld and money returned) were observed in 518 incidents, together with the characteristics of the situation and the person involved. Webb, however, does not observe directly but uses vandals' self-reports of their behaviour, to elicit exciting information as to the variables affecting their decisions to damage maliciously. He shows how the decision to vandalise in a particular location may depend on the risk of surveillance, the availability of an escape route, etc. Lawrence uses teachers' reports of vandalism arising in the context of incidents of disruptive behaviour for her studies. Dunning and his colleagues base their sociological analysis of football hooliganism upon a study of historical documents of various kinds (newspaper accounts, football club records, etc.), while Shannon uses police records of violent property destruction and self-report figures, in his study of the role of vandalism in delinquent careers.

Each paper contributes ideas on the nature of vandalistic behaviour, in particular on its meaning for the participant, thus offering an explanation for it in terms of intelligent activity, rather than chance. Thus, for Moser, vandalism in the telephone kiosk relates to an environment which frustrates the user, preventing him from making his call, in a situation in which recourse to the administration is difficult. The degree of frustration is shown to be significant in the fact that aggressive behaviour occurred in 70% of the cases overall where the money was withheld and in only 30% of those where the telephone returned his coin to the user. The differences found between the frequency of aggression in Paris and its lower level in the provincial town studied suggests an impact, too, from a wider, frustrating (?) environment, i.e. the city. Other explanations suggested by this research include the user's knowledge, based on experience, that banging the telephone may indeed restore it to use, as well as a negative perception of the functioning of public telephones. In general, then, the user maltreats the object which denies him control over his environment.

Webb's phenomenological approach to vandalism in council housing areas leads him to an explanation of the relation between vandalism and environmental design in terms of 'vandalism as opportunity'. From interviews with 12 to 16 year old boys which allowed the researchers to focus on the influence of variables of house and road surveillance and escape route upon the likelihood of four different types of vandalism occurring in 12 settings generated by these variables, they conclude that rational considerations such as the perceived chance of escape affect such a likelihood. They thus suggest that in interpreting vandalistic behaviour, issues need to be indentified which are important to the young vandal, notably the ways in which he conceptualises particular settings as more or less appropriate places for vandalism. One explanation of vandalism is thus that the specific built environment offers an opportunity for it; of particular interest is the importance of the perception of an escape route.

For Lawrence the perspective on vandalism, and the explanation of it, derives from the ecology of the individual school, its unique patterning, the psychological climate which synthesises interpersonal relations and attitudes, organisational style, and type of control and maintenance, which is critical. Teacher and pupil perspectives are all important, helping to make sense of vandalistic incidents, though for Lawrence they are viewed against a more general background of disruptive pupil behaviour. This study is searching for critical school differences, i.e. those factors within the school which make for differences in outcomes, behavioural outcomes, rather than outcomes of educational attainment. However, she acknowledges also the role of society outside the school itself, in washing its disorder into the school, and in general submits that different socio-environmental situations appear to encourage the development of different forms of vandalistic or disruptive behaviour.

For Dunning and his colleagues the explanation of football hooliganism is in terms of its providing for a 'violent masculine style' for members of working class communities (the 'lower working class') in which certain features tend toward this style, and as a consequence of the location of these communities in the wider social structure.

Following Suttles' notion of 'ordered segmentation' to explain how normally segmented parts of larger neighbourhoods regularly combine in an ordered way in the event of opposition and conflicts, and applying the notion to football hooligans, Dunning adds to this notion an explanation as to how the structure of 'adolescent and street-groups' leads to the genesis and maintenance of 'violent masculinity' as one of their dominant cultural characteristics. The combination of these two features yields an explanation of football hooligan violence, whose incidence is seen to vary over time depending largely on the degree to which the working class with its recent differentiation can be said to have become 'incorporated' into the mainstream of British social life, and Dunning argues thus that an explanation of this phenomenon requires its location in the structural setting within which the generation of the norms and values that underlie it takes place.

Finally, Shannon studies the way in which vandalism fits into delinquent and criminal careers and tentatively concludes that the vandals and those who engage in violent property destruction may differ from people who are not destructive of property but not significantly so; the vandal thus emerges as a juvenile miscreant rather than as a 'vandal', so that coping with vandalism becomes coping with crime. Indeed, running through the whole of this section is the idea, expressed in different forms, but substantially the same, that an understanding of vandalism is arrived at through an understanding of crime, and its location, and the interpretation of the environment by the vandal, rather than through an overfocus upon the characteristics of the 'vandal' himself. Crime as intelligent activity and crime as socio-environmentally derived are the predominant themes.

CHAPTER 10

Everyday vandalism

User behaviour with respect to malfunctioning public telephones

G. MOSER

Telephone call boxes are frequently vandalised. Statistically speaking, each public telephone box in France was damaged once in 1981. A distinction should be drawn between gain motivated damage, i.e. forcing coin boxes with a view to theft, and damage in the absence of theft. It is in fact the latter type of depredation which is most common and which we refer to as vandalism: in 1981, 70% of the damage recorded by the French Telephone Service fell into this category.

How can such apparently gratuitous acts be explained? One possible reason is the frequent malfunctioning of telephones, which could incite users to behave in a rough and aggressive manner. More generally, vandalism may, at least in part, constitute the reaction of individuals placed in an inadequate environment and thus the implementation of their plans is hindered by an object which does not fulfil its function. In the case of public telephones, this inadequacy may be highlighted by the fact that individuals feel that the Telephone Authority, and hence the remedy for their plight, is remote.

Furthermore, varying degrees of control may exist, depending on whether malfunctions consist of a missing dialling tone with the return of the inserted change or a missing dialling tone associated with the loss of the user's coin. A plausible hypothesis is that a user's reaction depends on the degree of malfunction and in particular on the extent to which the system fulfils some of its functions. Lack of control is particularly acute when it involves loss of money for the individual. Vandalism may thus be viewed as an attempt to regain control of an inadequately functioning system (White, 1959; Allen and Greenberger, 1980).

It is important not to neglect the role of the particular environmental context in which the act is perpetrated. Research has consistently shown that the behaviour of inhabitants of major cities is characterised by lack of cooperation (e.g. Milgram, 1970) and by the speed of their movements and gestures (e.g. Lowin et al., 1971). It may well be that aggressive reactions to telephones are stronger and more frequent in a city like Paris than in small towns.

The present study sought to test these hypotheses by accurately describing user behaviour in the case of telephone malfunctioning in four different situations, defined by two pairs of parameters: Paris/small town (Angers and Cholet) and malfunction with/without coin return.

Ten telephone boxes were selected for observation. All were isolated, i.e. no other box could be seen from them and they were not part of a double or triple box set. Furthermore, all boxes were apparently in a good state of repair, as observations were discontinued once aggressive users had occasioned clearly visible damage to the boxes. In all, 518 observations were made in the following way: each time someone tried to use the telephone, a hidden observer noted down three sets of data: concerning the characteristics of the situation, of the would-be user and of his behaviour. Specifically, the urgency of a given call was assessed on the basis of the user's manner (rushed or casual), while user characteristics (sex, approximate age, outward appearance) were noted. User behaviour within the telephone boxes during attempted calls were recorded under three headings, viz.

(i)   *standard operation* (e.g. pressing the money return button, replacing the receiver);
(ii) *'rough' handling,* such as blows of the hand or fist;
(iii) *violent handling,* such as striking with the whole weight of one's body or kicking the apparatus.

The distinction made here between 'rough' and 'violent' handling corresponds to that commonly drawn between instrumental aggression (having a non-aggressive objective) and hostile aggression. In the present context, some of the rough handling could in fact be aimed at restoring normal working order. In the following discussion, the term 'aggressive behaviour' will be used to cover both violent and rough handling.

Data were gathered on total time spent in the telephone boxes and on the number of attempts to make the call. In addition to the categorisation of behaviour, data were also gathered on the objects manipulated (e.g. money return button, receiver, receiver rest, telephone set, box) together with their chronological order.

All observations were then compared according to user characteristics, type of town and type of malfunction.

Is it possible to state that some groups were more aggresive than others? Table 1 shows the overall percentage recorded as roughly or violently handling on at least one occasion as a function of age, sex and overall appearance. Men were more frequently aggressive than women, mature adults slightly more so than either young or old persons, as were those who appeared to be less well-dressed. Furthermore, users in a great hurry tended to be more aggressive than their more casual counterparts.

In Paris, more than half of those observed (58%) reacted in a rough or violent manner. These figures should be considered in relation to a survey of

Table 1. Characteristics of users who behaved roughly or violently on at least one occasion, by sex, age and deportment.

Men (N = 298)	177	59%	chi^2 = 15.02, p < 0.001
Women (N = 218)	91	42%	
Young people (N = 284)	136	48%	
Mature adults (N = 171)	102	60%	chi^2 = 4.98, not significant
Old people (N = 63)	30	48%	
Favourable appearance (N = 250)	146	54%	chi^2 = 8.08, p < 0.01
Unfavourable appearance (N = 268)	122	49%	
Very rushed (N = 109)	74	68%	
Rushed (N = 285)	171	60%	chi^2 = 9.44, p < 0.01
Casual (N = 124)	60	48%	

200 Parisian users: 55% of those interviewed claimed to feel angry when faced with a telephone out of order, while 69% of respondents confessed to shaking the apparatus or roughly handling it in such circumstances.

In the provincial towns of Angers and Cholet, the frequency of rough and violent handling was noticeably less (42%), the difference being significant at the 0.001 level ($\chi^2 = 12.8$).

The hypothesis that aggressive reactions are more common in large towns is thus confirmed. This fact certainly justifies more detailed analysis: is there a different life style in such towns? Are small towns characterised by less individual anonymity, more respect for the environment or stricter norms? These questions are difficult to answer, but it should be borne in mind that there was a similar proportion of users in a hurry in the provinces as in Paris.

When the frequency of rough and violent handling is compared according to type of malfunction, a considerable difference emerges. In 70% of the cases where the telephone failed to return the user's money, aggressive behaviour followed. This proportion fell to 30% in the case of telephones which did not work but which automatically returned the coin ($\chi^2 = 82.4$, significant at the 0.001 level).

Table 2. Number of users behaving roughly at least once.

	Paris	Small towns	All
Malfunction/money withheld	134/147 (91%)	64/136 (37%)	198/283 (70%)
Malfunction/money returned	46/141 (29%)	24/74 (32%)	70/235 (30%)
Total	180/308 (58%)	88/210 (42%)	268/518 (52%)

Table 3. Average time spent in call box.

	Paris		Small towns
Malfunction/money withheld	115.4 sec.	↔	66.0 sec.
	min.: 20 sec.	$t = 6.77$	min.: 20 sec.
	max.: 3 min. 40 sec.	$p < 0.001$	max.: 3 min. 25 sec.
			↕ $t = 1.62$ n.s
Malfunction/money returned	43.4 sec.	↔	56.8 sec.
	min.: 15 sec.	$t = 2.53$	min.: 16 sec.
	max.: 2 min. 30 sec.	$p < 0.02$	max.: 3 min. 20 sec.

When both these variables (town and type of malfunction) are considered jointly (see table 2), the difference due to the malfunction type is much more striking in Paris than in the provinces. In Paris, 91% of those users who found themselves deprived both of the use of the phone and of the money inserted resorted to rough handling, whereas in the provinces this outcome is found in only 47% of users, only slightly exceeding the frequency of rough behaviour when money was returned (32%).

A more detailed analysis of the observed behaviour makes it possible to explain these differences. In Paris, the *average time* (in seconds) spent in the call box was three times as long when there was loss of money as when the money was returned. Moreover, in the latter case users spent less time manipulating the telephone in Paris than in the provincial towns (see table 3).

This analysis is borne out by the data concerning the *number of attempts* made by the users in the case of malfunctions associated with money return: those who retrieved their coins made several more attempts to get through (see table 4).

Thus far, we have only considered data computed on an individual basis. It is also possible, of course, to examine the distribution of the various reactions by town and by malfunction.

In Paris, when coins were returned, three quarters of the reactions were standard operations, whereas rough and violent behaviour occurred in 50% of cases when money was lost. In the provincial towns, on the other hand, no difference was found between the behaviour of users encountering different

Table 4. Breakdown of subjects according to number of attempts when money not withheld.

	1 attempt		2 attempts		> 2 attempts		Total
Paris	74	46%	63	39%	24	15%	161
Small towns	15	20%	33	45%	26	35%	74

Table 5. Breakdown of different types of telephone handling.

	Standard		Rough and violent		Total
Paris					
Malfunction/money withheld	886	49%	906	51%	1972
Malfunction/money returned	383	75%	139	25%	522
Small towns					
Malfunction/money withheld	813	85%	149	15%	962
Malfunction/money returned	379	89%	49	11%	428

types of malfunction (see table 5). Furthermore, violent reactions as such when money failed to be returned were restricted almost exclusively to Paris.

Lastly, it is possible to account for the temporal sequence of reactions by using two different indices: the cumulative abandonment rate and the number of rough and violent actions at each attempt.

Abandonment was defined to have occurred once the user left the call box; the cumulative abandonment rate indicates the total percentage of users having given up after each manipulation. The cumulative abandonment rate for Paris and for the small towns is shown in fig. 1. For Paris, behaviour clearly differs with respect to type of malfunction. When money was returned, all users had given up by the tenth manipulation, while more than 60% had given up by the fourth manipulation. When money was withheld, abandonment occurred much later: 60% of users gave up at or prior to the fifteenth attempt while others

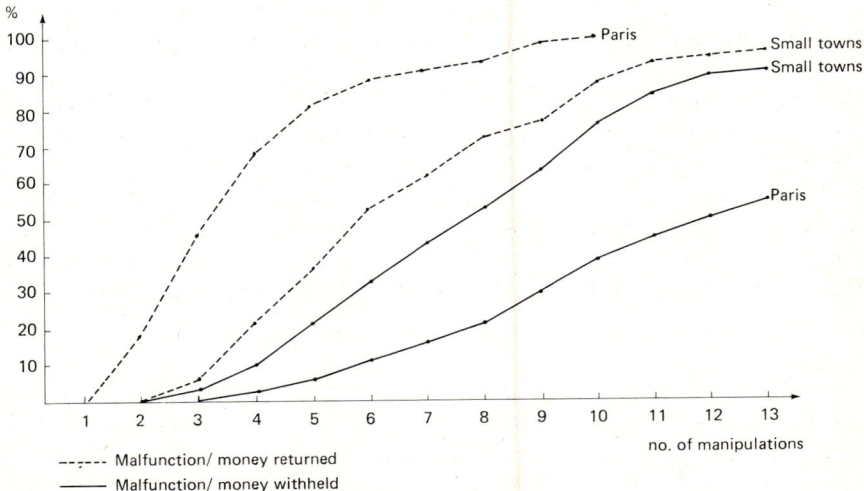

Figure 1. Cumulative abandonment rate: Paris/small towns.

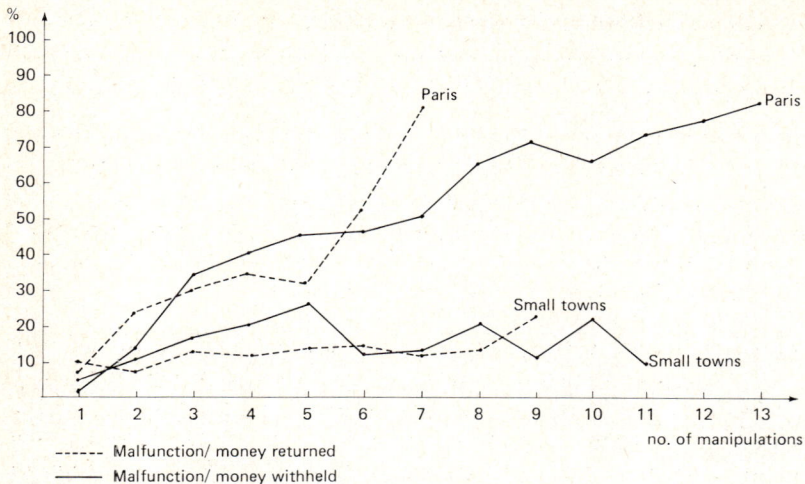

Figure 2. Rate of rough and violent handling: Paris/small towns.

made up to 36 attempts before leaving the box. In the provincial towns, on the other hand, abandonment rates did not vary with the situation.

In summary, in Paris the user either left quickly (when the money had been returned) or stayed much longer (when the money had been withheld).

Figure 2 shows the number of rough and violent manipulations as a function of all actions for each successive attempt to place a call. In Paris, more than 60% of the reactions are aggressive by the seventh or eighth manipulation, whatever the circumstances. The percentage of aggressive behaviour does, however, increase more quickly in the case of returned money than in that of money withheld.

No difference appears as between the two situations in the small towns. Moreover, the percentage of rough and violent handling never exceeds 25% of total manipulations.

In Paris, then, aggressive behaviour was observed to become gradually preponderant in user behaviour. The point made earlier (see table 5) that, overall, fewer rough actions were observed in the case of money being returned may be accounted for by the time spent in the box, which was less than in the case of money being withheld.

The conclusions to be drawn from the above are unequivocal. More than half the users exhibited aggressive behaviour with respect to telephones when they failed to work. Moreover, such behaviour was not limited to any particular social group: the same proportion of users was seen to handle roughly or violently telephones whatever their age, sex or appearance. Three explanations may be advanced to account for this behaviour: (i) behaviour reinforcement; (ii) user attitudes; (iii) lack of alternatives to the malfunctioning telephones.

Behaviour reinforcement. Several times during the period of data collection, malfunctioning telephones (for whatever reason) were observed to start working normally again following one or more violent blows. Clearly, a user who has seen the effectiveness of violent behaviour will experience behaviour reinforcement inasmuch as he will tend to reproduce this type of action, i.e. to continue to treat malfunctioning telephones with violence.

User attitudes. Two surveys were carried out in Paris while observations for the present research were being made. These surveys provide information concerning user attitudes towards telephones: 84% stated that telephones were frequently out of order, while almost all interviewees (94%) had already come across the problem. Insofar as the perceived reasons for such malfunctions are concerned, 23% of the users attributed them to technical defects and 47% to 'deliberate damage'. Furthermore, 62% of those interviewed thought that the breakdowns were caused by dissatisfied users and only 15% attributed it to the work of 'vandals'.

Overall, Parisian users perceive the working of public telephones in an unfavourable light and this may, in their opinion, justify their aggressive behaviour.

Lack of alternatives to the malfunctioning telephones. When a telephone is out of order there is little the user can do about it: no indication is given as to the whereabouts of the nearest call boxes; it is impossible to inform the Telephone Service since this would involve knowing and memorising the number of the inoperative telephone; a fortiori, the user cannot retrieve the inserted money – indeed, only 26% of those interviewed stated that they knew how to go about getting their money back.

In conclusion, the fact that users are faced with the impossibility of making their call, do not know where to find another box or, above all, how to retrieve their lost money may explain to a large extent why telephones are treated roughly. Furthermore, the possibility of getting telephones to work again by violent means encourages users to resort to such methods every time they are confronted with a malfunctioning telephone.

The inadequacy of the environment gives rise to generally aggressive user behaviour. This behaviour is more aggressive the less the user's feels that he has control over the environment. Furthermore, city environments (anonymity? environmental overload?) seem to favour aggressive behaviour as well as perseverance to force telephones to give up what they insist on withholding.

References

Allen, V.L., D.B. Greenberger, 1980. Destruction and perceived control. In: A. Baum, J.E. Singer, eds., Applications of personal control. Advances in environmental psychology, vol. 2. Hillsdale (N.J.): Lawrence Erlbaum.

Lowin, A., J. Holtes, B. Sandler, M. Bornstein, 1971. The pace of life and sensitivity to time in urban and rural settings. Journal of Social Psychology 83, 247–253.

Milgram, S., 1970. The experience of living in cities: A psychological analysis. Science 167, 1461–1468.

White, R.W., 1959. Motivation reconsidered: The concept of competence. Psychological Review 66, 293–333.

Abstract: G. Moser, Everyday vandalism: user behaviour with respect to malfunctioning public telephones.

One possible reaction to an inadequate environment consists in the development of aggressive behaviour. This article seeks to test this hypothesis by analysing users' reactions to malfunctioning telephones. Two control levels (money returned or money withheld) and two different environments (Paris/small towns) were defined. In urban environments people were found to be more aggressive than in small towns: they handled telephones roughly more often, and they stayed in booths longer when money was withheld than when money was returned. In small towns, there was no difference in behaviour with respect to the two types of malfunction: average time spent in booths fell between the values obtained under the two specified conditions in Paris. These results are explained in terms of attitudes towards the Telephone Authorities, instrumental behaviour and inadequate environments. Lack of control over the environment appears to intensify aggressive behaviour in telephone booths, but only in urban environments.

CHAPTER 11

Is there a place for vandalism?

B. WEBB

Hope and Winchester (1979), in their analysis of the relationship between crime and the physical environment, usefully identify three approaches to the use of the physical environment in attempts to prevent or minimize vandalism. They are (1) target hardening, (2) environmental management, (3) environmental design. Each of these approaches to the problem of vandalism prescribes measures which are congruent with a particular conceptualization of the relation between man and his physical surroundings. It is my aim in this part of the paper to provide a rationale for the research reported below. In order to do this I shall briefly consider each of the approaches to the problem of vandalism identified by Hope and Winchester. It is my intention to show how each approach represents a different facet to a common issue – the contribution of the built environment in the emergence of 'places for vandalism'.

1.

1.1. Target hardening

Hope and Winchester define target hardening as measures which "aim to make an offence more difficult to commit or to increase the risk of detection while the offence is being carried out" (p. 5). The use of security devices, alarm systems, and damage resistant materials are examples of such measures (cf. Building Research Station, 1971).

A target hardening approach defines the problem of vandalism in technological terms. Such a definition leads to a concern more with the strengths and weaknesses of the built form than with the way people actually come to use and think of their surroundings. Consequently, there is concern in the literature that such an approach should be adopted cautiously (e.g. Repetto, 1976).

The concern is that a target hardening approach adopted without awareness of the cognitive and social-psychological processes involved in the use of space (cf. Canter, 1977) may, in fact, legitimize the very behaviour it was designed to prevent. Measures prescribed by a target hardening approach, although designed to make an act of vandalism more difficult to perpetrate, may suggest that this is an appropriate place or object for vandalism.

1.2. Environmental management

Hope and Winchester define environmental management as a crime prevention measure in the following way: "the development and management of human resources to change the way in which environments are perceived and used" (p. 11).

The standard and speed of maintenance of, and repair to, public housing is frequently cited as a factor in influencing levels of vandalism (e.g. Building Research Station, 1971; Wilson, 1978a). Leather and Matthews (1973) suggest that, through inadequate maintenance, features of the built environment become seen as appropriate targets for vandalism. They state that if damage, which may result through normal wear and tear, is not repaired quickly, the object in question may become "thought of as an artifact upon which it is almost acceptable and permissible to inflict damage, or is considered to be so dilapidated, and therefore useless, that it is completely destroyed or removed" (p. 171). Zimbardo (1973) provides some rare empirical evidence for this process, identifying the crucial role of 'releaser stimuli' in the process of stripping and vandalizing of abandoned cars.

Research on how people perceive features of their environment which may have sustained some damage is sparse. However, it would appear, from the evidence available, that the quality and speed of maintenance and repair of housing estates may influence a great deal the way people perceive and use their environment. If vandalism is about the use and abuse of the environment (as Ward, 1973, defines it) then the state of repair of features of the physical environment may serve to communicate just what is considered to be appropriate and inappropriate use.

1.3. Environmental design

The issues and processes discussed in relation to target hardening and environmental management are echoed in the literature concerned with the relation between crime, vandalism and environmental design.

Jacobs' (1961) work, although criticized for its lack of empirical evidence, raised a number of themes which were later developed in a more structured and detailed fashion by Newman (1972). Relating crime rates in different housing projects with characteristics of physical design Newman propounds his concept of 'defensible space'. He claims that housing projects suffering from a higher crime rate can be shown to lack defensible space characteristics as he defines them. Newman identifies four features of environmental design, each of which, he suggests, contributes to the defensibility of space.

(1) The capacity of the physical environment to create perceived zones of territorial influence.

(2) The capacity of physical design to provide surveillance opportunities for residents and their agents.
(3) The capacity of design to influence the perception of a project's uniqueness, isolation, and stigma.
(4) The influence of geographical juxtaposition with 'safe zones' upon the security of adjacent areas.

Newman's declared aim is to define those factors of environmental design which encourage residents to adopt proprietary attitudes towards the public areas of their estates. Defensible space can be defined as the extent to which residents feel they have responsibility for, and control over, the spaces surrounding their dwelling places and the extent to which outsiders perceive the defensible qualities of these spaces. Newman claims that design along defensible space principles, as he defines them, will act as a deterrent to would-be wrong-doers since it gives a clear message of what is and is not appropriate use of space.

Empirically, Newman's principles of defensible space do not receive the strong support they demand. Research gives some support to the hypothesis that differences in levels of vandalism relate to differences in defensible space characteristics. However, the data is weak and, in many cases, statistically non-significant. The general outcome of these studies is that factors other than those features of the physical environment identified by Newman are more strongly related to indices of crime and vandalism. For example, Wilson (1978b) identifies child density as an important factor affecting rates of vandalism to housing blocks. Mawby (1977a) finds that the most significant variable relating to the amount of vandalism received by telephone kiosks is degree of use. Mayhew et al. (1979) find that the type of tenure surrounding telephone kiosks is significantly related to the level of telephone kiosk vandalism. Exploring residents' perceptions of what are and are not acceptable activities in outside spaces Ellis (1979) identifies the importance of a process of 'economic calculation'. The individual weighs his perceptions of spatial resources available in the area against his knowledge of the extent of the demand for the use of such resources.

Methodologically, Newman's work has received heavy criticism. Critics point out that social and socio-economic factors are not adequately controlled and that Newman's use of criminal statistics is too uncritical (e.g. Hillier, 1973; Bottoms, 1974; Mawby, 1977b). The consensus is that Newman's data is far too weak to support his dramatic conclusions and recommendations.

On a theoretical level Newman has been taken to task for his use of the concept of territoriality. Hillier (1973) cites archeological and anthropological evidence which, he claims, discredits the theory of territoriality in man. Territoriality, argues Hillier, is a misinformed view of human behaviour and can serve only to preclude any real understanding of the relationship between

social behaviour and the physical environment. Similarly, Ellis (1979) indicates
that Newman devotes very little time and space to discussion of any social-psychological processes which may be involved in people's responses to defensible
space. Defensible space, argues Ellis, may be better understood as a phenomenological concept. What may be construed as territorial behaviour cannot be
explained purely in terms of a set of responses to characteristics of the built
form. The concept of defensible space can only be understood by reference to
the social reality experienced by those involved.

The purpose of this introduction has been to identify a common concern
throughout the literature, that is to identify features of the built environment
which contribute to the conceptualization of a place or object as a suitable and
appropriate target or setting for vandalism. Research has been largely observational and correlational in nature. The architect and policy-maker concerned
with tackling the problem of vandalism can only draw upon information based
on very sparse, and often conflicting, empirical data. Nowhere has there been
any structured attempt to explore the relationship between vandalism and the
built environment as the vandal sees it himself. Defensible space, following
Ellis' (1979) argument, is here construed in phenomenological terms. Consequently, it is argued that the role of environmental design in the occurrence of
acts of vandalism can most fruitfully be explored phenomenologically.

2. The population: who is the vandal?

It is first necessary to identify those who may be more likely than others to
have experienced vandalistic activities, directly or indirectly.

Cohen (1973) indicates that the stereotype of the vandal as a working class,
male adolescent is less than useful. He considers that a conception of the
vandal as a 'homogeneous type' is not concordant with the many kinds of,
and reasons for, vandalism that exist. Belson (1975), using a self-report
technique, reports that differences between social class groups existed not in
whether but in what they stole. Gladstone (1978), using a similar technique,
does report a weak tendency for involvement in vandalism to be related to
social class. Among boys whose fathers' jobs were classified as unskilled or
semi-skilled 42% reported a high level of involvement in vandalism as against
30% of those with higher status fathers. Baldwin and Bottoms (1976) report
from their studies in Sheffield no significant differences in the distribution of
young male offenders aged between 10 and 19 years according to social class.
Mawby (1977a) concludes that his data indicates a difference in kiosk vandalism rates between council and private housing areas. Mayhew et al. (1979)
suggest from their study that the presence of 'council boys' influences the
amount of damage to kiosks within an area.

Table 1. Variables selected for study.

Variable A	House surveillance	High / Low
Variable B	Road surveillance	High / Low
Variable C	Escape route	(x) Alley blocked by 10′ wall / (y) Open road / (z) Twisting back alleys
Variable D	Type of vandalism	Damage to telephone kiosks / Damage to lamp posts / Damage to fences / Graffiti

The data is fragmentary and conflicting. However, for the purposes of the present study it was decided to interview 12 to 16 year old boys living in areas of council housing. It was anticipated that this would maximize, on present evidence, the change of including those with direct or indirect experience of vandalistic activities.

3. Research method

The first stage of the study involved pilot open-ended interviews with known vandals. As a result of the issues raised in these interviews it was decided to explore, in a more structured and controlled fashion, the influence of a number of variables on judgements made by a selected population concerning the likelihood of the occurrence of vandalism. The variables selected for study and their constituent elements are summarized in table 1.

Fifty boys were then individually interviewed. They were drawn from a total of four youth clubs serving four different areas of council housing in the Guildford area. Each interviewee was asked to assess the likelihood of each different act of vandalism (given by variable D in table 1) occurring in each of 12 different settings. Figure 1 indicates how variables A, B, and C combine to generate these 12 settings.

As shown by figure 1, settings varied in terms of the amount and kind of surveillance opportunities present and the kind of escape route available. Each

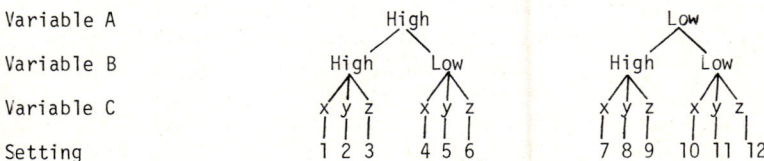

Figure 1. Generation of settings.

setting was described verbally. As examples of the settings generated, setting 4, in figure 1, is described in the following way: "The boys are in a place where they can be seen clearly from the nearby houses but they cannot be seen from the road. If someone decided to investigate their activities they could escape only by running off down a narrow straight alley which has high brick walls along its sides and which is blocked at the end by a ten foot high brick wall".

Setting 9, in figure 1, is described thus: "The boys are in a place where they cannot be seen from any houses but they can be seen clearly from the road. If someone decided to investigate their activities they could escape only by running off down lots of twisting back alleys and paths and by jumping over back garden fences".

Each of the 12 settings was presented to each interviewee, the order of presentation being randomized for each person. The order of the acts of vandalism each individual was asked to consider within each setting was also randomized. Each interviewee was asked to evaluate the likelihood of each type of vandalism occurring in each setting by rating it on a 7-point scale. The scale ranged from 'definitely not at all' (1) to 'definitely would' (7).

At the end of each interview the interviewee was asked to rank order the three escape routes. He was asked to state which, in his estimation, provided the best chance of successful escape (rank 1), the second best chance of successful escape (rank 2) and the worst chance for escape (rank 3).

4. Analysis and results

An analysis of variance for repeated measures was carried out on the data. The analysis revealed each variable to be statistically significant at the 0.001 level.

Table 2. Mean scores under each condition.

Variable		Means
A – House surveillance	High	3.91
	Low	4.70
B – Road surveillance	High	3.95
	Low	4.66
C – Escape route	Alley blocked by 10' wall	4.04
	Open road	4.09
	Twisting alleys	4.78
D – Type of vandalism	Damage to telephone kiosk	4.12
	Damage to lamp post	3.91
	Damage to private fence	4.34
	Graffiti	4.85

Scale: 1 = definitely not at all; 2 = very probably would not; 3 = probably would not; 4 = 50/50 chance; 5 = probably would; 6 = very probably would; 7 = definitely would.

Table 3 gives the means, indicating the significant influence of each variable on the judgements made. As the scale in table 2 shows, a higher mean score indicates greater perceived likelihood of vandalism.

Table 2 indicates that vandalism is considered more likely in those settings which provide only a low level of surveillance than in those settings where a higher level of surveillance is possible. Table 2 also shows that those settings which provide an escape route involving the use of lots of twisting back alleys and back garden fences are considered more likely to attract vandalism than those settings where alternative modes of escape are available. Table 2 indicates that the type of vandalism under consideration is also a significant influence on judgements. Graffiti is judged more likely to occur, in general, than damage to lamp posts or telephone kiosks.

The analysis did not reveal any significant interactions, indicating that, together, the variables act in an additive way. Each of the variables concerning surveillance and escape combine to produce settings which are construed by the sample as more or less conducive to vandalism. As such, it is more useful to consider settings, defined by a combination of variables, than to consider the variables independent of each other. Table 3 illustrates the very powerful additive nature of the variables, defining those settings construed as the most, and the least, conducive to vandalism.

Comparing the means in table 3 with those in table 2 it is clear that these variables in combination account for a greater variance in judgements than when considered independently. As table 3 shows, the setting in which vandalism is judged most likely to occur is that where surveillance both from the road and from nearby houses is minimal and where an escape route is available which involves the use of lots of twisting back alleys and back garden fences. The setting where vandalism is judged least likely to occur is that where maximum surveillance is afforded both from the road and nearby houses and

Table 3. Mean scores identifying those settings judged the most, and the least, conducive to vandalism.

Type of vandalism	Type of Setting	
	High house surveillance High road surveillance Alley blocked by 10′ wall	Low house surveillance Low road surveillance Twisting back alleys
Telephone kiosks	3.08	5.66
Lamp posts	3.02	5.30
Fences	3.16	5.82
Graffiti	4.14	6.12

Scale: 1 = definitely not at all; 2 = very probably would not; 3 = probably would not; 4 = 50/50 chance; 5 = probably would; 6 = very probably would; 7 = definitely would.

where escape is physically impeded. Graffiti is considered the form of vandalism most likely to occur in all settings.

The data in tables 2 and 3 reveals that features of the built environment significantly influence perceptions concerning the likelihood of vandalism. Further analysis of the data was carried out to test the hypothesis that this association could be construed in terms of perceived opportunities for vandalism.

Table 4 gives the frequency with which the different escape routes were placed into the ranked categories of perceived chances for successful escape. A chi square test on this data produces a value of 48.82 which, for four degrees of freedom, is significant at the 0.001 level.

Table 4 indicates that the type of escape route available is significantly associated with perceptions concerning the potential success of escape. Most people considered that twisting back alleys and back garden fences provided the best chance of escape. The narrow alley blocked by a ten foot high brick wall was perceived, by most people, as offering the worst route for successful escape.

It was hypothesized that, of those who considered the 'alley blocked by a ten foot high brick wall' to offer the best chance for successful escape, a greater proportion would consider vandalism to be more likely in settings incorporating this type of escape route than those who considered it to afford rather less opportunity for successful escape. Consequently, analysis was carried out on the judgements made by three groups of people (those who ranked the 'alley blocked by ten foot wall' as 1, 2, or 3) concerning the likelihood of vandalism in those settings involving this form of escape route. Within each of these groups the number of mean scores, in relation to these particular settings, above and below the mean for the total sample (4.04; cf. table 2) was calculated. Within each group, a higher proportion scoring above the mean for the total sample would indicate a greater perceived likelihood of vandalism in these settings. Conversely, a greater proportion scoring below this value would indicate that vandalism is judged less likely. Table 5 presents the distribution of these frequencies.

Table 4. Frequency of rank ordering of escape routes.

	Alley blocked by 10' wall	Open road	Twisting back alleys etc.
Rank 1	11	5	34
Rank 2	14	23	13
Rank 3	25	22	3

Scale: Rank 1 = best chance of escape; Rank 2 = second best chance of escape; Rank 3 = worst chance of escape.

Table 5. Frequency and distribution of mean scores above and below mean for total sample in relation to those settings incorporating the 'alley blocked by 10′ wall' escape route.

	Frequency above mean for total sample	Frequency below mean for total sample
Those who rank this escape route as 1	9	2
Those who rank this escape route as 2	6	8
Those who rank this escape route as 3	7	18

Scale: Rank 1 = best chance of escape; Rank 2 = second best chance of escape; Rank 3 = worst chance of escape.

The data in table 5 shows that 82% of the mean scores of those who ranked the 'alley blocked by ten foot wall' as offering the best chance of escape exceeded the overall mean. 72% of those who considered this escape route to offer the worst chance of escape gave judgements which fell short of the overall mean. The mean scores of those who ranked this escape route as 2 are fairly evenly distributed around the overall mean. A chi square test on the data in table 5 reveals the relationship between perceived chance of escape and judged likelihood of vandalism to be significant at the 0.01 level. These results strongly indicate that the better the perceived chance of escape from a place the greater the perceived chances of vandalism occurring in that place.

5. Discussion

5.1. 'Vandalism as opportunity'

As was noted earlier, research on the relation between environmental design and vandalism has been largely guided by Newman's theory of defensible space. Consequently, it was argued, the identification of 'places for vandalism' has been severely hampered by the concept of territoriality underlying Newman's work, leading to an oversimplification of the nature of crime and vandalism. A phenomenological approach to the problem adopted by the present study provides a more satisfactory account of the role of environmental design in the occurrence of vandalism. This study has gone some way to identifying issues which are important to the young adolescent in the perpetration of an act of vandalism. As such, it has been possible to describe, to some extent, the ways in which particular settings become conceptualized as more or less appropriate places for vandalism.

In the light of the present study and the work of the Home Office Research Unit (e.g. Mayhew et al., 1976, 1979) it is considered that the 'vandalism as opportunity' perspective offers a much more satisfactory framework within which to consider the relation between vandalism and the built environment. The H.O.R.U. proposes that, from such a perspective, the concern is with not only how the offender perceives his chances of being seen but also how he assesses the consequence of being seen. Of course, it can be argued that Newman addresses exactly the same issues. However, as has been argued, the concept of territoriality is severely lacking in its ability to account for the role of environmental design in this process. The H.O.R.U. states that a clearer understanding of the process by which surveillance achieves its effect is necessary. With this goal in mind they advocate greater concern for the vandal's perception of the situation, how he perceives the risk of intervention and what he considers the consequences of being seen might be. They state that the concept of opportunity provides a more realistic approach to the study of vandalism and affords a greater understanding of the nature of defensible space.

The data in tables 2 and 3 indicates that these boys were very concerned about the chances of being seen. At the same time, the 'escape route' and 'type of vandalism' variables suggest that they were also concerned with the consequences of being seen. However, the characteristics of urban design implied by the 'escape route' variable indicate that this anticipatory process can best be understood from an 'opportunity' perspective rather than a 'territorial' one.

The data given in tables 4 and 5 suggests that the 'escape route' variable may operate by influencing the perceived chances of successful escape. The greater the opportunity for successful escape the greater the likelihood of vandalism occurring. It is also worth noting that the open-ended interviews revealed that known vandals considered themselves far more likely to engage in acts of vandalism in an area they knew well (both socially and physically) than in an area they were not familiar with at all. The reasons given could generally be interpreted as indicating that they were less able to calculate the consequences of being seen in unknown areas.

It should also be noted from the open-ended interviews that escape routes were often described in terms of how much fun they were to use. Indeed, in many instances it was apparent that acts of vandalism had been perpetrated in order that a particular escape route could be coursed – the thrill of the chase. It was considered an obstacle course and provided the impetus for the vandalism.

The 'vandalism as opportunity' perspective would suggest that the type of vandalism under consideration is important because it also affects the perceived consequences of being seen and apprehended. Unfortunately, no data is available in the present study to indicate how this variable influences this process. However, Gladstone's (1978) study suggests that acts of vandalism can be distinguished in terms of their seriousness. If this is so, one would expect that engaging in less serious acts would, if seen, entail rather less serious consequences than more serious offences. Also, Cohen (1973) indicates that the nature of the object of vandalism may be important in identifying classes of witnesses more likely to take effective, intervening action. Thus, one would expect an interaction between the nature of the offence and the type of surveillance opportunities. Given one type of act of vandalism, the offender may be more concerned with avoiding surveillance by particular classes of witnesses (those people who would be committed in some way to defending the property under threat) than with avoiding surveillance altogether.

5.2. Implications for design and future research

Although the present study is rather limited in respect of the data collected it is considered that some suggestions for urban design and, in particular, for future research in this area can be made.

The present study suggests that the amount, rather than the type of surveillance is an important feature in the emergence of 'places for vandalism'. However, given the comments above on the importance of the nature of the act of vandalism, it would appear of value to explore the interactional effect of type of surveillance and type of vandalism in greater depth.

It is considered that perhaps the most valuable aspect of this study is the emergence of the 'escape route' as an important feature of urban design in the occurrence of vandalism. However, the data available permits only a crude analysis of this variable. It is suggested that a particularly fruitful avenue for future research would be to elaborate the environmental constituents of this facet in greater detail.

Bearing the tentative nature of this study in mind, it is possible to draw from it some implications for design aimed at minimizing the occurrence of vandalism. Firstly, we can suggest that, whenever possible, housing estates should be designed in such a way that they do not become perceived by children and young adolescents as obstacle courses. Design which involves a maze of paths, alleys and easily accessible back gardens should be avoided, particularly when the population of the estate is to include a large number of children.

Secondly, we can suggest that the layout of housing estates should maximize surveillance in vulnerable places and inhibit easy (or exciting) escape from these places by physical barriers and, of course, by ensuring surveillance and the possibility of intervention along the exit routes.

This study has shown that, not only is it useful to explore the way in which these boys conceptualize settings where vandalism occurs, but also that it is possible. The issues identified (one of them for the first time) and explored in this study suggest several potentially fruitful lines of enquiry for future research. More generally, this study provides encouraging evidence for the usefulness of an 'opportunity' perspective on the relation between environmental design and vandalism.

6. Conclusion

It is concluded that 'vandalism as opportunity' offers a more fruitful conceptual framework within which to consider the relation between vandalism and the built environment. Such a perspective leads to a concern more with the situation as the vandal sees it, how he perceives the chances of being seen and how he assesses the consequences of being seen. In the present study it was found necessary to consider the variable of surveillance in relation to other variables such as the nature of the act of vandalism and the escape route afforded by the setting. Surveillance is but one feature, encouraged or inhibited by the physical environment, within a complex 'opportunity structure' to which other physical and social factors contribute.

References

Baldwin, J., A.E. Bottoms, 1976. The urban criminal: A study in Sheffield. London: Tavistock.
Belson, W.A., 1975. Juvenile theft: The causal factors. London: Harper and Row.
Bottoms, A.E., 1974. Book review of 'Defensible space'. British Journal of Criminology 14, 203–206.
Building Research Station, 1971. Wilful damage on housing estates. Building Research Station Digest 132.
Canter, D., 1977. The psychology of place. London: Architectural Press.
Cohen, S., 1973. Property destruction: Motives and meanings. In: C. Ward, ed., Vandalism. London: Architectural Press.
Ellis, P., 1979. Conceptions of outside spaces in housing areas. Paper presented at the International Conference on Environmental Psychology, University of Surrey.
Gladstone, F.J., 1978. Vandalism amongst adolescent schoolboys. In: R.V.G. Clarke, ed., Tackling vandalism. London: H.M.S.O.
Hillier, B., 1973. In defence of space. Journal of the Royal Institute of British Architects, November, 539–544.
Hope, T.J., S.W.C. Winchester, 1979. The targets of crime: Some research on the relationship between crime and the physical environment. Paper presented at the International Conference on Environmental Psychology, University of Surrey.
Jacobs, J., 1961. The death and life of great American cities. Harmondsworth: Penguin.
Leather, A., A. Matthews, 1973. What the architect can do: A series of design guides. In: C. Ward, ed., Vandalism. London: Architectural Press.
Mawby, R.I., 1977a. Kiosk vandalism: A Sheffield study. British Journal of Criminology 17, 30–46.
Mawby, R.I., 1977b. Defensible space: A theoretical and empirical appraisal. Urban Studies 14, 169–179.
Mayhew, P., R.V.G. Clarke, J.N. Burrows, J.M. Hough, S.W.C. Winchester, 1979. Crime in public view. London: H.M.S.O.

Mayhew, P., R.V.G. Clarke, A. Sturman, J.M. Hough, 1976. Crime as opportunity. London: H.M.S.O.

Newman, O., 1972. Defensible space: People and design in the violent city. London: Architectural Press.

Repetto, T.A., 1976. Crime prevention through environmental policy. American Behavioral Scientist 20 (2), 275–288.

Ward, C., ed., 1973. Vandalism. London: Architectural Press.

Wilson, S., 1978a. Updating defensible space. Journal of the Royal Institute of British Architects, October, 274.

Wilson, S., 1978b. Vandalism and 'defensible space' on London housing estates. In: R.V.G. Clarke, ed., Tackling vandalism. London: H.M.S.O.

Zimbardo, P.G., 1973. A field experiment in auto shaping. In: C. Ward, ed., Vandalism. London: Architectural Press.

Abstract: B. Webb, Is there a place for vandalism?
A common theme is identified in the literature concerned with minimizing vandalism through use of the physical environment: what are the environmental constituents of 'places for vandalism'?

The present study sought to address this issue more directly than has been done previously. It is argued that a more comprehensive understanding of the relation between vandalism and environmental design is afforded if the question is explored phenomenologically. Fifty boys aged between 12 and 16 years were individually interviewed. They were asked to evaluate a number of verbally described settings in terms of the perceived likelihood of a number of different acts of vandalism occurring within them.

The results suggest that the 'vandalism as opportunity' perspective provides a far more satisfactory conceptual framework with which to consider the role of environmental design in the emergence of places for vandalism. The implications of the present study for design are considered together with suggestions for future research.

CHAPTER 12

Vandalism and disruptive behaviour in schools: some relationships

J. LAWRENCE

However important and valuable it is to study vandalism as a discrete phenomenon, it is clear that there is utility in considering it as a type of behaviour, such as a form of aggression, or equally as a form of disruptive behaviour. This approach is now particularly helpful as it has recently become feasible to study at close hand disruptive behaviour in schools, especially secondary schools. Previously, this was scarcely possible because it was considered to be too sensitive a topic for research. Teachers had fears of being called incompetent, while head teachers had fears of their school acquiring the reputation of being difficult. The climate has now changed so that it has been possible for my colleagues David Steed and Pamela Young and I to develop a technique for the systematic monitoring of patterns of disruptive behaviour in secondary schools, taking the disruptive incident as our focus.

1.

Incidents of disruptive behaviour (using criteria agreed between the researchers and the teachers) are reported, on a questionnaire, by the teacher to the researcher, who collates and analyzes the data, which he supplements through teacher interviews and other data-gathering techniques. Information about many types of disruptive behaviour, including vandalism, can be gathered in this way. If only one school is studied only a small number of vandalism incidents are collected, perhaps ten per cent of the total number of incidents, but larger scale survey work over many schools could yield a sufficient number to make generalization possible.

Methodologically, the incident of disruptive behaviour is a 'natural' focus for research, for several reasons.

Teachers remember incidents, even after long intervals, and so do children. Teachers, senior staff, and head teachers all deal with incidents. They are crisis points in 'disruptive behaviour', leading often to reporting onwards, and to entry for the child and the teacher into the official system for dealing with disruptive behaviour. They are often quoted in relation to official sanctions such as suspension and exclusion. Incidents are noted events in the life of a school. Incidents are useful in that where they are frequent, patterns may emerge which place the incident in the context of the whole life of the school: its timetable, administration, curriculum, staffing strength, pupil intake, etc. They offer therefore an opportunity for taking a global perspective on the school, and on disruptive behaviour itself. Above all, an incident occurs only when the behaviour or occurrence involved is seen as significant by a spectator or participant, so that it has an intrinsic meaning. The seriousness of the reported incident is not imputed, as in so-called 'objective' research, but is experienced.

We have studied disruptive behaviour, through the monitoring of disruptive incidents, in two schools (Lawrence et al., 1978, 1981) and have found the technique useful. The agreed definition of disruptive behaviour was 'behaviour which interferes seriously with the teaching process and/or seriously upsets the normal running of the school. It is more than ordinary misbehaviour in the classroom, playground, corridors etc. It includes physical attacks and malicious destruction of property'. The definition was adapted from NAS survey research (Lowenstein, 1975). As can be seen from this definition, teachers were invited to report incidents involving vandalism, i.e. malicious destruction of property.

Incidents of disruption were described on a standard form, asking for details of the class (including size, subject taught and type of activity) and details of the incident, including seriousness, time, length, number, sex and name of pupils involved, to whom the incident was reported, and full details of the incident itself.

Both the schools were 'problem' schools in that they were expected by the staff and by the local education authorities to yield a large number of incidents for study. Both were in outer London boroughs, both were multiracial. The first school was a boys' school with few signs of vandalism visible, but which was difficult in the sense that more boys were suspended from that school, than from any other school in the area. The second school was a mixed school, of unkempt appearance and signs of vandalism and clearly more difficult than the first. In the first school, over two one-week periods 101 incidents were reported, and 11% of them were described as 'very serious'; in the second school, over a one-week period 145 incidents were reported, 21% of them being described as 'very serious'. These figures are without any doubt underestimates, and point to the very large task which teachers face in coping with disruptive incidents in a difficult school, a task for which there is at present little or no formal training.

In relation to vandalism, it was clear that vandalism occurred both in and out of the classroom but did not constitute a major problem for the teachers in general. In the incidents reported there were rarely incidents which concerned vandalism as such, but there were a number where vandalism was quoted as one element in a complex incident (e.g. an incident of 'rowdy' behaviour), and there were a further number where, though destruction of property was not involved, damage to property or potential damage was, but the teacher was not explicit in designating it as vandalism, or sounded doubtful about doing this. It is clear from our data that the relationship between vandalism and disruptive behaviour in schools is complex, a grey area in which teachers often have difficulty in defining what is vandalism and what is not. Is a 'water-bomb' vandalism? Is throwing books 'vandalism', for example? Is the misuse of already damaged furniture 'vandalism'? Cases which we monitored where vandalism was the main component of the incident included the explosion of a firework, the setting off of a fire extinguisher, damage to parquet flooring through pupils 'riding' on chairs around a room, and the breaking of crockery through the rocking of a table. Cases where vandalism was part of the problem included the lighting of paper in a classroom, and the throwing of a bag out of a window.

The teacher's difficulty is illustrated by this example: is the boy who does the following, vandalizing the furniture? In this incident, the teacher did *not* describe the behaviour as vandalism: "Ten minutes from the end of the lesson, he begins his usual attempts at showing off to the girls. He gets an audience. Today he is an American baseball player. He takes position behind the open door of a locker, aims his fist and crashes it into the steel door. There is a loud din. He enjoys it and more so the loud laughter – goes back a few paces and does it again, he then nurses his knuckles and gleefully disappears as the buzzer goes, ignoring me while I ask him to stop. Pops back, 'Sorry, sir', and disappears". The teacher described this behaviour as 'rowdy behaviour' and 'disobedience' yet it is vandalism. The data we have suggests therefore that teachers are sometimes less sensitive to vandalism than to other behaviours in a 'vandalism' incident which are more threatening to them – for example, disobedience, and that general disorderliness, often called 'rowdy behaviour', in school incidents frequently contains elements of vandalism. Thus, a study of disruptive behaviour may contribute to the study of vandalism.

It may be helpful to distinguish between two types of vandalism: inactive or 'found' vandalism, and active or 'disruptive' vandalism. Inactive vandalism is that which is commonly studied as vandalism, i.e. major pieces of vandalism, which are 'discovered', often with the vandal being absent at the time of the discovery. While such cases of vandalism are frequently found in difficult schools, they are very rare in most schools compared with what we wish to call 'active' or 'disruptive vandalism'. Disruptive vandalism consists of relatively large numbers of minor acts of vandalism and is an integral part of some disruptive incidents; it occurs in all schools. The characteristics of such vandalism are as follows:

(1) It is *experienced* by the teacher, who observes it, may provoke or precipitate it, and who has to deal with it.

(2) It appears in the context of a *cluster* of other disruptive behaviours (e.g. rowdiness, refusal to obey, and temper). It may, or may not be, the most significant of those behaviours for the teacher.

(3) We have elucidated that factors leading to the teacher reporting the incident onwards to senior staff as serious, include:

a. stresses on the teacher at the time of the incident;
b. the repetitive nature of the elements of the incident;
c. the teacher feeling that the pupil's behaviour is directed against him personally, i.e. is malicious;
d. the teacher regards the incident as seriously disrupting the teaching process and/or disturbing the running of the school (according to the agreed criterion of what constitutes 'a disruptive incident').

In relation to the study of vandalism it is thus clear that there is the closest relationship between active vandalism and disruptive school behaviour, so that not only can the monitoring of incidents be used as a means of measuring and studying vandalism but, through the study of such incidents, the reasons can be seen why teachers often do not report vandalism (e.g. other behaviours in the incident 'hurt' the teacher more than the vandalism). Furthermore, the technique of analyzing incident data for whole schools, so as to reveal the patterning of incidents, may shed light on the patterning of acts of vandalism in schools if several schools are studied. Data becomes available through the technique, concerning time of day, day of week, location, activity in progress, children involved, objects concerned, reason for the report etc., and these data may suggest administrative, curricular, and teaching strategies which can reduce the vandalism and other forms of disruptive behaviour. Measures designed to reduce disruptive behaviour are likely to reduce vandalism.

An interest in the means which teachers have at their disposal for coping with their most difficult pupils, has led me to the development of a check-list approach to work with such children, among whom vandals and potential vandals will figure. A study of experienced teachers' responses to such children led to the notion that a larger number of resources of teacher skill and school practices was available for this work than was commonly realized (Lawrence, 1980). Teachers could use a list of these resources to plan programmes of work with such children, and since each item on the list (see table 1) can be used in a variety of combinations with other items, an enormous number of different programmes can be developed.

Anyone concerned with reducing vandalism and disruptive behaviour in schools will be interested not only in how teachers may work with individual difficult pupils, but also in studying difficult groups of children, and of course difficult schools, and how they develop. I have developed a technique for studying difficult classes in secondary schools (Lawrence, 1980) which uses a behaviour profile of each child in the class, which is completed by all the

Table 1. Behaviour problem checklist.

A. Classroom procedures

1. Apology: give opportunity for
2. Behaviour modification: encouragement etc.
3. Behaviour modification: contract
4. Causes: ask for
5. Causes: inspect records
6. Friend/s: get friend/s to help him
7. Gentle: be extra gentle
8. Ignore misbehaviour
9. Increase attention
10. Increase praise: private/public
11. Jolly along
12. Leader: use as
13. Medical reasons? e.g. sit near board
14. Monitor: use as
15. Place change: seat/group
16. Point out other behaving well

17. Previous good conduct: refer to
18. Private chat
19. Reasoning
20. Reprimand: private/public
21. Rules: reminder
22. Sanctions: minor (E.G. detention)

23. Send out of room
24. Send to other staff

25. Special help with work
26. Teaching approach: modify
27. Work: change work

B. School procedures

1. Attach to influential staff
2. Class change
3. Communicate with other staff re areas of good behaviour, preferred subjects, etc.
4. Counselling: formal (counsellor)
5. Counselling: from tutor/other
6. Counselling: preferred teacher
7. Curriculum revision
8. Medical?
9. On report
10. Parent contact: letter
11. Parent contact: invite to school
12. Parent contact: visit
13. Records. Check general record
14. Records. Check medical record

15. Sanctions: major a. cane
                  b. suspension
                  c. exclusion
                  d. expulsion
16. School: transfer of school
17. Sibling: contact
18. Social services?
19. Special educational treatment
20. Special unit: referral to
21. Supplementary tuition
22. Testing: school
23. Testing: educational psychologist

teachers who teach that group. The profile contains a mixture of positive and negative items which yields a score that describes the degree of cooperativeness of the child, for that particular teacher. The scores of all the children as seen by all their teachers, yield a matrix which reveals patterns of difficulty, and a measure of the general difficulty of that class, which can be used also to measure the effectiveness of strategies used to reduce disruptive behaviour among these children.

There are various ways in which our work could be developed in relation to vandalism. There could be macro-research, that is large scale studies of disruptive incidents in many schools, which would yield sufficient data on disruptive vandalism to permit pattern-analysis. One member of the research team could focus on vandalism. (There could also be micro-research, that is video-taping etc. of disruptive incidents (Clarke et al., 1981) to study the effectiveness of control techniques for difficult pupil behaviour, including aggression and vandalistic tendencies.) The check-list approach could be adapted for use with vandals specifically, and the behaviour-profile matrix could be adapted to measure the vandalism-potential of groups and classes of pupils.

In general, there is a need for teachers to be trained to be sensitive to vandalism in general so that they sensitize children to it. Disruptive vandalism usually relates to minor acts of vandalism, which are easily disregarded, but because these minor acts occur when a teacher is present, *teaching* can occur, i.e. the child is seeing an adult respond to vandalism and can and often will *learn* from this response. Thus, teachers need to be made sensitive to these acts, and must take the frequent opportunities they offer to teach children appropriate attitudes to premises and property. For coping with disruptive vandalism they need training, as they do for coping with other forms of disruptive behaviour.

In 1981, we began an inquiry into disruptive behaviour in schools in Western Europe. Describing the situation as we see it in England at the present time, we asked a number of experts in Western Europe to describe the situation in their own countries. We spoke of the considerable increase in concern in England among teachers, head teachers, and school administrators over the last ten years, about disruptive pupil behaviour, especially in city areas. We gave a list of types of pupil behaviours which were the basis for this concern; these included vandalism, and we asked whether respondents in their own country had noted a serious or very serious concern about each of these behaviours. We asked whether there were special units for disruptive pupils, as we have them in England, where they are on the school site or outside it, and where they are a recent, proliferating phenomenon. We also asked whether, as in England, local inspectors and advisers, and educational psychologists help teachers in their work with difficult pupils, by running courses of training at teachers' centres and by visiting schools to give advice on how to handle these children. Finally, we asked what are considered in the respondent's country to be the main causes of disruptive behaviour in schools, and the best means of controlling or reducing it.

Comparisons with other countries are fraught with difficulty, but so little is known of disruptive behaviour in European schools, that we thought it was appropriate to initiate an investigation into the issue. We were very much aware that the problems associated with comparisons are numerous: what is an appropriate conceptual framework for the analysis? What unit of comparison should be used? For example, countries like Denmark are in terms of size and homogeneity more comparable to some U.K. local authorities or French prefectures than they are to the U.K. or German countries as a whole. In this research, however, we raise such matters for future discussion.

It is apparent that those of us who are interested in and concerned with disruption need to explore one another's explanations and resultant strategies very carefully, not so much for a possible harmonization of policies where misbehaviour is concerned, but to benefit from shared knowledge and expertise. Why, for example, is England unique in its growing number of autonomous off-site units for disruptive pupils? Is this the most appropriate way of coping with disruption when we look at what other European countries are doing?

In the remainder of this paper the results of our enquiry are set out in summary form. It needs to be borne in mind that most of those whose opinions are summarized have a psychological bias: they are heads of research institutions, heads of special schools, professors of child psychiatry and educational psychology. The information was gathered from initial contacts with embassies and education authorities, who were asked for names of those known to them who had research or other interests in disruptive behaviour in schools. All those named were contacted, except that a selection was made where certain towns or areas were over-represented. Response was approximately 25%, and proved to be from a wide scattering of locations within each country. Information became available from France, West Germany, Switzerland, Denmark, Austria and Belgium.

2.

2.1. Definitions of disruptive behaviour

Many respondents accepted the authors' definition of disruptive behaviour, but the group as a whole demonstrated very clearly that enormous difficulties are involved in attempts to define it. These difficulties create problems for the very study of the topic.

Certainly it is difficult to draw lines of demarcation between disruptive behaviour and related concepts. The outstanding example of confusion is that between disruptive behaviour and maladjustment, or as a West German respondent put it, "between mental disturbance in the sense of neurosis and bad behaviour with a clearly defined origin, in the parents' upbringing of the child". The incorporation of 'disruptive' children within 'maladjusted' children and consequent confusion is also common in England and has contributed to the inclusion of disruptive pupils as a category of child with special educational needs.

The term 'disruptive' itself generated considerable interest, particularly among French-speaking respondents. Thus, some in Switzerland pointed out that the term 'disruptive' belongs properly, in French, to physics and is not used in the psychological field. Instead, expressions such as 'behaviour problems', 'disturbed child' are used. A few years ago the expressions 'troubles caractériels' or 'comportement caractériel' were very fashionable. In France itself, several terms are used in relation to disruptive behaviour e.g. 'comportements inadaptés' (maladjustment) and 'T.C.C.' i.e. 'troubles (importants) du comportement et de la conduite' (serious behavioural disturbances and conduct disorder). The diversity in the use of terms is well illustrated by one French psychiatrist who states that she never uses the term 'disruptive behaviour' and wonders whether it relates to what in France is called 'psychopathie'.

As a final illustration of the difficulties involved in definition, in Belgium, a group of head teachers and psychologists working in a special school declared that they had no specific definition of a disruptive child: the theoretical concept is not clear and the manifestations are debatable!

Though there was confusion in the use of terms, there were features in disruptive behaviour on which there was good agreement. These were, that its defintion depends on perception, that it departs from the norm and that it has bad consequences.

Unsurprisingly, most of the responses, given the strong representation of educational psychological services and advisory services, strongly emphasize clusters of disturbed behaviour which enable the identification and treatment of disruptive children. Sometimes the organizing theoretical framework which enables this identification is explicit in, for example, the Danish consultant to an observation class who refers to Erikson and "children lacking structure and norms"; at other times the terms used indicate the particular theoretical perspective being applied – narcissist, extrovert, introvert, passivity.

One important question on which opinion varied among respondents, was the involvement of the school in causing, exacerbating or triggering off disruptive behaviour. One West German opinion was that "the term at present is used with the meaning of a problem caused by 'outside' factors and therefore not one to be tackled through pedagogic intervention". In contrast, a French respondent commenting on the variation in teachers' levels of tolerance, from time to time, insists: "The school situation, against which the child is disruptive, is part of the picture".

2.2. Concern

A substantial body of opinion in France and West Germany agrees that their situation is similar to that in England in relation to anxieties about disruptive behaviour in schools, i.e. that there has been a considerable increase in concern among teachers, head teachers and school administrators, especially in inner-city areas. In other countries there were some statements suggesting a quantity of concern, occasionally said to resemble the British situation, but its degree would appear from others to be less severe, or more scattered. Thus, in Switzerland, concern seems currently to be centred upon violence rather than disruptive behaviour in general. Two Geneva researchers, concerned particularly with the 'Cycle d'Orientation', report expressions of concern at the increase in pupil violence from teachers and administrators, especially in relation to acts of vandalism against school premises and materials. In Denmark, only two of 22 respondents indicated that there was no concern, while two commented that the situation was "just like in England".

Concern for the problem has, in general, led to official recognition of it and various attempts to measure and control it, through socio-political initiatives (e.g. in West Germany the establishment of the 'Will to Educate' society [Mutzur Erziehung], in France the establishment of the 'Association de l'éducation en milieu ouvert' [Association for education in an open environment], and in Denmark the 'adoption' of the problem by a new political party, the 'Fremskridtspartiet' [Progress party]).

Concern may be located among pupils themselves (e.g. in France a strike by secondary school pupils against acts of peer violence), school staffs, parents, government and of course the media. Parental concern may be exacerbated where, as in France for example, great importance is attached to grades, examinations and school achievement in general. A French professor of psychiatry who raises this point and who recognizes, as do other respondents, that anxiety is now being felt concerning children of younger and younger age, emphasizes that "this anxiety is part of a wider concern about violence in general. Three years ago, a national committee was set up to study violence, with representatives from all over France, and it is possibly at this level that the concern is greatest. The mass media reflect it, and reinforce it, as can be seen by their treatment of child vandalism".

A widespread and recurrent theme is that the phenomenon of disruptive behaviour in schools, once restricted to pupils within secondary schools, where it was associated with the onset of adolescence, is now starting to be seen among younger children, and thus in the primary schools, and even at the preschool stage. This fact appears to be generating considerable concern in all the countries studied, though the precise types of disruptive behaviour in younger and older children are sometimes seen as different (e.g. restlessness in primary schools, but intentional destruction of property and places, i.e. vandalism, at the secondary stage). There is general agreement that concern centres more upon inner-city schools than others, though other schools may also be affected (e.g. through amalgamations). Very large schools, schools with migrant workers' children, and schools with many children from neglectful homes, special schools, 'secondary modern' schools and others are pinpointed as loci of concern.

Most of the data gathered points to a growth in concern at the problem, but the point was occasionally made that the increase in disruption may not be a real one, but merely perceived, and a note of cautious optimism was sounded by one or two respondents.

2.3. Types of behaviour

Respondents were asked to indicate by ticks those forms of disruptive behaviour which were said to be causing serious or very serious concern in their country. The results for France, West Germany, Switzerland and Denmark are shown in table 2, together with results for England, based on a population of 135 senior teachers from four outer-London boroughs, attending an in-service course on the 'Education of children with special needs'.

There are several points of interest arising from the data in table 2. Bullying or physical violence to other children is first or second in importance in four of the five countries, and vandalism is ranked high or very high in all of them. There is also a good measure of agreement concerning the importance of truancy (West Germany, Switzerland and Denmark) and refusal to obey the teacher (third or fourth rank for all countries except Switzerland, where it is only slightly lower, at seventh rank). Difficult classes are concerning all countries; this is an interesting finding in the light of current European concern at group disorder (e.g. rioting and football hooliganism). There may, however, be comfort to be found in the relatively low rank of disruptive behaviour in the larger educational grouping, i.e. whole schools ('difficult schools'). The clashing of gangs was mentioned, for West Germany.

Table 2. Types of behaviour causing concern: rank order.

	France	West Germany	Switzerland	Denmark	England
1. Bullying or physical violence to other children	2	1	9	2	1
2. Vandalism	1	2	4	5	4
3. Rowdy behaviour	8	3	9	5	13
4. Truancy from school or lessons	9	4	3	1	6
5. Refusal to obey teacher	3	4	7	3	3
6. Difficult classes	3	5	1	5	5
7. Boredom	9	6	5	11	7
8. Temper	9	8	12	8	12
9. Verbal abuse or bad language	5	9	2	4	2
10. Extreme late arrival at lessons	13	10	9	12	11
11. Alcoholism	14	10	13	12	15
12. Talking/chatting	15	12	5	8	8
13. Difficult schools	9	13	14	12	10
14. Stealing	5	14	8	3	9
15. Physical violence to teachers	5	15	15	15	14

For France, West Germany and Switzerland, drug-taking was mentioned as causing serious or very serious concern, and there are some very recent indications in the British educational press that this may start to figure among teacher concerns in this country.

2.4. Provision and facilities

Information was gathered in relation to special provision for disruptive pupils, in terms of special units, etc. and help for teachers from advisers and psychologists, etc. It is clear that provision for maladjusted pupils overlaps that for disruptive pupils, in all countries, probably because of the definition problems referred to in section 2.1.

The major distinction in provision for disruptive pupils appears to be that of integration and separation/segregation; in other words, the issues involved and the complexities mirror the debate around provision for children with special educational needs, in general. Since disruptive children are by and large seen as a group requiring special educational help, although – and here they are clearly distinguishable from other groups – underlying their consideration may be a question of deterrence and punishment, the issue is whether help should come to them in the ordinary classroom, or in a special unit closely attached to the ordinary school, or in some more segregated setting. In parts of Europe (e.g. Denmark and France), signs of the development of an integrated solution are more apparent; in others, segregation is favoured. Thus in England there is, at secondary level, a proliferation of off-site autonomous units for disruptive pupils. Unlike any units in the rest of Europe, they can operate outside the control of the schools' psychological services. In contrast, at primary level, France is developing the 'Groupes d'aide psychopédagogique' and Denmark a classroom observation system, both of which take help for disruptive pupils into the ordinary classroom.

Special classes for disruptive pupils have existed inside schools in a number of European countries for many years.

Other interesting features of provision include the developed form of the West Germany teacher-counsellor system.

The extent of teacher support for work with disruptive pupils varies, but services for this appear to be more developed in England than elsewhere, in that, for example, the Schools Council is currently preparing a 'disruption pack' of materials and techniques for teachers, following upon a nationwide enquiry into aids for the problem (Wilson and Evans, 1980). Similarly, there is a substantial programme of courses for children with special needs, sponsored by the Department of Education and Science which includes reference to disruptive pupils.

There are frequently expressed regrets in the European data that more is not done to train and help teachers at all stages in their career for work with disruptive pupils.

2.5. Causes and cures

In attempting to ascertain the reasons why schools seem now to be experiencing more disruptive pupil behaviour, our respondents agree in locating specific causes, whether they relate to home or school, within a broad framework of societal change. This framework is that of modern life, seen as a spoilt, polluted environment with associated problems of emotional and physical deprivation, particularly in the city. Life today is seen as reflecting a breakdown of authority, the destruction of ethical and moral values and in general a lack of direction. Social problems abound within this picture, whether they refer to unemployment, migrant populations, or impaired family relationships. In this context, it is obvious that poor behaviour in school will frequently emerge from poor parenting or disadvantage of various kinds, triggered off by exacerbating factors within the school, for example inappropriate demands upon the child.

Often, as in West Germany, schools are seen as too academic, too competitive, large, anonymous, bureaucratic. The curriculum is seen as overcrowded, boring and irrelevant, not responding to emotional needs. Basically, many schools have not responded appropriately to societal change and to our period of questioning goals, norms and values.

There was also broad agreement among respondents as to the 'cures' available for this situation. The need is seen for intensive individual help at the primary stage, and for psychologically healthy climates in secondary school classes, in which children's needs can be met, and social learning take place and in which, above all, the child is accepted for what he is. As for curriculum, this should have meaning for the child, in terms of the society in which he is living.

For all this, teacher education must be improved, so that teachers develop insight, and become concerned with the whole of the child's development. Earlier identification of children's problems is needed, so that intervention can become more effective. The need is seen for close cooperation between parents and teachers, without, however, specific suggestions being offered as to ways in which this might be achieved.

3. Conclusion

Our work suggests that vandalism is usefully viewed in the context of the disruptive behaviour in school. Though this has the disadvantage of appearing to make the problem of vandalism more complex, it has the advantage of locating vandalism in the nexus of school differences which may have an impact on disruptive behaviour in general. Thus it points to the need for schools to examine their processes and procedures, their curricula, their styles of teaching, the training of their staff, and the many features which go to make up a busy school. This examination may have outcomes which are potentially more fruitful than concentration on major causative social factors which are less susceptible to manipulation. As can be seen from the first part of this paper, techniques can be made available to schools which wish to undertake the painful but useful task of self-analysis and diagnosis.

The second part of the paper suggests the need for collaboration between countries in this field. Without minimizing the difficulties of this, and the situation-specificity of educational structures and systems, it is clear that we have much to gain from a sharing of information and a reflection upon similarities and differences.

References

Clarke, D.D., et al., 1981. Disruptive incidents in secondary school classrooms. A sequence analysis approach. Oxford Review of Education 7(2), 111–118.

Lawrence, J., 1980. Exploring techniques for coping with disruptive behaviour in schools. Gold-smith's College, Educational Studies monograph 2.

Lawrence, J., D. Steed, R. Young, 1978. Monitoring incidents of disruptive behaviour in a secondary school. Durham & Newcastle Research Review 41, 39–43.

Lawrence, J., D. Steed, P. Young, 1981. Dialogue on disruptive behaviour. A study of a secondary school. South Croydon (Surrey): PJD Press.

Lowenstein, L.F., 1975. Violent and disruptive behaviour in schools. National Association of Schoolmasters.

Wilson, M.D., M. Evans, 1980. Education of disturbed pupils. Schools Council Working Paper no. 65. London: Methuen.

Abstract: J. Lawrence, Vandalism and disruptive behaviour in schools: some relationships
The paper reports on recent researches into disruptive school behaviour which facilitate the study of vandalism in this context, as it arises within incidents of disruptive behaviour. The incidents are reported during periods of monitoring disruption throughout the school. It also describes other techniques developed by the author for use by teachers, as part of an analytical, diagnostic approach to reducing disruption. Finally, the paper reports on a collaborative research into disruptive behaviour in schools including vandalism, as described by approximately one hundred experts with a psychological bias, in six West European countries.

CHAPTER 13

The sociogenesis of football hooligan violence

E.G. DUNNING, J.A. MAGUIRE, P.J. MURPHY and J.M. WILLIAMS

Although it tends to be widely regarded as a predominantly English 'disease', the phenomenon of 'football hooliganism' is currently more or less firmly established in a number of European countries. Hooligan incidents also appear to be increasingly occurring in the context of international matches, both at the club and inter-country levels. Accordingly, it is a problem regarding which sociological analysis and research are urgently required. This paper reports some of the findings of a research project on football hooliganism that we have been engaged in for the past four years. [1] Hopefully, the fact that the phenomenon currently appears to be spreading may make an analysis of British data of interest to an international audience.

Our analysis traces the phenomenon up to what might be termed its 'take-off' point as a cause for national concern in the early 1960s. It takes as a starting point two persistent features: firstly, the fact that football hooliganism is overwhelmingly a male preserve; and secondly that, for males who attract the 'football hooligan' label, Association football forms a focus for aggressive behaviour, more specifically, for expressing norms of 'aggressive masculinity' or what one might call a 'violent masculine style'.

Variations on these norms are found at all levels in the social stratification hierarchy but they appear to be generated in a particularly clear and unrestrained form in the lower working class. Thus the literature on working class youth stresses the cultural centrality in the 'rough' working class of the ability 'to look after oneself', i.e. to fight. We hypothesize that this distinctive 'violent masculine style' is principally a consequence, firstly, of certain features inherent in the structure of working class communities, and, secondly, of the location of these communities in the wider social structure.

1.

1.1. The social origins of football hooligans

Information on the social origins of fans who fight at football matches is currently scarce but data on those convicted of football hooligan offences

[1] The research reported in this paper was supported by the Social Science Research Council. It is continuing to be funded by the Football Trust.

suggest that the phenomenon is predominantly the preserve of the lower working class. Of course, there is often a degree of arbitrariness about who is and who is not arrested in a football context. As a result, such figures have to be treated with caution. Nevertheless, the emerging pattern is sufficiently strong and geographically consistent to make it difficult to believe that the figures significantly distort the social class distribution of football hooligans. This raises the question of what it is about the structure of lower working class communities and the position they occupy within the broader network of power relationships that generates and sustains the standards of aggressive masculinity that are displayed in the football context and elsewhere.

1.2. Lower working-class communities and the sociogenesis of a 'violent masculine style'

In lower working-class communities relatively little pressure is exerted upon individual members to exercise self-control over recourse to physical violence. The higher levels of violence which are characteristic of internal relations in these communities in turn foster and sustain higher levels of tolerance towards violence. Other central aspects of the structure of these communities seem to work in the same direction. For example, the relatively rigid division of labour between the sexes and the dominance of men over women both serve to minimize the consequences of softening female pressure. Indeed, since many women in these communities grow up to be relatively violent themselves and to expect violent behaviour from their menfolk, this further serves to compound to violent propensities of the latter.

These standards of aggressive masculinity manifest themselves in many aspects of community life, but they find their strongest expression in the 'street corner gang'. These gangs, or 'alliances', emerge, in part, as a consequence of the comparative freedom from adult control experienced by lower working-class children and adolescents. This leads to relatively violent forms of interaction and to the development of dominance hierarchies based on age and physical strength. Moreover, the conferral of prestige on males who can fight encourages these males to develop a love of fighting and to come to see it as a central source of meaning and gratification in their lives.

In short then, lower working-class communities of this type appear to be characterized by a constellation of processes which serve to heighten the willingness and desire to resort to physical violence – especially on the part of young males.

These communities are internally divided but they gain a degree of overall unity as a result of the threat, or perceived threat, posed by 'outsiders'. Such outsiders include more powerful groups, particularly 'the authorities', but the most continuous threat is perceived as coming from similarly placed groups in adjacent lower working-class communities – communities which have been subject to similar socialization processes and which experience similar structural constraints. Thus, while these communities are characteristically divided by internal conflicts, they possess the capacity to combine in the event of an external challenge. Indeed, it is the nature of this external threat which appears to determine the level of alliance formation. For example, just as, at the community level, otherwise hostile groups combine in the event of disputes between rival estates, so, at football matches, our observation is that estates stand side by side in the cause of 'end' solidarity. If the challenge is perceived in regional terms then, again, enemies join forces. For example, Northern fans visiting London often complain about confrontations with combined 'fighting crews' from a number of local clubs. Southerners visiting the North voice similar complaints. Finally, at the international level, club and regional rivalries are subordinated to national reputation. At each of these levels, and particularly if the opposition groups are not present in sufficient strength, lower-level rivalries are apt to re-emerge. The central point is that the nature of the opposition seems to determine the level at which the temporary alliance is formed.

So far, we have argued that street gangs and a distinctive violent masculine style are characteristically generated by specific structural features of lower working-class communities and the manner in which these communities are integrated into the wider social structure. The areas in social life outside lower working-class communities where these relatively violent standards have found expression have tended to shift under the influence of changing fashion and circumstances. In Britain since the Second World War, a number of working-class 'youth subcultural fashions' have emerged to be perceived as a general threat to social order. Football hooliganism, although it is not entirely distinct from the others, is one in that series. If football hooliganism has a distinguishing feature, it is the length of time over which it has preoccupied the authorities and the media. Is there anything inherent in the structure of Association football which accounts for its attractiveness as a venue for the expression of aggressive masculinity?

1.3. Professional football and the working class

Working class men have traditionally been attracted to soccer, partly because it injects an element of excitement into their otherwise routinized lives, and partly because masculine values have been intrinsic to its development. That is, the game is basically a 'play-fight', a socially legitimized struggle with a ball in which two groups of men fight within a set of rules to establish dominance over one another. It is an activity in which a constellation of attributes valued in and expected of men over and above skill at the game *per se*, e.g. strength, stamina, courage, determination and group loyalty, can be tested. As such, the match forms an arena in which masculine reputations are at stake. At the same time, the inherently oppositional character of the game means that it lends itself readily to group identification and the enhancement of in-group solidarity in opposition to a series of easily identifiable out-groups, the opposing teams and their supporters. The identifications mobilized by the professional game are mainly working class because the majority of teams are the named representatives of the towns, cities and sections of cities where the industrial working classes live. Moreover, players and managers, the socially most visible proponents of the game at this level, tend to have working class origins and, for the most part, to display cultural attributes that are working class.

   This complex of characteristics serves to explain the appeal of soccer to male members of the working class. Viewed as a total configuration, each match is a struggle for superiority principally between the male, working class members of two communities. It is a struggle in which some participants, the players, are directly involved, whilst others, the spectators, managers, etc., take a less direct though not necessarily less active part. The game brings regularly into the areas lived in by such groups and into the stadia they regard as their preserves, teams that represent other, similar collectivities, together with a variable number of their supporters. Opposition is inherent in this total configuration on two distinct levels: that of the match itself and that of the 'territorial invasion' represented by the visit of the opposing team and its supporters. The opposition between rival fans can find expression in anything from the display of colours and insignia, through the expression of vocal support for one's own team and denigration of the opponents, to physical confrontation. The conflict is liable to remain on the level of more or less friendly rivalry to the extent that the personnel involved are accustomed by their socialization and position in the overall system of social interdependencies to behaving in a more or less courteous and tolerant way towards strangers, that is, in what might be termed a 'cosmopolitan' manner. Group fighting becomes more probable to the extent that fans are drawn from communities which tend to view 'outsiders' with hostility and adhere to an aggressive masculine style. This suggests that the changing class composition of football crowds and the degree to which the working class have been 'incorporated', i.e. have internalized the values of dominant groups, are of central importance as determinants of long-term variations in the rate of fan disorder.

1.4. The changing class composition of football crowds and the rate of fan disorder

Association football dates from the foundation of the Football Association in 1863. At first, the game was the preserve of the upper and middle classes but, from the 1870s, it began to spread down the social scale. While the administration of the game as a whole and the control of the professional clubs remained mainly in the hands of the upper and middle classes, by the 1890s the 'terraces' had become largely the preserve of the male working class. Evidence as to the precise composition of this working class support is slight and inconclusive. Nevertheless, there is a high degree of unanimity among historians who have researched this field.

In this context it must suffice to say that at the end of the nineteenth century, football crowds seem to have consisted largely of skilled manual workers, perhaps with a greater or lesser sprinkling of clerical workers in their ranks. That is, spectators appear to have been recruited mainly from the 'respectable' rather than the 'rough' working class. Our data suggest that, since this period and up to the present, an increasing number of those attending football matches have tended to be recruited from the more 'respectable' sections of the working class. One indication of this process is that there occurred, for a period, a decline in the rate and seriousness of football crowd disorder. However, in the late 1950s and early 1960s, a number of developments intersected which began to make the game more attractive than it had been hitherto to males from the 'rough' working class who came to define football stadia as places for expressing their masculinity norms. The rate of fan disorderliness correlatively increased. Crowd disorderliness as such at football was nothing new. It had occurred on a large scale before, particularly around the turn of the century. During the inter-war years, however, and for about a decade following the end of the Second World War, it seems to have decreased. The following discussion is an attempt to explain this apparently 'curvilinear' pattern.

2.

2.1. Fan disorderliness before 1914

The following examples have been selected to show the occurrence of football fan disorderliness in different forms and settings in the period up to the First World War. The first describes an attack on the players of a visiting team; the second alludes to attacks on rival supporters; the third describes a fight between fan groups away from the ground; and the fourth shows the level of destructiveness that was sometimes involved.

1885: Aston Villa v Preston
On the North End team leaving the field, they were mercilessly attacked by a gang of, if appearances go for anything, *bona fide* Brummagem roughs, who mobbed them and used sticks, stones and every available missile with which to wreak their vengeance on the visitors...(*Saturday Night* [Birmingham] 9 May 1885)

1889: Small Heath (Birmingham) v West Bromwich Albion
The lower element of the partisans of the Small Heath Football Club are a particularly objectionable lot. Not content with resorting to disgusting expletives, they not infrequently molest strangers when the chances of the Coventry Road team are vanishing. (*Birmingham Daily Mail* 6 May 1889)

1889: Nantwich v Crewe

An exciting scene took place at Middlewich Station on Saturday evening, after a match between Nantwich and Crewe for the Cheshire Final. Both parties assembled on opposite platforms waiting for trains. They commenced operations by alternately hooting and cheering, and then one man challenged an antagonist to a fight. Both leaped on the metals and fought desperately until separated by the officials. Then a great number of the Nantwich men ran across the line, storming the platform occupied by the Crewe men. Uninterested passengers bolted right and left. The special then came in and the police guarded them off, many of them carrying away marks that will distinguish them for some time. (*Liverpool Echo* 1 April 1889)

1909: Hampden Park, Glasgow

About six thousand spectators tore up goalposts, fences and pay-boxes, set fire to them and danced around them in the middle of the pitch. Police, firemen and ambulancemen were stoned, fire-engines damaged and hoses slashed. The police, after throwing the stones back at the rioters, finally cleared the ground at seven o'clock, at a cost of fifty four constables injured and the destruction of virtually every street-lamp around Hampden. (*Glasgow Herald* 19 April 1909; paraphrased in Hutchinson, 1975)

Examples such as these do not give an idea of the *rate* of disorderliness in this period. That is another complex issue. It must be enough in the present context to illustrate the fact that it was relatively high by reference to the conclusions of historians who have studied the issue. According to Hutchinson (1975):

"Riots, unruly behaviour, violence, assault and vandalism appear to have been a well-established, but not necessarily dominant pattern of crowd behaviour at football matches at least from the 1870s".

Green (1953) writes of "the growth of uncontrolled partisanship" among football spectators in the 1880s and 1890s. In short, it seems that in this period, disorderliness was a fairly regular occurrence at football grounds across the country, engaged in by a sizeable minority of the 'typical' crowd.

2.2. Fan disorderliness in the inter-war years

As the following examples show, fan disorderliness at football matches was not unknown in the inter-war years.

1920: Report of the action taken against Birmingham City FC by Frank Hare, an oxy-acetylene welder from Birmingham

The affair happened on 'Spion Kop' ... Immediately after the interval, 'bottles were flying around like hailstones'. Witness tried to get away, but he was struck on the head, and received an injury which necessitated seven stitches. He had seen other disturbances on 'Spion Kop', and on one occasion a week or so before he was injured, he saw men using bottles as clubs instead of using their fists. The bottles used were half-pint stout bottles. (*Birmingham Daily Post* 14 October 1920)

1930: Clapton Orient v Queen's Park Rangers

Towards the end of the match at Homerton between Clapton Orient and Queen's Park Rangers, the police had to stop fighting between rival spectators behind the goal which the Rangers were defending. There was no demonstration against the referee or the players. Only last Wednesday, the Rangers ground was closed owing to the unruly conduct of their supporters during the match with Northampton Town. (*Birmingham Daily Post* 24 February 1930)

1934:Return of Leicester City fans from a match in Birmingham
After a thorough search of all the coaches, it was found that the communication cord had been pulled ... It was ascertained that the hooligan element sometimes found on the trips had caused not a little damage to the rolling stock, some of it almost new. Windows were smashed, seats cut and torn, and the leather window-straps slashed with knives. (*Leicester Mercury* 19 March 1934)

These few examples go some way towards dispelling the romanticism which tends to cloud assessments of football crowd behaviour in this period. Like those cited for the period before the First World War, they do not give an idea of the rate at which disorderliness was occurring. They do, however, suggest that it was geographically quite widespread, continuing as a regular 'subterranean' occurrence and not just an occasional affair. At the same time, the balance of evidence for the period suggests that the rate of disorderliness was declining. Although it cannot be regarded as conclusive, let us review the evidence which points in that direction.

Descriptions of Cup Final crowds in the inter-war years, for example, convey the impression of relatively orderly assemblies. Fans were frequently depicted as 'invaders' or as 'taking over' the streets of the capital, but, almost invariably, their antics were excused as the expression of 'high spirits' or 'raucous good humour'. Even when official arrangements broke down, crowds were seen as remaining disciplined and generally well-behaved. *The Report of the Departmental Committee on Crowds* (1924), for example, commented on the exemplary behaviour of spectators at the 1923 final (the first at Wembley) when a considerably more than capacity crowd turned up. Again, after the 1928 final, an editorial in the *Leicester Mercury* (23 April) favourably compared current crowd behaviour with crowd behaviour in the past. It reads:

There seems to have been more than the usual favourable comment on the good behaviour of the Wembley crowd. Students of people in mass will probably tell us that we make merry nowadays without the discreditable manifestations that were at one time thought to be inseparable from these public rejoicings. Rejoicing and sobriety go hand in hand, and great crowds distinguish themselves with a sense of discipline that is creditable all round. May we infer that we are an improving people?

Other evidence suggests that the perceived civility of Wembley crowds was not just a reflection of the special status of the FA Cup Final but indicative of a more general perception. For example, a report in the *Leicester Mercury* (10 January) of disorder at a match in Belfast in 1928 claimed that such behaviour no longer occurred in England:

... the half-time interval in a cup-tie between Celtic and Linfield was given to a diversion which introduced the storming of the musicians in the band, and the intervention of the police who used their truncheons to keep the more heated rivals in the crowd apart ...

In many centres in England during the next few weeks the big issues at stake in the Cup and the League will unite thousands of people in a single thought ... And happily all these things will be duly settled without a single policeman having to raise his truncheon to preserve the peace.

Another indication that football grounds were not defined as 'unduly danger-ous' in this period is provided by the increasing attendance of women at matches. The *Mercury* (23 April) coverage of the 1927 Cup Final, for example, reported that

a remarkable feature was the number of women who had accompanied their husbands and sweethearts. Many mothers carried babies in their arms and confessed they had brought them to see the Cup-tie.

Two years later, on the occasion of the Bolton v Portsmouth Final, the *Mercury* (27 April) reported in less surprised tones that a

feature of the crowd was the number of women who were making the trip to Wembley, at least 50% of the train loads being of that sex.

It seems, moreover, that women were not just attending Cup Finals. Thus, such was the size of the female contingent who travelled to support Brentford in a cup match against Leicester that the London side were referred to as 'the ladies' team' (*Mercury*, 11 January 1936). It is reasonable to suppose that women would not have attended matches in large numbers if serious crowd disorder had been a regular and unavoidable occurrence.

2.3. Fan disorderliness after the Second World War

The decline in crowd disorderliness seems to have continued in the decade and a half following the end of the Second World War. That is not to say that this period was devoid of incidents. Take, for example, the two following cases:

1949: Millwall v Exeter City
The referee and linesmen reported that, when 50 yards from the Millwall ground after the match, they were subjected to abuse and hostility by a crowd numbering 150-200 people. The referee received a blow in the back and tea cups were thrown at the three officials. (FA Disciplinary Committee; Minutes of meeting held in January 1950)

1954: Everton Reserves v Bolton Wanderers Reserves
The referee ... reported also that several hundred spectators came on to the field during the match. Fireworks were thrown and one of the linesmen was kicked. (FA Disciplinary Committee; Minutes of meeting held in December 1954)

A detailed reading of the Football Association minutes and of Birmingham, Leicester, South East London and selected national newspapers for the period suggests that such disorders were relatively rare up to about 1960 but that, somewhere around that time, a marked increase began to occur. This impression is confirmed by figures reported by the Chester Committee in 1968. Thus, between 1946 and 1960, 195 cases of "disorderly behaviour by spectators" were brought to the attention of the Football Association, an average of thirteen per season. By contrast, "in the following six seasons 148 cases were reported, an average of 25 per season". In our view, this increase was partly an artefact of the 'moral panic' over football hooliganism generated in the 1960s but also partly a 'real' phenomenon. The 'perceptual' and the 'real' dimensions of the problem seem to have contributed to a process of mutual escalation, the moral panic leading to an increase in the rate of football hooliganism and the increase of football hooliganism intensifying the moral panic. Let us briefly explore the dynamics of this process.

2.4. The emergence of football hooliganism as a national 'cause of concern'

Our findings lead us to believe that, from the first predominantly proletarian crowds of the 1880s and 1890s until the emergence of football hooliganism as a national 'cause for concern' in the early 1960s, there occurred a gradual decline in the rate of football crowd disorder. This process was not continuously 'progressive' but short-term fluctuations need not concern us here. In order to gain an adequate understanding of it, one needs, above all, to avoid an *ahistorical* view of the working class. By this, we mean that it seems likely that, around the turn of the century, a greater proportion of the membership of that class would have lived under social conditions and adhered to standards of behaviour that approximate to those of the present-day 'rough' working class than is currently the case. If this supposition is correct, it helps to account for the frequency of football crowd disorder in a period when the majority of spectators were from the 'respectable' working class. In the course of the twentieth century, however, the upper strata of the working class have undergone a process of increasing incorporation, that is, the standards to which they adhere have moved closer to those of the dominant social groups. While the lower strata of the working class have not been unaffected by this process, they have remained *relatively* untouched.

This general process and the concomitant differentiation of the working class are deserving of at least a paper in themselves. In this context, however, it must suffice to say that the gradual incorporation of the upper working class appears to have occurred relatively slowly during the inter-war years and to have accelerated after the Second World War, particularly from the mid-1950s with the emergence of the so-called 'affluent worker'. A consequence was that members of the upper working class who attended football matches, and who constituted the majority of the crowd, not only increasingly refrained from disorderly conduct themselves but came to view with growing distaste the diminishing sections who continued to disrupt matches. The discrepancy between the diverging standards of these groups reached a critical point towards the end of the 1950s. At that conjecture, the growing antagonism between the increasingly 'respectable' majority and the 'rough' minority, which had parallels in other areas of social life, began to find expression in the press. Incidents of disorder which, to varying degrees, had long characterized the professional game, began to be presented in dramatic relief. Match days and football grounds came to be portrayed, albeit inadvertently, as times and places at which fighting could be engaged in and aggressive masculinity displayed with relative impunity. As a result, the game began to attract growing numbers of youthful members of the 'rough' working class.

Other developments in the early 1960s worked in this direction, too. For example, before that time, little or no action seems to have been taken by the state and local authorities to curb unruly behaviour by football spectators. That is, fan disorderliness was defined as a problem to be dealt with by the football authorities on their own. Nor is there any evidence before that period of a 'moral panic' on this issue, that is, of a widespread perception of soccer grounds as 'dangerous' places and, as such, symptomatic of a serious 'social problem' for which state intervention was urgently required. However, as Cohen (1973) has noted, starting in the 1960s, "... there was a steady build-up of an image of football hooliganism as a massive new national problem, one that was increasing and becoming more intense".

The preparations for the World Cup staged in Britain in 1966 were of some significance in this regard, for this event meant that British crowds were about to come under scrutiny from the international press. As a result, newspapers began to focus on football hooliganism as a threat to national prestige. Around the same time, too, they started to send reporters to matches specifically to cover crowd incidents rather than the match itself. Television coverage was increased as well and TV commentators focused increasingly on the crowd. In this way, the subterranean current of spectator misbehaviour which, as we have shown, has never died out, was highlighted. An 'amplification spiral' was set in motion and, in that context, the media resorted increasingly to a rhetoric of violence, frequently exaggerating the level and extent of the violence that was actually involved. Widespread publicity was given to a definition of match days and football grounds as times and places where 'real' fights regularly took place and, as an unintended consequence, football became publicly defined in a manner that made it consonant with the norms and values of violent masculinity. Hence, the attractiveness of the game to adolescent and young adult males from the lower working class increased. In consequence, they started attending matches more regularly and more frequently than ever before.

3. Conclusion

We have outlined above a hypothetical structural explanation of football hooligan fighting. We have supported it by means of a sociological diagnosis of some crucial aspects of football as a spectator sport and by reference to historical data about crowd disorderliness and the social composition of football crowds. It is important to stress that our hypothesis does not assert that all youths who engage in football hooligan fighting come from what one might call segmentally structured communities or that all youths who come from such communities engage in football hooligan fighting. It merely implies that such youths are the most *centrally* and *persistently* involved. As such, particularly given the intensive coverage of their activities by the media, they may have come to form a reference group for some disaffected youths from 'respectable' working class and middle class backgrounds.

Our approach to football hooliganism differs considerably from that of other contributors to the field. Ian Taylor and John Clarke, for example, have both, to varying degrees, underplayed the fact that crowd disorderliness has been a more or less constant feature of the Association game. Taylor (1971a) sees it as the response of a 'subcultural rump' to a decline in the 'real' or, more likely, the perceived 'participatory democracy' that used to characterize the professional game. By contrast, we have argued that present-day football hooligans come mainly from a section of society which has traditionally had weak ties with the 'soccer subculture'. Clarke (1978) views football hooliganism as an entirely new phenomenon, a consequence of the widening generation gap in the period after the Second World War and of the correlative decline in adult supervision and tutelage of young supporters. We have argued that the central participants come from communities where young males have traditionally been left very much to their own devices.

Our approach also differs from that of Marsh et al. (1978). Their central thesis is that football hooligan fighting is ritual in character and thus not seriously violent. We agree that it contains ritual components but our data suggest that it is also, on occasions, seriously violent. In short, in our view, ritual violence and serious violence are not mutually exclusive alternatives as Marsh and his colleagues seem to imply. Press accounts have tended to exaggerate the seriousness of football hooligan violence. The work of March et al., however, tends to minimize its seriousness. In that way, they have inadvertently served to obscure the social roots of the phenomenon. It is our view that an adequate understanding of football hooliganism requires the location of this kind of behaviour in the structural setting within which the generation of the norms and values that underlie it takes place.

References

Clarke, J., 1978. Football and working class fans. In: R. Ingham, ed., Football hooliganism. London: Inter-action Imprint.

Cohen, S., 1973. Campaigning against vandalism. In: C. Ward, ed., Vandalism. London: Architectural Press.

Department of Education and Science, 1968. Report of the (Chester) Committee on Football. London: HMSO.

Departmental Committee on Crowds, 1924. Report; Cmnd 2088. London: HMSO.

Elias, N., 1978. The civilizing process, vol. 1. Oxford: Blackwell.

Green, G., 1953. A history of the Football Association. London: Naldrett.

Harrington, J.A., 1968. Soccer hooliganism. Bristol: John Wright.

Harrison, P., 1974. Soccer's tribal wars. New Society, 5 September.

Hutchinson, J., 1975. Some aspects of football crowds before 1914. In: The working class and leisure. Proceedings of the Conference of the Society for the Study of Labour History, University of Sussex.

Marsh, P., E. Rosser, R. Harré, 1978. The rules of disorder. London: Routledge.

Mason, A., 1980. Association football and English society 1863–1915. Brighton: Harvester.

Robins, D., P. Cohen, 1978. Knuckle sandwich. Harmondsworth: Penguin.

Suttles, G.D., 1968. The social order of the slum. London: University of Chicago Press.

Taylor, I., 1971a. Football mad: A speculative sociology of football hooliganism. In: E.G. Dunning, ed., The sociology of sport. London: Cass.

Taylor, I., 1971b. Soccer consciousness and soccer hooliganism. In: S. Cohen, ed., Images of deviance. Harmondsworth: Penguin.

Trivizas, E., 1980. Offences and offenders in football crowd disorders. British Journal of Criminology 20 (3).

Vamplew, W., 1979. Ungentlemanly conduct: The control of soccer crowd behaviour in England, 1888–1914. In: T.C. Smouth, ed., The search for wealth and stability. London: Macmillan.

Walvin, J., 1975. The people's game. London: Allen Lane.

Abstract: E.G. Dunning et al., The sociogenesis of football hooligan violence
This paper is a resumé of our research into football hooliganism in Britain. It argues that this phenomenon can be appropriately depicted as a form of aggressive masculinity and that this activity is predominantly the preserve of lower working class youths. The paper sets out to explain the sociogenesis of these distinctive standards of aggression in terms of the characteristics of lower working classes communities and the position they occupy in the broader social structure. It considers the traditional attractiveness of Association Football to sections of the working class and relates long-term changes in the rate of spectator disorder to changes in the social class composition of the crowd, a phenomenon which is itself connected to the broader process of working class 'incorporation'. Finally, we briefly place our thesis in the context of other work in the field.

CHAPTER 14

The role of vandalism in delinquent careers

L.W. SHANNON

The visibility and high cost of vandalism has focused attention on this offense in recent years. [1] Between 1970 and 1980 the vandalism arrest rate increased by 52.3% for the U.S., 55.8% for cities, and 58.4% for rural areas. During the same period the total arrest rate increased 8.5% for the U.S., 4.6% for cities, but 62.6% for rural areas, although the arrest rate for the latter still remained considerably below that for cities. [2]

Although vandalism has been usually considered a juvenile offense (in 1971 persons under age 18 were arrested in a ratio of almost three to one to those over 18), arrest trends for this offense have been up far more sharply during the period from 1970 to 1980 for persons aged 18 and over (almost equal numbers of persons were arrested under and over age 18 in 1980). At the same time, the percent of those charged with vandalism who have been convicted has increased and the percent of those charged with all offenses who have been convicted has declined.

Still, one must recognize that vandalism plays only a small part in all offenses which result in arrest and being held for prosecution. Of those arrested in the United States in 1970, vandalism arrests comprised only 1.72% of the total and had increased to only 2.41% by 1980. During the same time period, however, the percent of youthful arrests (those under 18 years of age) for vandalism increased from 4.91% to 5.71%. Although persons over age 18 made up a larger proportion of all persons who were arrested for vandalism, this offense rose from 0.64% to still only 1.56% of their total arrests. The proportion of all male arrests that were for vandalism increased from 1.83% in

[1] The data for this paper were collected under Grants Number 77JN-99-0019 and 79 JN-AX-0010 from the Office of Juvenile Justice and Delinquency Prevention, U.S. Department of Justice. Points of view or opinions in this document are those of the author and do not necessarily represent the official position of policies of the U.S. Department of Justice. Judith McKim (Senior Research Assistant) and Lawrence Haffner (Programmer) of the Iowa Urban Community Research Center assisted in the analysis. A lengthier version of this paper including statistical tables and maps may be obtained from the author.
[2] All references in this paper to offense rates in the United States have been taken from or calculated from data in the *Uniform Crime Reports for the United States*, Federal Bureau of Investigation, U.S. Department of Justice, Washington, D.C., 1970 through 1980.

1970 to 2.61% in 1980 while a lesser increase from 0.90% to 1.32% was registered for females. Similar changes were found in the cities and in rural areas of the United States, although vandalism constituted even a lower proportion of both male and female arrests in the latter.

No definitive effort has been made to determine how vandalism fits into delinquent and criminal careers. And that is because most research reports are on vandalism rather than the lives and careers of vandals. Are vandals just vandals? Are there some who are only vandals and some for whom vandalism is only a part of their larger repertoire of delinquent and criminal behaviors? Do vandals have more continuity in their careers than non-vandals? Is vandalism early in one's career predictive of a longer and more serious career? Is vandalism intertwined with other juvenile offenses among those who are continuously involved in miscreant behavior?

What do we know about the ecology of vandalism – is property in some areas more likely to be vandalized and are those who are socialized in some areas more likely to be vandals than are others? It is our intention to answer all of these questions as the story of our research unfolds.

1. Racine, the belle city of Wisconsin

Racine, Wisconsin, is a city of 100,000 population situated on the western shores of Lake Michigan some 70 miles north of Chicago. In 1908 Racine had a crime index of 6,981.5, New York an index of 8,952.8, and Chicago one of 5,721.8. Thus it fell between two major cities.

During the period 1949 to 1961, Part I or Index Offenses in Racine were fairly stable, less than 40 per 1,000 persons per year, but commencing in 1962 they started to rise sharply, continuing to a peak of around 170 per year in 1974–1976, then commencing to fall. A similar trend was found for arrests for Part I offenses during this period, paralleling those for the United States during the same period. Racine's increasing proportion of persons charged with violent property destruction (1.28% in 1965 to 2.27% to 3.70% in 1977) suggests that it has been increasing at a pace comparable to that in other urban areas in the United States. [3]

2. Vandalism and violent property destruction in three birth cohorts in Racine

2.1. The birth cohort data

The data on vandalism and violent property destruction to which we now turn are derived from official police records on three Racine birth cohorts and from

[3] Persons Charged with Offenses, Racine Police Department, 1965–1977.

self-reports on persons from two of these cohorts. Only those 4,079 persons who had essentially continuous residence in the city from the age of six to the year that data collection in their cohort ceased (age 33 for the 1942 cohort, 26 for the 1949 cohort, and 21 for the 1955 cohort) are included in this analysis. Official records for three birth cohorts and self-report data about the 889 persons whom we interviewed from two of the cohorts (1942 and 1949) enables us to see how serious and continuing delinquent and criminal careers develop for a small proportion of each group, a group of 5% with two or three felonies each who account for roughly 85% of the felonies and many of the other offenses that bring people from each cohort into contact with the justice system (Shannon, 1980).

2.2. Violent property destruction and vandalism: police records

Less than 1% of all police contacts were for violent property destruction (this includes, for both juveniles and adults, arson and destruction of property by the use of explosives and, for adults, criminal damage to property), with the age period 18–20 being that in which this offense made up the greatest proportion of all offenses. This percentage looks small in comparison with the proportion of all police contacts that are for Part I or Index Offenses (6.5% for the 1942 cohort, 10.0% for the 1949 cohort, and 20.5% for the 1955 cohort). Furthermore, its proportion of all offenses has scarcely increased from cohort to cohort by comparison. Less than 1% of each cohort have had a police contact for this offense alone. Only 1.7%, 1.5%, and 2.1% of each of the three cohorts respectively had a violent property destruction contact at any point in their careers.

Only 6.56% of the 1955 cohort had had a recorded police contact for vandalism during the juvenile period. Of the total number of contacts by this cohort, only 2.51% were for vandalism, a figure which, although not an arrest figure, is reasonable because it is quite comparable to the proportion that vandalism constituted (approximately 2%) of all arrests in cities in the U.S. or to the 1.89% in 1970 and 3.04% in 1980 for cities with a 50,000–100,000 population in the U.S. It is also comparable, when transformed into a rate per 100,000 (93.1), to the 83.9 in 1970 to 141.3 in 1980 for other cities of this size in the United States.

2.3. Vandalism: self-report

Direct comparison of the Racine self-report data with other studies is difficult for a variety of reasons. We had only 16 broad offense categories while other self-report studies have had as many as 47. Differences in wording also make comparability problematic. For example, in the self-report study by Short and Nye, their category, 'Purposely damaged or destroyed private or public property', was broader than our 'Have you ever intentionally destroyed, damaged,

or marked up any property that would cost *more* than $20 to repair or replace?'
Consequently, when 60.7% of the high school Midwestern boys and 44.8% of
the Western boys (21.7% and 13.6% of their girls) responded in the affirmative,
it was not comparable to our 15.3% for the 1942 cohort and 16.0% for the 1949
cohort for the ages 6–17. On the other hand, our question on taking a car
without the owner's consent was sufficiently comparable that their 11.2% and
14.8% for boys and 5.4% and 4.5% for girls can be compared to our 8.0% for
the 1942 cohort and 10.0% for the 1949 cohort.

More recent self-report studies using definitions as broad as those of Short
and Nye have continued to show similar levels of high involvement in
vandalism by males and females and, even when a national sample aged 11–17
was questioned about their activities during the past year (Ageton and Elliott,
1978), 24% of the boys and 10% of the girls admitted property destruction.
Turning back to Racine self-report data, it is interesting to note that while
13.9% admitted vandalism during the age period 6–17, only 2.6% acknowledged it during the age period 18–20.

But to put vandalism in perspective we must also note that 39.9% admitted
shoplifting, 9.2% auto theft, 12.0% burglary, but only 2.1% armed robbery. The
most frequently admitted offense was drinking under age, 56.0%, and the least
frequently admitted offense was drugs, although the latter rose from 1.8% in
the 1942 cohort to 13.8% in the 1949 cohort for ages 18 through 20. Thus,
while we are concerned about vandalism, it is not even one of the most
frequently admitted offenses on self-report forms.

That self-report vandalism for the juvenile period is intertwined with official
records of police contact is shown by the fact that of those who admitted
engaging in vandalism (15.3% and 16.0%) during this period, 58.8% of the 1942
cohort had official records of police contact, as did 61.8% of the 1949 cohort.
Thus, only 9.0% and 9.9% of the two cohorts admitted vandalism and also had
official records of any police contacts. But of those who did not admit
vandalism, only 32.6% and 43.3% had official records of police contacts for
any reason.

2.4. Vandalism and career seriousness

This brings us to the question of whether or not persons with official records of
vandalism have extensive involvement in other types of delinquency and crime.
Table 1 suggests that persons with a police contact for vandalism as juveniles
do indeed have more serious careers than persons who have not had such
contacts.

The average seriousness of juvenile careers for those with at least one
vandalism contact is considerably higher than that for those who had police
contacts but no vandalism contact. This difference is maintained in each
succeeding age period. Furthermore, the average accrued seriousness for per-

Table 1. Mean seriousness of careers at various age periods for persons with and without vandalism contact ages 6–17: 1955 cohort.

	6–17	18–20	21 +	All age periods	N
No juvenile police contacts	0.00	0.72	0.27	0.99	1202
Police contacts but no vandalism	8.00	4.33	1.17	14.27	806
Police contacts including vandalism	37.01	10.57	2.73	50.26	141

sons with vandalism contacts as juveniles is three times as large as is that for those who had only other types of police contacts. While it is agreed that this is a rough indicator of the larger involvement of those who had police contacts for vandalism as juveniles, 58.9% of the 141 persons from the 1955 cohort who did have vandalism contacts as juveniles were in the top 10% of the seriousness distribution for that cohort at ages 6–17, 34.0% at 18–20, and 28.4% at the 21 and older age period. For all age periods combined, 53.2% of those who had a police contact for vandalism as juveniles had career seriousness scores which placed them in the top 10% of the seriousness distribution.

Put differently, when vandalism 6–17 was used as a predictor variable in a regression analysis, it accounted for 24.3% of the variation in juvenile seriousness scores, but only 6.3% of the variation in age 18–20 seriousness scores, only 3.4% of the variation in seriousness after 21, and 21.1% of career seriousness scores. By adding race, sex, contacts other than vandalism, and a variable indicating inner city vs. other areas to the equation the variance accounted for increased to 33.5% for juvenile seriousness, 14.7% for 18–20, 10.1% for 21 and older, and 33.0% for career seriousness. In other words, vandalism contacts during the juvenile period were responsible for over two-thirds of the variance in seriousness scores accounted for by it and four other variables combined.

3. The spatial distribution of vandalism by place of offense and place of residence of the vandals

3.1. The spatial distribution of delinquency and crime

Although ecological succession in Racine has not generated concentric circles of relatively homogeneous land use, distinctive 'natural areas' have evolved as the city has grown and developed. The poorest housing may be found adjacent to and intermingled with commercial-industrial areas, other residential areas are interspersed among large park and public use areas, and housing quality generally changes from that which is traditionally found in inner city slums to finer homes which surround the city on much of its periphery. In spite of the irregularity of these areas it was possible to delineate 65 neighborhoods, some of which are primarily commercial-industrial, others a mix, and still other predominantly residential.

Police contact rates for all cohorts during the 1970s by neighborhood of contact and by neighborhood of residence were highest in the inner city and transitional areas and generally lowest in the more peripheral residential areas. While continuity in offense rates by neighborhood of contact and by neighborhood of residence has resulted in the 'hardening' of the inner city, new areas of delinquency and crime have been developing following changes in the spatial distribution of the population, social institutions, and targets for delinquency and crime. We have, indeed, found that prior offense rates, land use, housing quality, and target density are the most powerful variables in explaining around 95% of the variation in neighborhood offense rates in the 1960s and 1970s (Shannon, 1981).

3.2. The spatial distribution of vandalism

The distribution of juvenile police contacts for vandalism by members of the 1955 cohort was similar to the distribution of all police contacts during the 1970s. Vandalism contacts were concentrated in the inner city and interstitial areas but there are also some high contact areas toward the periphery related to target density (the number of taverns, restaurants, grocery and convenience stores, liquor stores, and automotive service stations). When the proportion of all contacts in the neighborhood that are for vandalism and the proportion of all contacts that cohort members residing in the neighborhood have had for vandalism, regardless of where the contact took place, were considered, a rather irregular picture was generated, some of the stable and peripheral residential areas having surprisingly high relative proportions of their police contacts involving vandalism. Thus, even though vandalism rates are the highest among juveniles in neighborhoods where juveniles have high rates for other offenses, this differs markedly from its proportion of all offenses by place of occurrence and by neighborhood of residence of those who engage in vandalism.

Let us now be more specific. There were eight neighborhoods in which *none* of the juveniles who resided there had a police contact for vandalism. All except one of those neighborhoods included were peripheral better residential neighborhoods. At the opposite extreme were 21 neighborhoods in which at least 10% of the 1955 cohort members had at least one vandalism contact. There were only two in which less than 50% of the 1955 cohort members had no police contacts. These 21 neighborhoods were widely distributed throughout the city with seven on or near the periphery. The remainder had a range from

25% to 75% of their members with no police contacts but with only from 2% to 8% with a vandalism contact included in their records.

Although the vandalism rate of juveniles who resided in the inner city and interstitial neighborhoods was generally much higher than that for persons who resided elsewhere in the city, the contribution of vandalism to the careers of those who had police contacts or to the occurrence of vandalism as a proportion of neighborhood delinquency showed much less spatial concentration.

3.3. The spatial distribution of violent property destruction

The spatial distribution of police contacts for violent property destruction by cohort members was even more concentrated in some respects than that for vandalism, 27 neighborhoods not having difficulty with cohort members for this reason. In only 16 neighborhoods were 1% or more of the police contacts by cohort members for violent property destruction. (Three had no cohort residents but cohort members from other neighborhoods had such contacts there.) But, these neighborhoods were scattered throughout the city with more than half consisting of stable middle class or better residential neighborhoods on the city's periphery and others located in the inner city or transitional area.

There were also 24 neighborhoods whose cohort residents did not have any police contacts for violent property destruction (six were excluded because they did not have at least five cohort members) and 13 in which over 1% of the police contacts by those who resided there were for violent property destruction. Only two of these neighborhoods had also had more than 1% of the cohort contacts which took place in the neighborhood occur for violent property destruction. Two-thirds of the neighborhoods whose cohort residents had sufficient violent property destruction contacts to equal at least 1% of their contacts were again stable middle class or better residential areas on the periphery of the city. Of the 14 neighborhoods whose cohort members had no police contacts for violent property destruction, 14 also had less than 1% of their in-neighborhood contacts by cohort members for this reason. These neighborhoods were, with one exception, outside the inner city and transitional areas.

When the members of each cohort were considered cohort by cohort, it was significant that those who had a violent property destruction contact in their careers could be found in only eight neighborhoods for the 1942 cohort, 14 neighborhoods for the 1949 cohort, but in 30 neighborhoods for the 1955 cohort. Only three of these neighborhoods with persons involved in violent property destruction were outside the inner city and interstitial areas in the 1942 cohort, four in the 1949 cohort, but 15 were outside the inner city and interstitial areas in the 1955 cohort. This increasingly greater dispersion in residential location of those who engaged in violent property destruction was found whether the juvenile or adult or total career was considered. Even taking into consideration the growth of the city and the addition of new peripheral neighborhoods from cohort to cohort, this is an indication that persons who are destructive of property are spread throughout the community much more widely than before.

4. The delinquent and criminal careers of persons with contacts for vandalism

Thus far, we have been concerned with the extent and distribution of vandalism, some of the characteristics of vandals, the distribution of vandals by place or residence, and the relationship of vandalism to seriousness and continuity in careers. Now for a look at some of the vandals, a preliminary look that will sensitize us a bit to different types of vandals.

4.1. A vandal

Take the case of Buddy Butz, born in 1955, the son of a teacher and later principal in some of the better peripheral schools in Racine. Their home was also in a good residential area. In January of 1973 at the age of 18 he was apprehended for vandalism, accused of committing physical damage of 46 motor vehicles in the City of Racine on 14 different days between November of 1972 and January of 1973. A hearing was held in February and the petition was dismissed upon agreement to pay over $500, half of the sum to be collected from Nippy Knox, who was also involved in the vandalism of these autos. Through September 1977 Buddy had only two further contacts, one a minor traffic accident and the other for driving without a license. This case is a good example of episodic juvenile vandalism and certainly cannot be considered a career.

4.2. Two delinquent boys

The next two cases are for boys who lived in the same block or within a block or two of each other in the inner city at the ages of 11 through 14 and were in company and in difficulty for the same offenses on numerous occasions. The records indicate that they vandalized property, stole things, ran away from home, burglarized homes, and later together violated the terms of their supervision by the juvenile court.

One of the two boys, Andy Oleson, had acquired 25 police contacts, the first being for vandalism at the age of 11, for a total of eight vandalism contacts during the next three years. Interspersed with these were contacts for minor offenses but as he grew older contacts for theft and burglary appeared on his record. He was also truant from school and a runaway from home on several occasions before reaching the age of 18. By the age of 21 he had also acquired several moving vehicle citations including a hit and run accident. Although he had been placed under supervision of the court as a juvenile, his only offenses as an adult were five traffic violations, for which he had paid substantial fines, over $100 on the last occasion. His juvenile seriousness score was 59, a score which placed him in the top 2% of the cohort. His father was a machine operator.

Roger Jones, his companion, had a similar but more serious career. His father was a factory worker at American Motors. His 33 police contacts include five for vandalism. His first police contact was at the age of 10 but not until his fourth police contact at the age of 11 was he, according to the records, involved in vandalism. Most of the vandalism offenses were not serious (breaking school windows with stones) but his other difficulties, including theft (shoplifting), burglary, truancy from school, and uncontrollable behavior (he was judged wayward and habitually disobedient), resulted in his being placed under court supervision at the age of 14 and then at the age of 15 being placed on formal probation for two years. He and Andy were apprehended for burglary while under supervision. He later ran away from home while on probation. At no time was he institutionalized. His most recent police contacts were for moving vehicle violations, for which he was fined. His juvenile seriousness score was 77, placing him in the top 1% of the 1955 cohort. But neither Andy nor Roger continued on to have careers in adult crime, insofar as we know.

4.3. Boys who continue into adult crime

John Johnson had 39 police contacts, 35 as a juvenile. His father was employed as a laborer at American Motors and the family resided in a middle class area near the edge of the city. His first contact at the age of six was for theft and his second at that age for the first of seven vandalism contacts, this for breaking school windows, for which his mother punished him. In the course of his career, he stole or assisted in the theft of at least six automobiles, for which he was placed on two years probation, had his driver's license suspended, and was required to make restitution for damages to the automobiles. Within two weeks of the auto thefts disposition he was charged with burglary of a residence, required to make restitution, and had his probation continued. Within a year and a half probation was terminated. It was reported that his school record was good, he had a part-time job, and had stayed out of trouble since the last offense for which he had been continued on probation. In addition to those offenses already mentioned, in the course of his career he was charged with a wide variety of other offenses including assault and disorderly conduct. His juvenile seriousness score of 108 placed him in the top 1% of the cohort.

Although it appeared that he had ceased to be a problem at the age of 17, at the age of 18 he was again in trouble and continued to remain in trouble, even after marriage, for such offenses as disorderly conduct and theft.

The case of Larry Lumpkin is even more complex. Larry's father was a bartender. The family always resided in the inner city. Larry had 44 police contacts as a juvenile and 12 as an adult. Only ten persons in the entire cohort had higher career seriousness scores. Of all his police contacts, however, only five were for vandalism. It also turns out that he was involved with Andy and Roger in several escapades. But the main point here is that vandalism played a small part in his delinquent and criminal career. His first three contacts, commencing at the age of seven, were for theft. From then on he was continuously in trouble, thefts interspersed with other reasons for police contact, including burglary. At the age of 13 he was first involved in vandalism (with Andy and Roger) and at that age he had his run of contacts for vandalism. His record reveals that more of his contacts were for theft than any other offense, several each year during the early teens. On numerous occasions he was also involved with other youths suspected of marijuana use.

From the age of 15 on he was either on probation or involved in various programs designed to resocialize youth of this type. His father was uncooperative with the authorities and all attempts to place Larry in a home where he would experience a structured environment were rebuffed. On several occasions petitions alleging delinquency were dismissed. It was not until the age of 17 after numerous referrals that he was finally found delinquent and placed on probation for one year. At the age of 18 he was apprehended for attempted rape. He was also charged with burglary at that age but the petition was dismissed when he agreed to pay restitution.

After reaching 18 he continued to be a source of trouble in the community, frequently receiving fines for disorderly conduct, but as often having the charges dismissed. When follow-up on the 1955 cohort ceased he was managing to get into trouble as frequently as before, having received three years' probation and 60 days in the County Jail at the age of 21 for burglary.

His father and mother had been continuously in contact with the police for difficulties of one sort or another of their own and it would appear that the home atmosphere was one of frequent disturbances – the home and tavern combining to create a violent milieu in which the boy had been socialized.

These cases lead us to the conclusion that vandalism is simply one of many offenses committed by persons with delinquent careers, careers that may or may not lead to adult criminal careers.

Having examined a few cases in which vandalism played a small part, a fairly substantial part, or most of the misbehavior of a juvenile career, we turn to the multivariate analysis which should permit a more definitive statement.

5. The multivariate analysis

Preliminary to the discriminant function analysis described in this section it was found that there was very little difference between persons with vandalism contacts and those with only misbehavior other than vandalism by race, head of household's occupational level, several measures of place of residence as inner city and interstitial vs. stable and peripheral residential areas, and land use in neighborhoods. Persons with vandalism contacts had significantly more police contacts at an earlier age, had more official dispositions of their contacts as juveniles, had been more severely sanctioned as juveniles, had more offenses against persons, property, public disorder, and status offenses than did those who had not had vandalism contacts.

In a series of preliminary multiple discriminant function analyses with variables entered in groups, the relationship of these variables to vandalism took on a different light. Persons with vandalism contacts had earlier first contacts but less serious reasons for contact, more status offenses, were not the children of white-collar workers, and resided in lower SES neighborhoods. In the next stage, only those variables which had consistently discriminated were included; age at first police contact, number of contacts as a juvenile, and seriousness of contacts as a juvenile remained as one basis for classification, while number of offenses against persons, property, and status offenses remained as another.

In the first instance, the canonical discriminant function could be used to correctly classify 56.7% of those who had reported vandalism and 89.3% of those who did not; the total correct classification was 84.5%. Since there were only 141 persons with vandalism contacts and the above percentages involved classifying 61 persons who had vandalism contacts incorrectly as non-vandals and 86 persons as having vandalism contacts who did not, there was a total of 147 errors, six more than would have been made if all had been classified as non-vandals. The latter would have resulted in only 14.9% error, or 85.1% correct classifications. In the second instance, type of other contacts during the juvenile period resulted in correctly classifying 86.5% of those involved (10% more than chance), a very slight increase over the prediction based on the modal category of the marginals, i.e., that no one would have had vandalism contacts during the juvenile period.

Although those members of the 1955 cohort who had vandalism contacts in their careers differed in other respects in terms of their careers from those who did not have vandalism contacts, the early onset, number of police contacts, and less serious nature of their careers did not permit any sizeable decrease in classification errors beyond those which would be made by assuming that none had vandalism contacts in their careers.

The same approach was utilized in an effort to better predict the inclusion of violent property destruction in the official careers of members of the combined cohorts and with almost identical results, the only difference being that age of first police contact was later rather than earlier for persons with violent property destruction in their official records.

6. Summary and conclusions

Although vandalism in the United States has been considered an offense more characteristic of youth than adults and remains so, the sizeable and disproportional increase in arrest rates for this offense must be attributed to an increase in vandalism by persons age 18 and older. Still, it plays only a small part in the total arrests of persons of all ages in the United States and remains a predominantly male offense.

Official records from Racine, Wisconsin revealed that very few of the persons in each of the birth cohorts have police contacts for violent property destruction as part of their delinquent and/or criminal careers. Only 6.56% of the 1955 cohort even had a police contact for vandalism during the juvenile period and only 2.51% of their contacts were for vandalism. While it is admitted that much of the youthful vandalism goes unnoticed officially, only 15% and 16% of the 1942 and 1949 cohorts even admitted engaging in vandalism as juveniles.

On the other hand, persons with both official and self-report vandalism had more serious official police records than those who did not have vandalism as part of their careers. While vandalism contacts during the juvenile period accounted for only 24.3% of the variation in juvenile seriousness scores, it accounted for more variation than did other variables in a multiple regression analysis.

Although vandalism, as do other police contacts, has a higher rate of occurrence in the inner city and interstitial areas, it does not play a disproportionate part in the careers of persons who reside in these areas nor does it constitute a disproportionate number of the total police contacts by neighborhood of residence or neighborhood of contact of cohort members.

Police contacts for violent property destruction by the combined cohort members were concentrated in one-fourth of the neighborhoods (16) but these were scattered throughout the city, as were the even fewer neighborhoods (13) in which cohort members resided who had police contacts for violent property destruction. However, it should be noted, and this is important because it relates to the increasing concern about vandalism and violent property destruction, that persons with violent property destruction in their careers were found in an ever-widening group of neighborhoods from cohort to cohort, eight, 14, and then 30 by the 1955 cohort, with exactly half of these neighborhoods outside the inner city and interstitial areas for the latter cohort.

Perusal of the complete records of a group from the 1955 cohort with police contacts for vandalism during the juvenile period again revealed that vandalism is one of many offenses committed by persons with delinquent careers that may or may not lead to adult criminal careers, although there are some persons with serious juvenile and/or adult careers whose contacts consist almost entirely of incidents of vandalism.

In the last section of this paper, the data were analyzed following the multiple discriminant function routine in an effort to determine if the characteristics of those persons in the 1955 cohort who had vandalism contacts in their juvenile careers were sufficiently different from those who had only non-vandalism contacts to permit classification with fewer errors than would be made by assigning everyone to the modal category of the marginals. Little or no improvement was made in classification accuracy over that obtained by assuming that there were no vandals. Similar findings were made for members of the combined cohorts who had juvenile contacts for violent property destruction. In essence, there are so few persons in these categories that they are not sufficiently discriminated to be separable from that vast group of juvenile miscreants who make continuous research on juvenile delinquency and adult crime an important endeavor if we are to ultimately reduce the cost of delinquency and crime to society.

References

Ageton, S.S., D.S. Elliott, 1978. The incidence of delinquent behavior in a national probability sample. Boulder (Colorado): Behavioral Research Institute.

Federal Bureau of Investigation, 1970 through 1980. Uniform crime reports for the United States. Washington, D.C.: U.S. Department of Justice.

Shannon, L.W., 1980. Assessing the relationship of adult criminal careers to juvenile careers. Washington, D.C.: U.S. Department of Justice.

Shannon, L.W., 1981. The relationship of juvenile delinquency and adult crime to the changing ecological structure of the city. Final Report to Department of Justice.

Short, J.F., Jr., F.I. Nye, 1958. Extent of unrecorded juvenile delinquency: Tentative conclusions. Journal of Criminal Law, Criminology and Police Science 49, 296–302.

Abstract: L.W. Shannon, The role of vandalism in delinquent careers
Official police records from Racine, Wisconsin, are utilized in determining the relationship of vandalism and violent property destruction to other forms of delinquency and crime. Very few of the persons in each of three birth cohorts (born in 1942, 1949, and 1955) have police contacts for violent property destruction. Only 6.56% of the 1955 cohort had a police contact for vandalism during the juvenile period and only 2.51% of all police contacts by this cohort were for vandalism. Only 15% and 16% of the 1942 and 1949 cohorts admitted engaging in vandalism as juveniles. Those with both official and self-report vandalism had more serious official police records than those who did not have vandalism as part of their careers.

Although there are some persons with serious juvenile and/or adult careers whose contacts consist almost entirely of incidents of vandalism, it is one of many offenses committed by persons with delinquent careers that may or may not lead to adult criminal careers. A discriminant function analysis differentiated between vandals and non-vandals but little or no improvement was made in classification accuracy over that obtained by assuming that there were no vandals. Similar findings were made for members of the combined cohorts who had juvenile contacts for violent property destruction.

PART FOUR

Public attitude towards vandalism

INTRODUCTION

The public's perceptions of vandalism

S. COHEN

The dimension of 'public attitudes' is crucial whether one approaches the subject of vandalism with the theoretical interest of a social scientist or the practical interest of a policy maker (or victim).

The social scientist should be aware that vandalism, like any other form of deviance, is behaviour which is perceived and categorized in many different ways. These perceptions both depend on and determine the dominant modes of understanding the phenomenon – whether in the media, public opinion, the control system or the professional theories which social scientists themselves use. All these groups are thus not just passive audiences, but active participants in the drama of vandalism: they make fateful decisions, they influence the gathering of statistics and they allocate priorities. They determine where and how vandalism is placed on the agenda of any particular society.

This leads to the policy interest. Both at the organizational level (schools, public housing authorities, services) and at the overall political level, decisions are routinely made on the basis of a real or imaginary sense of what 'the public' wants or thinks. These decisions (overall budgeting, manpower, whether or not to repair destroyed property, use of surveillance techniques) are just as often based on prejudice, tradition and guesswork as they are on a firm knowledge of public opinion. If we look, for example, at the more restricted criminological debate on vandalism, it is not at all clear whether the demand for 'justice' in the abstract sense is as important in the public mind as it is in the world of criminal justice politics.

The four papers in this section provide us with interesting material both for the social scientist and the policy maker. Christensen deals with the day-to-day perceptions, guidelines and preferences of managers in one rather special type of setting: parks and recreational facilities in the Western United States. She shows the extreme variability of these responses in what appears to be such a 'simple' setting. Her picture is somewhat incomplete, however, as it does not give us any idea of how *users* (the public) perceive these various impacts and solutions. No solution is really a solution unless its costs are weighed up, both in financial and value terms. The question is not so much whether 93.3% (or whatever) of managers are in favour of "increased patrolling of area by law enforcement", but how much of this sort of solution can be tolerated before it gets worse than the original problem. Vandalism can easily become the sort of social problem where the costs and unintended consequences of the intervention simply create more problems: a case of social policy becoming what Spieber calls a "fatal remedy".

Mawby's research in Sheffield gives us a much clearer sense of the actual context in which attitudes to vandalism are formed and expressed. In addition to other interesting findings about the distribution of the behaviour itself, this research shows us how vandalism becomes defined as a local issue and how it is perceived in terms of the more general problem of living in high rise estates. Residents clearly do not like living in these places and whether or not vandalism is actually *caused* by this dislike, it is clearly the case that vandalism is a constant and visible reminder of just how unpleasant this type of living can be. The "self-perpetuating spiral of decline" which Mawby describes is characteristic of many other forms of vandalism.

These, of course, are the sort of implications for planning, design and management already well discussed in the vandalism literature. But the Sheffield research also hints at another type of policy implication: the punitive response based on some notion of reparation. Vandalism appears often to evoke a public demand for 'paying back' – both in the retributive sense and in the sense of compensation or restoration.

The question of whether vandalism is more or less likely than other offences to stimulate this response, relates to the broader interest in criminology in the public ranking of offences in terms of their seriousness and suitability for certain types of punishment. This interest must in turn be related to the now fashionable so-called 'back to justice' movement. The argument – increasingly dominant in criminal justice politics in the West, particularly the United States – is that punishment should be allocated directly and only in terms of the perceived seriousness of the offence. The obvious empirical questions then arise whether there is consensus about offence 'seriousness' and if so, how this might be affected by situational factors (such as the nature of the victim).

These are the questions addressed by the two related French papers included in this section. They approach the problem, though, not from the criminological perspective but from a number of well-established traditions in psychology: classical psychological work on scaling; the newer interest of cognitive psychologists in how people perceive and attribute meaning to phenomena; and the socio-psychological concern with the variability of social judgements. Moser, Girault and Lévy-Leboyer thus show us patterns of both constancy and variability in the seriousness with which vandalism is rated by different groups and under different conditions. Bideaud and Coslin then locate the judgement of vandalism in terms of the overall processes through which moral judgements are formed.

The results show what sociologists would call 'situated' or 'negotiated' morality. It is not simply that abstract norms or rules (in this case, against property damage) are perceived differently according to variables such as age or class, but rather that invariably highly particularistic and situational judgements (the private or public character of the property destroyed, the consequences of the damage, etc.) are used. These two papers, then, contain data not just of intrinsic interest, but of great potential relevance to the whole 'justice' debate. There is also a wider social policy question indicated by these findings about tolerance and normalization: when and how can behaviour be seen as a 'social problem' or as 'deviant' if it is not in fact perceived as such by the public?

And finally – a less obvious connection – these findings about public perception might also be related back to the behaviour itself. A 'delinquent' group, as Moser et al. show, will have similar attitudes to the offense as a 'non-delinquent' group. They both draw on a common cultural reservoir of motivational accounts in order to justify the behaviour. We thus return to one of the standard problems in the sociology of deviance: how might people break rules while not questioning their general legitimacy?

CHAPTER 15

Vandalism and public perceptions of vandalism in contrasting residential areas

R.I. MAWBY

"For anyone living in one of our large cities vandalism is an inescapable fact of life" (Clarke, 1978: 2). During the 1970s especially, researchers and policy makers were forced to acknowledge that while vandalism was afforded little recognition in criminal statistics, and for the most part incidents involved little cost, it could be distinguished from other crimes as one pervasive urban problem.

There were a number of reasons why vandalism became defined as a serious social problem. Thus, it was readily visible (Cohen, 1973) and extremely common (Clarke, 1978), to the extent that the overall cost of vandalism was considerable. Moreover, whilst the public appeared to have a somewhat vague notion of what vandalism was, most agreed that it was a serious problem (Research Bureau Limited, 1977). Official recognition was also accorded by the Department of the Environment and the Home Office, who, with the death of optimism over penal policies, saw preventive research as a possible solution to the rising tide of crime, and identified the issue of vandalism on publicly rented estates as one to which research could be directed (Burbridge, 1981; Clarke, 1978; Wilson and Burbridge, 1978).

In fact, whilst, as Clarke (1978: 4) diagrammatically illustrates, explanations for vandalism may be sought at a variety of levels, very little research has centred on those who commit acts of vandalism. This is partly because of the low clear-up rate for offences of vandalism, even where these are reported to the police and recorded. However, self-report studies have shown a link between vandalism and parental supervision and social handicap (H. Wilson, 1980, 1982) and between vandalism and peer group activity, parenting, and school achievement (Gladstone, 1978).

Instead, by far the most research has concentrated on the targets for vandalism. On the one hand, there is the finding that vandalism against public rather than private property is common (Sturman, 1978; S. Wilson, 1978). On the other, the design features of modern developments have been noted (Leather and Matthews, 1973; Miller, 1973).

Most especially in this respect, researchers have followed Newman (1973) in considering the extent to which 'defensible space' is an explanation of the amount of vandalism. Newman's work has been criticised on a number of empirical and theoretical grounds (Bottoms, 1974; Herbert, 1982; Mawby, 1977a, 1977b; Mayhew, 1979), but there is nevertheless some evidence that with regard to vandalism – if not crime in general – both feelings of ownership and responsibility and visibility may affect vandalism levels (Mayhew et al., 1979). Certainly, vandalism more than any other offence-type appears to be a feature of public sector housing, and most especially high rise accommodation (Mayhew and Clarke, 1982).

Vandalism is only one of the variety of criminal and quasi-criminal incidents considered in our own research in Sheffield. In summarising the research from the perspective of its relevance to vandalism research, this has both disadvantages and advantages: for while the amount of detail on vandalism is restricted, at the same time we have been able to consider a variety of measurements of vandalism within *specific areas*, in a way which is not always possible in other studies, and we have been able to compare, with other crime, rates of vandalism and perception of vandalism.

This paper is therefore in three parts. In the following section, the research project as a whole is discussed, with particular reference to aspects of the research which covered incidents of vandalism. Then the data are described in terms of the extent of vandalism in the areas covered by the study. Finally, a less common perspective is introduced, namely material on the perception of and attitudes towards vandalism of those living in these different residential areas of the city.

1. An introduction to the Sheffield research

The Sheffield research into urban social structure and crime commenced in 1969 with a study of area variations in indictable crime statistics throughout the city, ultimately establishing patterns for both offence rates (Baldwin and Bottoms, 1976). One problem with this type of analysis, however, is that its dependence on official statistics raises the question of the reliability and validity of such data as measurements of crime (Cicourel, 1968; Douglas, 1979; Kitsuse and Cicourel, 1963). Consequently, the second stage of the research focused on the social processes involved in the creation of crime statistics, through an analysis of policework and the use of a variety of measurements of crime (Mawby, 1979). Ultimately, a household interview survey was conducted in seven residential areas of the city, including both a victimisation study and a series of questions aiming to tap respondents' attitudes towards different crimes (Bottoms et al., 1981).

Because indictable crime statistics for Britain only include malicious damage offences where the cost of the damage is more than £20, most incidents of vandalism were by definition excluded from the first stage of the research. However, in the second stage, data were collected on all criminal or quasi-criminal incidents recorded by the police, as well as other agencies, and these allowed a more detailed consideration of information on vandalism.

In particular, records kept by the Post Office, on damage to public telephone kiosks, provided a detailed account of one aspect of vandalism which avoided problems of under-reporting or under-recording (Mawby, 1977b). In other respects though, official records were of limited validity. Analysis of police recording suggested that, unless an offender was identified, it was extremely unlikely that incidents would be recorded, and consequently acts of vandalism appeared only rarely in police data, even for incidents defined as non-criminal (Mawby, 1979: ch. 2 and 6).

What then of other ways of measuring the occurrence of offences involving criminal damage? At this juncture an attempt was made, for certain areas in the publicly rented (council) sector, to get information from public officials such as estate managers and caretakers. However, the more conventional methods of gaining statistical detail of the 'dark figure' of unrecorded crime are the use of self-report and victim studies. Consequently, in 1975 we carried out a self-report survey of juveniles aged 11–15 from three publicly rented areas of the city, including four items on vandalism (Mawby, 1980). Shortly after this, the household survey in seven areas of the city was completed. This included one question directed at experience of vandalism within the past year, and a number of other questions referring to perceptions of the frequency of vandalism, and appropriate ways of responding to vandalism.

The data from these different sources have been collated in the following two sections. Before detailing them, it is perhaps useful to describe briefly the areas covered in the analysis. The first stage of the research covered the whole of the city of Sheffield, a northern British city concentrated on the steel industry. However, subsequent more detailed analysis was confined to selected *residential* areas within the city. These were distinguished according to three criteria considered important in the early analysis: the offender rate (according to official indictable crime statistics), the predominant tenure type of the area (owner occupied, privately rented, and council owned/publicly rented), and, for the publicly rented sector, age. In fact, this latter distinction was subsequently made a more important feature of the research when, following the publication of Newman's (1973) *Defensible space*, we included two estates of post-war public sector development, both high rise blocks of flats, one with a high offender rate (CFH), the other with a low rate (CFL). [1] In addition, three estates of pre-war conventional public sector housing were included, one with a

---

[1] The three-letter code has been used throughout the second and third stages of the project. The first letter refers to the tenure type of the area (council, rented privately, or owner occupied); the second letter refers to the design type predominating in the area (houses, flats); the third letter refers to the offender rate of the area, using the 1971 standard list file data (high, medium, low).

high official offender rate (CHH), one with a medium rate (CHM) and one with a low rate (CHL). In the privately rented sector, we included one area with a high offender rate (RHH) and two with low rates (RHL and R'HL). Finally, one area of owner occupied housing was selected which had, in common with other such areas in the city, a low offender rate (OHL).

The survey of police and other official records covered these nine areas, and seven (excluding CHM and RHL) were selected for the household interview survey. However, the self-report study was confined to the three areas of pre-war public sector housing (CHH, CHM, and CHL). Thus, while the following sections provide a comprehensive series of data on vandalism, the majority only cover seven of the areas and the self-report survey is restricted to three areas.

2. Vandalism in contrasting residential areas of the city

With the exception of the self-report data, all our information is of incidents occurring in the areas, not of offences by residents of the areas. One further distinction, of course, which is central to much of the literature on vandalism, is that between offences against individuals' property (including property rented by the individual) and vandalism of public or corporate property.

The data collected from the Post Office on kiosk vandalism provided a comprehensive picture of damage to one such public corporation, during 1973–74. The results have been described in detail elsewhere (Mawby, 1977b). However, for present purposes it is perhaps useful to summarise the findings:

(i) Vandalism to kiosks was not anything like as extensive as public outrage implies. In Sheffield as a whole during the period, kiosks were repaired on average about three times per year, at an annual cost of about £7 per kiosk. Moreover, while in the nine survey areas damage was more common, this still amounted to under 3% of kiosk income.

(ii) Comparing incidents in each area, there was no evidence of more vandalism in the high rise flats. However, two other patterns were evident: vandalism in the high offender rate areas was more common than in the low rate areas (with the exception that RHH had a relatively low rate of vandalism), and vandalism in the council sector was greater than in the private sector.

(iii) Relating vandalism to the 'publicness' of the kiosk, there appeared to be two contrary trends. On the one hand, kiosks in more public locations, i.e. open to more public scrutiny, appeared relatively well protected. On the other hand, and more strikingly, kiosks which were used the most were the most likely to be vandalised, leading to the defensible space paradox that "greater use of public space may be provided, not only more witnesses, but also more potential offenders" (Mawby, 1977b; 45).

The fact that telephone kiosks in the high rise areas were not especially likely to be vandalised suggests that the notion of defensible space can be more meaningfully related to specific targets than to whole areas. This was well illustrated both by discussions with council officials and observations of the public-sector housing. Whilst open, publicly owned targets were more common than, say, windows of houses or flats (in both pre-war and post-war estates), and damage in the high offender rate areas exceeded that in the low rate areas, the most notable feature was the extent of damage in the high rise sector. Here, in line with the findings of other researchers, damage to the lifts, graffiti in the corridors and stairways, and broken lights in the public spaces between and within blocks were common. The high rise flats thus provided both more public targets for vandalism and a greater range of poorly protected targets than were evident in the more conventional estates.

While vandalism against public targets is more common than against individuals' property, we were able to consider the latter for the seven areas included in the household survey. Each respondent was asked about specific types of offences of which he or she might have been the victim during the previous 12 months. Subsequently, residents were asked a series of questions concerning up to nine incidents (no more than three from any one offence category). In all, 11% of respondents said that they had been the victim of vandalism during the past year, a figure exceeded only by thefts from outside the dwelling (e.g. on doorstep or from garden). However, as is clear from table 1, while those areas with high offence rates generally also had high rates for vandalism against residents' property, there is no evidence of more vandalism against individuals' property either in the high rise areas or in the council areas compared with the privately rented and owner occupied sector.

This point is an important one, since it has not been made forcibly by earlier writers. Thus, while it seems that council areas, and high rise blocks, have particularly high rates of vandalism, this is restricted to what we have elsewhere described as "the estate outside the dwelling" (Bottoms et al., 1981). There is no evidence here that vandalism against household units (i.e. individual flats/houses, gardens, garages, etc.) is more common in these types of area.

The *extent* of vandalism is, of course, only one aspect of the issue. A more detailed consideration of the incidents themselves reveals that most are of a minor nature. For example, only 13% involved damage costing ten pounds or more, whereas 19% involved no apparent cost. Again, if we assume that willingness to report incidents to the police is an indication of perceived seriousness, again it appears that most vandalism is minor in nature. Thus, only 11% of incidents were reported to the police, compared with 21% of other offences. Indeed, the most common reason for non-reporting, given on 38 occasions, was that the offence was too trivial.

With regard to incidents occurring in the areas, then, the picture is of

Table 1. For the seven areas in the household survey, vandalism reported in the survey compared with all offences reported in the survey and police crime figures.

	CHH	CHL	CFH	CFL	RHH	RHL	OHL
Percentage reporting vandalism	16	10	18	10	16	5	5
Percentage reporting any crime	42	27	58	44	53	27	26
Official indictable offence rate against residents, 1971	85	24	31	20	114	18	10
Official indictable offender rate, 1971	97	32	77	22	142	23	5

vandalism against individuals' property being relatively common, but rarely serious. While some public targets, like telephone kiosks, do not appear to be vandalised as frequently, or as extensively, as might be anticipated, other public targets in the high rise sector, like lifts and lights, are frequently the object of damage. This far, however, we have no detail of the offenders. What then do we know of those who commit damage offences?

In fact, the household survey included, for each victimisation, a question on the offender. For acts of vandalism, 37% of victims alleged they knew who the culprit was, a figure not markedly different from that for other offences. Overall, where an offender was identified he was generally said to live within the area. This was especially the case for vandalism, with 88% of offenders said to live in the area, compared with 66% of offenders for other offences. This suggests that vandalism is especially likely to be a local offence, and supports the overall finding of a correspondence between offence and offender rates in an area.

This is, however, only partly supported by the findings from the self-report study. Comparing data for juveniles from the three pre-war areas of public housing (CHH, CHM and CHL), area differences in offending rates broadly corresponded to the official picture. Thus, for the 19 offence items included in the questionnaire, juveniles from CHH admitted to committing approximately one more offence item than their counterparts from CHL (table 2). With regard to vandalism, the picture was far less clear. Indeed, overall it appeared that social class, age and area differences in admitted vandalism were negligible. On the other hand, as has been shown elsewhere for juveniles from *one* school in the locale, sex differences were considerable (Mawby, 1980). Moreover, as in earlier studies, it is clear that vandalism is closely related to the offending in general – those who commit vandalism are particularly likely to commit other offences.

Table 2. Mean number of items admitted by juveniles from the three areas.

| | Male | | | Female | | |
	CHH	CHM	CHL	CHH	CHM	CHL
All incidents (total 19)	6.02	5.65	5.02	3.10	2.53	2.30
Vandalism incidents (total 4)	1.58	1.46	1.34	0.84	0.42	0.67

Table 3. Percentage who admitted committing each item of vandalism.

	Males	Females
Broke or smashed property	52.9	14.9
Writing on walls	48.1	45.5
Firework vandalism	31.1	3.0
Arson	13.4	3.0
At least one vandalism offence	69.6	50.5

What is clear, and supports other self-report data (Gladstone, 1978), is the extensiveness of vandalism. As is illustrated in table 3, three of the four items included on vandalism were cited by a number of boys, and overall over two-thirds of boys and half the girls admitted committing at least one of the items within the last year. For girls, though, only graffiti vandalism was *common*.

From the data on vandalism in the areas covered by the survey, what then can we say about the extent and distribution of vandalism? On the one hand, it is evident, from both victim survey data and self-report questionnaires, that minor vandalism is extremely common. On the other hand, area differences are not consistently shown. For example, in the pre-war, publicly rented estates rates from the self-report study showed little inter-area variation, while offence rates varied between areas only for certain types of vandalism. In particular, it seemed that the excessive amount of vandalism in high rise and publicly rented areas was restricted to incidents involving 'the estate outside the dwelling', and kiosk vandalism was more common in council areas but not especially high rise estates. Thus, as we turn to consider the impact of this on perceptions of and attitudes towards vandalism, the implications of these findings will be developed.

3. Perceptions of vandalism

It is, of course, commonplace to observe that incidents or seriousness of a problem does not necessarily equate with *perception of* seriousness (Mawby,

1983), and it has already been suggested that the visibility of such vandalism and the extensiveness of minor damage may create an environment within which vandalism may be defined as a problem of considerable magnitude.

In the household survey, three series of questions were asked which were of direct relevance to the current discussion. First, we gave respondents a list of offence types and asked which they felt 'happen most often *round here*'. One of the incidents included related to vandalism, being 'committing vandalism, such as breaking windows, lights or fences, or writing on walls'. Then, later, we introduced series of vignettes and asked householders to respond to each. One vignette described a situation where 'A lot of areas have petty vandalism – like boys smashing windows, breaking fences, and things like that'. Finally, we asked respondents about two hypothetical incidents directly involving themselves, one a burglary, the other vandalism. In the latter case, we described an incident where 'two boys who live down the road/block smash a window or doorpanel in your house/flat. You see them do it'.

In essence, we asked respondents how common they felt vandalism was, what they felt about it, and what they would do about it.

Referring first to estimations of the *extent* of different types of offence, we found that vandalism was identified as common by 66% of householders, more than twice that of any other incident. In contrast, theft from garden or doorstep, the most common offence mentioned in the victim survey sections, was cited by only 28% of the respondents. Moreover, three patterns of inter-area variation were noticeable. First, those living in the flats cited vandalism more often than those living in conventional housing; second, those from the high rate areas mentioned more than those from low rate areas; finally, those from the council sector saw vandalism as more common than did those from the privately rented and owner occupied sectors. Thus, vandalism was cited by 95% of CFH residents, 83% of CFL residents, 80% of those from CHH, 69% of those from RHH, with the remaining areas below average.

The vignettes covered a rather wider range of quasi-criminal and deviant activities, but again vandalism was identified as the most common, with 55% of respondents seeing it as happening very or quite often in their neighbourhood, followed in order of incidence by drunk and disorderly behaviour (36%), television licence evasion (31%), shoplifting (17%) and domestic violence (13%). Here the most notable contrast was between high and low rate areas, but again the council sector, and particularly the high rise estates, stood out. Thus, at the extreme, 92% of CFH householders saw vandalism as common.

The seriousness, rather than the extent, of vandalism can be judged if we consider what respondents felt should be done about the incident. We asked what they would do if they were to see a similar incident occur to someone else's property. Some 30% replied that they would inform the police, although the most common reply was that they would 'tell off' the offender, mentioned by about half the sample. At the extreme, only 7% said that they would do nothing. The most notable variation between areas was that those from the owner occupied sector (OHL) were especially likely to say they would involve the police.

If we compare answers here with equivalent ones for the other vignettes (where appropriate), an interesting pattern emerges. Basically, a similar proportion *said* they would inform the police or other officials if they witnessed the shoplifting or domestic violence, but only a small proportion said that they would do so if they knew of a case of license evasion. However, a far higher proportion in the vandalism example said that they would do *something*. Thus, five times as many people said they would do nothing if they saw an incident of shoplifting, six times as many if they witnessed domestic violence, and nine times as many if they knew of a case of licence evasion. These answers suggest that the public may be more willing to become involved because of the nature of the offenders (i.e. boys rather than adults), because they consider the offence serious, or because they see it as the public's business (as opposed to the example of domestic violence – see Pizzey, 1974).

Another indication of perceived seriousness is gleaned from answers to the question of what the police ought to do if they caught the offenders. Here, at one extreme, about one-fifth of respondents suggested the police should unofficially warn the offenders, while at the other extreme a quarter favoured prosecution. Respondents from the privately rented sector favoured the former, those from CFH the latter, suggesting a link between perceived frequency of offence and attitudes towards police response. It is also worth noting that unofficial warnings were seen as more appropriate in each of the other vignettes (drunken conduct, domestic violence and licence evasion). However, prosecution was also considered *least* appropriate in the case of vandalism, and other alternatives to prosecution (for example, making the offenders pay for the damage) were more likely to be considered than for other incidents.

Responses to the vignette might, of course, be coloured by ideas that since the incident involved other people, it was another person's problem. We therefore also asked about a situation where the respondent was the victim, and compared this with a similar incident involving burglary of a relatively small item (a transistor radio). In fact, although the minority who said they would do nothing shrank to about 1%, the proportion who said they would call the police was approximately the same as before. Interestingly (in contrast to the earlier question), those from the owner occupied area were least likely to say they would involve the police. However, as before, there was no indication that those living in the high rise blocks, with more vandalism, were more inclined to call the police.

In fact, whereas four-fifths of householders said they would call the police in the event of a minor burglary, the most common response to the vandalism item, given by about two-thirds of the sample, was to tell the offenders' parents. The difference is explicable if we consider the reasons given in each case. While between a quarter and a third of respondents were motivated by a deterrent or punitive philosophy ('This sort of thing wants stopping' and 'They deserve punishment'), the most common reason cited for behaving in a particular way, given by one-third, was that this was the most effective means of getting the damage paid for. In contrast, while a smaller proportion said they would call the police to the burglary because they 'want this sort of thing stamped out' or 'want the offender caught', the most common reason for involving the police was to get one's possessions returned.

A number of practical issues arise from the survey data. First, it is clear that if high rise flats evidence poor defensible space qualities as far as vandalism is concerned these are largely restricted to the public areas – lifts, stairs, lights, etc. – not the flats themselves. However, perceptions of the extent of vandalism as a problem are clearly coloured by damage to the area 'outside the dwelling'. Elsewhere (Bottoms et al., 1981) we have stressed the degree to which these flat-dwellers saw their flats in favourable terms, but in marked contrast defined the rest of their area unfavourably. While vandalism is only one element in this concern with 'the estates outside the dwelling' it is clearly an important one, and our findings parallel those of Wilson (1978) in pointing out the self-perpetuating spiral of decline in physical standards. Thus, while the overwhelming unpopularity of the flats, and especially CFH, among residents (which we have detailed elsewhere, Bottoms et al., 1981), cannot be attributed solely to vandalism, damage is a highly visible and constant reminder of the problematic features of high rise living.

These implications are of direct relevance to those involved in planning, design and estate management. Additionally, some of the findings from the household survey can be considered from the viewpoint of those concerned with penal policy. The hypothetical questions on reactions to vandalism suggest that the two primary concerns of the public are for punishment/deterrence and compensation. That is, in line with recent thinking within the criminal justice system, there is some support here, from those principally affected by vandalism, that more needs to be done about the problem, where a solution might be based on reparation, involving both punishment for the offender and compensation for the victim.

References

Baldwin, J., A.E. Bottoms, 1976. The urban criminal. London: Tavistock.
Bottoms, A.E., 1974. Review of 'Defensible space'. British Journal of Criminology 14, 203–206.
Bottoms, A.E., R.I. Mawby, P. Xanthos, 1981. Sheffield study on urban social structure and crime. Part 3. Report to Home Office.

Burbridge, M., 1981. Priority estates project: Improving problem council estates. London: DOE, HMSO.

Cicourel, A., 1968. The social organization of juvenile justice. London: Heinemann.

Clarke, R.V.G., ed., 1978. Tackling vandalism. HORS no. 47. London: HMSO.

Cohen, S., 1973. Campaigning against vandalism. In: C. Ward, 1973.

Douglas, J., 1979. The social meaning of suicide. Princeton University Press.

Gladstone, F.J., 1978. Vandalism among adolescent schoolboys. In: R.V.G. Clarke, 1978.

Herbert, D.T., 1982. Residential crime and urban environments. In: M. Hough, P. Mayhew, 1982.

Hough, M., P. Mayhew, eds., 1982. Crime and public housing. Research and Planning Unit Paper 6, H.O. London: HMSO.

Kitsuse, J., A. Cicourel, 1963. A note on the use of official statistics. Social Problems 11.

Leather, A., A. Matthews, 1973. What can the architect do: A series of design guides. In: C. Ward, 1973.

Mawby, R.I., 1977a. Defensible space: A theoretical and empirical appraisal. Urban Studies 14, 169–179.

Mawby, R.I., 1977b. Kiosk vandalism: A Sheffield study. British Journal of Criminology 17 (1), 30–46.

Mawby, R.I., 1979. Policing the city. Farnborough: Saxon House.

Mawby, R.I., 1980. Sex and crime: The results of a self-report study. British Journal of Sociology 31 (4), 252–543.

Mawby, R.I., 1983. Fear of crime and concern over the crime problem among the elderly. Journal of Community Psychology, forthcoming.

Mayhew, P., 1979. Defensible space: The current status of a crime prevention theory. Howard Journal 18, 150–159.

Mayhew, P., et al., 1979. Crime in public view. HORS no. 49. London: HMSO.

Mayhew, P., R.V.G. Clarke, 1982. Crime prevention and public housing in England. In: M. Hough, P. Mayhew, 1982.

Miller, A., 1973. Vandalism and the architect. In: C. Ward, 1973.

Newman, O., 1973. Defensible space. London: Architectural Press.

Pizzey, E., 1974. Scream quietly or the neighbours will hear. Harmondsworth: Penguin.

Research Bureau Limited, 1977. Vandalism research: A survey of the general public. London; Job No. 11381.

Sturman, A., 1978. Measuring vandalism in a city suburb. In: R.V.G. Clarke, 1978.

Ward, C., ed., 1973. Vandalism. London: Architectural Press.

Wilson, H., 1980. Parental supervision and delinquency. British Journal of Criminology 20, 203–235.

Wilson, H., 1982. Delinquency and public housing: Initiatives for future research. In: M. Hough, P. Mayhew, 1982.

Wilson, S., 1978. Vandalism and 'defensible space' on London housing estates. In: R.V.G. Clarke, 1978.

Wilson, S., M. Burbridge, 1978. An investigation of difficult to let housing. Housing Review, July-August, 100–104.

Abstract: R.I. Mawby, Vandalism and public perceptions of vandalism in contrasting residential areas This paper reports on those findings of the Sheffield Survey on Social Structure and Crime which pertain to vandalism. The three main sections cover a brief discussion of the wider research project and the methodologies employed, a description of data on vandalism in the residential areas covered by the research, and an analysis of public perceptions of the extent and seriousness of vandalism. Overall, some contrasts were noted in the distribution of vandalism, particularly vandalism of publicly defined property, between areas. However, perhaps the most interesting findings relate to the degree of concern voiced by residents at what appear to be a large number of relatively minor incidents of vandalism. Vandalism thus becomes symbolic of the various issues underlying the popularity or notoriety of an area. In this context, the public appeared concerned that steps should be taken to combat vandalism, but saw reparation as well as punishment and deterrence as a justifiable aim of criminal justice policy.

CHAPTER 16

The evaluation of acts of vandalism

G. MOSER, N. GIRAULT and Cl. LEVY-LÉBOYER

The concept of vandalism is a somewhat vague one. In France, for instance, juvenile courts place the breaking up of school furniture, the smashing of windowpanes in public buildings and breaking and entering into one and the same category. Some police reports refer to acts of vandalism as thoughtless, thereby indicating that they believe them to be irrational or even of a pathological nature. The French Postal Service classifies all breakages under the same heading whether or not theft or a forced entry has taken place.

While there is clearly abundant disagreement as to the meaning of the term, the evaluation of the various acts referred to as vandalism, not to mention the seriousness attributed to such acts, is even more subject to debate. It is probably safe to say that acts such as the scribbling of graffiti or the smashing of a school bench would probably be generally perceived as trivial or puerile while others, such as the defacing of an artistic masterpiece, for example, would be widely condemned. However, what would be the general reaction to the carving of initials on trees, the destruction of telephone booths or the trampling of a flower bed?

The research reported in the present article looks at the evaluation of acts of vandalism as a function of two variables, the presumed originator of the act in question and the age and social status of the person assessing the seriousness of the behaviour.

Forty acts of vandalism were defined for the present study on the basis of two criteria, viz. the damaging or destruction of environmental objects associated with the apparent absence of motives of immediate, obvious gain. The 40 selected acts involve target-objects which may be classified under five headings: the built environment, private property, school buildings, the natural environment and transport facilities. A list of the 40 acts of vandalism was presented to subjects who were then asked to evaluate each act on a 4-point Likert scale varying from 1 (not serious) to 4 (very serious). This procedure generated the following data set for each group of subjects:

- a total score, representing the overall seriousness of the acts of vandalism,
- a seriousness score for each act thereby enabling acts to be classified in descending order of seriousness,
- a typology of acts of vandalism as a function of evaluation similarity, obtained by hierarchical grouping of the vandalistic acts.

The questionnaire required but little time to complete, and was used with two aims in mind. We wished:
(1) to see if the presumed description of vandals influenced the evaluation of the seriousness of the act;
(2) to study the variability of the evaluations provided by groups of different age and social status.

1. Vandal identity and seriousness of acts

Four equivalent subgroups from a population of students completed the questionnaire: each subgroup received one of four sets of additional information specifying that the acts had been carried out by:
– a young person acting alone;
– a young person acting in concert with a group;
– an adult acting alone;
– an adult acting in concert with a group.
Table 1 presents the average score obtained corresponding to each of the preceding sets of additional information: none of the differences between these scores are significant. Furthermore, differences were not significant when data were grouped to test the influence of the alone/group and young person/adult variables.

It may be concluded therefore, that, on the whole, acts of vandalism are not evaluated as a function of the persons carrying them out. The evaluation of the seriousness of the act depends on its nature and is independent of the person having perpetrated it and of the social context in which it took place.

It was also felt to be of interest to test for the existence of differences between vandal types with respect to specific acts of vandalism. In only one case ('kicking toilet door to pieces') was the act evaluated to be more serious in the case of a younger than an older person ($M = 3.01$ and 2.2; means significantly different at the 0.01 level). Three acts were evaluated differently according to the social context in which they were perpetrated: 'drawing or writing on train or underground seats' was found to be significantly more serious in the case of an individual acting alone ($M = 2.65$ and 2.36, $t = 2.32$, $p = 0.01$).

Table 1. Average seriousness score according to age and social context.

Vandalism perpetrated by:	A young person	An adult
Alone	$M = 2.94$ ($N = 57$)	$M = 2.84$ ($N = 67$)
In a group	$M = 2.88$ ($N = 71$)	$M = 2.92$ ($N = 57$)

Table 2. Average evaluation score when perpetrator of act presumed young and acting alone.

Acts of vandalism perpetrated by:	Young person alone (N = 57)	Others (N = 195)	Student 't'
Ripping off railway timetables	2.62	2.95	$t = 2.2; p < 0.05$
Walking through wheatfields before harvest time	3.07	3.36	$t = 1.98; p < 0.05$
Tearing up a vegetable garden	3.32	3.59	$t = 2.3; p < 0.05$
Defacing masterpieces in an exhibition	3.67	3.85	$t = 2.3; p < 0.05$

This may reflect the fact that a single individual drawing on seats sets an example and incites others to imitate him/her. On the other hand, two acts were perceived to be significantly more serious when perpetrated in a group, viz. 'ruining flowers in a public garden' and 'walking through a wheat field before harvest time' (3.05 and 3.32; $t = 2.65$ significant at the 0.01 level; and 3.17, 3.43; $t = 2.43$ significant at the 0.01 level, respectively). These acts are fairly unusual and occasion greater damage when perpetrated by a group; the evaluation of their consequences probably predominates in the perception of their seriousness.

The subgroup which evaluated vandalism supposedly perpetrated by young persons acting alone was less critical in the case of four acts (see table 2) which were perceived by the others to be serious. Perhaps this is due to the fact that such acts are rare, cannot give rise to imitation and evoke a judgement of irresponsibility with respect to the young people involved in them.

Overall, the salient feature of the preceding analyses is that these differences are exceptional. As a general rule, vandalism is judged *per se* and is independent of the person perpetrating it and of the circumstances in which it took place. Consequently, it was felt worthwhile to analyse the data gathered for the second part of the study wherein we sought to throw light on the basis of respondent evaluation and to see whether the same fundamental principles apply to all the different groups.

2. Age of respondents and severity of judgement with respect to vandalism

For this part of the study the questionnaire was, in the absence of information concerning those perpetrating the acts described, completed by four groups differing with respect to age, namely:

Table 3. Evaluation of seriousness of vandalistic acts as a function of age.

		Student 't'
Lycée pupils (N = 87)	2.52	$t = 4.86$, significant difference at $p < 0.001$
Students (N = 244)	2.86	
Working adults (N = 27)	2.98	$t = 2.45$, significant difference at $p < 0.005$
Retired people (N = 36)	3.13	

(i) 'lycée' pupils between 15 and 18 years of age,
(ii) students between 20 and 25 years of age,
(iii) working adults between 30 and 45 years of age,
(iv) retired people over 65 years of age.

Table 3 shows the overall seriousness score for each of these different samples. It can be seen that relative tolerance falls off noticeably with increasing age, although these differences are not as significant as those between each pair of subgroups taken successively. 'Lycée' pupils are the most tolerant and students more so than retired people. Age, then, or rather generation, plays a role in the assessment of the seriousness of acts of vandalism.

3. Social status and the evaluation of acts on vandalism

In this case the questionnaire was completed by four very different groups. The 'neutral' version of the questionnaire was used, i.e. no information was provided as to the nature of the person perpetrating the acts evoked.

In addition to the 'lycée' pupils, students and working adults who were used for the age comparisons described above, it proved possible to obtain responses from 25 young delinquents (15 to 18 years of age), from 31 foreign

Table 4. Evaluation of the seriousness of vandalistic acts by different groups.

		Student 't'
Lycée pupils (N = 87)	2.52	$t = 4.26$, significant at the 0.001 level
Delinquents (N = 25)	2.98	
Students (N = 244)	2.86	$t = 2.6$, significant at the 0.01 level
Foreign students (N = 31)	2.57	
Working adults (N = 27)	2.98	not significant
Local authority councillors (N = 393)	2.88	

students attending French educational institutions and from 393 town council-lors. These different subgroups may be compared: such a comparison, in terms of the overall scores, is presented in table 4.

The judgements of the young delinquents are significantly more severe than those of young people of the same age. This is scarcely surprising, since it is known that delinquents adopt rigid norms and are therefore more critical in their assessment of departures from the norm. Their overall seriousness score is consequently at a similar level to that of the working adults. On the other hand, the foreign students are less critical in their evaluations than their French colleagues. It may well be that this observation reflects the fact that foreign students perceive less clearly the nature of the norms applying in the host country and therefore manifest a greater degree of tolerance. Insofar as the local councillors are concerned, their evaluations are not significantly different from those of the working adults.

The preceding results as a whole – with respect to both age and social status – suggest a certain degree of homogeneity in terms of the evaluation of vandalistic behaviour. While it was seen that respondent age plays a role and that certain minority groups adopt more exacting norms (the delinquents) or manifest greater tolerance (the foreign students), differences between means are small, even in extreme cases.

In the light of the above it is possible that overall differences may arise from the existence of differing attitudes with respect to clearly specified acts. In other words, the evaluation criteria used by the different groups may not be the same. This hypothesis is examined in greater detail below.

4. Evaluation criteria with respect to acts of vandalism

An ascending hierarchical grouping procedure was used. This method enables inter-variable distances to be evaluated and a tree diagram to be produced in which intra-variable class homogeneity is maximised as far as possible, while inter-variable class heterogeneity is simultaneously maximised as far as possi-ble. This algorithm was applied to the two largest groups of respondents (244 students, 393 local councillors) whose overall evaluation scores were practically identical (2.86 and 2.88, cf. table 4).

Figure 1 shows the results of the application of the hierarchical grouping procedure to the local councillor data. The first split clearly differentiates between acts of vandalism giving rise to relatively inexpensive repair work (drawing, scribbling, knocking over dustbins, etc.) and those resulting in expensive and dangerous impacts on the community at large.

Within these two groups somewhat finer distinctions may be drawn: insofar as behaviour judged to be *non-serious* is concerned, it is possible to differenti-

NOT SERIOUS

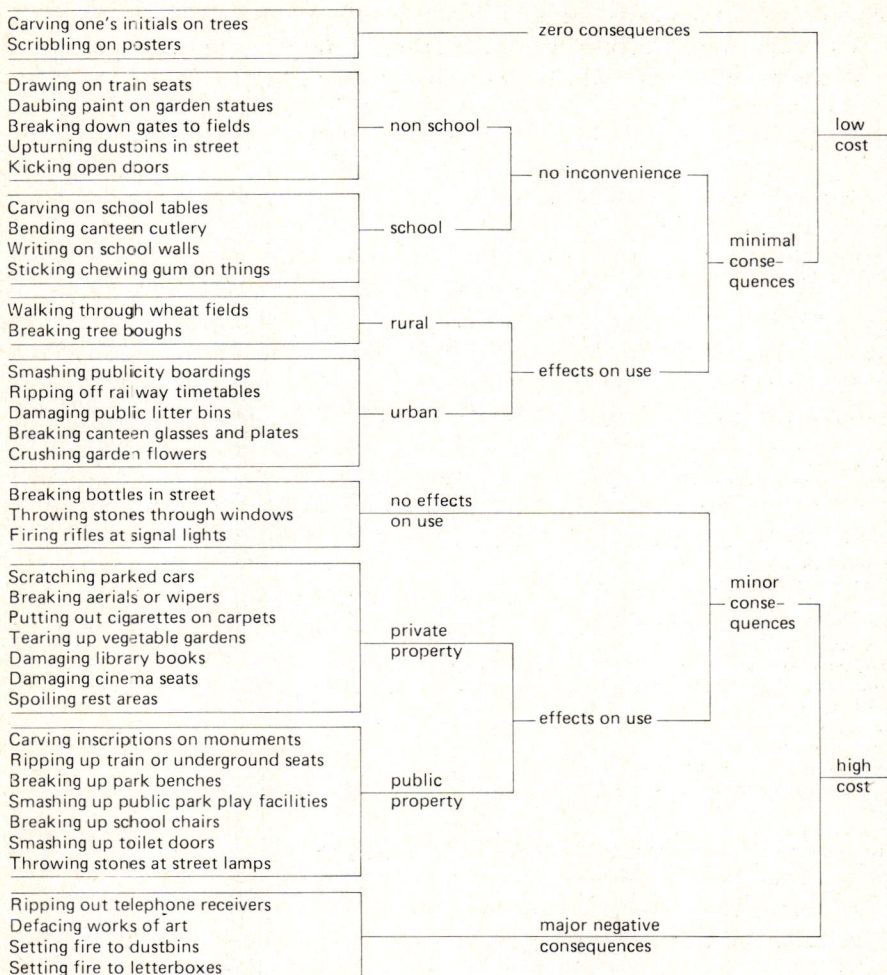

Fig. 1. Hierarchical response classification: town councillors.

VERY SERIOUS

ate the type of action and the environment under attack. Thus, 'scribbling', 'drawing' and 'carving' are viewed as trivial, no matter what the object on which they take place (e.g. posters, train or underground seats, school benches). On the other hand, vandalism within school buildings is not tolerated to the same extent as similar behaviour outside the school. Thus 'carving in school tables' is felt to be more serious than 'carving one's initials in a tree' or 'daubing statues in public parks'.

A second subset groups acts of vandalism which inhibit the subsequent use of a facility and in most cases involve irreversible damage: 'break', 'smash',

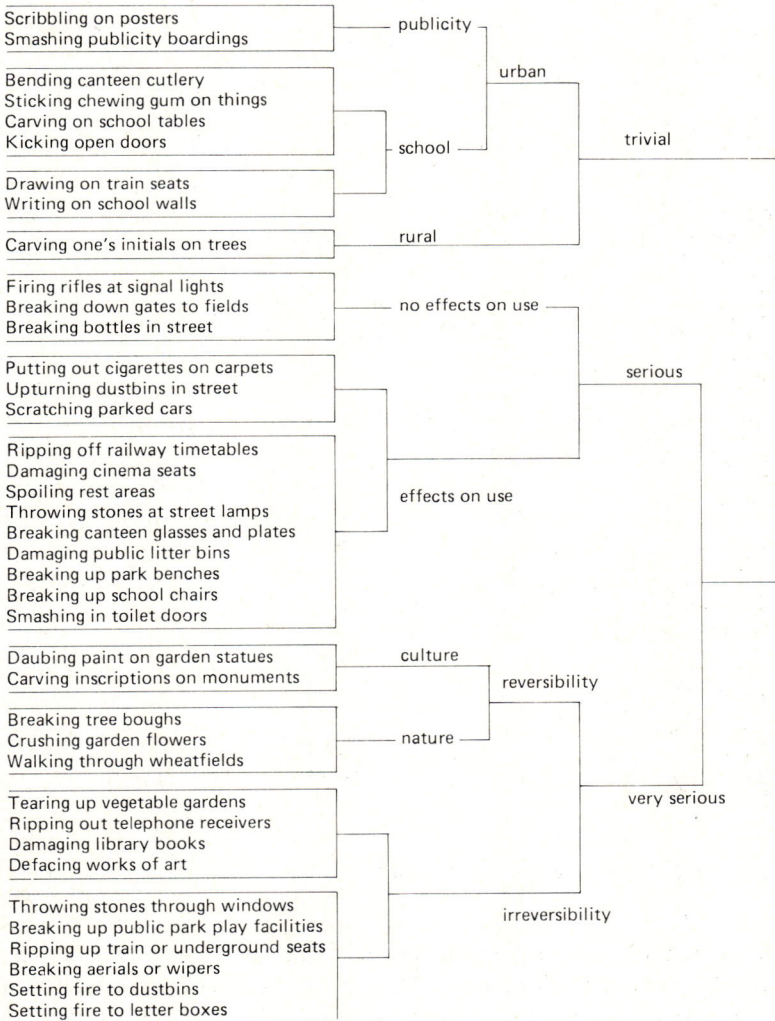

Fig. 2. Hierarchical response classification: students.

'rip off', 'damage'. Here again, however, such depredations are neither costly nor of great importance in terms of their consequences.

Acts of vandalism which are perceived as *serious* were divided into three classes which may be ordered in order of increasing seriousness:

(1) damage to privately owned and protected objects causing them to be subsequently unusable (e.g. books, windscreen wipers, cinema seats);
(2) damage to publicly owned property leading to community-born costs;
(3) dangerous acts of vandalism having potentially major negative consequences (e.g. setting fires, ripping out telephone receivers).

Figure 2 presents the results obtained by applying the same algorithm to the student data. The first split separates trivial acts of vandalism from those viewed as serious, as was the case with the town councillors. This time, however, the two classes are unequal in size, with relatively few acts being qualified as 'not serious' (nine instead of 18). Student tolerance is extended mainly towards the vandalising of downgraded objects. Thus, the vandalising of publicity panels is viewed as unimportant whereas the carving of one's initials in a tree (the least important item in the eyes of the local councillors) is felt to be more serious.

More detailed examination of the various subsets shows clearly that the evaluation criteria used by the students differ from those adopted by the preceding group. Four categories can be picked out with respect to those acts which were judged to be serious, namely, those directed against cultural artefacts, those having a negative impact on the natural environment, those having a negative impact on the community and those involving irreversible damage to the vandalised objects.

Were we to sum up the criteria used by the local councillors to make their evaluation of acts of vandalism in a few words, it could be said that they essentially take into account the cost of refurbishment and the extent of user inconvenience. The students, on the other hand, assess vandalism with respect to the value attributed to the damaged object and the irreversibility of that damage. While the overall evaluation scores of the two groups are similar, it is clear that their attitudes with respect to vandalism are profoundly different.

Two broad conclusions emerge from the study presented above. First and foremost, vandalism was generally considered to be serious (since the average score was almost 3 on the 4-point scale) and this was so for all respondent groups. Secondly, acts of vandalism were not assessed as a function of those perpetrating them nor of the circumstances in which they took place. Rather, were they judged in a transactional perspective, i.e. as a function of the relationship holding between the individuals involved and their environment – cost and inconvenience in the case of the councillors responsible for protecting the environment of their respective citizens, value and damage irreversibility in the case of the students, whose relationship with the environment is of a more symbolic nature.

The data and analyses presented here enable attitudes with respect to vandalism to be explained and an orientation for the control of vandalism to be put forward. It is known that vandalism is frequently perpetrated in public by individuals, acting alone. If the public tolerates these acts and fails to react, then vandalism is becoming a familiar feature of our environment. The responses to our questionnaire show clearly that these acts are judged as a function of the object involved. The destruction of a valued, functional environment is condemned, whereas acts against objects of no psychological value, the absence of which will not give rise to inconvenience, are condoned.

There can be no doubt then that environmental protection – and thereby the collective fight against vandalism – must resort to the amelioration of the environment for those who use and inhabit it.

Abstract: G. Moser et al., The evaluation of acts of vandalism
The term 'vandalism' covers a wide range of different acts. This article seeks to clarify the concept of vandalism by analysing the evaluation of different acts in terms of the presumed perpetrators of the acts in question and the age and social status of the person assessing the seriousness of the behaviour in question.

It would seem that vandalism is generally considered to be serious regardless of those presumed to have carried out the acts or of the supposed circumstances in which they took place. Acts are evaluated as a function of the object involved. Their seriousness is assessed as a function of the relationship existing between the individuals concerned and their environment.

CHAPTER 17

Moral judgement and attitudes towards vandalism

J. BIDEAUD and P.G. COSLIN

The research presented in this article seeks to analyse the relationship between adolescents' attitudes to vandalism and their judgements with respect to pro-social behaviour. This approach is predicated on the hypothesis that one of the factors responsible for vandalism may be the replacement of the social responsibility norm by the reciprocity norm. In the first part of the paper the degree to which the study of vandalism can be undertaken in relation with moral judgement change as postulated by developmental research will be assessed. The second part summarises the main points of a study in which the attitudes of 15- to 18-year-olds towards specific types of vandalistic behaviour were compared to their judgements of acts with broader moral implications.

According to Kohlberg's model (Kohlberg, 1958, 1963, 1968; Kohlberg and Turiel, 1978), subsequently modified by Rest (1979), moral judgement develops in three successive stages. At the initial, pre-conventional stage some features of reciprocity do exist in the evaluation of social intercourse, but such reciprocity is interpreted quite pragmatically with the main aim being personal benefit. Conventional morality oriented towards law and order makes its appearance at the second stage although still with a view to personal benefit: an egalitarian concept of justice develops in correlation with peer group solidarity. The third and final stage is characterised by a change from this purely egalitarian concept of justice to a higher form of reciprocity: here personal acceptance of moral principles is based on a humanitarian ideal.

The model is a seductive one: it provides us with a harmonious growth of moral development from the subject-centred pre-conventional stage to the realisation of the existence of a universal ethical principle. However, a certain number of experimental results combined with facts of life in society, notably the spread of vandalism, are somewhat incompatible with the model and give rise to some pressing questions.

Firstly, let us look at some of the experimental data. Several studies have shown that, when judgements are called for, the social responsibility norm (e.g. helping someone in need without expecting any recompense) is well internalised by the age of six. Notwithstanding this, if subjects are placed in a situation where their requests for assistance are not satisfied, they subsequently no longer relate to this norm but subordinate pro-social behaviour to reciprocal behaviour (Bryan and Walbek, 1970; Harris, 1970; Peterson et al., 1977). Change with age would appear to be associated with conformity of judgement and conduct, although the reciprocity norm plays a role at all ages – particularly during adolescence.

Turiel (1974, 1977) has provided an explanation of this apparent regression. According to him, the changeover from one stage to another upon reaching adolescence (level 2 to level 3 in Kohlberg's terminology) is not continuous but includes a phase of disequilibrium wherein judgement and conduct modes are reassessed. Two sources of imbalance would appear to be present, one associated with the new relations between individual and social requirements and one corresponding to the questioning of universal moral principles. From this stems our hypothesis of the reversion to the application of the reciprocity norm in the case of judgements and behaviour. This norm would come into play at two levels: (1) society fails to respond to an individual's expectations and is therefore 'punished' by way of more or less continuously updated hostile or rebellious behaviour; (2) assistance is only given to a limited peer group which temporarily backs the individual's revolt by responding to the latter's need for approval and consolation.

It is clear that vandalism can occur during this period of imbalance should it be accentuated or lengthened, for various reasons, and work out negatively. Consequently, depending on the extent to which the social responsibility norm, which usually goes back to educational models, has been affected, and the degree to which the reciprocity norm has been accepted at both levels (realisation of potential social sanctions, realisation of the fragility of the group's structure), vandalism will take on a variety of forms which will differ both with respect to their significance and to their seriousness. Notwithstanding the preceding, this hypothesis would seem to stand in need of modification in the light of the context and characteristics of acts of vandalism. The term vandalism, in fact, covers a multitude of sins and apparently 'senseless' behaviour of this type is underpinned by highly complex motives differing considerably according to the context and characteristics of the acts perpetrated.

It is by no means an easy matter to define vandalism. It was originally considered to be a state of mind favourable to the defacing or destruction of works of art or of other 'things beautiful'. Over the last ten years or so, however, vandalism seems to have become much more commonplace whilst society has apparently become inured to it despite the high costs incurred. Thus, vandalism is used to refer to non-accidental damage to school buildings and facilities, to more or less aimless damage to call boxes, to damage to public or private property or, again, to the more trivial act of setting fire to dustbins. At the same time, all this behaviour with its diverse meanings has generally come to be associated, if not with young people as a whole, then at least with a good proportion of the adolescents dwelling in major population centres.

A number of different social attitudes are engendered by this diverse behaviour. They are linked with several variables found in the vandalism attitude scale recently perfected by Lévy-Leboyer et al. (1982) which may be summarised as follows:
- the social context in which acts are perpetrated (work or school, cultural or recreational, etc.);
- the public or private nature of the vandalised object;
- the reversible or irreversible nature of the act;
- the act's involuntary or deliberate nature;
- the serious or innocuous nature of the potential consequences of the act (in the short or long term).

Attitude relativity depending on these diverse variables is based on taking into account the various motives behind the different types of vandalism. Consequently, there is a variability in the moral judgements made in this respect by adolescents which corresponds to a finer resolution with respect to vandalistic behaviour definition as a function of the variables listed. This finer resolution, then, appears to stem from modifications in the application of the reciprocity and social responsibility norms.

It appears to be possible to assess fluctuations in these norms during adolescence by means of Rest's Defining Issues Test (DIT, 1979). This test is predicated on Kohlberg's theory and makes use of his different stages and characteristics. The method used is, however, different from Kohlberg's clinical approach which is based on interviews built around dilemmas involving a norm together with justified individual needs. In the case of DIT, the subject chooses his responses from a set of 12 issues following each of the six dilemmas selected by Rest. Since the test is standardised this choice enables the level of the moral judgement to be determined directly without the necessity of having recourse to the interpretation of a 'judge'. Moreover, the responses obtained are comparable as between respondents; the situation is the same for all those involved and the interviewer/subject variable, with all its potential bias, is eliminated.

The aim of the present research is then to investigate the relationship between moral judgements as measured by the DIT and attitudes towards different types of vandalism as measured by the Lévy-Leboyer scale.

The population used consisted of 40 adolescents in French secondary schools in Paris. These adolescents were divided up into two groups of 20:
(1) secondary school pupils in the 'troisième' class, average age = 15;
(2) secondary school pupils in their final year, average age = 18;

Each adolescent had to complete the DIT and then proceed to the vandalism attitude scale. These operations took place on a group basis and lasted about 90 minutes. All subjects were volunteers and were guaranteed confidentiality.

The instructions and the first of the six items on the DIT together with the instructions and the first five of the 40 items on the Lévy-Leboyer scale are given in the appendix.

The data gathered was then analysed in such a way as to obtain for each adolescent:

(1) A Kohlberg moral judgement level defined on the basis of the six stages assessed by the DIT:

(I)   Pre-Conventional Level
  – stage 1: punishment and obedience orientation,
  – stage 2: instrumental relativist orientation.
(II) Conventional Level
  – stage 3: interpersonal concordance of 'good boy–nice girl' orientation,
  – stage 4: law and order orientation.
(III) Post-Conventional, Autonomous or Principled Level
  – stage 5: social-contract legalistic orientation,
  – stage 6: universal ethical principle orientation.

(2) Attitudes with respect to acts of vandalism capable of being categorised according to several dimensions which are not exhaustive:

Dimension A: irreversible nature of the act (inversely A': reversible)
  – daubing paint on statues in parks;
  – destroying a vegetable garden;
  – damaging books in public libraries;
  – defacing works of art in an exhibition;
  – carving one's initials on a tree;
  – breaking off flowers in parks;
  – breaking tree branches;
  – trampling down wheat before harvest time;
  – setting fire to letter boxes.
Dimension B: dangerous nature of the act (inversely B': harmless)
  – ripping out telephone receivers in public call boxes;
  – throwing stones through windows;
  – breaking down fences to fields;
  – deliberately breaking bottles in street;
  – breaking publicity hoardings (e.g. in bus shelters);
  – deliberately smashing canteen glasses and plates;
  – throwing stones at street lamps;
  – breaking car wipers and aerials;
  – setting fire to dustbins;
  – firing at road signs;
  – setting fire to letter boxes.
Dimension C: accidental nature of the act (inversily C': deliberately committed)
  – kicking open the door of a block of flats;
  – putting out a cigarette on the carpet of a waiting room;
Dimension D: vandalised objects at work or in school
  – carving things onto tables at work;
  – deliberately smashing canteen glasses and plates;

- writing on walls at work;
- breaking up chairs at work;
- bending canteen cutlery;
- smashing in school toilet doors.

Dimension E: vandalised objects in cultural or recreational contexts
- daubing paint on park statues;
- damaging books in public libraries;
- defacing works of art in an exhibition;
- breaking off flowers in public parks;
- carving inscriptions on the walls of monuments;
- breaking play facilities in parks.

Dimension F: act perpetrated in a rural context (inversely F': in an urban context)
- breaking down fences to fields;
- destroying a vegetable garden;
- damaging lay-by facilities;
- carving one's initials on a tree trunk;
- dirtying washing hung out to dry;
- firing at road signs;
- trampling down wheat before harvest time.

Dimension G: act perpetrated on personal possessions (inversely G': communal property)
- throwing stones through windows;
- breaking down fences to fields;
- scratching parked cars;
- kicking open the door of a block of flats;
- destroying a vegetable garden;
- dirtying washing hung out to dry;
- breaking car wipers and aerials;
- trampling down wheat before harvest time;
- setting fire to letter boxes.

These attitudes were measured on a 4-point numerical scale.

(3) Reasons given to justify responses

- tolerant attitudes, or expression of agreement with act;
- reasons referring to intentions (relativity of the intention behind an act, attempted explanations of acts, criticisms of institutions and of society);
- reasons invoking consequences of acts (defamatory consequences, consequences for human life, material consequences, cost of damage)
- subjective remarks

The data obtained were first of all analysed in terms of the variables selected and then as a function of the adolescents' justifications of their attitudes with respect to vandalism.

1. Analysis of data as a function of the different variables

1.1. Social context in which the act was perpetrated

Here, acts of vandalism were first of all contrasted according to whether they took place in a work or school context (the D dimension of the Lévy-Leboyer scale) or in a cultural and recreational context (dimension E of the scale).

Damage to the latter milieu was judged by all subjects to be notably more serious. The degree of seriousness, however, was observed to increase as a function of age: average scores on the E and D dimensions were 2.79 and 2.46 respectively for the 15-year-olds while the 18-year-olds produced corresponding averages of 3.28 and 2.24. On the other hand, the degree of seriousness declined as a function of level of moral judgement: adolescents at level III on the Kohlberg scale (the post-conventional level) tended not to differentiate between acts of vandalism classified according to context, whereas lower level adolescents (conventional level: law and order orientation) perceived acts perpetrated in a cultural or recreational context as more serious.

It was also felt worthwhile to compare subject attitudes with respect to acts of vandalism perpetrated in rural contexts (dimension F) and in urban contexts (dimension F'). The outcome of this comparison was that neither differences between perceived seriousness nor interactions between context (rural or urban) and subject's age or between context and the adolescents' moral judgement level appeared to exist.

1.2. The communal or personal nature of the vandalised object

The results obtained showed that attacks on private property (dimension G) tended to be judged slightly more severely than attacks on public property (dimension G'), especially in the case of the younger adolescents. The corresponding mean scores for the 15-year-olds were 2.99 and 2.69 whereas those of the 18-year-olds only varied from 2.75 to 2.65.

These are only tendencies of course, but they do suggest that the perceived seriousness of vandalistic acts falls off with increasing age and also as higher levels of moral judgement are attained.

1.3. Consequences of acts of vandalism

All subjects perceived acts giving rise to irreversible consequences as more serious than those resulting in reversible consequences (dimensions A and A'). This increased severity was associated with age: the difference was negligible in the case of the 15-year-olds (2.72 for reversible consequences v. 2.79 for irreversible ones), but became quite considerable in the case of the 18-year-olds where it rose from 2.56 to 2.98.

1.4. Intention relativity

The results obtained showed that if an act is accidentally committed, the seriousness was minimised in the eyes of all subjects (dimensions C and C').

Here again, however, a tendency towards interaction between this variable and subject age appeared: although the average seriousness score increased only slightly in the case of the 15-year-olds (2.59 to 2.77) it made quite a jump in the case of the 18-year-olds, from 2.21 to 2.71.

This factor also showed a tendency to interact with the level of moral judgement attained by the adolescents: the accidental character of acts minimised perceived seriousness mainly for subjects who had attained a high level of moral judgement.

1.5. Consequences of acts

The seriousness of the consequences of vandalism (dimensions B and B′) seems to have an important effect on adolescent attitudes, at least in the case of the younger subjects where the average score varied from 2.60 to 2.93 according to the consequences associated with different acts. The difference was markedly less in the case of the older pupils (2.67 and 2.78).

Subjects having attained the conventional level of moral judgement (level II) would appear to be more sensitive to the consequences of acts of vandalism than those having evolved as far as level III. The latter probably gave greater weight to the intentions accompanying vandalism.

2. Reasons advanced by respondents for their judgements

The analysis of adolescents' reasons for vandalistic conduct appears to have been of greater value. Not only did it confirm the facts and tendencies appearing both in the DIT and the Lévy-Leboyer attitude scale data, but it also enabled some of them to be generalised and explicated. Such analysis, for instance, brought out not only the part played by the level of moral judgement in determining attitudes towards vandalistic behaviour, but also its partial interaction with age. Thus an analysis of the reasons put forward by the older adolescents (final year pupils) showed that their degree of tolerance augments along with their level of moral judgement. [1]

This comes out in the DIT results obtained by level III subjects where less reference was made to the costs of damage and to other material consequences as indices of the seriousness of vandalistic acts. Thus, reasons for the seriousness of damaging theatre seats such as 'it increases the price of tickets' gave way to statements such as 'it's a pity to spoil seats but seats as such do not really matter all that much'.

Nevertheless, the same subjects perceived an element of risk for potential victims of vandalism as a determining factor when assessing the seriousness of acts, e.g. 'it's a serious matter throwing a stone through a window as it might hit somebody'.

Moreover, again in the case of the older subjects, reasons related to act causality and to relativity of intentions increased as a function of moral

---

[1]   Not all final year students were at level III of the Kohlberg scale. In our sample, only 11 out of 20 reached this level.

judgement level. For instance, in the case of damaged call boxes, 'I think the problem is much more complex than the ripping out of the apparatus'.

It is clear that older subjects of a higher moral judgement level were referring in general to the responsibility norm. On the other hand, there is the paradox that these were the only respondents to come forth with anti-institution reasons. This never occurred in the case of the younger subjects.

These younger subjects were also characterised by increasing tolerance of vandalism and by a decreasing number of references to material consequences as their level of moral judgement increased. Notwithstanding the level attained, however, they were almost never observed to proffer relativity or intention based reasons for acts of vandalism. It is almost true to state, in fact, that these adolescents did not really come out with any reasons at all.

3. Conclusions

The hypothesis that the judgements and attitudes of adolescents manifest a return to the application of the reciprocity norm stands in need of modification.

The social responsibility norm was clearly present among the older members of our sample, even if it occurred along with anti-institution reasoning manifesting a certain degree of reciprocity: society is punished or at least undergoes judgement because it does not match up to people's expectations. The reciprocity norm was more apparent in the case of the younger respondents but was applied more in terms of their moral judgements than in terms of their attitudes with respect to vandalism where social responsibility was involved in some cases.

It would appear, then, that the two norms coexist during adolescence, just as moral judgement levels and the various attitudes with regard to vandalism coexist.

The appearance of one norm rather than the other would seem to depend on the type of vandalism and the type of moral act being judged. For example, vandalising cultural resources is always judged to be very serious and the fact that these are part of our mutual cultural heritage is invoked, thus bringing into play the social responsibility norm. When it is a question of everyday facilities, however, such as call boxes, reference is made to social problems: society is perceived to be responsible and is, in a way, punished by reciprocity.

A further important point emerging from our research is the constant link which was observed between the level of moral judgement and the varied assessment of acts of vandalism. The higher the level, the greater the reference to the social responsibility norm and the stronger the influence on respondents' attitudes. Paradoxically, as was pointed out earlier, this can even give rise to a degree of relative tolerance with respect to certain acts of vandalism. These observations raise the problem of the relations between moral education, civics and delinquency in the broadest sense of the word.

It is pertinent to note in this context that the last two decades have witnessed a renewal of interest in the study of the internalisation of moral principles in the course of development. The spread of delinquency has raised questions in terms of psychology, pedagogy, sociology and politics which have been incorporated into the school curriculum by laying stress on moral education and civics. It is clear that an attempt is under way to heighten the value attached to the norm of social responsibility, and this is clearly of significance in terms of the prevention of vandalism.

Appendix

(A) Defining Issues Test (Rest, 1979: 2–3).

Opinions about social problems

This questionnaire is aimed at understanding how people think about social problems. Different people often have different opinions about questions of right and wrong. There are no 'right' answers in the way that there are right answers to math problems. We would like you to tell us what you think of several problem stories. The papers will be fed to a computer to find the average for the whole group and no-one will see your individual answers.

In this questionnaire you will be asked to give your opinions about several stories. Here is a story as an example.

Frank Jones has been thinking about buying a car. He is married, has two small children and earns an average income. The car he buys will be his family's only car. It will be used mostly to get to work and drive around town, but sometimes for vacation trips also. In trying to decide what car to buy, Frank Jones realised that there were a lot of questions to consider. Below there is a list of some of these questions.

If you were Frank Jones, how important would each of these questions be in deciding what car to buy?

Instructions for Part A: (sample question)

On the left-hand side check one of the spaces for each statement of a consideration. (For instance, if you think that statement no. 1 is not important in making a decision about buying a car, check the space at the far right.)

Importance:

Great	Much	Some	Little	No
				×
×				
		×		
				×
×				
				×

1. Whether the car dealer was in the same block as where Frank lives. (Note that in this sample, the person answering the questionnaire did not think this was important in making a decision.)

2. Would a *used* car be more economical in the long run than a *new* car? (Note that a check was put at the far left to indicate the opinion that this is an important issue in making a decision about buying a car.)

3. Whether the colour was green, Frank's favourite colour.

4. Whether the cubic inch displacement was at least 200. (Note that, if you are unsure about what 'cubic inch displacement' means, this should be marked 'no importance'.)

5. Would a large, roomy car be better than a compact car?

6. Whether the front connibilies were differential. (Note that if a statement sounds like gibberish or nonsense to you, it should be marked 'no importance'.)

Instructions for Part B: (sample question)

    From the list of questions above, select the most important one of the whole group. Put the number of the most important question on the line below 'Most important'. Do likewise for your second, third and fourth most important choices. (Note that in this case the 'Most important' choices will come from the statements that were checked on the far left-hand side – statements no. 2 and no. 5 were thought to be very important. In deciding what is the *most* important, a person would reread nos. 2 and 5, and then pick one of them as the *most* important, then put the other one as 'second most important', and so on.)

Most *important*	*Second most* *important*	*Third most* *important*	*Fourth most* *important*
5	2	3	1

Heinz and the drug

In Europe, a woman was near death from a special kind of cancer. There was one drug that the doctors thought might save her. It was a form of radium that a druggist in the same town had recently discovered. The drug was expensive to make, but the druggist was charging ten times what the drug cost to make. He paid $200 for the radium and charged $2000 for a small dose of the drug. The sick woman's husband, Heinz, went to everyone he knew to borrow the money, but he could only get together about $1000, which is half of what it cost. He told the druggist that his wife was dying, and asked him to sell it cheaper or let him pay later. But the druggist said, 'No, I discovered the drug and I'm going to make money from it'. So Heinz got desperate and began to think about breaking into the man's store to steal the drug for his wife.

Should Heinz steal the drug? (Check one)

_ Should steal it   _Can't decide   _ Should not steal it

Importance:

Great	Much	Some	Little	No	
					1. Whether a community's laws are going to be upheld.
					2. Isn't it only natural for a loving husband to care so much for his wife that he'd steal?
					3. Is Heinz willing to risk getting shot as a burglar or going to jail for the chance that stealing the drug might help?
					4. Whether Heinz is a professional wrestler, or has considerable influence with professional wrestlers.
					5. Whether Heinz is stealing for himself or doing this solely to help someone else.
					6. Whether the druggist's rights to his invention have to be respected.
					7. Whether the essence of living is more encompassing than the termination of dying, socially and individually.
					8. What values are going to be the basis for governing how people act towards each other?
					9. Whether the druggist is going to be allowed to hide behind a worthless law which only protects the rich anyhow.
					10. Whether in this case the law is getting in the way of the most basic claim of any member of society.
					11. Whether the druggist deserves to be robbed for being so greedy and cruel.
					12. Would stealing in such a case bring about more total good for the whole society or not?

From the list of questions above, select the four most important:

Most important _   Second most important _
Third most important _   Fourth most important _

(B) Attitude scale (Moser et al., 1982)

Instructions
    This is a survey about the quality of life. We should like you to fill out this questionnaire. Below is a list of activities. Please rate their seriousness by circling 1, 2, 3, or 4.

For instance, if you believe that spitting on the ground in the street is *not serious*, circle the number 1:

    'Spitting on the ground in the street ...'   ①   2   3   4

If you believe that it is *very serious*, circle the number 4:

    'Spitting on the ground in the street ...'   1   2   3   ④

After each sentence, give a short explanation of your decision.

References

Bryan, J.H., N.H. Walbeck, 1970. The impacts of words and deeds concerning altruism upon children. Child Development 41, 741–757.

Harris, M.B., 1970. Reciprocity and generosity; Some determinants of sharing in children. Child Development 41, 313–328.

Kohlberg, L., 1958. The development of modes of moral thinking and choice in the years ten to sixteen. University of Chicago (doct. diss.).

Kohlberg, L., 1963. The development of children's orientation toward a moral order. Vita Humana 6, 11–33.

Kohlberg, L., 1968. Stage and sequence: The cognitive developmental approach to socialization. In: D.A. Goslin, ed., Handbook of socialization theory. Chicago: Rand McNally.

Kohlberg, L., E. Turiel, 1978. Moralisation, the cognitive developmental approach. New York: Rinehart and Winston.

Moser, G., N. Girault, C. Lévy-Leboyer, 1982. Attitudes du public face au vandalisme. Communication au Colloque International sur le Vandalisme, Paris, 27–29 octobre 1982.

Peterson, L., D.P. Hartmann, D.M. Gelfand, 1977. Developmental changes in the effects of dependence and reciprocity cues on children's moral judgments and donation rates. Child Development 48, 1331–1339.

Rest, J.R., 1979. Revised manual for the defining issue test, an objective test of moral judgment development. Minnesota Moral Research Projects.

Turiel, E., 1974. Conflict and transition in adolescent moral development. Child Development 45, 14–29.

Turiel, E., 1977. Conflict and transition in adolescent moral development, II: The resolution of desequilibrium through structural reorganisation. Child Development 48, 634–637.

Abstract: J. Bideaud and P.G. Coslin, Moral judgement and attitudes towards vandalism
This chapter presents the results of a study of the relationship between adolescents' attitudes towards vandalistic behaviour and their judgements of prosocial conduct. The hypothesis underpinning the research was that one of the factors responsible for vandalistic behaviour could be the masking of the social responsibility norm by the norm of reciprocity applied almost exclusively to the group to which the vandalising individual belongs. Kohlberg-type moral dilemmas and the Lévy-Leboyer vandalism attitude scale were successively administered to a sample of 40 15- to 18-year-olds. The main outcome of this experiment was the modification of our hypothesis: it would appear that reciprocity and prosocial norms coexist during adolescence, just as different levels of moral judgement and various attitudes to vandalism coexist. Apparently, the norm applied varies according to type of vandalism and type of moral act being judged.

CHAPTER 18

Vandalism: an exploratory assessment of perceived impacts and potential solutions

H.H. CHRISTENSEN

Guidelines for mitigating vandalism and other depreciative actions were identified by recreation managers, researchers, and educators as one of the top ten recreation research issues in the United States (U.S. Department of the Interior, 1981; Samdahl et al., 1982). The problems with vandalism and other violations of rules extend across the recreational opportunity spectrum (Clark and Stankey, 1979) and include impacts in urban parks, developed campgrounds, roaded forest areas, roadless backcountry, and wilderness areas (Clark et al., 1971a, 1971b; Hendee et al., 1978; Shafer and Lucas, 1978; Westover and Chubb, 1979).

National or international data on the trend of costs of vandalism are not available. The costs of vandalism, theft, and other depreciative behaviors are, essentially, in the initial stages of documentation. The $2 billion-a-year reported costs from vandalism in the United States and Sweden are discussed elsewhere in this compendium by Phillips and Donnermeyer, and Roos. National Parks Canada reports that vandalism costs taxpayers in Canada between $1 and $1.7 million dollars annually (Bronson, 1981, 1982). The USDA Forest Service reports that vandalism and littering in the National Forests cost taxpayers more than $7 million in 1974 (U.S. Department of Agriculture Forest Service, 1975). [1] For California, the USDA Forest Service reports that vandalism and littering costs were nearly $1.6 million during 1974. One area that experiences more severe problems allocates as much as 10% of their budget to repair or replace vandalized facilities. Other government agencies have similar impacts (U.S. Department of the Interior National Park Service, 1979a, 1979b).

As Van Vliet points out (ch. 1 in this compendium), one of the problems in research on vandalism is the lack of consensus as to what constitutes vandalism. The definition of vandalism is problematic (Christensen and Clark, 1979). There is a great deal of confusion about the true nature of vandalism. Many times an illegal act, as defined by a manager, may be appropriate from a recreationist's perspective. In other instances, recreationists who have little

---

[1] Costs of vandalism and littering were collected service-wide on a one-time basis only during 1974 (U.S. Department of Agriculture Forest Service, 1975).

contact with a particular recreation setting may not know the rules or guidelines for that particular setting. Some may know but disagree or not care; for example, carving initials on tables and benches. The lack of consensus between users and managers results in vandalism by definition only. Research has documented this difference in perspective (Downing and Clark, 1979; Clark, 1976a).

The kinds of impacts found in recreation areas are well known and include:
– vandalism at trailheads such as breaking and entering recreationists' cars;
– bullet damage to directional or prevention signs that can obliterate the message and affect public safety;
– theft of personal and public property such as users' backpacks, camping equipment, or signs;
– theft of historical or cultural artifacts; and
– vandalism to restroom facilities.

Private and public land managers and users are concerned about this disregard by users for regulations and the rights of others (Alfano and Magill, 1976; Clark, 1976a; Dreissen, 1978; U.S. Department of the Interior, 1978).

In response to the concerns of managers about vandalism, theft, littering, and other impacts, the USDA Forest Service, in cooperation with universities and other agencies, is conducting a series of descriptive and evaluative studies in the Western United States. [2] The objective is to develop management and administrative guidelines for the prevention and control of depreciative behaviors. The problem under study is complex and will involve planners and researchers from various disciplines.

The purpose of this paper is to describe managers' perceptions of vandalistic impacts and potential solutions for a variety of outdoor recreation settings. The data came from a pre-test of a study on perceptions and opinions of managers about vandalism and the effectiveness of control strategies. In the larger study, additional issues are addressed: perceptions about user safety and victimization; contributing factors to vandalism and depreciative behavior problems such as theft and littering; and involving the recreational user in the management of vandalism such as reporting witnessed infractions to the authorities.

One of the areas under investigation is the managers' perceptions of and experiences with vandalism and other depreciative behaviors on the lands they manage. No accurate summary of this data is presently in existence. The information will assist managers and researchers to understand the process and

---

[2] Cooperating agencies in the Western United States are: U.S. Department of Agriculture, Forest Service; U.S. Department of the Interior, Bureau of Land Management, National Park Service, and Fish and Wildlife Service; U.S. Army Corps of Engineers; University of Washington, College of Forest Resources; Portland State University; and Western Washington University, Department of Sociology.

dynamics of the vandalism problem in recreation environments. It will provide data on trends so changes that have occurred over time can be evaluated: it will identify the kinds of changes and the conditions under which they occurred. This information will help to assess perceptual similarities and differences between managers from various agencies. It will be compared to user perceptions of the problem in order to identify differences and develop programs for resolving the differences. Last, this information will provide baseline information from which evaluation studies can be developed, experimentally tested, and monitored. Strategies perceived effective will be evaluated to specifically determine under what conditions alternative control strategies work.

1. Methods and framework for analysis

During June and July 1982, questionnaires were mailed to a stratified, random sample of 70 recreation resource people working for the USDA Forest Service, National Park Service, and Bureau of Land Management in the Western United States (California, Oregon, and Washington). Two follow-ups were made with a postcard reminder. Fifty-one questionnaires were returned for a response rate of 72%.

The Recreation Opportunity Spectrum (ROS) will be used as a framework in the analysis to identify impacts and potential solutions within specific environments that range from urban (developed) to primitive (backcountry and wilderness). The ROS was recently developed to facilitate planning, management, and research activities (Clark and Stankey, 1979; Brown et al., 1979; Driver and Brown, 1978). The framework was formalized and adopted by two federal resource agencies in the United States and is being considered by agencies in Australia and New Zealand. Readers are also referred to Australian Parks and Recreation (1982) for a compilation of writings on applying the ROS.

Clark (1982) states, the Recreation Opportunity Spectrum (ROS) is a "conceptual framework that helps to clarify relationships between recreational settings, activities, and experiences. The assumption underlying the ROS in that quality is best assured through the provision of a diverse array of opportunities. The ROS recognizes that opportunities sought by recreationists range from easily accessible, highly developed areas with modern conveniences to undeveloped primitive areas in remote locations (wilderness). A wide variety of opportunities is possible between these extremes".

2. Characteristics of the respondents

Respondents are from the USDA Forest Service (34%), the National Park Service (34%) and Bureau of Land Management (32%) in Washington, Oregon,

Table 1. Percent of managers reporting impacts of vandalism as 'very important' or 'somewhat important' across the Recreation Opportunity Spectrum.

Reported impacts	Recreation Opportunity Spectrum							
	Developed areas (modern-urban)[a]		Semi-developed areas		Dispersed areas		Backcountry/ wilderness areas (primitive)	
	%	Total N	%	Total N	%	Total N	%	Total N
Vandalism to resources or habitat	96.6[b]	29	97.3	37	88.6	35	85.7	35
Vandalism to park facilities	96.6	29	97.3	38	73.5	34	58.8	34
Vandalism to users' equipment	72.4	29	56.7	37	41.2	34	31.4	35
Specific kinds of impacts								
Carving on trees	82.8	29	81.1	37	75.7	33	52.8	36
Damage to trees such as nails in trees, axe scars, wire around trees	93.4	30	89.7	39	82.8	35	69.5	36
Graffiti using pens, pencils or other media	83.4	30	71.1	38	36.3	33	28.6	35
Carving on tables	96.7	30	89.1	37	29.0	31	19.4	31

[a] *Modern-urban areas* are defined as developed with easy access by paved roadways, high interaction between recreationists, extensive modification of the setting for recreation use such as facilities to accommodate trailers and motorhomes, flush toilets, and running water. *Semi-developed areas* are defined as natural appearing areas with less well-maintained roadways, low-to-moderate interaction between recreationists, and minimal comforts or conveniences provided for recreationists such as pit toilets or centrally located water. *Dispersed areas* are defined as semi-primitive areas with less well-maintained roadways, much off-road vehicle use, low interaction between recreationists' and no formal recreation development or facilities. *Backcountry/wilderness areas* are defined as semiprimitive or primitive non-motorized areas removed from the sight or sound of motorized roadways or developed sites, concentration of recreationists is low, and no site modifications or development except for minimal safety of users.

[b] To obtain percent in which respondents reported 'not at all important' or 'don't know' subtract 96.6 from 100.0 percent.

and California. These individuals work as recreation specialists, planners, resource or recreation managers, and interpreters. All work daily at a particular recreation area, rather than at regional offices, and have direct contact with recreation users, on-site concerns, and physical and social impacts.

3. Perceptions about vandalism

Respondents were provided a list of problems such as 'vandalism to park facilities' and asked: 'How important are each of the following problems in your recreation area?' Response categories included 'not at all', 'somewhat', 'very much', or 'don't know'. Table 1 summarizes the impacts of vandalism perceived by managers to be 'very important' or 'somewhat important' across various recreation environments.

The number of impacts and their intensity increases toward the modern-urban end of the ROS. Vandalism is perceived by managers as an important concern across a variety of settings; however, as we move closer to the modern-urban conditions of the spectrum, impacts increase and are perceived as more important (see table 1). In other words, impacts are perceived as more important in developed settings as compared to primitive environments. This might be expected because of the greater density of users at the developed end of the spectrum and the presence of more facilities. For instance, 97% of the managers perceived 'vandalism to park facilities' in developed and semi-developed areas as a problem; however, fewer managers perceived vandalism to facilities as a problem in other areas with fewer facilities (74% in dispersed areas and 59% in backcountry/wilderness areas). It is still a problem, however, as over half of the managers report 'vandalism to park facilities' in primitive areas. Damage to signs and trail boardwalks are some of the concerns in these areas.

'Vandalism to resources or habitat' such as illegal firewood gathering, polluting the water, or harrassing wildlife is a concern to managers across all settings. Vandalism to users' equipment such as destruction to recreationists' cars or campstoves is perceived important toward the modern-urban end of the ROS but not as important as in other areas.

We asked about specific kinds of vandalism. 'Carving on tables', for instance, was perceived by managers as an important concern across the spectrum (ranging from 83% in modern-urban settings to 53% in primitive settings). Similarly, 'damage to trees from nails or axe' was perceived as important (ranging from 93% toward the developed end of the ROS to 70% in primitive settings). Furthermore, we asked about 'graffiti using pens and other media' and 'carving on tables'. They were perceived by managers as more important toward the modern-urban than the primitive end of the ROS.

Table 2. Percent of managers reporting potential solutions to vandalism as 'very important' or 'somewhat important'.

Perceived solutions	Recreation Opportunity Spectrum							
	Developed areas (modern-urban)		Semi-developed areas		Dispersed areas		Backcountry/ wilderness areas (primitive)	
	%	Total N	%	Total N	%	Total N	%	Total N
Increased visibility of interpretive, maintenance, fire patrol, and other personnel	96.7	30	100.0	39	100.0	36	88.9	36
Better communication of reasons behind the rules	93.5	31	94.8	38	91.5	35	88.3	34
Stricter enforcement of rules	93.4	30	94.9	39	86.1	36	82.9	35
Increased patrolling of area by law enforcement	93.3	30	97.4	38	86.6	35	85.7	35
Use of vandal-resistant materials	93.3	30	92.4	39	82.8	35	73.6	34
Reporting by the public of	93.3	30	92.3	39	91.7	36	86.2	36

...programs	90.4	31	89.7	39	69.4	36	71.5	55
Increased maintenance of the area	90.0	30	94.7	38	83.3	36	76.4	34
Stricter convictions by the courts	86.7	30	89.8	39	94.4	36	91.6	36
User involvement to determine their needs and how they may differ from agency goals and programs	86.7	30	87.2	39	83.3	36	80.5	36
Presence of host or volunteer at recreation site	86.6	30	92.1	38	54.5	33	62.5	32
Educational programs at schools and clubs	86.2	29	89.4	38	91.7	36	86.1	36
Entry station with full-time attendant	83.9	31	62.1	37	33.4	33	40.7	32
Incentives to users for proper behavior	83.3	30	80.6	36	66.7	33	75.8	33
Separation of site for different types of activities	76.7	30	82.1	39	67.6	34	54.5	33
Increasing user involvement in monitoring areas	86.6	30	87.1	39	86.1	36	77.7	36
Fees to use the area	66.6	30	67.6	37	34.3	35	37.5	32
Closure of isolated problem sites	46.5	28	59.4	37	50.0	34	44.1	34

Results suggest that vandalism is perceived by recreation managers as important across all settings. The perceived importance is relative and varies from 'important' in modern-urban environments to 'less important' in primitive settings. In primitive settings, however, 31% of the managers still perceive vandalism to be an important concern. To mitigate these impacts, managers, planners, and researchers need to better understand the nature of the facilities or resource impacted, the characteristics of the setting, and the kinds of situations in which the environment is destroyed.

4. Perceptions about prevention and control strategies

Respondents were asked 'In your judgment, do you believe the following strategies would be effective in reducing problems which are occurring at your recreation area?'. Response categories were: 'Not al all', 'somewhat', 'very much', or 'don't know'.

'Increased visibility of the authority figure' was the management strategy consistently perceived as most important for the prevention and control of vandalism across all settings (table 2). This practice is already used in many recreational areas that have recreation and/or fire patrols. Because many incidents of vandalism occur when park employees are not present, increasing patrol times or adjusting patrol hours to match hours when users are present may reduce some impacts.

Some strategies are perceived as more important than others in certain settings; for example, in dispersed areas and backcountry/wilderness areas, 'reporting by the public of illegal incidents' and 'stricter convictions by the courts' were perceived as important strategies. In these settings, control strategies that are subtle, indirect, and take place off-site – use of the courts, better communication of the rules, and public involvement – are considered especially important.

In developed and semi-developed areas where park personnel monitor users more closely, managers reported all solutions as effective. Most strategies were endorsed by over 75% of the recreation managers as effective. The presence of an entry station with a full-time attendant was endorsed by 83% of managers for mitigating some problems but by fewer (62%) in semi-developed areas. Hosts or volunteers currently reside in many semi-developed areas during the recreation season. The practice is well-received by the public and perceived effective by managers in preventing some vandalism.

Across all settings of the ROS, closing isolated problem sites was the one strategy perceived less effective than other strategies in mitigating vandalism. Closing sites may remove the opportunity or target from the potential vandal – it may be a consequence if not a solution. Closing sites results, however, in the majority of recreationists suffering for the actions of a few vandals. In some situations, closing sites may invite vandals rather than deter them.

5. Conclusions

This paper has described the importance of vandalism and perceived solutions as reported by recreation managers in the Pacific Northwest and California. Managers are expressing concern about vandalism across the recreation opportunity spectrum. Damage to resources and habitat is apparent, and concern about damage to facilities and users' equipment is especially strong in areas toward the more developed end of the spectrum.

Resource managers do not see one approach as a total solution. Rather, they advocate a variety of practices to mitigate the impacts of vandalism. Littering and anti-littering research is a good example of a systems approach that uses empirical testing of the effectiveness of different strategies. Research has shown the relative effectiveness of education, litter cans and bags, using incentives, and involving the public (Clark, 1976a, 1976b; Clark et al., 1972a, 1972b; Christensen, 1981). More research of this type – developing and testing a comprehensive approach – is needed to reduce vandalism.

Little is known about the real effectiveness of these strategies in mitigating vandalism. Evaluation studies are needed to determine the conditions in which various strategies are effective. Different strategies may work for some kinds of vandalism but not others; and some strategies will work only in certain settings.

To understand vandalism and its prevention and control, managers, planners, and researchers need to identify why some settings are vandalized and others are vandal-free. Why, for instance, are some facilities destroyed or damaged and others are not? What kinds of management strategies reduce specific kinds of impacts?

The results of this analysis are suggestive only – an investigation based on a larger sample of agency personnel will allow for a more comprehensive analysis of the relations between environments, impacts, users, and management practices.

Effective methods of controlling vandalism and other destructive activity in natural environments will help managers develop and maintain quality recreation opportunities and minimize conflicts between forest users. The potential payoff of such research is high and would result in reduced drain on operating budgets of managing agencies and reduced environmental and social impacts. This information will increase the quality of recreational opportunities and experiences by improving safety and security for visitors while they are on forest and range lands.

Acknowledgement.   The assistance of Diane M. Samdahl, Linda D. Sims, and M. Kevin Burke is gratefully acknowledged.

References

Alfano, S.S., A.W. Magill, eds., 1976. Vandalism and outdoor recreation: Symposium proceedings. Gen. Tech. Rep. PSW-17. Berkeley (CA): U.S. Department of Agriculture, Forest Service, Pac. Southwest For. and Range Exp. Stn.

Australian Parks and Recreation, 1982. Applying the recreation opportunity spectrum. Canberra, (Australia): Royal Australian Inst. of Parks and Recreation.

Bronson, D., 1981. Vandalism in national parks: A preliminary report. Interpretation and Visitor Services Division, National Parks Branch, Parks Canada.

Bronson, D., 1982. Vandalism in national parks, phase two. Interpretation and Visitor Services Division, National Parks Branch, Parks Canada.

Brown, P.J., B.L. Driver, D.H. Bruns, C. McConnell, 1979. The outdoor recreation opportunity spectrum in wildland recreation planning: Development and application. In: Proceedings, First Annual National Conference on Recreation Planning and Development, vol, II, pp. 527–538. New York: American Society of Civil Engineers.

Christensen, H.H., 1981. Bystander intervention and litter control: Evaluation of an appeal-to-help program. Research Pap. PNW-287. Portland (OR): U.S. Department of Agriculture, Forest Service, Pac. Northwest For. and Range Exp. Stn.

Christensen, H.H., R.N. Clark, 1979. Understanding and controlling vandalism and other rule violations in urban recreation areas. In: Proceedings of the National Urban Forestry Conference, 1978, November 13–16, Washington, D.C.

Clark, R.N., 1976a. Control of vandalism in recreation areas – fact, fiction, or folklore? In: S.S. Alfano, A.W. Magill, eds., Vandalism and outdoor recreation: Symposium proceedings, pp. 62–72. Gen. Tech. Rep. PSW-17. Berkeley (CA): U.S. Department of Agriculture, Forest Service, Pac. Southwest For. and Range Exp. Stn.

Clark, R.N., 1976b. How to control litter in recreation areas: The incentive system. Portland (OR): U.S. Department of Agriculture, Forest Service, Pac. Northwest For. and Range Exp. Stn.

Clark, R.N., 1982. Promises and pitfalls of the ROS in resource management. Australian Parks and Recreation, May, 9–13.

Clark, R.N., G.H. Stankey, 1979. The recreation opportunity spectrum: A framework for planning, management, and research. Gen. Tech. Rep. PNW-98. Portland (OR): U.S. Department of Agriculture, Forest Service, Pac. Northwest For. and Range Exp. Stn.

Clark, R.N., R.L. Burgess, J.C. Hendee, 1972a. The development of anti-litter behavior in a forest campground. Journal of Applied Behavioral Analysis 5 (1), 1–5.

Clark, R.N., J.C. Hendee, R.L. Burgess, 1972b. The experimental control of littering. Journal of Environmental Education 4 (2).

Clark, R.N., J.C. Hendee, F.L. Campbell, 1971a. Depreciative behavior in forest campgrounds: An exploratory study. Res. Note PNW-161. Portland (OR): U.S. Department of Agriculture, Forest Service, Pac. Northwest For. and Range Exp. Stn.

Clark, R.N., J.C. Hendee, F.L. Campbell, 1971b. Values, behavior and conflict in modern camping culture. Journal of Leisure Research 3 (3), 143–159.

Downing, K., R.N. Clark, 1979. User's and manager's perceptions of dispersed recreation impacts: A focus on roaded forest lands. In: R. Ittner, D.R. Potter, J.K. Agee, eds., Recreation impact on wildlands: Conference proceedings, 1978, October 27–29, pp. 18–23. Seattle (WA): U.S. Forest Service and National Park Service, Pacific Northwest Regions.

Dreissen, J., 1978. Problems in managing forest recreation facilities: A survey of field personnel.

Missoula (MT): U.S. Department of Agriculture, Forest Service, Equipment Development Center.

Driver, B.L., P.J. Brown, 1978. The opportunity spectrum concept and behavioral information in outdoor recreation resource supply inventories: A rationale. In: Integrated inventories of renewable natural resources, pp. 24–31. Gen. Tech. Rep. RM-55. Fort Collins (CO): U.S. Department of Agriculture, Forest Service.

Hendee, J.C., G.H. Stankey, R.C. Lucas, 1978. Wilderness management. Misc. Publ. No. 1365. Washington, D.C.: U.S. Department of Agriculture, Forest Service.

Samdahl, D.M., H.H. Christensen, R.N. Clark, 1982. Prevention and control of depreciative behavior in recreation areas: Managerial concerns and research needs. In: Forest and river recreation: Research update, pp. 52–54. Agricultural Exp. Stn., Miscellaneous Publication. Univ. of Minnesota.

Shafer, E.L., Jr., R.C. Lucas, 1978. Research needs and priorities for dispersed recreation management. Journal of Leisure Research 10 (4), 311–320.

U.S. Department of Agriculture, Forest Service, 1975. Recreation information management system. Washington, D.C.: RIM Center.

U.S. Department of the Interior, 1978. National urban recreation study. Executive Rep. Washington, D.C.: Heritage Conserv. and Recreation Serv.

U.S. Department of the Interior, 1979a. Memorandum – Servicewide crime statistics, 1978. Washington, D.C.: National Park Service.

U.S. Department of the Interior, 1979b. Ranger activities and protection division report. Washington, D.C.: National Park Service (mimeo).

U.S. Department of the Interior, 1981. A national agenda for recreation research. Washington, D.C.: National Park Service.

Westover, T.N., M. Chubb, 1979. Crime and conflict in urban recreation areas. Presented at the Second Conference on Scientific Research in the National Parks, 1979, November 26–30, San Francisco (CA).

Abstract: H.H. Christensen, Vandalism: an exploratory assessment of perceived impacts and potential solutions

For nearly two decades, managers have reported concern about vandalism, littering, and other depreciative behaviors in outdoor recreation environments. As part of a larger research effort, recreation managers of the USDA Forest Service, the National Park Service and Bureau of Land Management, U.S. Department of the Interior in the Western United States were asked to report their perceptions of and experiences with vandalism. Results suggested that impacts varied across a variety of settings ranging from developed to backcountry and wilderness. The perceived importance of impacts was greater toward the developed side of the spectrum. Furthermore, managers perceived a variety of strategies as effective in reducing vandalism – the courts, the public, schools and clubs, and recreation managers.

PART FIVE

Tackling vandalism:
the lesson of action research

CHAPTER 19

Vandalism in residential areas in England: Oldham case study

An architect's view

J.K. WAWRZYNSKI

The contents of this paper are largely based on research carried out in 1979 and 1980 by my colleagues and me in Oldham Metropolitan Borough in conjunction with Manchester University and Manpower Services Commission.

1. Aims of the study

Our major task was to give assistance to a local authority which had become concerned with an increasing level of vandalism on their council estates (publicly owned, rented housing). The general statistics of vandalism nation-wide were, at the time, very alarming. In 1971, in England and Wales, there were 27,000 reported cases of criminal damage (assuming that vandalism has been classified under this definition). In 1979, this figure had reached 250,000 and in 1980, 320,000, at the estimated cost of £100 m. p.a. In Greater Manchester alone, the increase in criminal damage between 1975 and 1980 was estimated at 153%.

The choice to study the town of Oldham was justified in two ways: firstly, the problem generally and the amount of vandalism appeared to be fairly 'typical' for the North-West of England, and, secondly, the local authority was keen on establishing links with academics in the hope of working out a policy based on the commissioned report. The expectations of the study were as follows:
— to discover the incidence of vandalism and to try to define it;
— to explain vandalism in terms of physical design and to find a relationship between physical factors and the incidence of vandalism;
— to recommend preventive action, both in terms of design changes and materials, which may be taken by Local Authority.

Any explanation of vandalism solely in design terms can only be a partial one, as it considers only the opportunity to commit damage and not the *motive* of the person committing the damage. If, however, a hypothesis is formulated that physical factors play an important role in the occurrence of vandalism on housing estates, two broad areas of consideration could be considered: firstly, the *macro-scale* approach, dealing with the 'defensible space' concept, and, secondly, the *micro-scale*, dealing with the specification of actual materials and finishes.

2. Selection of study method

The approach adopted was based on a small number of 'visually deteriorating' and vandalised estates in Oldham. This allowed us to keep the research at a manageable level and, therefore, to spend time on examining the chosen example in detail, to analyse the findings and to produce a detailed report to the authority.

In terms of both macro- and micro-scale, three points had to be considered:

(1) *What areas were to be investigated* within the residential development selected for the study? It was decided that this would include not only the external area immediately around the block(s) (including car parks, pedestrian and vehicular access routes, childrens' play areas, landscaped areas and front gardens), but also semi-public areas within the buildings (vertical and horizontal access, i.e., decks, galleries, lifts, etc.). Damage to the interior of dwellings has been excluded.

(2) *What damage should be recorded as vandalism?* As the term 'vandalism' is used to describe a wide range of conditions it was decided to record not only willful damage (insofar as it can be determined in accordance with the Criminal Damage Act 1971, Sect. 1, para 1), but also general degradation of the environment specified in the above paragraph, for it might be difficult to separate those two factors.

(3) *How was damage to be recorded?* The method of direct observation and interviews with tenants was adopted to ascertain all aspects of poor environmental quality. It was impossible to refer to the local authority housing repair records because these did not distinguish between 'wear and tear' repairs and vandalism repairs. It should be noted that the level of damage recorded reflected the efficiency (or inefficiency) of the maintenance or caretaking services.

As suggested above, the aim of the survey was to look at several (previously selected) estates and determine whether their 'bad' appearance could be attributable to vandalism, lack of maintenance or general wear and tear. Whilst certain elements (such as the number of broken window panes) could be noted directly, other elements were assessed and measured on a scale which indicated condition. This unavoidably involved a certain degree of subjectivity, but by using a stringent set of criteria, the problem was reduced to a minimum.

Of the four investigated estates, we decided to explore further Pearly Bank in Sholver, as it presented a typical case of a rapidly deteriorating deck access development (regarded by the Local Authority as a 'priority area') and also of extremely 'bad' appearance, with clear symptoms of vandalism and general neglect.

3. Pearly Bank case study

3.1. Historical background

The building of Pearly Bank contains 134 flat units ranging from four-bedroom maisonettes to one-bedroom flats, built between 1968 and 1970, approximately three miles from the town centre of the Sholver II estate. The original application to build at Sholver was at first turned down by the Minister on the grounds of severe climatic and environmental conditions. Sholver is one of the highest sites for large scale council development in the country and therefore greatly affected by strong winds, rain and frost. Subsequently, pressure was exerted on the Minister to reverse his decision, the reasons mainly being attributable to the fact that within the borough there was no alternative site. Finally, permission was granted for building 1,400 homes at Sholver, in two phases. Included in the plans were sites for a community centre, a public house, shops, a library as well as a primary school to be built on the Lower Sholver site. The responsibility for the detailed design of Lower Sholver (Pearly Bank) was assigned to a private practice who had undertaken other housing developments in Oldham.

Following the report of an independent consultant, the final choice of the type of construction was Bison prefabricated elements, a system of moulded concrete panels over a concrete superstructure. The whole development consisted of two medium-size deck access blocks. This, it was concluded, was the cheapest, most efficient and least time-consuming method of construction.

As a result of a lack of co-ordination and delays in the provision of services, houses on the estate were completed, handed over and tenanted long before even the area in which they were located was tidied up and finished. Plans for a comprehensive residential community centre (cinema, library, sports facilities, etc.) were abandoned and total occupation of the site took place before a small shopping centre was built. As a result of this, the estate experienced a sharp decline in environmental terms and an increased level of vandalism. This view was echoed by architects and planners in the Local Authority who felt that "the tenants, instead of feeling proud of having been offered new accommodation did, in fact, feel that they had been 'fobbed off'". It was their opinion that "this lack of a complete scheme had led to most of the vandalism on this site".

Some of the previously mentioned facilities had later been provided, but the fact remains that at the time when our research started Pearly Bank (and Sholver generally) was difficult to let. This dissatisfaction had been further augmented by problems of expensive electrical underfloor heating, condensation and rising damp which have all contributed to the particularly 'bad' image of this block.

286   *J.K. Wawrzynski, Oldham case study*

3.2. *Survey of internal semi-public areas* (carried out in 1978/79)

Our detailed survey of stairwells, internal lights, refuse chutes, doors and windows along decks, and lifts, revealed that the block suffered extensively from various kinds of vandalism. Internal lights were found to be not working (45%; see table 1) all glass had suffered extensively, 23% of all door windows were damaged (table 2) and 25% of all windows adjacent to the decks were either broken or boarded up.

The stairwells and the decks themselves were in poor condition, the doors were nearly all missing and the windows generally had no glass in them, and much of the lead flashing had been removed. The lifts were rarely working during our visits and one of them had been out of order for a long time (18 months). There was extensive graffiti on all stairwell walls (see table 3).

Table 1. Internal lights in stairwells.

Condition	Pearly Bank	Wilkes Street
Total number of internal lights	30	26
Total number of lights not working	12 (9) [a]	3 (3) [a]

[a] Figures in brackets refer to numbers of lights previously observed in working order.

Table 2. Condition of door windows and windows along decks.

Condition	Pearly Bank	Wilkes Street
Door window damaged [a]	16	5
Window damaged	7	3
Window boarded	6	1
Total number of flats	125	111

[a] 'Damaged' refers to windows that are cracked, smashed or temporarily boarded up. Percentage affected: Pearly Bank 23%, Wilkes Street 8%.

Table 3. Graffiti on walls and ceilings in semi-public areas.

	Pearly Bank	Wilkes Street
Walls		
Number of walls on landings	34	30
number affected by graffiti	27	14
Number of stairwell walls [a]	30	26
number affected by graffiti	24	19
Ceilings		
Number of ceilings below stairwells	26	22
number affected by graffiti	17	7

[a] Two sides counted as one wall.

In terms of cost, the expenditure on *lifts* alone during the 18-month period of our research was over £4,000 and about a third of this sum was used for repairing damage caused by vandals.

3.3. Survey of external (public) areas

This included investigation of the condition of footpaths adjacent to the block, car park, and general landscaping. The result was equally depressing. The general impression was one of neglect; littered and virtually impassable footpaths, glass littered car park (see fig. 1), and very poor landscaping with broken trees and damaged street furniture.

Figure 1. Glass-littered entry to the car park.

3.4. Conclusions of the surveys

The surveys revealed substantial damage to the environment on top of *other* known problems such as a high turnover of tenants, difficult to let flats, frequent 'break-ins' etc. The following points had to be considered.

(1) The *type of layout* used undoubtedly contributed to the high degree of vandalism. It is symptomatic of the deck-access systems that the semi-public space is not only large but also very difficult to control as decks run the entire length of the building and become difficult to supervise 'through corridors' (see fig. 2). These passageways are therefore a perfect example of 'indefensible space', they do not appear to belong to anybody in particular, strangers would not be challenged, and a high degree of privacy is offered to the vandal to operate undetected.

The semi-public nature of the access-ways also helped to explain the high level of 'break-ins'. The burglars were able to enter and move around freely. This might in turn help to explain the excessive number of dogs (and the associated problems, e.g. dirty decks) as people may have attempted to protect their property.

(2) The level of vandalism reflected also the use of *inappropriate materials*, e.g. the smooth paint surfaces in stairwells were very easy to write on with felt pen or crayon, it could also be disfigured by scratching the paint surface with a knife. This type of finish is particularly unsuitable in a stairwell. The use of

Figure 2. Long decks become 'through corridors' and provide an opportunity for vandals.

Figure 3. Inappropriate materials provide an opportunity for vandals.

glass along semi-public decks as well as most of the other fittings were found to be inappropriate. This provided the opportunity for acts of vandalism (see fig. 3).

(3) The problem of rubbish and litter in the communal areas was partly related to poor design, e.g. inadequate openings in the rubbish chute system, difficult to clean surfaces, etc.

(4) Other problems included a high turnover of tenancies; therefore, the tenants adopted a negative attitude to their environment and did not show any pride in living there. Statistics show that 69% of tenancies ended in less than two years and only 5.8% tenancies had been maintained for five years or more. By contrast, in other Oldham estates it was evident that only 26% of tenancies were for less than two years and 55.8% had remained for over five years.

4. Options for Pearly Bank (May 1979)

In order to deal with the problem the following options were put before the Council:

(1) Environmental improvement scheme, including improved management and maintenance services (suggested by our team).
(2) Demolition or partial demolition followed by replacement of dwellings of a different design not necessarily on the site.

(3) Outright sale to an interested developer without any improvements.
(4) Sale to a housing association on condition that the scheme would be improved.
(5) Comprehensive improvement by the Authority and then sale of individual units.

4.1. Environmental improvement scheme

In a report submitted to the council, the university team suggested the following:
- establish more direct identification for each tenant with his part of the block;
- provide opportunities for the tenants to contribute to the quality of their environment.

The concept was based on the introduction of *defensible space* into the block, i.e. to allow residents to control and supervise (visually) access to and use of the stairwells/lifts and decks.

In general, the amount of semi-public space would then be reduced and a number of semi-private spaces would be created (which could easily be supervised). The aim of the proposal was to increase the responsibility of the caretaker over the semi-private spaces, create more *private* spaces (fenced back gardens) as well as to improve the quality of materials/finishes and the general maintenance level. Consideration should also be given to better quality landscape.

The following therefore was proposed in terms of *physical design*:

(1) Alteration of access. Two different types of access were proposed: (a) main entrance, (b) fire escape (door opened only from inside). The whole block would be divided into two parts. This would involve a wall/barrier across the decks with a connecting door for emergencies only.

(2) Main entrance in each section equipped with entry-phone. This would also involve constructing a lobby supervised by the caretaker who would be available at certain times.

(3) General upgrading of decks. Planting boxes, use of colour, suitable materials to facilitate cleaning were suggested.

(4) Provision of private back gardens.

(5) The provision of children's (5–15 years old) play area, *away* from the building, was recommended. The proposal did not include any equipment.

On top of this, the team suggested changes in management with regard to tenants allocation policy (high ratio of children was found to be inappropriate in this type of layout), as well as improved maintenance services.

Although this option involved a high capital outlay on capital expenditure, long-term benefits might have been gained, i.e. increase in rent revenue. Also, unlike the demolition of the block, it did not involve a reduction in the council housing stock and consequently the cost of new dwellings.

The cost of the scheme was estimated in the region of £500,000 (including some improvements *inside* the dwellings).

In general terms, the fundamental aim of this proposal was not only to introduce defensible space into the blocks but also to improve the quality of design, materials and finishes as they alone have a significant part to play in enhancing the communal areas of the block. It was hoped that these measures would generate greater pride and responsibility amongst the tenants so that they in turn would play a more active and positive role in the upkeep of the block.

4.2. Results

It was the Council's decision (minutes of the council meeting in Jan.–March 1980) not to implement fully our recommendations as the estimate for the works was said to be too high. Instead, they opted for partial demolition and proposed the removal of two upper storeys, claiming that what will be left (two-storey 'traditional' block) would be both manageable and aesthetically satisfying. In order to proceed with the demolition (costing £70,000) the tenants were evacuated in April 1980. In May, however, as a result of a change of political power (Conservatives lost the local election and Labour took over), it was decided to halt the operation and not proceed with the alteration. The inevitable happened and the block (unoccupied) was left exposed to further attacks of local vandals and soon became a 'vandals' paradise' (see fig. 4). At

Figure 4. The development has become a 'vandals' paradise'.

the beginning of 1981, all that was left was a completely devastated shell with all internal fittings removed or destroyed (see fig. 5).

The newly elected Council had to shelve the plan of partial demolition when they learned that due to the condition of the whole block the scheme would cost £1.2m (including refurbishing of flats). As an alternative to total demolition they have tried (May 1981) to attract the attention of a private developer by offering the whole complex freehold for £1, but no offers had been received. In August 1981, the total cost of the demolition (the only realistic option), including the payment of the 50-year loan, was estimated at £1.7m. The site after clearance was to be offered to developers for luxury private housing. The block was finally demolished in November 1981 at the total cost of £2m to the ratepayers, and negotiations started with regard to the sale of the plot.

5. Final remarks and conclusions

In concluding the above case study, I would like to present a couple of general observations which might put more light on the mechanism of our research in Oldham as well as explain our failure insofar as we failed to persuade the Council to adopt our policy and implement our recommendations.

Analysing the whole strategy which had been presented to the Authority in terms of preventive action, it would appear that they failed to combine the

Fig. 5. View of Pearly Bank in 1980, showing the escalating deterioration.

'social' and the 'design' aspects of our approach, even in the case of Pearly Bank which came to be seen as 'the problem'.

Even here, the discussion concerned itself almost entirely with devising those modifications in the *physical* design and layout which would be most likely to reduce the level of vandalism. Our point, that the actual nature of these physical modifications is valid only in conjunction with consultations with tenants, as well as radical changes in management, was largely ignored.

In conclusion we pointed out that *preventive* rather than defensive measures were needed. This incorporates modification of the design and layout on housing estates, caretakers to provide supervision and a housing allocation policy and management which distributes families with children more equably.

It seems perfectly natural that in most of the cases the architects/planners should confine themselves to common-sense precautions and select finishes and materials that work and provide little opportunity for the vandal. A design guide based on these precautions should therefore be produced and used in all local authorities nation-wide, as the problem is not confined to specific geographical areas.

To give guidance to protect architects in the future, we ought to investigate the influence of building design in relation to vandalism and even produce *standard* details of layouts for areas particularly liable to attack. The creation of 'defensible' space is crucial here. Damage occurs most frequently where there is little surveillance. It also occurs in areas where ownership is ambiguous, the no-man's-land for which nobody is responsible. To this extent, the amount of vandalism a building/layout suffers is related directly to the amount of 'indefensible space' it has.

As pointed out before, tenure (ownership) may be as important as territory. There is evidence that council estates (public sector) suffer generally more than private ones, irrespective of their layout and design.

The correct management should also be considered as a priority issue. This has to be based on a co-operation of all parties concerned: planners, architects, housing departments, maintenance departments, caretakers and tenants.

References

Boys, J., 1978. The quality of life on council estates. Building Design, 3 March, 2.

Brown, A., 1978. Vandalism – who is to blame? Planning 258, 10 March, 12.

Broxap and Corby, 1981. A designer's approach. In: Proceedings of the Vandalism Conference, Warrington New Town, June.

Clarke, R.V.G., 1978. Tackling vandalism. Home Office Research Unit, Research Study no. 47. London: HMSO.

Clarke, R.V.G., P. Mayhew, 1980. Designing out crime. Home Office Research Unit. London: HMSO.

Department of Environment, 1981. Priority estates project 1981. London: HMSO.

Fagg, J., 1977. Defensive design. The Architect, July.

Gladstone, F., 1980. Home Office report, 5 November.

Halton Borough Council, 1976. Halton anti-vandalism campaign: Final report. Widnes: Halton B.C.

Home Office Standing Committee on Vandalism, 1975. Protection against vandalism. London: HMSO.

McKean, C., 1978. Vandalism and building form. The Architects' Journal, 12 April.

Mawby, R.I., 1977. Defensible space: A theoretical and empirical appraisal. Urban Studies 14.

Newman, O., 1973. Defensible space. London: Architectural Press.

Oldham Metropolitan Borough Council, 1979a. Minutes of the Council meetings in September–December 1979.

Oldham Metropolitan Borough Council, 1979b. Minutes of the Treasurer's financial appraisal of various options re: Pearly Bank. 18 Dec. 1979.

Oldham Metropolitan Borough Council, 1980. Minutes of the Council meeting in January. Point on deck access blocks – Pearly Bank and Wilkes Street.

Pease, K., E.J. Reade, J. Wawrzynski, 1979a. Vandalism in residential areas in Oldham, pp. 170–186. Oldham Metropolitan Borough and Manchester University.

Pease, K., E.J. Reade, J.K. Wawrzynski, 1979b. Vandalism in residential areas in Oldham, Section 3, pp. 103–111. Oldham Metropolitan Borough and University of Manchester.

Schrerrer and Hicks, 1979. Report on upgrading of Sholver (Oldham). North British Housing Association (internal).

Sykes, J., ed., 1979. Design against vandalism. London: The Design Council.

West Pennine Housing Association Ltd., 1979. Pearly Bank rehabilitation (internal).

Wilson, S., 1977. Vandalism and design. Architectural Journal, 26 October.

Wilson, S., 1978. Updating defensible space. Architectural Journal, 11 October.

Wilson, S., A. Sturman, 1976. Vandalism research aimed at specific remedies. Municipal Engineering, 7 May, 708–713.

Abstract: J.K. Wawrzynski, Vandalism in residential areas in England: Oldham case study

The study, based on research carried out in one of England's North-West municipalities, attempts to rationalise the occurrence of vandalism in housing estates and to suggest possible modifications in physical design in order to combat the problem. The relationship between housing estates' macroscale (layout) and microscale (detailing, finishes) physical design is evident from a number of previous research studies. Our aim was to define the degree to which a particular neighbourhood suffered from vandalism and to offer practical solutions in design terms.

Having investigated a number of neighbourhoods as to their public and semi-public space, a medium-high-rise development was selected (Pearly Bank, Oldham) as a suitable area for the research. The detailed physical survey showed a high degree of vandalism and general neglect, and the accompanying social survey revealed problems symptomatic of 'sinking estates'.

The suggested remedies concentrated on an environmental improvement scheme as opposed to e.g. demolition, suggested by the Council. The scheme proposed various ways to reduce the semi-public space in the layout as well as in the blocks themselves in favour of semi-private spaces which would be easier to maintain and supervise. The proposal was never implemented: the block, left unoccupied for some months, deteriorated so badly that finally demolition was the only option left.

CHAPTER 20

Social urban design in Los Angeles' skid row

G. RAND

This is a study of vandalism and negative social behavior from an urban design perspective. It is based on the premise that in order to account for differences in individual behavior, even in a minimal manner, one must take into account a range of physical, social, and cultural variables. While vandalism is most certainly an individual impulse, it always is a response to an environmental context. Accounting for vandalism reveals the limits of psychological theories that do not also propose a theory of the environment, including the form of the environment and its genesis. Vandalism is only a part of the manifold interactions between organism and environment. It has to be understood in the context of an ongoing dialectic between environmental design, creation and destruction, all this at the scale of the individual, the social group and the society as a whole.

The particular subject of this paper is Los Angeles' Central City East, an area of low-income social services in downtown Los Angeles which has become known as 'Skid Row'. The area is subject to a great deal of vandalism and serves to underline a general pattern of social neglect. The streets have been the target of petty criminals eager to prey on the weakness of elderly low-income residents who live in a myriad of run-down hotels. The police enforcement of the area has been more concerned with clearing the streets of thousands of people who live without means than with protecting the rights of people to use the public streets in safety. Recently, a series of landmark court decisions have resulted in a new interpretation of the statutes concerning public drunkenness. No longer can police merely jail people for being drunk in public. They must now take them to medically oriented detoxification facilities which offer rehabilitation services.

Vandalism is a complex response to an extremely complex set of conditions. In the Skid Row area of Los Angeles that which we take to be vandalism is a normative response of a large number of residents in the community. This is true because the indigent residents of the community are living largely as 'hunter-gatherers' in what otherwise is an advanced industrial-capitalist society. Their concerns are simply defined and expressed. The basic need for water is hard to even imagine in a modern city. It is everywhere, pulsing underground, in taps in restaurants, homes, etc. But for the indigent resident who cannot enter any building because of his/her unsightly appearance it is like an urban desert. Bathrooms are not available and when they are they offer questionable security from robbery for the user.

Food is a major problem. Paradoxically, food is readily available in the form of cast-offs from the large produce market which offers wholesale service to the city. Though it is nearby and puts to waste about 20% of incoming produce as 'unsaleable', these foods are not available to the areas' indigents.

Shelter is not difficult to obtain in the relatively mild climate of Los Angeles and, in addition to old hotels, people find it in parks, doorways to abandoned stores, and small planted areas alongside freeways. Security in these places is very poor and people often wake up minus their shoes or other articles of clothing.

Much that passes for vandalism is a direct effort to see to these needs in an environment which does not make them directly available.

- water is potentially available all over the community by employing stand-pipes on streets;
- bathrooms could be made out of simple self-composing toilets designed to provide privacy while offering enough visibility to insure freedom of use;
- clothing changes (and showers, shaves, grooming) can be made available at missions making it possible to clean up for a period of time;
- new shelter opportunities are possible by building low-cost housing units, rehabilitating hotels, etc.;
- recreation opportunities and safe, supervised lounging areas can be designed to avoid the spectra of men and women using the public sidewalks as recreation areas.

The net effect of these efforts would be to allow the 'hunter-gatherer' lifestyle to continue in parallel with the more ordered commercial activities which occur in the area. A 'social service' zone can be created which can exist in harmony with a 'commercial' zone that occupies the same space. If the physical area and operational programs are defined properly, these parallel uses can co-exist with a minimum of conflict. Further, we would suggest that vandalism is a product, in large measure, of this tendency to mix 'social' and 'commercial' modes of organization in the same zone without considering the ways in which they contradict one another. This study attempted to elucidate some of these conflicts and experimented with a series of actions designed to resolve the conflicts between the 'hunter-gatherer' and 'industrial' uses of the city.

1. Urban design

Conventional urban design in a *commercial* context is concerned with 'exchange' value and the consumption of goods and services. Therefore, space is treated abstractly. Public investments in settings (e.g. plazas, streets, infrastructure costs) are justified by means of return on investment, the accumulation of tax-increments, the creation of new jobs and new households.

In a 'social service' zone, value is achieved by the production of settings which are supportive of human welfare, and not *via* consumption of goods and services. For example, currently, many residents of Central City East receive about $400/month individually in social service payments from the government. These payments barely cover the costs of lodging and meals. If communal kitchens were available and residents learned to share in their upkeep and use, there would be great dollar savings as well as the added security of human contact. For the most part, services of this kind are not provided. Commercial hotels, restaurants, clothing stores and pawn shops largely take advantage of residents despite their limited means. All the 'overhead' and 'profit' from these ventures is taken out of the community inasmuch as these facilities are owned and operated by people who do not reside in Skid Row.

Missions and other direct Social Service provisions are overburdened. They have industrialized the provisions of social services in order to deal with the large indigent populations that appeal to them endlessly for food, health care and lodging. Residents are routinely put through the cycle – deloused, lectured to, fed, allowed to sleep and then evicted. This is an oversimplification, of course, to put in relief the problems facing what otherwise are well-meaning and over-taxed organizations.

In point of fact, the thousands of indigents in the community bring millions of dollars per month into it in the form of relief payments, to say nothing of salaried employees who work for service agencies. These monies are largely taken out of the community or are not directed adequately to serve the needs of indigent residents.

This report is an account of a five-year effort to address this conflict in patterns of urban development ('commercial' vs 'social development' objectives) in Central City East. The leading agency in undertaking to achieve a new synthesis of objectives has been the Los Angeles Community Redevelopment Agency. The entire area of Central City East is under the authority of the agency's development powers and subject to review by its public Board of Directors. It is charged both with the need to insure economic stability in the areas and to guarantee the growth of the social support system for indigent residents in the community. This became the basis for a novel kind of urban design approach. The CRA has made commitments in the past five years to the following projects:

- construction of 270 units of low-cost, very small apartment units (25 square meters each) for indigent residents. A key feature of the project is a large courtyard which provides safe and secure outdoor space for residents, and a communal kitchen which provides one meal per day for residents;
- building of two small parks for neighborhood residents providing water,

toilets and limited recreation and outdoor seating;
- rehabilitation of run-down hotels (the first is already completed) to provide additional low-cost housing in the community;
- providing support for local self-help efforts. This has been done in the form of subsidizing the formation of the Skid Row Development Corporation.

This Agency has spurred a number of commercial ventures which provide jobs and services that are compatible with the needs of local residents. The Skid Row Development Corporation has built and leased with Federal assistance, "a light industrial center", that allows industries employing local residents (e.g. a bakery, or the recycling of aluminum and other materials) to survive and to operate at a lower overhead rate than market rates. The Skid Row Development Corporation has also founded Transition House, a shelter providing social services and temporary lodging for men and women.

The CRA has also acted indirectly to support the network of service agencies in the community, including missions, and philanthropic organizations. It has used its powers of persuasion and its economic powers to prevent the take-over of large areas of Central City East by outside industries which are incompatible with the social development objectives they have set for the community.

2. Social studies of Central City East

In 1978, I had the opportunity to carry out detailed studies of the physical context of Skid Row and to chart its impact on residents. The context is a large 50-block area bounded by an industrial area (the garment district) on the South, an entertainment and residential area on the north (Little Tokyo), business and shopping areas of downtown Los Angeles on the west, and railroad yards, and massive concrete flood control channels on the east. The population is estimated at about 15,000 residents, including an increasing number of families with children. As many as 5,000 additional people are estimated to live on the streets, parks and roadways in surrounding areas and use Central City East. They use this area as a location to make contact with social service agencies and for basic social supports like clothing changes, showers, minimal health care, alcohol, etc. The typical resident is 50 years or older, although this is changing with the recent increase in ultra-poor families with children. A base population exists of white males over 50. It is this population, many of whom are alcohol dependent and committed to the area as a matter of 'life style', to which the name Skid Row most readily applies.

An increasing percentage of minority residents of all origins is beginning to dominate the area. As a result, the community has come to resemble other communities of 'last resort'. With minor exceptions these ethnic and racial minorities each maintain separate 'turfs' in the community. Seventh Street is largely dominated by Latino (mostly Mexican) men, women and families. Sixth Street is almost totally occupied by black men. Fifth Street is a major spine of activity in the area and the hotels along it and in side streets near it are occupied by elderly white men, mostly war-veterans and pensioners.

Over the course of six months, our small research team kept close records of the 'staining' of streets, the presence of garbage, graffiti, broken glass and other products of human occupancy. This was done by carrying out systematic observations on more than 100 sites in the area which were sampled repeatedly at different times of the day and different days of the week during sampling periods separated by a four-month period. These physical measures were augmented by more intensive qualitative evaluations at the beginning and end of this research period of 20 individual 'behavior settings' in the community. These evaluations entailed 'participant observation' by the research team (dressed in the manner of local residents) in bars, day-labor centers, street-corners, sex shops, the bus station, a donut shop, a 'thieves market' and other important neighborhood 'haunts'. Finally, interviews were held with 15 'homeless' indigents, men who live on the streets or in small temporary shelters in alleys or doorways.

In general, it was discovered that a small number of street stains or areas of destruction can have an impact on the way a community is perceived that goes far beyond their actual significance. In point of fact, the appearance of Skid Row is created simultaneously by the appearance of dirt, graffiti or garbage and the presence of 'street people'. A small number of 'street people' can produce the appearance of occupancy of the community by this group and suggest to the passer-by or the expert that the community has been taken over by undesirables. Studies of the behavior of 'street people' and of physical evidence of their presence throughout the area suggested that they occupied only small islands of space throughout the area and that small signs (glass fragments, street stains) were enough to make their presence *felt* throughout. Also, many instances of what appeared to be vandalism and destruction were by-products of incompatible uses. For example, many stories were related about how 'street people' broke windows and destroyed plants and trees. These stories failed to indicate the accidental nature of the destruction. Hundreds of men are forced to line up nightly and wait for two or more hours for food or lodging. They dare not leave these lines for fear of losing their place. As a result, many lose control of vital functions, faint, become incontinent, become embroiled in conflicts, etc. The people of this community are constantly being lined up, rousted, moved and evicted from their locations, and this provides a different backdrop against which to judge their alleged vandalism.

2.1. Interviews with homeless indigents

In order to gain insight into the actual use of urban space by Skid Row indigents, a survey instrument was created in the style of Kevin Lynch's 'Image of the city' survey from his 1959 study of Los Angeles. Fifteen individual face-to-face interviews were conducted with subjects in the hall of St. Vincent Center between 9:00a.m. and 3:00p.m. on weekdays. People come into this hall from a lineup on the street: the doors open at 7:00a.m. and they are served donuts and coffee. There is a shower and bathroom through which people are cycled. Behind the 'cage' is the center's staff which metes out supplies (such as shaving cream and razor-blades) and stores possessions of street people for a short time in small wire racks. The men (and some women) sit around playing cards or checkers or watching TV inside a chain-link fence box. In the back of the large room there are 20 cots built by stringing a heavy plastic material across a frame made of plumbing pipe. Interviews lasted between 30 minutes and one hour and followed the course of questioning established in an interview outline as follows:

Cognitive mapping survey

  1. What first comes to mind when you hear the words Skid Row?
  2. How would you describe Skid Row to a stranger to Los Angeles?
  3. Where do you sleep at night?
  Tell me all the places you go during the day! Describe to me the sequence of things you see along the way from early in the morning until late at night. What do you see, smell, hear? Who do you talk to or interact with along the way? What buildings, places, or landmarks do you notice?
  If your routine is different on the weekend, tell me about it. Saturday? Sunday? Special days?
  4. Are there certain places on the trip during the day where you feel especially comfortable and like to stay as long as possible? Why?
  Are there places you like to get past as soon as possible? Why?
  5. Which elements of Skid Row are most distinctive and easy to remember? They can be large or small, well-known or very personal places.
  6. How would you describe [a certain landmark place] in a physical sense? What makes it such a distinctive place? (list of landmark places).

Although it is hardly surprising in retrospect, the first result of these interviews that is worthy of note is the degree of consensus that is apparent. Each of the men interviewed operates on his own with one or two compatriots at best and no two men live in the area in an identical fashion. Yet, all of them indicate a clear conception of Skid Row as having an 'urban form'.

For the most part, the range of settings mentioned by the subjects is not very different from that which would be significant for a conventional elderly population. The appearance of their typical behaviors is very different due to their low socio-economic status. They are elderly and disabled people who are simply not in harmony with their environment. Further, their behaviors are visible to the public because they do not live behind the closed doors of a private dwelling in a suburb. The conventional elderly person can regulate bodily functions, seek rest, eat food or sit in the sun in a manner that is in harmony with the environment. For the indigent people, taking a rest during a walk means sitting or lying on the ground rather than stopping at a cafe for a drink. Lack of access to toilets makes them appear incontinent and their poor diet and irregular eating habits as well as illness contribute to their lack of bodily control.

The settings which they identify as primary resources all contribute to fulfilling these basic goals. The sites identified by more than 50% of interviewees in their descriptions of Skid Row are as follows:

Midnight Mission	Volunteers of America
Union Rescue Mission	The Hospitality Kitchen
St. Vincent Center	Pershing Square (a major downtown park)

These elements form an urban context around the streets of Skid Row for men and women who live on the streets. A number of other sites are mentioned less often, but contribute to an overall pattern. The following are mentioned by 25% or more of the interviewees:

Harbor Light Mission	Victory Liquor
Los Angeles Mission	Greyhound Bus Terminal
Soul Clinic	The Blood Bank
El Rey Hotel	The Los Angeles Central Public Library
MacArthur Park	The Los Angeles Convention Center parking lot
The Singapore Bar	Winston Street Alley
Almar Bar	

There is an underlying consensus about the meaning, location and use of each of these sites. These and others form a *cognitive structure*, the physical context of Skid Row. Each interviewee established a pattern of daily use which is related to the Skid Row context. Their ways of life are remarkably similar to conventional uses of urban settings.

Conventional elderly settings	*Skid Row elderly settings*
sleeping/resting	sleeping in doorways
waiting for bus	lingering at bus stop
sitting in park	sleeping in park
grocery shopping	scavenging for food
laundering clothes	exchanging clothes at mission
post-office/banking	checking bags at terminal
department store visits	Thieves' Market – Russ Hotel
social center visits	day center
movie-going	Main Street all night movies
attending lectures, discussions	'ear-banging' services

organized trips	travel to East L.A./other areas
church	–
physician visits	Hospitality Kitchen
library	reading papers in library
gardening	–
home maintenance	–
cooking	tending open fires
entertaining at home	bottle gangs in alley

Some of the interview summaries are instructive about the texture of the community and the modes of adaptation of Skid Row residents to an extremely impoverished environment. For an illustration of this, see the appendix, where the responses of five interviewees are presented. For each of the cases presented, the freehand drawing (figures 1–5) is an attempt to represent pictorially the responses of subjects to the survey questions. The regular geometric shape intersecting these drawings is the actual boundary of Central City East's 51 square blocks in downtown Los Angeles.

3. Summary

In 1950, the average population of Skid Rows in American cities was 7–9,000; by 1970, this had dropped to 2,500–3,000. Lifestylers who lived on Skid Rows – middle-aged white men – were displaced by the lack of labor options to sub-nuclear areas, usually a series of smaller Skid Row-like areas in each city. While there is no reason to suspect the absolute size of the homeless, unemployed populations has diminished, the territories they occupy have shrunk.

Fear seems definitely on the rise and stores and hotels in the communities seem less protective of residents than in earlier times. Credit options are more difficult to find. People complain that they can no longer trust the streets to be safe.

There is a need to cut through the stereotypes concerning who lives in the area and why they live there. Hopefully, a new 'image' may begin to emerge which depicts the population as a community of last resort, made up of the poor elderly and disabled, men and women and small poor families with children. Central City East is a resource for dealing with the needs of this community. While traditional Skid Rows were supported by the need for occasional labor, the new 'Skid Row' is a social service community; money exists in the form of public assistance payments and social security supplements.

The area should begin to transform services from alcoholism treatment to concern with a broader range of needs – psychiatric counseling, health care and social support. The tasks of the local agencies (missions, charities) can gradually be broadened to include concern with the development of the community attempting, where possible, to coordinate services and expand the degree to which they maintain common records and to keep track of people who use overlapping services; in short, to become a 'halfway community' in which services offered are modified to match the diagnosed needs of the community.

4. Toward a new coalition

The problem with current processes of urban redevelopment is that they attempt to 'freeze' evolution at its present stage. The internal turbulence in our current urban system is too great to allow this type of control to be effective. As Beer says, in *Platform for change*, "We are no longer capable of solving our mounting problems". This does not mean all is despair. Rather, we cannot force their solution by mechanical problem-solving or resolve them by a simple technological breakthrough. We have to flexibly change the course and allow our perception of the attainable goals to be transformed – not denied us. We need to invent the future out of the present and not try to carve it out of images of the future imagined in another time for another set of actors.

The context of this paper is Los Angeles' Skid Row. Such areas are symptomatic. For many years – throughout the era of urban renewal and urban redevelopment – we asserted the necessity of planning and goal-setting. The systems we used for analyzing the problem generated environments designed to lend expression to these themes. Time-saving freeways and work-saving high-rise offices became *metaphors* of the production of human experience. In the interest of saving time and effort we industrialized our own experience.

What we need are urban design strategies which call attention to this paradox. American cities were created, on an industrial basis, along river edges and at the crossings of market roads in agricultural valleys. In the 19th century, the spreading of industry and the exploration of associated routes of commerce gave form to cities and surrounding regions. Downtown areas were concentrations of populations centered around railroad terminals and ports. Hotels sprung up to support these movements of people and products.

The post-industrial city is a product of the cybernetic metaphor. New generations of cities are the cybernetic derivative of the industrial city. Theoretically, their form is open to wide variation subject only to constraints of what is 'believable' as a coherent life setting. Like a caricature in art, the forms of buildings and neighborhoods are generalizing abstractions built on the diagrams of past buildings and neighborhoods.

Conceived this way, urban design is not the special province of those who bring to the analysis of cities the faded memories and borrowed, albeit time-tested metaphors of Europe and classical antiquity. All actors in the downtown drama are capable of contributing to the design of the future. It necessitates an attitude of forging new settings for a new society which are born out of old settings. Like the art of Japanese flower arrangement, it is a process of response of the arranger to the immediately preceding step and not the engineering of a solution based on a set of prescribed objectives.

With the removal of the working class from the central business districts came the general removal of all life, and in some instances business itself. Urban renewal programs ended up serving the needs of a small number of clients and surrendering the central city to commercial interests.

Once again, the tide has begun to turn back toward the central city: suburbanites have been drawn back to the center of life and culture, braving the risks of crime and vandalism in the central city. Living systems involve this dynamic flow between opposites, the force of the city and the force of the country.

The goal is to guide the dialog with a gentle tiller. The future of Skid Row requires a certain degree of protection from exploitation and rapid development, and yet sufficient impetus to sustain its transformation into a high-performance, socially effective zone offering genuinely human services and contributing to human well-being.

Through simply 'being there' in the community, one begins to grasp it as a totality. Out of this experience of the community comes a sense of what is central and what is peripheral to its inner workings, of what could be removed without consequences, of what additions or changes would require special explanation. Finally, comes a direction of development through dialog about the collective intentions of the community.

Appendix

Herbert, 54 years old, white, from Pt. Mills, West Virginia (figure 1)

The Police Station... they won't let him walk in front of the building or on the sidewalk.

He sleeps outside in the weeds... near the Hollywood Freeway. He might go up to the library to read or to the St. Vincent Center during the day. If he is brave he will sit in the park (Pershing Square) on the weekend.

He is an alcoholic and seems to have control of his relationships to other people. He buys liquor at 5th and Main. Goes to 3rd and Main to drink, Pocket Park.

When he sleeps in hotels, he goes to the Russ Hotel, the Panama Hotel, or the Lorraine Hotel, walking past the Hard Rock Cafe. He tries to avoid this area because he feels that it is dangerous. He noticed a knife fight there last week and the police didn't do anything. He claims that they don't care about his area. However, if the police cars are out, they will scare people away and the merchants in this area suffer.

Goes to the Blood Bank twice a week to give blood and get drinking money.

Favorite place is Graumman's Theatre in Hollywood.

Has never slept in the missions and shuns them because of the 'ear-banging' (sermons).

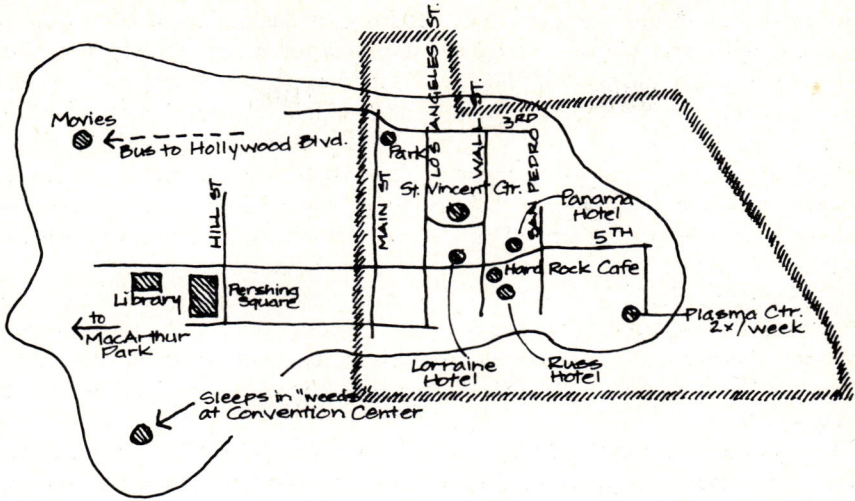

Figure 1.

Jim, 41 years old, white, born in Iowa (figure 2)

Left his wife 18 months ago. Has been on Skid Row since. Sleeps in 'The Weeds' outside of The Convention Center (bushes) or at the Union Rescue Mission.

Skid Row is "friendly", streets are dirty, run-down area, buildings not maintained, but the people are kind.

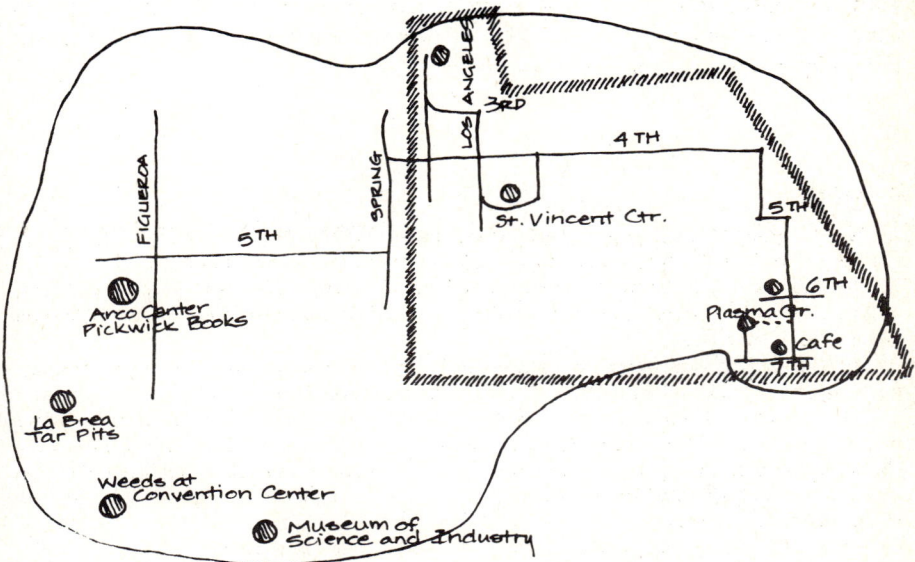

Figure 2.

Did not exhibit any daily pattern because he changes his sleeping places so often. However, he stated that he avoided Fifth Street from Los Angeles Street south but does use Fifth Street above Spring Street. He uses Winston Street, coming down Third or Fourth Streets from Main. He goes to the Hippie Kitchen for lunch every day or occasionally Seventh and Gladys. He does not use Pershing Square but rather prefers the alleys because they are safer from police.

He often goes to the Arco Center in the afternoon but is at St. Vincent center in the morning. He uses Fifth or sometimes Sixth to get there. He buys books at Pickwick. He goes into doorways of banks and buildings along Figueroa to drink and sometimes sleeps there as well. He goes there because it is safe. States that because an area is black, people think that it is dangerous but he goes there because he is safe.

He once went to Montana Reds, the Alcoholic Recovery Center, for a 12-step program but he left only four hours later.

He sells his blood at The Plasma Center once a week.

Saturdays he spends at The Arco Center listening to the bands play and sometimes goes to the City Mall for the same.

Sundays he goes to the Hyatt House or to Exposition Park. He travels as far as the Museum of Art, Science, and Industry, The Los Angeles County Museum, and Southgate.

His idea of what is inside the Police Station: a booking desk, a drop tank, 6-8 hours of observation, like the Glass House. He thinks that the new police station will alleviate the crime in the area by 25%.

Don, 35–40 years old, Chippewa Indian from Chicago   (figure 3)

Has been on Skid Row since 1970. Has a son in City of Commerce, not married, but the mother takes care of the son and he sometimes visits them both.

Skid Row: "the back door of yesterday". He can tell that it is Skid Row by the fumes and odors, the lower quality buildings, and police arrest more people for being drunk in public.

He sleeps outside on a mattress and pad, has been doing this for two weeks. He hides them so that no one will steal them.

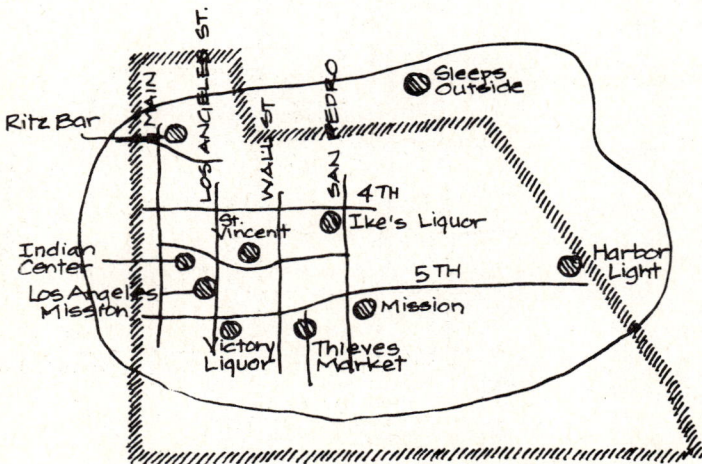

Figure 3.

Five favorite places: 5th and Los Angeles Street, liquor stores; 5th and San Julian, Thieves Corner, can buy anything there; 5th and San Pedro, Mission has the best beef stew; 4th and San Pedro, Ike's Liquor Store – holds on to guys' money for them and deducts their fees for drinks; and 3rd and Main, the Ritz Bar.

He also has an alley where he goes to drink and sits on the window sill of the Los Angeles Mission where it is safe.

On Saturdays and Sundays he panhandles. Saturdays, The Indian Center at 118 Winston Street and on Sundays he makes out the best he can.

In the Police Station: "there are the Vice Squad, The Narcs, and Blues".

Distances: from 2nd Street to 7th on Main, to the Union Rescue Mission. Has gone twice to MacArthur Park, Harbor Light Mission, Little Tokyo. Stays around 5th and Wall most of the time.

Howard, 62 years old, white   (figure 4)

Was drunk when I interviewed him. Hasn't worked for ten years. Has lived in missions since 1960.

"The L.A. Police Department poisons people's minds. They knock you in the head and they beat you up and you got to go to the County Hospital. And you're lucky to be alive. The State of California are a pack of liars, including Governor Brown".

Goes to Long Beach to get out of Los Angeles, to get away from "the stupid tramps". Goes to all but the Union Rescue Mission, stays at the Baptist Mission, The Soul Mission, and the Midnight Mission. And down in Long Beach at the Union Rescue Mission and the Wilmington Mission to see all his old drinking buddies.

"Skid Row stinks because there are too many fish markets".

Last night he slept in Whittier at the Rose Hill Cemetery, walked back to L.A. this morning.

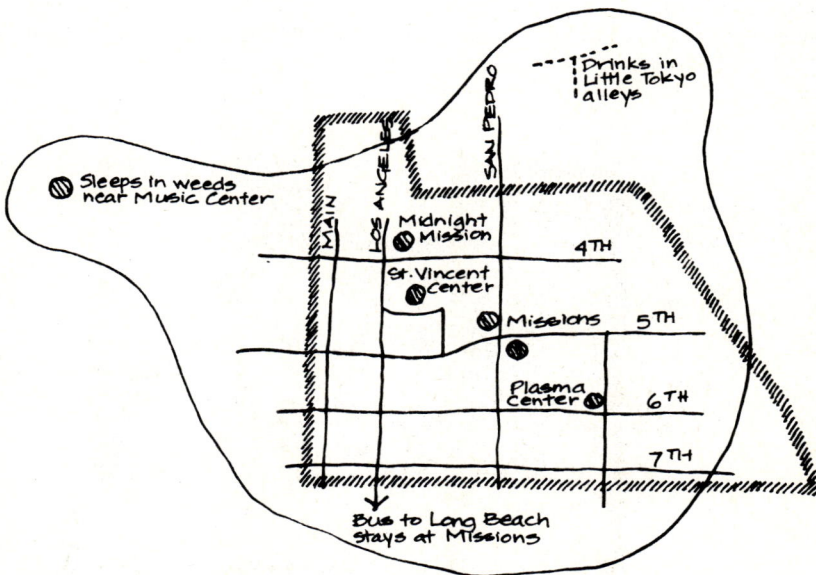

Figure 4.

His wife died ten years ago. He also sleeps near the Hollywood Freeway under the Music Center. Walks 25–30 miles every day. Goes to Little Tokyo to drink in the alleys, walks all over the Skid Row area. Goes to Santa Monica, Long Beach, and has been to Santa Barbara twice as well as Santa Ana. "Because the people here will kill you for two cents".

Avoids the Police Station, hasn't been in a police station for six months. Goes to the Blood Bank for money to buy liquor, gets $12. Will use it to go to Chicago or Arizona and work for the Salvation Army.

"Police jackroll the bums to steal their money".

Ed, 49 years old, white, from Detroit, Michigan (figure 5)

Sometimes sleeps in hotels and sometimes in Missions. Currently staying at the Golden West Hotel on 5th and San Pedro. Has prepaid and has a room for the next few days at $16.00/week. Uses 5th Street, up and down, and Main and Los Angeles Streets, Volunteers of America, The Union Rescue Mission and The Midnight Mission on Main.

Hotel is a "flophouse". Does not like The Los Angeles Mission; doesn't like the people or the ministry. Their attitude is bad, they "run you down". The meal is bad, beans aren't cooked. "Ear-beating" is tiresome. Has had his share. Hotel is not very clean, 10×12 size. Bed, dresser, and sink. No tub. Prefers taking bath or shower at the missions. Washes clothes at the Volunteers of America.

Sleeping outside is dangerous; too much thievery. Hippie Kitchen for lunch when he is broke; to the Midnight Mission at night for an evening meal. Gets up at 6:00a.m., walks down 5th to Wall, down Wall to Winston, Winston to St. Vincent Center to get a free cup of coffee. Sticks around and watches T.V. or plays cards. Takes this route to avoid 5th Street and the Singapore Bar where there are "coloreds", homosexuals. "Loaded with homosexuals, in my hotel, all over".

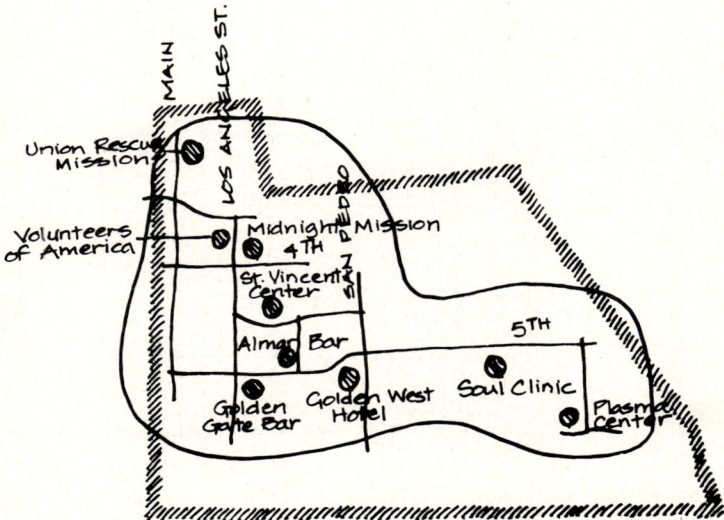

Figure 5.

For lunch, cuts over to San Pedro, then goes back down 5th to Towne or Sanford and uses the alleys to get to the Kitchen...the shortest distance. At night takes the long way to be safe, does not use the alleys at night. When he has money he "generally sits at the bar on Wall and 5th Street, The Almar Bar". In afternoons sits in the hotel lobby and watches T.V. Goes to the Soul Clinic sometimes for dinner, on Sanford. Has no friends, just acquaintances. Strictly on his own, less trouble.

Saturdays and Sundays...Volunteers of America or stays in bars when he has money. Never goes to the Hard Rock Cafe or The Singapore. Goes to The Almar or The Golden Gate, the 258 or the Valleria. Confined to the area, only goes outside to go to a doctor or to Little Tokyo.

Abstract: G. Rand, Social urban design in Los Angeles' skid row
This is the report of an action research project conducted in Los Angeles in the downtown Skid Row area. The study involved extensive observations and analysis of informal uses of streets by indigent people and resulted in recommendations to the City agency responsible for managing the redevelopment of downtown Los Angeles. The recommendations contributed to a process in which new parks, a 270-unit ultra-low-cost housing project and rehabilitated hotels were developed in the area for its residents. The study conceives of and provides evidence to support the belief that Skid Row dwellers are 'hunter gatherers' living in a commercial city and that this mismatch of needs and styles accounts for what appears to be vandalism in the area.

CHAPTER 21

British Telecom experience in payphone management

C.L. MARKUS

This paper looks at a large public organisation in the UK, British Telecom, which suffers from vandalism of its payphones, the attitude and policies of its managers towards the problem and the results, if any. The aim of the paper is to point towards further areas of research and maybe priorities.

1. The scale and nature of vandalism to British Telecom public payphones

Vandalism is defined for the purposes of this paper as destruction and damage without the clear motivation of fraud or theft. It is 'malicious damage', say our statistical returns, already hinting at the attitude of managers. Of course, our statistics of vandalism are as unreliable as others and there is a well-known overlap between vandalism and theft or fraud (e.g. a payphone may be smashed in an unsuccessful attempt to steal or coin chutes may be blocked to try and collect the coins and yet none are present), but cases of direct theft are so low in the UK that they can be ignored for all intents and purposes. Payphone vandalism, as defined, is widespread, severe and variable and there are some interesting correlations which will be apparent between vandalism and other variables. With 77,000 payphones, there were 230,000 recorded incidents of destruction and damage, excluding graffiti and urination and other acts of which, for obvious reasons, the statistics were not recorded. Figure 1 is not untypical of a filthy graffiti covered kiosk. What is interesting is: the level of vandalism measured in the number of incidents has not changed greatly over the last 20 years or so, despite the measures, one form of vandalism replacing another, as 'the problem' was partially solved.

The damage from vandalism is serious to British Telecom and to the community. It costs over £2.5m a year in replacing damaged material and labour to install it, around £4m in defensive measures, armouring handsets and such like and a vast amount of lost revenue in that the payphones often cannot be used. For example, there is evidence in Liverpool of takings from a less vandalised 'Oakham type' payphone (figure 2) increasing from £600 to £1800 p.a. compared with its highly vandalised predecessor. Revenue was said to increase by 25% in 200 'Oakham booths' which replaced traditional kiosks in areas of North West England. The level of vandalism generally in UK appears

Table 1. Scale of vandalism in 1982.

	UK	France
No. of public payphones	77,000	104,000
Theft of cash (incidents)	1,016	32,000
Vandalism (incidents)	230,000	84,000
Vandalism incidents per payphone	3	0.8

Sources: British Telecom and French PTT national statistics.

from the broadly comparable statistics of British Telecom and the French PTT (table 1) to be four times the level of that in France. This is in itself disturbing. A damaged payphone is, moreover, a poor advertisement for British Telecom and the neighbourhood and, if out of service, frustrating to the user. Vandalism to payphones cannot be ignored and for the last ten years in particular a series of radical measures have been attempted to deal with 'the problem'.

The label 'vandalism' conceals a variety of attacks and a variable and complex phenomenon. Table 2 shows what was attacked, according to British Telecom's national statistics in 1982. We make a worthy contribution to the British glass industry with 52,000 panes a year being replaced, the peak achievement being 62,000, and we add to the print of directories (when was one last seen intact in many payphones?). Vandalism statistics are unreliable, and so we looked in early 1983 at a sample of 100 urban and 100 rural payphones in Southern England and 90 payphones at London main line railway stations as well as in particular at selected payphones in Newcastle and Leeds in Northern England and in Slough, near London, to obtain first-hand

Figure 1. Graffiti.

Figure 2. The 'Oakham type' payphone.

Table 2. Kiosk vandalism: types of damage, number of incidents.

	Type of damage	No. of incidents
Glass	broken	52K
Coin runways [a]	blocked by rubbish,	50K
Coin entry slots [a]	damaged by wires,	40K
Reject chutes [a]	knives, liquids, etc.	20K
Handset and *cords*	cut, broken or dismantled	20K
Cash compartments	broken into	1K

[a] Includes attempted fraud and theft.
Excluded are numerous incidents of: graffiti, fouling, fires (of directories or rubbish), torn notices.
Source: British Telecom national payphone statistics.

data to supplement our 1982 national statistics of payphone vandalism. The statistics gathered in our survey were not always as expected and raise questions about the nature and incidence of the vandalism: in the 100 urban payphones, for example, only six were not working and among the 100 rural ones only one. Vandalism is thus fundamentally an attack on the kiosk. Of the glass smashing, 43 rural payphones had broken glass, only seven urban ones. We must, therefore, treat generalisations with the reserve they deserve.

In our research we were also conscious of the local differences in the extent of vandalism and looked for explanations. The average rate of vandalism is, according to our 1982 national statistics, 3 incidents p.a. per kiosk and most sites experience a modest degree of vandalism. A few, however, have a very severe degree of localised vandalism – for example, Glasgow, the most vandal prone city in the UK from the point of view of payphones, had 12.4 incidents in 1982. This is a different order of vandalism to the second worst area in parts of central London with 9.71 incidents. In the rural areas around Glasgow, the incidents fell to 1.43 p.a. Even in city centres, the level was variable – 1.72 in the West End/Hampstead parts of Central London compared with over 9.0 in adjacent areas and yet 9.12 in the typical surburban areas of South London, the third worst area in the UK for payphone vandalism. Faced with the onslaught of the variable vandals, what did British Telecom do and what conclusions can be drawn?

A number of general points emerge from our 1983 survey. Vandalism is related in a rather interesting way to the degree of use of payphones. Indeed, even including marked graffiti, urination and other so-called anti-social behaviour on the fringe of vandalism, the heavily used kiosks suffer relatively little. These kiosks are often sited at railway stations, in airports and in city centres, perhaps in shopping precincts. The degree of use and public visibility at these sites may discourage vandalism as does the protection from the general public outside busy times. It is also interesting that vandalism appears to be related to the area in which the vandals live. As few people, if any, live in the vicinity of typical high usage kiosks this, too, may discourage vandalism. Typically, vandalism seems to be related to the medium usage, neighbourhood kiosks – being relatively low in the high usage payphones and also in the rarely used rural payphones, although it is present as a phenomenon in all sites, viz. the breaking of glass in our survey of rural kiosks. We were, indeed, unable to discover an unvandalised kiosk!

More research needs to be done on the local phenomenon of vandalism. We have not examined in depth why payphone vandalism is worst in Glasgow (with 12.4 incidents p.a.) and lowest in Colchester (with 0.07). These marked variations between areas in the UK are perhaps a fruitful subject of further study. Just as vandalism is not a reflection of the degree of use, it is not a question of location in town or country. Both suffer from vandalism to some extent and inter-urban variations, even within London, appear much more significant. Vandalism of payphones appears simply as part of a general problem in certain residential areas, for example, in, say, Newcastle, within the public housing estates or the older terraced housing. There was no correlation found with levels of unemployment, although vandalism was high in some areas of high unemployment (e.g. Strathclyde), it was low in others (e.g. South Wales). It was when we looked at the local environment of the kiosk that the closest correlations emerged. Vandalism of kiosks was relatively high near schools and the type of graffiti and other damage appeared clearly the work of children. There was also often a close relationship with the degree of public housing and the general appearance of the neighbourhood. The Strathclyde case and evidence from North East England seem to support this conclusion.

2. Policies towards vandalism

Policies towards vandalism went through four stages which are still continuing. Today, all these stages of policies are operating. First, defensive measures were tried, then exposing the vandals by making them more visible as they worked, next improving the environment and finally involving the community. Academics will see that even a large public organisation is not immune to their theories! What happened and why?

2.1. The concept of the senseless vandal and defensive measures of containment

The word that many of our managers apply to vandalism is 'senseless'. This is a way of saying whatever motivates them is outside our managers' experience or at least their remembered experience! Most of our payphones are of a ·

design known as 'Pay on Answer' which first saw service in 1958. A few years after its introduction, Pay on Answer equipment began to suffer quite badly from theft. This took the form of attacks on the cash compartment, which was broken open and the contents removed. This was successfully overcome by strengthening the cash compartment, manufacturing it of 10mm steel instead of a 4mm aluminium casting and strengthening the lock. The payphones also began to suffer from loss of handsets and dials. Of course, some of the handset loss, especially in busy locations, is due to purely accidental damage. People moving their heads about whilst they talk undeniably puts a strain on the handset cord for instance. But many of the handsets are simply snipped off, and the dials ripped away from the payphone. At the same time, kiosk windows are smashed, graffiti are daubed on payphones and kiosks. Unpleasantly, many kioks were being used as public lavatories. Our managers of British payphones realised that this activity had little to do with theft or gain. It was 'senseless', they decreed. Our managers were encouraged in the defensive strategy of dealing with the 'senseless problem' by the great success in virtually eliminating theft from cash containers (although not in eliminating fraud from the coin refund chutes) of payphones by using 10mm steel casing and robust locks.

But these defensive measures had a limited success, as far as vandalism was concerned. For example, the number of handsets and cords destroyed declined from 52,000 in 1980 to 20,000 in 1982. And one of the most successful defensive measures has been the Oakham booth, an indestructible, sold steel booth with an armoured payphone. This robust housing has been installed in increasing numbers in vandal prone locations – 50 in the worst areas of Newcastle, 20 in Leeds, 200 in North West England as a whole. Out in the open, it seems, the vandal feels insecure and, faced by the largely indestructible housing, usually turns his attention elsewhere – perhaps to other British Telecom sites. The only pleasure left to a vandal at the site of an Oakham booth is to cover the payphone with the typical black felt tip pen graffiti and this is done with gusto. Overall, the conclusion drawn was that, in aggregate, vandalism has stayed at much the same level – it should be emphasised – whatever has been done, although aggregate statistics are not particularly interesting.

2.2. The visible vandal

It was believed that the vandal seen practising his craft might feel less secure and so be deterred. 24-hour lighting was thus introduced at all payphones and some 2000 light bulbs p.a. lost! Also, the design of the telephone kiosk was changed. Previously, there had been no less than 72 small panes of glass in the 1920 traditional red kiosk (K6) (figure 3) designed by Sir Gilbert Scott, but three large toughened panes were used in the late 1960s (K8) replacement

Figure 3. The traditional red kiosk (K6).

Figure 4. K8, the replacement of K6.

(figure 4). What has been interesting is the much lower amount of glass smashing in the K8 kiosk. For example, in Slough, three of nine K6 payphones had their panes smashed or missing and none of the five K8s. This pattern was common in our survey. It may be that there is a certain reluctance to draw attention to the act of smashing glass on a large scale and perhaps there is a hierarchy of vandalism with smashing small panes considered by a vandal as less 'serious' than smashing a large pane and hence a more frequent occurrence of the 'minor' vandalism. The hierarchy of vandalism acts is an interesting area of research.

2.3. *Improving the environment*

A sustained drive has been made to improve the design of kiosks. The idea has been to make kiosks less attractive to casual vandals by making them modern, well designed and clean. There is a marked contrast between the new designs of kiosks and the standard on average, 40 year old, often rusting cast iron K6 red kiosks much beloved by the public. There is also some evidence that attacks on kiosks already damaged or covered in graffiti tends to be more frequent than those on kiosks in good condition. However, this is, by no means, always the case. In some sites, replacing the glass window of kiosks seems to stimulate further breakage – a game almost of breaking the glass. Indeed, in an experiment in Newcastle, it was found that leaving the kiosks without glass reduced vandalism on the payphone. One kiosk in Leeds was left without glass for three years and apparently suffered less vandalism than before, and less than did other kiosks with glass.

2.4. Kiosks as part of the community

More recently, kiosks have been fostered as part of the local community. Serving the community, they should be looked after by the community to keep them wholesome and in working order. The kiosks are not just public property, the hardware of an anonymous faceless organisation, but the community's property. This concept has been furthered in a, so far, limited way by two projects: involving young children, before they become seriously involved in vandalism in their pre-teens and teenage years and by encouraging whole communities to take over the running of their kiosks.

'Adopt a phonebox' involves school children in looking after their kiosk, reporting to British Telecom what is wrong with the payphone and the kiosk and British Telecom, in turn, responding to the children. Report books are provided, badges, certificates and such like and the children are told what has been done as a result of their reports. Moreover, they can see what is being done by British Telecom to keep their kiosk and payphone in good order. Naturally, the scheme depended on the local schools fostering interest and on the enthusiasm of the British Telecom local management and staff. The interest of the children was fairly assured and good publicity was fairly easily achieved. The problem in the scheme has been that enthusiasm is a quality in short supply and the scheme was sometimes obstructed by some trade unionists (very much a minority), who were worried that union cleaners might be criticised, and by some managements (again a minority), who said they had too much work already! Up to 90 schools and other groups have been involved. We plan to relaunch the scheme against an attitude which still says that the armoured defensive booth type payphone is a better investment than encouraging a constructive interest in vandal and pre-vandal age children. Such an attitude recently disbanded 1100 phone rangers in Dundee. Cardiff has shown what can be done. Here, there are 158 phone rangers in the most vandal prone location in the West. The idea of the phone ranger scheme is a long-term and general one to change attitudes and the lack of short-term pay-off has disappointed managers who have misunderstood the purpose and who are looking for quick solutions to the problem.

Another approach has been to involve the local community in running the kiosk, cleaning it, collecting the money (and paying British Telecom for the service), repairing the glass (if damaged) and even painting the structure. A series of flexible schemes for doing some or all of these jobs but, above all, taking some responsibility for the kiosk have been devised. But, again, it must be admitted, although it is early days of the scheme, interest has been limited. Enthusiasm and a desire for involvement, even if partly stimulated by a fear of losing the kiosk otherwise is hard to come by. There are, however, examples of successful schemes in North Wales at Llantysilio, Whirchall near Shrewsbury and Badenoch in Scotland.

3. Conclusion

Data on payphone vandalism is far from complete and often ambiguous, but a number of features are apparent. Kiosk managers dealing with vandalism have had, in the past, generally an uncomprehending attitude, using labels, referring to the 'senseless problem' and adopting a defensive policy, spending money on strengthening payphones and dabbling in a few palliatives which push 'the problem' away or try to do so. But this has not been too successful, even measured against criteria of reducing costs of vandalism locally, in numbers of cases of vandalism and other facets which might appeal to managers. A new approach has been to move gradually towards trying to understand what motivates the vandals, how they work, to analyse the problem at source and to view the payphone and its vandalism as part of the community in which it is sited. In parallel, we have made the payphones much less tempting to the serious vandal by producing simple, strong booths and highly visible, clean kiosks and, indeed, removing the temptation of cash, by installing cardphones which do not use coins. There is a good deal of data available to be analysed, there are the beginning of interesting social experiments and, through the symposium in Paris and these papers, a start at a dialogue between academics, managers and others concerned by the problem. Vandalism is not something that can be ignored even when applied to payphones – it is too costly to the victim, whether a large organisation or the community, and is part of a general degradation of the environment which is being and should be resisted in many different ways.

Abstract: C.L. Markus, British Telecom experience in payphone management
The study looks at the attitude and policies of British Telecom managers towards vandalism and the varying results and, sometimes, lack of results. It describes, quantifies and analyses the vandalism to BT public payphones. The label vandalism conceals a variety of complex and costly attacks. Some detailed analysis of vandalism in different parts of the country and a comparison between rural and urban vandalism underline the need to treat generalisations about this matter with reserve. There are, however distinct local variations in the extent of payphone vandalism in the UK. Around the most vandal prone city, Glasgow, there is a marked fall-off towards the rural areas beyond the city and there are interesting variations even within London. The general lack of vandalism in high usage kiosks in railway stations and city centres and the high levels of vandalism in the medium usage neighbourhood kiosks is one correlation to emerge from the study.

The paper also looks at four stages of policies developed towards vandalism starting in the late 60s/early 70s, when the 'senseless vandal' concept was prevalent and defensive measures of containment were applied. These succeeded in making it difficult to destroy the payphone but the vandal turned his attention to its housing, graffiti and such. Next we tried making the vandals more visible and there is some evidence that this reduced the level of attack. This was followed by improving the design of kiosks generally. Evidence is much less conclusive that this has yielded short term results. The thirst for short term results is a major problem in handling vandalism and this is evident from BT's recent policy to encourage the community to regard kiosks as part of themselves. Two schemes are described, one involving young children before they became seriously involved in vandalism, the other encouraging communities to take over the running of their kiosks. Both have met with a mixed amount of commitment.

CHAPTER 22

Vandalism in Amsterdam

B. VAN DIJK, P. VAN SOOMEREN and M. WALOP

Every research project ought to start with a definition of the phenomenon to be studied. The term 'vandalism' is relatively recent and was probably used for the first time in 1794 by Grégoire, bishop of Blois. Grégoire concentrated on the destructive acts against churches and cathedrals during the French revolution. On the other hand, it is of interest that acts such as the plundering during the religious wars in the reign of Louis XIV have never been labelled as vandalism.

Clearly, the use of this term has an ideological component. However, we will not deliberate upon these ideological aspects (see Cohen, 1973) and will rather confine ourselves to the following working definition: 'Vandalism is the damaging of the property of others, without material benefit to the offender'. [1] In this definition the term 'damaging' has the meaning of 'making an object useless for its intended function'.

1. The structure of the action research in Amsterdam

Pilot research on the extent of vandalism in The Netherlands (1979)

Before the end of the seventies little or no research had been done on vandalism in The Netherlands. Therefore, our pilot research concentrated on the extent of and increase in Dutch vandalism. The results showed that vandalism was rising sharply and that further research would be useful. Moreover, the results showed that Amsterdam would be a suitable city.

Part 1: Research on the geographical distribution of vandalism in Amsterdam (1980)

To begin with, the spatial distribution of vandalism in Amsterdam was analysed. In a way, the explanations for this distribution pattern can be seen as the hypothesis underpinning the next part of the research. Moreover, the neighbourhoods where this next part of the research took place, were selected on the basis of the spatial distribution of vandalism. In section 2 we will describe the first part of the research.

---

[1] The addition of 'without material benefit to the offender' means that, for example, the wrecking of a parkingmeter to obtain the coins is not covered by our definition. However, there are authors who now use the term 'acquisitive vandalism'.

Part 2: Research on vandalism in two neighbourhoods (1981 / 82)

In this part, interviews were held with youths, headmasters and youth workers in two Amsterdam neighbourhoods. The relationship between the built environment and vandalism was also investigated. The main results of the second part of the research are dealt with in section 3.

Part 3: Anti-vandalism experiments in one neighbourhood of Amsterdam (1982 / 83)

The results of the second part of the research were used as a basis for setting up and carrying out a number of anti-vandalism experiments (among others: school projects on vandalism, a workshop for mopeds, a bicycle cross course and target hardening measures). These experiments were based not only on the second part of the research, but also on experience with vandalism prevention elsewhere in The Netherlands (Van Dijk et al., 1981; Van Dijk and Van Soomeren, 1981a).

Part 4: Evaluation of the anti-vandalism experiments

At the moment we are working on the evaluation of the experiments and the policy directions that resulted from the evaluation. In the summer of 1983, evaluation and policy directions, together with a summary of the whole research, will be published in a final research report.

However, in this article the pilot research, the experiments (part 3) and evaluation of the experiments (part 4) are not dealt with. Besides, the description of the second and third parts had to be very short. This means that we do not explicate our theoretical framework and the research results regarding the relationship between the built environment and vandalism. In the course of 1983, a more detailed synopsis of our research will be available (Van Dijk et al., forthcoming).

2. Spatial distribution of vandalism in Amsterdam

2.1. Goals and methodology

As was already mentioned in the introduction, before 1979 little research had been done on vandalism in The Netherlands. The first part of our research in Amsterdam must therefore be conceived of very much as an exploratory study. [2] Two central questions were posed:
(1) In the first place we were interested in the geographical distribution of the

---

[2] This was the only way to get a picture of the distribution of vandalism. In Amsterdam, only about 75 'vandals' get caught annually, so that this does not give a good picture of the distribution of vandalism. Moreover, it would have been too time-consuming for us to carry out and process victim surveys.

amount of vandalism in Amsterdam. In other words: *where* does vandalism occur and to what extent?
(2) Subsequently we asked ourselves how the discovered pattern could be explained. In other words: *why* did vandalism occur in some places less and in other places more?

2.1.1. Data

To answer our first question, we collected information about destructive acts to public property (Van Dijk and Van Soomeren, 1980). In general, these figures are difficult to obtain, because most municipal departments do not keep a separate 'vandalism file'. After a lot of counting we eventually succeeded in acquiring the following figures:
- for vandalism to lampposts (from March 1 to December 31, 1979), the tally was 2535;
- for vandalism to stopsigns for public transport (from September 1 to December 31, 1979), the tally was 483;
- for vandalism to trees (in 1978 and 1979), the tally was 208.

2.1.2. Maps

For each of the vandalistic acts it was known where it had occurred. This made it possible to chart about 3000 vandalistic acts on a detailed map (appr. $3m^3$). We will make do here with just a part of this map (map 1) and a map depicting the number of vandalistic acts per neighbourhood (map 2). [3] With these maps we have, in fact, the answer to the first central question.

The maps give the following impression: everywhere in Amsterdam a certain amount of vandalism does occur. However, there are neighbourhoods where there is distinctly more vandalism. This applies to neighbourhoods in the centre, the north and the far west of Amsterdam.

The answer to the first question (where does vandalism occur and to what extent) leads directly to the second question: how can the discovered pattern be explained? To answer this, one can choose one of two lines of approach.

In the first place, one can start from the psychic environment as, among others, Newman (1973) and Jeffery (1971) (the godfather of the so-called environmentalist movement in criminology) do. As stated in the introduction, we will not discuss this approach here. [4]

In the second place, the social characteristics of neighbourhoods can be taken as a starting point, as in the socio-ecological tradition of the Chicago school (Shaw and McKay, 1969). We use this line of approach in section 2.2.

---

[3] We have opted for a presentation of vandalistic acts per neighbourhood without applying a weighting for neighbourhood size. Such a weighting would hardly alter the picture.
[4] The reader who is interested in our testing of the environmentalist ideas may consult Van Dijk and Van Soomeren (1980, 1981b).

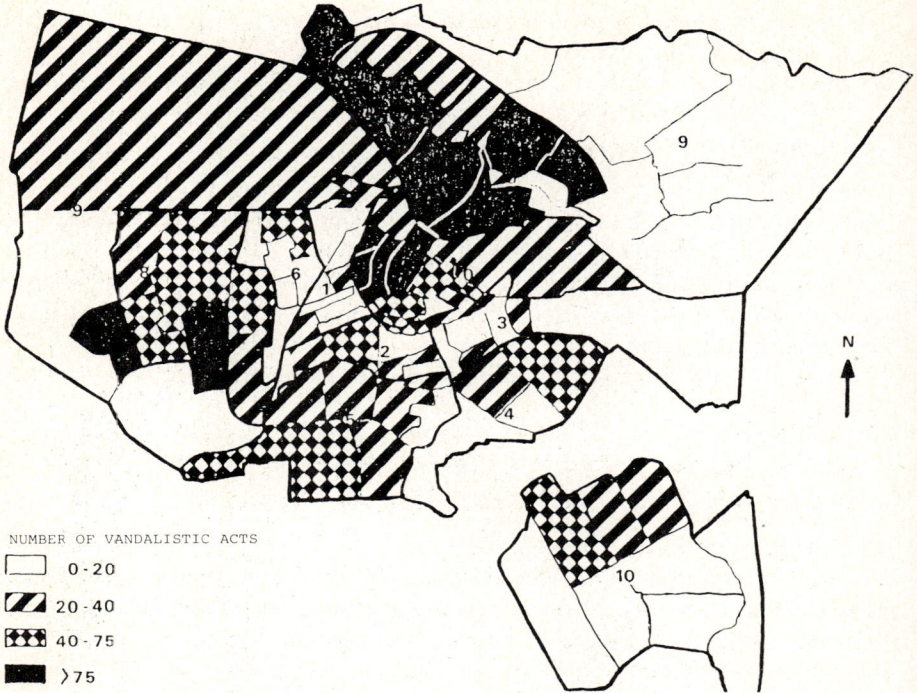

Figure 1. Map showing the distribution of vandalistic acts per area.

2.2. Analysis at the neighbourhood level

For the purposes of a socio-ecological approach, it is necessary to collect data on vandalistic acts at the neighbourhood level (map 2). Consequently, it can be determined whether correlations exist between the number of vandalistic acts on the one hand and demographic and socio-economic characteristics of neighbourhoods on the other. The idea behind this is that youths who grow up in certain neighbourhoods are more likely to commit acts of vandalism than youths from other neighbourhoods.

This means that in the following analysis the number of vandalistic acts is used as an indicator for numbers of vandalising youth. The analysis of data on vandals caught in Amsterdam proved that the place of residence and the place where the crime is committed generally lay close together. [5] There was,

---

[5]   It is evident from other research also (Turner, 1969; Mawby, 1982) that youths often commit destructive acts not far from their homes. There is therefore no reason to assume that the amount of vandalism forms an unreliable surrogate for the number of vandals.

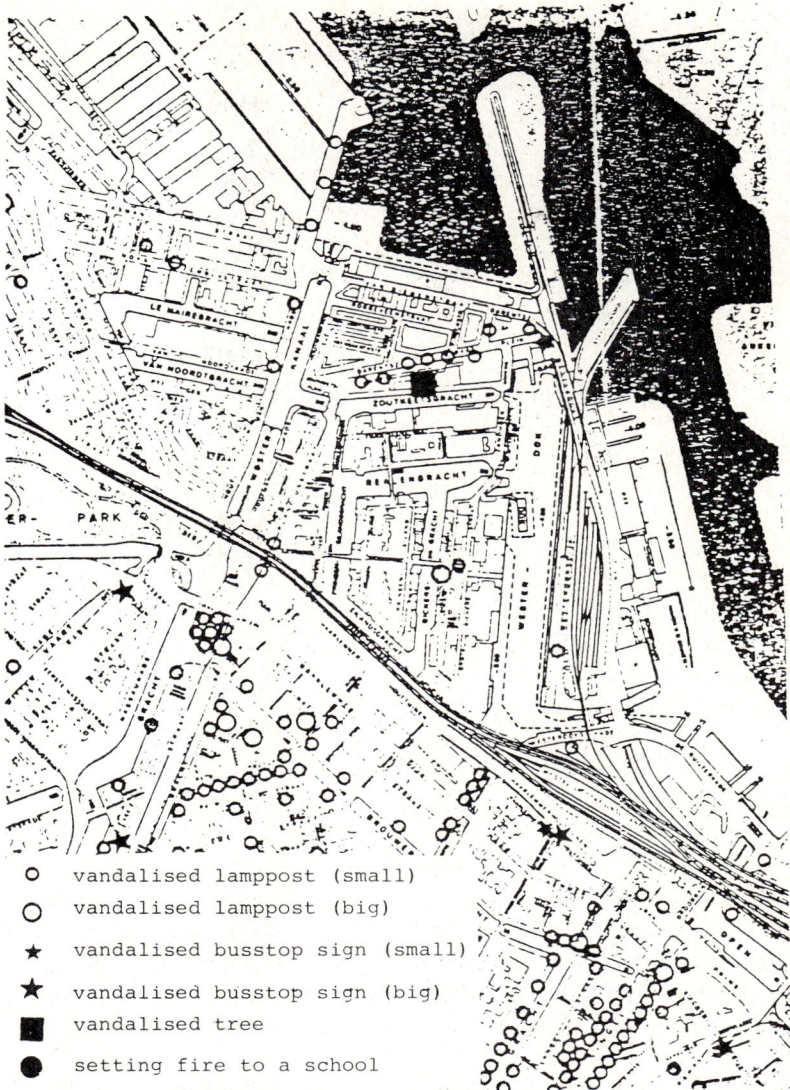

○ vandalised lamppost (small)

◯ vandalised lamppost (big)

★ vandalised busstop sign (small)

★ vandalised busstop sign (big)

■ vandalised tree

● setting fire to a school

Figure 2. Map showing the amount of vandalism in Amsterdam.

however, one exception to this pattern: the offenders in the centre of Amsterdam came from all parts of the city.

On the basis of criminological theories we expected that the socio-economic status of a neighbourhood, the quality of the neighbourhood as a living environment (as measured by the variables 'average owner-occupier rate' and

'moving frequency') and the demographic structure would be related to the number of vandalistic acts. The analysis produced the following results:
- there is no correlation between socio-economic status and the number of destructive acts;
- there is no correlation between the number of vandalistic acts and the variables that indicate living-environment quality;
- there is a clear, positive correlation between the percentage of resident youths of 10–19 years old and the number of destructive acts.

Again, the city centre is the exception: the number of vandalistic acts is high, but few youths live in this area.

On the basis of these results the following tentative conclusions can be drawn:

– In the first place, it seems that vandalism is not a phenomenon that manifests itself mainly in neighbourhoods of low socio-economic status. The strong correlation between the percentage of resident youths and the number of vandalistic acts points to the conclusion that vandalism in particular is a phenomenon that many youths (from different socio-economic strata) are guilty of. The theories that see youth criminality as a consequence of the deprivation of lower-class youths (e.g. Cloward and Ohlin, 1962; Cohen, 1955) therefore do not seem to offer an explanation for (mild forms of) vandalism. The theories that see youth criminality as a fairly common phenomenon that in some way 'belongs' to a certain age (e.g. Crane, 1952; Matza and Sykes, 1962) are probably more useful.

– In the second place, it is clear that vandalism is not a phenomenon that occurs especially in neighbourhoods characterised by poor living conditions. This can also be seen on map 2: in the neighbourhoods directly around the centre (the so-called 19th-century belt) where the living conditions are generally not good, there is relatively little vandalism – even when controlled for the percentage of resident youth.

– There is a lot of vandalism in the city centre. Our explanation for this is in line with a recent Dutch study on youth criminality: a lot of (young) people go to the centre for an evening out and it is especially during this going out (of which alcohol consumption and the showing of bravado are important ingredients) that a lot of criminality takes place (Van Dijk and Steinmetz, 1982).

Map 2 also shows that, in addition to the centre, the periphery and relatively new neighbourhoods of Amsterdam also have a lot of vandalism. A goodly portion of this can be explained by the high percentage of youths in these neighbourhoods. Apart from this, it can be noted that in these neighbourhoods a sort of 'overflow' problem probably plays a part. The families that come to live here often have social ties (friends, club activities) in the neighbourhoods where they originally lived. The parents are – in contrast to their children – often mobile enough to maintain these contacts.

Furthermore, it is also easier for the parents to, for example, shop or look for recreation outside the new neighbourhood. They will therefore generally hardly be involved in the social life of their new neighbourhood. This brings with it the fact that social control in these neighbourhoods is limited. On the other hand, the youths have far fewer opportunities to amuse themselves outside the neighbourhood; the long distance to the centre of Amsterdam undoubtedly plays a role herein. In their new, predominantly grey, home neighbourhood there is little to experience and, because social control is limited, the committing of vandalism is an obvious way of getting out of the rut of routine.

2.3. Conclusions

The most important conclusion resulting from this first part of our research can be summarised as follows: vandalism in Amsterdam is widespread. In the centre and the outer (new) belt of the city vandalism occurs more ofen. The large number of vandalistic acts in the centre can largely be explained by the fact that many youths go out there.

3. Research among youth, youth-workers and headmasters

3.1. Goals and methodology

In this second part of our research, interviews were held with youth, youth workers and headmasters in two neighbourhoods of Amsterdam. The main objective was to gain insight into the reasons why youth do or do not vandalise things.

The best 'experts' in the domain of vandalism are the youths themselves. Consequently, we held extensive interviews with a total of 239 youngsters, who were contacted via the schools and youth centres. Pupils from 28 schools were selected via random sampling. Non-school going youths were approached via youth centers. The sample of non-school going youths in both neighbourhoods is, of course, not completely random. However, all (six) youth centres in both neighbourhoods co-operated.

The age of the interviewees varied from eight to 23. [6] Because we acquire more information about vandalism from boys, more boys than girls were selected (the proportion of boys–girls was 2 : 1). The interviews took place with three youths simultaneously, each interview lasting about an hour and usually

---

[6] Marshall's (1976) research in Blackburn showed that over one-third of the 'vandals' caught by the police were children. That is one reason why eight-year olds were also interviewed. It is remarkable that most self-report studies are confined to the somewhat older youth. In the English study of Gladstone (1978), ages varied from 11 to 15. American researchers (Phillips and Bartlett, 1976; Richards, 1979; Phillips and Donnermeyer, 1982) interviewed youths in their late teens.

Table 1. Vandalism and age.

Age	Vandalism [a]	No vandalism
8–10	32 (64%)	18 (26%)
11–12	32 (55%)	26 (45%)
13–14	22 (57%)	17 (43%)
15–16	20 (47%)	23 (53%)
17–18	9 (30%)	21 (70%)
19–23	1 (6%)	18 (94%)
Total	116 (49%)	123 (51%)

[a] Vandalism – admitted to committing one or more vandalistic acts in the past year.

proceeding in a very open and relaxed manner. Our questions referred to, among other things, leisure activities, group membership, parental control, attitudes towards school, work and the neighbourhood. Of course, vandalism was also discussed. The interviews were taped and processed afterwards. [7]

Other experts are youth workers and headmasters. They are confronted with the consequences of vandalism in youth centres and schools and also work with youths on a professional basis. We held interviews with 11 youth workers and 28 headmasters.

Some of the more general findings from this research are presented in section 3.2. In the literature on vandalism most attention is paid to the *meanings* of or the *motives* behind vandalism. Our findings with respect to this are discussed in section 3.3.

The question of why youths do *not* vandalise might be just as interesting. We distinguish two types of barriers to youthful vandalism:

(1) an internal barrier; one may feel that vandalism is simply 'not done', for instance because one feels that vandalism is a 'waste' or that vandalism is 'childish';

(2) an external barrier; one might not vandalise things because of the risk of being caught and punished.

We discuss these barriers in section 3.4.

3.2. General findings

Most of the interviewed youths did not regard vandalism as an unusual pastime. Table 1 shows that it mainly involved youths up to 16 years of age. Moreover, a clear correlation was found between vandalism and *sex*. In the three age categories the relationships were as follows:

[7]   This part of the research is more comprehensively dealt with (in Dutch) in Van Dijk et al. (1981 [part 3], 1982, where our theoretical framework is explained).

- children (8–12): of the boys, 69% admitted to having committed acts of vandalism; this figure was only 40% in the case of girls;
- teenagers (13–16): boys 58%, girls 40%;
- young adults (17–23): boys 31%, girls 17%.

For the most part, these differences can be explained by different leisure activity patterns as between boys and girls. It also appears that motives and barriers are often sex-determined. We will examine this further in sections 3.3 and 3.4.

We observed that no correlation exists between vandalism by youths and the *socio-economic status* of the parents. Youths from lower-class families therefore do not vandalise things more or less than youths from middle-class families.

It does appear that vandalism is strongly connected with impulsiveness. Youths whose behaviour patterns show that they act fairly impulsively and satisfy their needs quickly (e.g youths who spend their pocket money on sweets or chips) appear to vandalise more often than those who can defer their needs longer (e.g. setting aside their pocket money for longer-term goals, like saving for a bicycle). This correlation between spending pocket money and vandalism is significant and appears to agree with the ideas of Allen and Greenberger (1978) who see the 'hedonistic component' as an important feature of vandalism.

From most of the interviews with the youths it became clear that vandalism usually occurs when the available forms of leisure activities (like a game of football) begin to become boring. Youths then think of something to dispel this boredom. An exciting (and preferably 'forbidden') activity is most appropriate for this. In this context, the youths themselves talk about 'looking for thrills'. The smashing of windows ('a nice sound'), followed by a 'chase by one of those security guys' satisfies the natural demand for action and excitement.

3.3. Meanings and motives

When describing the motives and meanings of vandalism, Cohen's (1973) typology is often used. Cohen distinguishes five types of 'conventional' vandalism: acquisitive vandalism, tactical vandalism, vindictive vandalism, play vandalism and malicious vandalism. His typology was aimed at undermining the stereotyped picture of vandalism as 'senseless behaviour'. Cohen has certainly succeeded in this. However, his typology was only partly useful for a classification of our research material. [8]

---

[8] Certain motives (like 'prestige') are not mentioned by Cohen. One thing coming out of our interviews was that different motives can play a role in a single vandalistic act. These motives often appear to be age-determined. Therefore we shall mention the most common motives by age group.

Table 2. Vandalism and attitudes towards school (children).

Attitudes towards school	Vandalism	No vandalism
Positive	21 (47%)	23 (53%)
Neither positive nor negative	12 (60%)	8 (40%)
Negative	23 (79%)	6 (21%)

With *children* (8–12) vandalism mostly boils down to:
– a direct expression of anger, the reason for the anger being clear to the child itself. Example: "During a street football-game, I had to take a penalty. Because of a sudden gust of wind the ball was blown away for a second and I missed the shot. I was so angry that I kicked the first parked car I came to" (boy/12). [9]
– An expression of *vindictiveness*. Vandalising something belonging to somebody else because you are angry with him. Example: "During the weekend we had made a lovely hopscotch course on the street. We could hopscotch on it beautifully. But it was in front of the milkman's door and he didn't want us to play there during the week. He rubbed our course away himself. Well, we hated him so much that we slashed the tyres of his car that evening" (girl/11).
Motives like anger and vindictiveness are found to about the same extent in both boys and girls. The damage involved is generally not so great.
Another meaning of children's vandalism can be described as *'exploration of the environment'*. This meaning is particularly common among boys, and almost exclusively in a group context.
This exploration can be related to the *physical* environment. For example, children play on a building-site and light a fire there, whereby, unexpectedly, some bricks suddenly crack. 'Exploration' can also be related to the *social* environment. Children know that vandalism is 'forbidden' by adults. Yet, it is not clear if – and if so how – adults will take action. This also makes vandalism 'exciting'.
In connection with this it is important to mention that vandalism appears to be interchangeable with other activities, whereby it is very exciting to see 'how far you can go'. Therefore, children often mention the committing of vandalism in the same breath with "the teasing of neighbours".
Apart from the above-mentioned motives there is another background factor closely related to vandalism, namely *attitudes towards school*. Table 2 shows that there is an obvious correlation between attitudes towards school and vandalism. Children who dislike school commit vandalism much more

---

[9] This quotation and the following quotations are from interviewed youths.

often than children who enjoy going to school. A possible explanation for this correlation is that children who dislike going to school work off the dissatisfaction and tension that originate from this by vandalising things. This could also partly explain the large amount of vandalism to school buildings. It is also possible that disliking school is an experience the children have in common and that they form groups on the basis of this common experience. After school they will feel the need to experience something that is nice and exciting at last. 'Looking for thrills' then becomes obvious.

We mentioned 'the exploration of the social environment' as one of the reasons why children vandalise things. We see this perhaps even more strongly in teenagers (12–16 years), namely as *a way to test the existing norms and the authority of adults*. Through daring to vandalise things one gets to know the (social) potentialities and at the same time one checks how adult norms (like 'vandalism is not done') are upheld. It appears that, just as with children, vandalism is interchangeable with other activities that are forbidden by adults, like: 'bullying a teacher' or 'daring to shoplift'. The confrontation of teenagers with (the authority of) adults has another aspect. With activities like 'bullying a teacher' and 'daring to commit vandalism', teenagers place themselves in an independent position with respect to adults. Through this, respect (*prestige*) can be won in one's peer group.

For example: "I smashed a telephone box. We came from the disco with a whole group – about ten of us. And you want to be part of it, don't you? We all picked up stones, and threw them through the windows. Then we pulled the telephone out. Then the older boys – about sixteen, seventeen years old – went and started standing on cars. I was the youngest and if you don't join in, they call you a softy" (boy/13). This showing-off is especially important for boys in their teens. In a group within which vandalism occurs, girls often (but not always!) have the role of spectator.

With children we saw that 'disliking school' had a strong correlation with the committing of vandalism. We find this underlying factor with teenagers too: teenagers who dislike school commit more vandalism than teenagers who enjoy going to school. However, this correlation is slightly less pronounced than it is for children.

A smaller percentage of *young adults* (17–23) vandalise. In this age group, vandalistic acts are often coupled with 'an evening out' and having fights, provoked or otherwise. With young adults the underlying factor of 'dissatisfaction' plays a predominant role. With children and teenagers, this dissatisfaction surfaces in 'disliking school'. With young adults it takes other forms: those who are dissatisfied with their work situation vandalise things more often than those who are satisfied with it. Young adults who do not have any influence on the course of events in their youth centre also indulge in vandalising more often than those who do have a say in it.

3.4. Barriers

In this section, first the internal and external barriers for the different age categories (children, teenagers and young adults) are described. Next, we will go into the role that certain adults, headmasters, youth workers and parents, play in these barriers.

The majority of the interviewed *children* (59%) appeared to have vandalised something in the previous year. They were not very bothered about this: "Oh, it was just a game anyway" (girl/9); "That school will be pulled down anyway" (boy/10); "A window like that – there's sure to be an insurance on it" (boy/12). Statements like this indicate that the *internal* barrier is not very high. A minority of the children said they did not vandalise things because they felt it to be a waste when something got broken, especially because this would then cost money, and sometimes also because somebody would have to come especially to repair it.

The external barrier is not very high either. However, it appeared slightly higher in the neighbourhood with the most visual control possibilities.

The norm that 'vandalism is not done' occupies a different place for teenagers. For a number of teenagers the fact that this norm originates with adults is a reason for testing it (and its upholding). The infringement of this norm can be a motive for them. However, a lot of teenagers do accept this norm and for them the norm forms an internal barrier not to commit vandalism.

This barrier is put into words in different ways. According to a number of girls vandalism was mainly an activity for boys: "I always let my boyfriend do it. Let him do the busting. I could tell him 'don't do it' ten times, he'd still go on. I do enjoy standing nearby" (girl/15). Some teenagers do not vandalise things because this would only be done by a particular sort of youth: "I don't belong to that scum" (boy/16).

Five of the teenagers in our random sample had had dealings with the police because of vandalism. For all of them this was a reason to, at least temporarily, stop vandalising things. We may state therefore that after such confrontations with the police the external barrier rises. A few statements: "You know, when you were young, you just broke all the windows in that nursery school. It used not to be serious, you were not put in a cell. Now I have sat in a police car with handcuffs on. We'd stolen lead then, taken lead strips off those bars. We do watch out, now!" (boy/13). "We were bashing up everything here. Until we got trouble from those cops. We'd had it, then. It was then we said 'We're going to stop and never do it again'. It's been okay since then. Well, of course we write with crayons a bit, but then everybody does that. But it's not serious anymore: pulling benches out of the ground, bashing in telephone boxes, punching holes in car tyres and all that stuff. Very stupid things, but that doesn't happen anymore" (boy/16).

These findings seem to show that testing norms by means of vandalism loses its charm as soon as it is plain that these rules exist for the youths in question, and they feel that breaking the rules is too dangerous.

For *young adults*, the *internal* barrier plays an important role. Most of the young adults think that vandalism is not done. This is not only because it is a waste or causes damage, but especially because vandalism has become childish to them. They see it as an activity for adolescents that they have 'outgrown'.

Some young adults were part of (what is described in the English literature [10] as) a 'lower-class gang'. These youths have developed their own subculture, a way of life clearly distinguishable from others. They want a place where they can meet, where as much as possible is allowed and nothing is compulsory. They do not care for fixed rules and hate anything that bears any likeness to government, adult leaders and educators.

One could expect these youths to vandalise things a lot because the norm that 'vandalism is not done' does not have any meaning for them. Yet, it appears that only some of them do vandalise things. They usually find the risk of coming into contact with the police for something as daft as vandalism too great.

Vandalism for thrills is considered by them as too childish also: "You don't throw a stone through a window for 'kicks', maybe you do it to steal the Walkman behind it" (boy/18). This brings us back to the *external* barrier. This barrier is also very high for youths more 'adapted to society'. If they should acquire a criminal record by committing vandalism, their chances of getting a job decrease. The penal age-limit of 18 years makes it extra risky from this age onwards.

We also examined how *headmasters* and *youth workers* managed with these barriers. The interviews with headmasters showed that many of them use serious acts of destruction to the school building as an inducement to talk with the pupils, usually by making a round of the classrooms. This was mentioned mostly in primary schools. A number of other headmasters mentioned an increase in the involvement with the school building as being the best contribution towards the prevention of damage to that building. This can be done by making the school look well cared for (and, for example, by having cleaning-up campaigns in and around the school with the pupils). It seems that the raising of the external barrier (punishment) is seized upon comparatively sooner in secondary educational institutions.

The interviewed youth workers were generally a lot more laconic about vandalism, especially with regard to the vandalism that does not take place within youth centres. This more easy-going attitude can be explained from the point of view that youth workers often regard vandalism as a direct expression

---

[10]   See, for example, A. Cohen (1955), Corrigan (1976).

of dissatisfaction, or as one youth worker put it: "a healthy reaction to an unhealthy system". This does not alter the fact that the youth workers certainly do take measures to counteract vandalism within their own buildings.

As one of the barrier-raising factors they mentioned, among others, that they and the individual youths are more identifiable within the youth centre, for example, by their noticeable presence during activities and by working with membership cards. Like the headmasters, the youth workers also mentioned the importance of keeping the building in good order, because damaged things provoke fresh vandalism.

In summary, we can state that the imparting of the norm 'vandalism is not done' seems to occur mainly in primary schools and that among somewhat older youth more indirect methods are used to prevent vandalism.

3.5. Conclusions

The main results of the second part of our research can be summed up as follows:

(1) A lot of young people commit vandalism. There is no correlation between socio-economic status and vandalism. There are more children and teenagers than young adults engaged in vandalism.

(2) The following motives can be distinguished.
With *children*, vandalism is an expression of anger or vindictiveness or vandalism is an exploration of the social or physical environment.

In general, *teenagers* have other motives: vandalism is a way to test norms and the authority of adults, and vandalism is a way of gaining prestige in the peer group. These motives are closely related to each other.

Dislike of school is an important factor behind vandalism in the case of both children and teenagers.

Young adults: Dissatisfaction in a more general sense, for example with a job, or having little influence on the course of events in a youth centre, makes a major contribution to the explanation of vandalism committed by young adults.

(3) There are two barriers that can keep youngsters from committing vandalism: (a) the norm that vandalism is not done; (b) the fear of being caught and punished. In general, these barriers are only really high in the case of young adults. They are afraid to get a criminal record and, moreover, vandalism has become childish to them.

Acknowledgement

This article is a very brief summary of a part of the action research on vandalism we have undertaken over the past four years. Numerous people have assisted us during this research and to acknowledge them all would take several pages. We shall therefore name only the two institutions that played the most important role in carrying out the research: The Departments of Youth

Affairs and Education of the Municipality of Amsterdam and The National Crime Prevention Bureau (Ministries of Justice and of the Interior).

References

Allen, V.L., D.B. Greenberger, 1978. An aesthetic theory of vandalism. Crime and Delinquency 24 (3), 309–321.
Clarke, R.V.G., ed., 1978. Tackling vandalism. Home Office Research Study no. 47. London: HMSO.
Cloward, R.A., L.E. Ohlin, 1962. Illegitimate means and delinquent subcultures. In: M.E. Wolfgang et al., 1962.
Cohen, A.K., 1965. Delinquent boys: The culture of the gang. Glencoe (Ill.).
Cohen, S., 1973. Property destruction: Motives and meanings. In: C. Ward, 1973.
Corrigan, P., 1976. Doing nothing. In: S. Hall, 1976.
Crane, A.R., 1952. Pre-adolescent gang: A topological interpretation. Journal of Genetic Psychology no. 81, 113–123.
Dijk, B. van, P. van Soomeren, 1980. Vandalisme in Amsterdam. Amsterdam (mimeo).
Dijk, B. van, P. van Soomeren, 1981a. Vandalisme: Ideeën/onderzoek/preventie. Amsterdam: Kobra.
Dijk, B. van, P. van Soomeren, 1981b. Stedebouw en vandalisme. Stedebouw en Volkshuisvesting 4. The Hague (mimeo).
Dijk, B. van, P. van Soomeren, M. Walop, 1981. Rapportage actie-onderzoek jeugdvandalisme. Part 1: Inventarisatienota. Part 3 (with A. van Assema, M. van IJzendoorn): Interviews met jongeren, schoolhoofden en jongerenwerkers. Amsterdam (mimeo).
Dijk, B. van, P. van Soomeren, M. Walop (with A. van Assema, M. van IJzendoorn), 1982. Rapportage actie-onderzoek jeugdvandalisme. Part 4: Amsterdammertjes vernielen! Achtergronden van jeugdvandalisme. Amsterdam.
Dijk, B. van, P. van Soomeren, M. Walop, forthcoming. Vandalism: A Dutch perspective.
Dijk, J.J.M. van, C.H.D. Steinmetz, 1982. Victimization surveys: Beyond measuring the volume of crime. The Hague (mimeo).
Gladstone, F.J., 1978. Vandalism amongst adolescent schoolboys. In: R.V.G. Clarke, 1978.
Hall, S., R. Jefferson, 1976. Resistance through rituals. London.
Houchon, G., 1982. Criminologie du vandalisme. Paper presented at the International Colloquium on Vandalism, Paris.
Jeffery, C.R., 1971. Crime prevention through environmental design. Beverly Hills (CA).
Marshall, T., 1976. Vandalism: The seeds of destruction. New Society, June, 625–627.
Matza, D., G.M. Sykes, 1962. Techniques of neutralization: A theory of delinquency. In: M.E. Wolfgang et al., 1962.
Mawby, R.I., 1982. Vandalism and public perceptions in contrasting residential areas. Paper presented at the International Colloquium on Vandalism, Paris.
Newman, O., 1973. Defensible space. London: Macmillan.
Phillips, G.H., K.F. Bartlett, 1976. Vandals and vandalism in rural Ohio. Wooster (Ohio).
Phillips, G.H., J.F. Donnermeyer, 1982. Vandals and vandalism in the United States: A rural perspective. Paper presented at the International Colloquium on Vandalism, Paris.
Shaw, C.R., H.D. McKay, 1969. Juvenile delinquency and urban areas. Rev. ed. Chicago.
Turner, S., 1969. Delinquency and distance. In: Selling, M.E. Wolfgang, eds., Delinquency: Selected studies. New York: Wiley.
Ward, C., 1973. Vandalism. London: The Architectural Press.
Wolfgang, M.E., L. Savitz, N. Johnston, eds., 1962. The sociology of crime and delinquency. New York: Wiley.

Abstract: B. van Dijk et al., Vandalism in Amsterdam
Two parts of the action research on vandalism in Amsterdam are described in this chapter. The first part deals with the geographical distribution of vandalism in Amsterdam. It shows, among other things, that vandalism is widespread and is not concentrated in lower-class neighbourhoods. The second part contains the results of interviews held with youths, youthworkers and headmasters. The reasons why youths commit vandalism (motives and meanings) or do not commit vandalism (barriers) are clearly determined by age and sex. Most vandalism is committed not by young adults, but by children and teenagers (8–16 years). Dislike of school is an important underlying factor.

CHAPTER 23

Preventing vandalism: the experience of an action research project

T. HOPE

It is one thing to have ideas about how to prevent vandalism; but putting those ideas into practice may be quite another matter. In comparison with the range of theories about the causes of vandalism, our knowledge of how to prevent vandalism is severely limited. This chapter describes an action-research project undertaken by the Home Office to investigate ways of preventing vandalism to schools. The experience suggests that an awareness of practical and organisational issues in implementing preventive measures is just as important as a theory of vandalism causation.

1. The situational approach to vandalism prevention

Arguably, our understanding of how to prevent vandalism suffers from an excess of theory over practical knowledge and experience. In part, this may be due to a tendency to focus upon the motivation of those committing damage at the expense of developing an understanding of other aspects of vandalism. A bias towards motivational or dispositional explanations of vandalism has been apparent in both social scientists' and the public's perception of vandalism. Psychologists, for instance, have looked for the causes of vandalism in the maladjustment of individuals or their difficulties in coping with life, while early sociological explanations (cf. Cohen, 1955) saw vandalism arising from the role frustrations of youth, mediated by differential social class experience. As Clarke (1980) points out, this kind of dispositional bias has also been apparent in much theorising about crime in general. In addition, concern with the motivational aspects of vandalism also connected with public perceptions of vandalism as an expression, or symptom, of many of society's inherent ills and difficulties. Thus, for example, Kellmer-Pringle (1973) saw vandalism arising from, among other things, high density housing, unemployment, impersonal neighbourhoods, parenting difficulties, the influence of television and inadequate leisure provision.

The net effect of all this was to encourage an approach to vandalism prevention which sought to 'cure' offenders of their disposition to destroy while simultaneously seeking to create a society which would not inspire destruction. Yet, while it is probably true that the achievement of these aims would eradicate vandalism (and many other problems besides), little improvement seemed to occur in local communities. Local government, youth workers, residents, etc. continued to face the various consequences of vandalism; and continued to respond or react in a variety of ways. Little systematic evidence was available about preventive measures, nor suggestions as to which approaches might be most useful.

Perhaps in response to this gap between theory and practical experience a number of new perspectives on vandalism began to merge in Britain during the 1970s. While differing in many important respects, they shared a common concern to develop a more 'situational' or phenomenological interpretation of vandalism with greater practical relevance. Situational interpretations generally place much less emphasis on identifying deep-seated motives for damaging property and emphasise more immediate aspects such as the role of the environment in providing opportunities for vandalism (Clarke, 1978); the meaning of vandalism for those engaging in it (Cohen, 1973a; Corrigan 1979); and the various ways society reacts to vandalism (Cohen, 1973b). In their differing ways each sought to develop theories which more accurately reflected local communities' experience of vandalism and each of these interpretations made a conscious attempt to suggest ways in which local communities – whether local government or residents themselves – might act to discourage vandalism.

Ward's (1973) collection of essays, for instance, brought together architects, community workers and sociologists in looking at ways in which local communities and their physical environments might be improved. In similar vein, the Home Office Research Unit conducted a programme of research to inform thinking about prevention and concerned explicitly with situational aspects of vandalism (Clarke, 1978). The various studies highlighted a number of findings which were consistent with a situational interpretation of vandalism (Mayhew and Clarke; 1982): much vandalism consisted of relatively trivial acts of damage mainly against public property (Sturman, 1978), committed by many youngsters in the course of unsupervised play or exuberant behaviour (Gladstone, 1978), in environments which provided opportunities for property destruction because they were unsupervised (Wilson and Burbridge, 1978), easily damaged, or unsuitable for the needs of the young people and families who lived there (Wilson and Burbridge, 1978). The general lesson from this research was that it appeared to be possible to tackle vandalism in local settings and that much might be gained from directing preventive efforts to situations in which vandalism commonly occurs, without necessarily having to solve individuals' personal problems or society's deeper ills. Vandalism therefore seemed to be a local problem which communities might be able to solve themselves if they had sufficient guidance and support.

Nevertheless, the findings from Home Office research were of little immediate assistance to local agencies and residents; more practical evidence of the effectiveness of a situational approach to prevention was necessary. It was therefore decided to launch a small 'demonstration project' which might serve as a model for others to emulate. Vandalism to schools (a then relatively unexplored aspect of vandalism) was selected as a topic for the experiment, and the City Council and Police force of an inner city area in the north of England were invited to participate. An account of the early phases of the project is provided by Gladstone (1980); this paper reviews the course of the project as a whole. Unfortunately, the early promise of the project faded when research came to be put into practice.

2. The project

Drawing inspiration from the research programme, the project was envisaged as resting upon a thorough analysis of the conditions giving rise to vandalism at individual schools. This method would establish the conditions which encouraged vandalism in its particular settings and this in turn would suggest the kinds of measures which might be taken. Decisions as to the best courses of action would follow; the measures would be implemented and the results evaluated. There were therefore three aspects of the project: planning, decision-making and implementation.

2.1. Planning

The initial phase of the project seemed to confirm the utility of analysis in planning preventive measures. It quickly emerged that the education department of the City Council was not making the best use of available information and was consequently gaining a partial and distorted impression of vandalism in its schools. The Council recorded the cost of repairs for vandalism in each of its schools as part of its computerised and integrated accounting system but this was not used by the education department, which relied instead on a simpler system. Here a list was drawn up each month of schools having more than one 'incident' of vandalism. Unfortunately, each incident was in fact a report of one visit to a school by maintenance staff. Thus, an incident could vary between the repair of a single window-pane and the repair of 50 windows. Even the computerised system had its inadequacies since the recording of the costs of vandalism repairs was rather arbitrary, with much accidental damage and 'wear and tear' emerging as vandalism. It seemed sensible therefore to recommend the replacement of the current monitoring system with a better 'management information system', using data produced by the computerised accounting system, which would monitor the trend in more precise indices of damage at individual schools. Unfortunately, as will be seen later, this new system was never fully implemented.

There also seemed a need for a 'situational' analysis to identify the reasons for vandalism at individual schools. Local police crime prevention officers undertook surveys of school premises and advised the education department on crime prevention. However, it became apparent that their expertise lay more towards the prevention of burglary than vandalism. As their contacts with headteachers and staff was generally limited, this meant that their approach was dictated not so much by the actual problems suffered by each school as by a repertoire of anti-burglary methods which, however valuable in principle, were not especially appropriate for tackling vandalism (Gladstone, 1980). In contrast, the police were encouraged to use a more diagnostic approach during the project. It was found that much of what had passed as 'vandalism' was actually a consequence of young people playing without supervision in school grounds at evenings and weekends. Much of the damage seemed virtually 'accidental'. Many windows were broken, for instance, by footballs, and much of the damage to the external fabric of schools was caused by children clambering about on them. This suggested quite different strategies from those appropriate for dealing with 'malicious hooligans'. Two options presented themselves: *physical measures* to protect the exterior of the buildings from further damage; and improved *leisure provision* to direct youngsters into less harmful activities.

2.2. Decision-making

Planning must involve those who are to put the plans into effect, yet the dynamics of collaborative decision-making may play a crucial role in determining the outcome of such deliberations. It was decided to convene separate 'case conferences' of local officials, school staff and local police to discuss vandalism at each school. These groups were presented with the results of the situational analysis which suggested both physical measures and leisure provision. However, the groups invariably selected physical measures. Moreover, most of the measures were of a conventional 'target hardening' kind – for example, window grills, damage resistant glazing and high fencing. Only two measures were particularly innovative: a 'good neighbour' scheme to encourage local residents to keep a watchful eye over two adjacent schools; and a proposal to re-design a school's grounds to divert play to a less vulnerable area. Improved leisure provision was suggested for only one of the eleven schools where more evening activities were recommended.

It is difficult to know whether a bias towards physical measures reflects the most rational choice of preventive measures or arises for other reasons. On the one hand, it is possible that the groups were persuaded of the cost-effectiveness of physical measures. A body of research suggests that physical measures may be effective in reducing certain crimes (Clarke and Mayhew, 1980) and while youth services require continual expenditure, physical measures are usually once and for all investments. On the other hand, the groups may have been swayed by those whose province was physical crime prevention. This may have been because physical measures were usually deployed against vandalism by the buildings branch of the education department, who were recognised as having administrative and financial responsibility for dealing with vandalism. It may also have been because the expertise of local police crime prevention officers (who were seen as crime prevention experts) lay in the direction of physical measures. Whatever the reason, the project produced only a somewhat modified version of the customary response to vandalism in schools.

It was hoped that the situational approach would produce innovative responses to school vandalism, and the actual responses of the groups were discouraging (Gladstone, 1980). This experience perhaps illustrates one of the ironies of collaborative decision-making: that decisions which command the greatest support may often be those which are least innovative because they are least controversial (Rothman, 1974). In this project, it seems that the situational approach was lacking a strategy which secured agreement for recommendations and at the same time encouraged new responses.

2.3. Implementation

Unfortunately, the situational approach also failed to anticipate the difficulties of implementing the measures. After two years, only 15 out of 30 recommendations had been implemented and ten had been in effect for less than 12 months. More seriously, the groups had endeavoured to produce a consistent package of recommendations for each school but at only two were all the recommendations implemented. Incomplete implementation in the end meant that the situational approach had little impact on vandalism in most of the eleven target schools.

There were a number of reasons for failure during implementation. First, there were some *unanticipated technical difficulties*. The installation of damage-resistant glazing, for instance, proved difficult both because 'polycarbonate' materials were thought likely to give off toxic fumes and because the time taken to install 'toughened' glass seemed too lengthy in view of the need to replace broken windows rapidly. Consequently, not a single pane of either type of material was ever installed.

A second difficulty proved to be an *absence of control over local activity*. At one school it was proposed to divert play to a less vulnerable area by replacing the schools' original hard-surface playing area with flower-beds and re-surfacing another part of the grounds. However, misunderstandings and inadequate on-site supervision resulted in only half the proposed area being re-surfaced, without the replacement of the original area with flower-beds. Thus, vandalism at the school was much as it had been and there was an additional piece of tarmac which the school did not use. Similarly, a failure to properly advise staff at local repair depots meant that new procedures for recording vandalism (which were to be the main means of monitoring the effectiveness of preventive measures) failed to be adequately implemented. This resulted in the replacement of an imperfect record system by an inadequate one.

A third reason – *failure to co-ordinate local action* – led to the failure to launch the good neighbour scheme to encourage local residents to keep watch over two of the schools. A number of different branches of the education department and the police would have been involved, as well as the schools themselves, but no one was able or willing to take the lead. Fourth, many of the measures which were implemented took a long time to appear, mainly due to *competing priorities* for the education department's time and energies. Finally, failures occurred where the wider consequences of particular courses of action appeared to outweigh their immediate benefits – what might be called *'inhibiting consequences'*. In one school, a proposal to extend activities for children into the early evening was abandoned by education department officials on the grounds that they were likely to become embroiled in negotiations with the teachers' unions which might have wider repercussions. In another school, an apparently successful measure was abandoned because of its cost implications. Here, vandalism had been reduced by paying education department workers to patrol the grounds in their spare time. However, this proved too expensive, especially when other schools, and other workers, demanded to become part of the scheme.

It has been suggested that the views of those who had most experience or responsibility for dealing with vandalism prevailed in decision-making, but a similar explanation seems to apply to implementation as well. All the successful measures – such as window grills, intruder alarms and improved fencing – which were the sole responsibility of the buildings branch of the education department were implemented eventually, while none of those which involved other departments or agencies ever materialised. Neither procedures nor the means for agreeing on responsibility existed for those recommendations which involved inter-agency co-operation or the development of new methods.

3. Lessons

Why did things go wrong? In the first place, although the project broke new ground in attempting to discover the specific causes of vandalism at individual schools, it failed to alter, in any appreciable way, the response by the local authorities. In other words, it failed to alter the 'ownership' of the problem; vandalism prevention remained the province of those who customarily dealt with it – the buildings and maintenance departments, and local police crime prevention officers. Thus, the project acquired a distinctly 'target hardening' bias. Yet even so, a surprisingly large proportion of physical measures failed to materialise, or were delayed in implementation. There thus appear to have been two main implementation problems: resistance to innovation and inefficiency. How might these obstacles have been overcome?

It is not as though these two causes of implementation failure are unusual in social policy-making and in recent years a substantial body of work has appeared which attempts to understand policy implementation failure (cf. Barrett and Fudge, 1981). Two alternative solutions tend to emerge from this work. One solution can be termed the *programmed* approach; the other the *adaptive* approach (Berman, 1980). The programmed approach sees implementation failure arising because policy-initiators have insufficient control over implementors. A lack of control gives rise to difficulties in communicating policy objectives, failure to co-ordinate action, and resistance and inefficiency on the part of implementing agencies. The solution is therefore to devise clearly articulated plans and to ensure that these are adhered to. The adaptive approach, in contrast, looks at difficulties in implementation from the point of view of the agents charged with implementation. Here, implementors, as individuals and organisations, are seen as acting more or less rationally to achieve personal and organisational goals (Stone, 1980). These may not, however, coincide with the aims and objectives of policy initiators (Self, 1977). Attempts to impose greater external control will only be met with greater resistance. The solution is therefore to adapt policy to those situations in which it is to be implemented, and to negotiate agreement so that broad policy objectives 'evolve' into practical measures.

It is evident that the demonstration project fell somewhere between these two views. In being predicated upon a rational decision-making methodology, it clearly implied a programmed approach to implementation, yet it failed to provide any means of retaining control over decision-making and implementation. But, there was also insufficient recognition of the need to find out why things were customarily done in a particular way, and, just as important, how to detach implementors from their habitual practices.

It is likely, that the successful implementation of vandalism prevention programmes will require different approaches and emphases at different times (Berman, 1980). For certain problems, there may be a need to negotiate – suggesting an 'adaptive' approach to implementation; for other problems, greater clarity and control may be required, which would argue for a more 'programmed' approach. This suggests that it is necessary to pay more attention to the issues of implementing vandalism prevention measures. There is unlikely to be a recipe for successful implementation which could be applied to every circumstance and it is therefore necessary to develop implementation strategies applicable to individual situations.

Although the situational approach is valuable in directing attention to local circumstances, its scope needs to be broadened to include the organisational and political arena in which prevention is to be initiated. Above all, there is a continuing need to find a better fit between theory and practical experience. Situational approaches to vandalism prevention may have narrowed the gap between theory and practice, but the experience of this demonstration project, at least, suggests there is still a long way to go.

© Crown Copyright 1983.

References

Barrett, S., C. Fudge, eds., 1981. Policy and action. London: Methuen.

Berman, P., 1980. Think about programmed and adaptive implementation: Matching strategies to situations. In: H.M. Ingram, D.E. Mann, eds., Why policies succeed or fail. Beverly Hills: Sage Publications.

Clarke, R.V.G., ed., 1978. Tackling vandalism. Home Office Research Study no. 47. London: HMSO.

Clarke, R.V.G., 1980. Situational crime prevention: Theory and practice. British Journal of Criminology 20, 136–145.

Clarke, R.V.G., P. Mayhew, eds., 1980. Designing out crime. London: HMSO.

Cohen, A.K., 1955. Delinquent boys: The culture of the gang. Glencoe (Ill.): The Free Press.

Cohen, S., 1973a. Property destruction: Motives and meanings. In: C. Ward, 1973.

Cohen, S., 1973b. Campaigning against vandalism. In: C. Ward, 1973.

Corrigan, P., 1979. Schooling the smash street kids. London: Macmillan.

Gladstone, F.J., 1978. Vandalism amongst adolescent schoolboys. In: R.V.G. Clarke, 1978.

Gladstone, F.J., 1980. Co-ordinating crime prevention efforts. Home Office Research Study no. 62. London: HMSO.

Kellmer-Pringle, M., 1973. The roots of violence and vandalism. London: National Children's Bureau.

Mayhew, P., R. Clarke, 1982. Vandalism and its prevention. In: P. Feldman, ed., Developments in the study of criminal behaviour, vol. 2: Violence. London: Wiley.

Rothman, J., 1974. Planning and organizing for social change. New York: Columbia University Press.

Self, P., 1977. Administrative theories and politics. 2nd ed. London: Allen and Unwin.

Stone, C., 1980. The implementation of social programmes: Two perspectives. Journal of Social Issues 36, 13–34.

Sturman, A., 1978. Measuring vandalism in a city suburb. In: R.V.G. Clarke, 1978.

Ward, C., 1973. Vandalism. London: The Architectural Press.

Ward, C., ed., 1978. Tackling vandalism. Home Office Research Study no. 47. London: HMSO.

Wilson, S., 1978. Vandalism and defensible space on London housing estates. In: R.V.G. Clarke, 1978.

Wilson, S., 1979. Observations on the nature of vandalism. In: J. Syker, ed., Designing against vandalism. London Design Council.

Wilson, S., M. Burbridge, 1978. An investigation of difficult to let housing. Housing Review, July, 100–104.

Abstract: T. Hope, Preventing vandalism: the experience of an action research project
This chapter reports the experience of a demonstration project concerned with the prevention of vandalism to schools. The project was intended to test a 'situational' approach to vandalism prevention – an approach based on an analysis of vandalism in specific situations, and using local resources to tackle the problem. It was hoped to develop methods which local communities might adopt. Unfortunately, while the project was successful in casting new light on the problem, it failed to produce innovatory thinking and encountered obstacles in implementing preventive measures. It is argued that more attention needs to be paid to organisational issues when tackling vandalism, and that preventive efforts should be designed to overcome inevitable difficulties of implementation.

CHAPTER 24

Vandalism: overview and prospect

D. CANTER

The sub-title to the colloquium on vandalism was 'Behaviour and motivations'. This alone reveals that the objectives of the colloquium were to go beyond the naive views of vandals and acts of vandalism. The uninformed, popular view of vandals and vandalism as willfull and wanton acts of destruction, having little meaning and far less possiblity of explanation by civilized society, has now been truly opened to question. Similarly, the naive view enshrined in the work of Oscar Newman, that an area only has to be made defensible for crime to be pushed away is also challenged by many of the studies which are covered in earlier pages.

The purpose of this concluding contribution, then, is to draw together some of the threads and themes from the other contributions and to point to some of the directions for the future. This is a particularly inviting task because of the richness and variety of presentations. The diversity of contributions and the general methodological and theoretical sophistication they have shown indicate a vibrant area of research which has a wide geographical and cross-disciplinary distribution. This is not to say that there are not still great strides to be made. That is certainly the case. There are still many things we do not understand about vandalism, or indeed know about it. There are also many formulations which are unlikely to stand the test of time and further empirical investigation. In the following comments I will try and indicate where I see those strengths and weaknesses. However, I do think that these exist against a background of valuable and interesting research which holds great hope for the future.

1. Motivations for vandalism

In her opening comments and earlier writings on vandalism professor Lévy-Leboyer pointed out that one of the interests to applied social scientists of acts of vandalism is the way in which they are commonly defined as being motiveless. Indeed in the popular imagination this is the *sine qua non* of a vandal's act, that it appears to have no real purpose to it. As professor Lévy-Leboyer pointed out, this is a real challenge to conventional psychological theorizing. Motivation is regarded as integral to all human activity and therefore to conceive of an act as having no motivation raises some profound questions about the psychological mechanisms involved. Of course, professor Lévy-Leboyer need not feel too great a fear that studies of vandalism will bring the structures of psychology tumbling down. In the presentations in the present volume there is a veritable plethora of motivations being postulated to explain, or at least underlie, acts of vandalism.

These motives can probably be ordered from those which see the vandal's reacting because of something that has been done to him, what might be called 'stimulated vandalism', to those motives and explanations which see the vandals making a positive gesture possibly initiated by the vandal rather than by some external stimulus, what might be called 'assertive vandalism'. This range links to notions of locus of control where the vandal is seen as being motivated from within or essentially challenged from without to respond – Let us consider each of them in turn.

(1) Revenge. At one extreme is the explanation of vandalism as being motivated by a sense of injustice. A feeling that the individual has been hurt in some way by society and is therefore acting on it in order to express this injustice and to achieve some form of revenge for it. This is a form of motivation which puts vandalism clearly in the contexts of criminal actions, taking the law into your own hands.

(2) Anger. A slightly less actively conscious form of vandalism is explained in terms of persons feeling annoyed, now being able to get what they want. The anarchic or criminal element here is now not the source of explanation so much as the individual's own inadequacy and feelings of anger at not being able to get his own way. Clearly, this has a more juvenile form to it which may, to some extent, be seen as an attempt to cope with stresses and strains internal to the individual.

(3) Boredom. A number of the contributions talk about vandalism being associated with unemployment and lack of recreational facilities. It is interesting that in the rural mid-west of America as well as in northern English towns similar patterns are found of youths simply breaking things and destroying things in order to introduce some excitement and interest into their life. Of particular curiosity here, and importance in the understanding of vandalism, is the fact that the stimulating qualities of this type of activity are increased to some degree by the possibility of being caught. The 'fun of the chase' adds to the excitement engendered by this type of act.

(4) Acquisition. A further motivation of a more direct, and almost intelligent, kind is best illustrated by an example from the Soviet Union. It seems that a number of years ago, when electric guitars first became popular, there was a great rash of destructions in telephone kiosks. The reason for this was that the small microphone which could be placed inside the guitar in order to amplify the sound was not readily available in the Soviet Union, but that the

microphones inside public telephones did provide just the equipment needed. The industrious guitar player thus had a ready source for his equipment. A number of other detailed examples of this kind could probably be found in many other countries, but it can be seen that this type of behaviour might be interpreted as vandalism in many contexts when in fact it is directly a form of theft.

(5) Exploration. Some contributors have argued that a major motivation for vandalism is to see how the system works, often both physically and socially. By destroying objects some of their properties can be discovered. But also the search and the chase involved in trying to deal with acts of destruction can reveal to the individual the way in which a society operates. Many students of adolescence have demonstrated the importance of 'testing the limits' and this could be perceived as another type of similar activity.

(6) Aesthetic experience. It has been suggested by one or two contributors that the artistic community has always explored the possibilities of iconoclasm and destruction. Certainly early 20th-century art explored the possibilities of destruction as artistic creation to a great extent. Self-destructing artistic activities as well as forms of expressionism and abstract expressionism all could be viewed as forms of elite, institutionalized vandalism. It is therefore possible to argue that individuals in a less elite circumstance may still get some degree of aesthetic pleasure out of some forms of destruction.

(7) Existential exploration. It is possible to take the argument of search and exploration to an extreme where acts of destruction and various forms of vandalism become seen as almost existential in quality. It might even be suggested, following Descartes, that 'I smash therefore I am', although this may seem like a philosophical extreme. A strange means for the individual to try to come to terms with the possibility of his impact on society. It can be seen that some forms of attack on social institutions or physical objects can be a part of the personal growth for certain disturbed individuals.

What is fascinating about a list such as the one above is how far it takes us from the idea of vandalism being motiveless. Quite the reverse, it now becomes possible to think of it as a very complex, motivated series of activities. As such, it is quite likely that a number of different motivations run together in many acts of vandalism. Especially if the social element is introduced whereby the individual is revealing boredom but at the same time demonstrating his position within a social group and thus exploring his own concepts of himself. From this perspective vandalism can take its place with most other forms of human activity. The only problem that remains from this summary of potential motivations is how they can lead us to a distinct explanation of *vandalism* as opposed to other forms of delinquent or criminal-like behaviour.

Most of the motivations summarized above have been used at one time or another as explanations of a wide range of criminal behaviour, whether it be mugging or bank robbery. What is it that turns the individual to attack property rather than to attack other individuals? What gives rise to the wanton qualities of almost random attack on public objects as opposed, for example, to arson of a disliked school building or the theft of objects from a shop? Part of the answer to this question is likely to reside in the situation in which the individual finds himself, the opportunities which are available and part of the answer must lie in the nature of the individual, whether he is socially inept or physically inadequate. But this serves to emphasize that vandalism cannot be simply and clearly distinguished from other forms of criminal behaviour. Certainly in terms of its motivation it seems very possible that similar motivations in different situations may give rise in one situation to vandalism and in another situation to other forms of delinquent or criminal behaviour. One advantage of this formulation is that the literature on criminal and delinquent behaviour can be explored (vandalized might be too harsh a term!) in order to examine the contributions it might make to explaining this distinctly physical environmental oriented behaviour.

2. Why is vandalism now recognized?

Having seen the range of motivations and the possible overlap between vandalism and other forms of anti-social behaviour, the question must be answered 'why do we now recognize vandalism as a particular form of behaviour and what is it that has brought such a large number of people together in its study?'. There are a number of historical and social answers to this important question.

One possibility is that there has been a noticeable increase in vandalism over the last few years, drawing people's attention to it and to the need to do something about it. It is very difficult to know how valid this is because of the close association between a concern with vandalism and information being available as to its occurrence. History from the ancient world to the modern day shows that groups of people have always been prepared to express their dislike of existing establishments by destruction with various degrees of wantonness. Indeed, the very name 'vandal' is taken from the marauding hordes which destroyed the works of art and glories of the countries into which they moved. Given this prevalence, it is all too possible that as more statistics are collected there is an increasing awareness of the existence of the problem and a belief that parallels this increasing awareness which suggest that vandalism itself has actually increased.

So a question related to that of whether or not vandalism has increased is the question as to what has generated the increase in concern with vandalism. It could well be that this is part of a much more general development in our society of anxiety with the effects which disaffected groups can have. In a society in which there is more information widely available and in which incidents of any significance can be reported to a very large proportion of societies very quickly, it does seem likely that the effects of small disaffected groups can cause more concern than they might have done in the past. It is very important to unravel these issues. If there is essentially a more general anxiety with a society which has become too plural for comfort, then this demands different types of research exploration than if the development in interest in vandalism is because of a general increase in the destructive behaviour of adolescents. Although, of course, these two issues can never be completely separated.

The concern about groups on the fringe of society is part of a deeper and possibly more understandable concern with the way in which small determined groups can play havoc with monolithic or highly interconnected institutions. To put it another way, there is the underlying fear expressed by many individuals that if a vandal is given a weapon he may become an urban guerilla. This view is not as far-fetched as it might at first seem. The newspaper coverage of guerillas does suggest a strong ideological commitment and a determination based upon some form of rational analysis of the situation. So, in principle, reporting of guerilla activities does make it appear very different indeed from the wanton, random activity of vandals. However, although it is clear that the leaders of guerilla movements and their spokesmen do have serious political commitments, there is a growing amount of research to suggest that the rank and file of guerilla movements are often people who are not motivated by any profound political ideology but are finding an institutional framework in which to be destructive and to express far more personal conflicts with the world. It is thus possible that what is known of the far more dramatic urban guerilla groups may help us to understand something of the activities, certainly of large scale vandalism.

Another way of thinking about this relationship between vandalism and more overt and organized acts of violence is to ask for the link between vandalism and riot. For here again, there is some evidence that, whatever the initiating cause of a riot, it does suck into it many individuals within the community who would perform acts of destruction in other circumstances if they could get away with it. Indeed, within this context, the destruction by the Hitler Youth Movement and the Blackshirts of the property of private citizens, because it was condoned by the authorities, can be seen as institutionalized vandalism. In the present day the way in which destruction continues in Northern Ireland also suggests that there are individuals associated with these activities who are not strictly motivated by ideological or political reasons.

One of the reasons why it is important to emphasize these links, from relatively benign acts of minor destruction to large scale urban guerilla movements, is that it seems very probable indeed that the reasons why official authorities are prepared to support studies of vandalism and the reasons why it gets such a large amount of press coverage is because of these underlying associations in the minds of many people in positions of authority. As researchers we must be on our guard not to confuse these various issues and not to be drawn into studies which purport to look at vandalism, but in effect are looking at differences in ideological systems.

3. The importance of definition

It is thus important to explore the definition of vandalism and the borderline between it and other forms of anti-social behaviour for a number of reasons. Definition is not neutral. It takes a stand. Especially this is true when the definition involves an evaluation of whether the activity is bad or not bad. This is particularly the case with acts of vandalism because in many studies there is the implicit definition that these acts are bad but not too serious. If the act becomes serious and open to consideration as a criminal event then it is interpreted as a crime rather different from vandalism, in many studies. Thus there are examples of students destroying dormitories in a ritual way after football or rugby matches and this being condoned by the authorities and normally paid for through some institutional mechanism. On the other hand, some presentations have indicated, for example, that hanging washing lines on trees in US National Parks is an act of vandalism for which considerable resources should be expended in order to reduce.

There is also an important consideration that has psychological and legal implications. In law, the role of the intention of the individual to cause damage or to carry out a criminal act is regarded as being important. This refers us back to my opening comments on motivation. That if there is some intention, some clear motivation, associated with a particular piece of behaviour it begins to draw it more into the realm of criminal act than into the realm of accidental or unintentional damage, which may be interpreted by others as vandalism. Researchers will need to be clear in their own minds why they are defining the behaviour they are studying as vandalism and not criminal. As part of this they will need to explore rather closely what forms of intentions and motivation they see as being prevalent in the act involved.

Definition is likely to reveal some other overlaps and potential confusions with different types of activity. For example, what about industrial sabotage? It is well known that on certain production lines workers will introduce a break-down into the system in order to relieve the monotony. Is this a form of vandalism and should it be explored in relation to other, similar acts? What about destruction which people might cause in their home as opposed to damage of public housing property? Are these different issues or the same issues in a different context? What happens if we take schools as the focus? Is this any different from taking housing? Are there different processes involved here? Furthermore, when damage is caused by people finding it difficult to use particular equipment or facilities and this clearly has an ergonomic component, should this get classed as vandalism or not?

In all these considerations of definition we must be aware of the possibility of building in value judgements into our definition and thus weighting the likelihood of certain sorts of outcome as a consequence. This, of course, opens up one very interesting area for research. What types of activity get called vandalism and what types of activity are regarded as being just part of the continuum of anti-social, criminal behaviour?

4. Positive directions and actions for the future

Having indicated some of the common themes in the explanations for vandalism and my personal view of some of the reasons why vandalism is a legitimate area of study, it is appropriate to move on to a discussion of what are the fruitful future directions for study and the future possibilities for action to reduce vandalism.

There are still four fundamental questions that need to be answered about vandalism:
(1) What exactly is vandalism? At least the question must be answered, what forms does vandalism take?
(2) Where does vandalism occur and what are the qualities and properties of these locations?
(3) Who are the individuals who are responsible for the actions that are observed to occur and have been classified as vandalism?
(4) What can be done about it?

These four questions cover a very big research task. They also suggest that there are many different forms of vandalism which are likely to require very different types of solutions for their reduction. It also would be inaccurate to suggest that we do not have the beginnings of answers to many of these questions. As I have already indicated, we already have a number of hypotheses about motivations added to which more complex hypotheses are likely to develop. A number of researchers have also begun to find who is committing different acts of vandalism in different situations. We know for example, from the French research on destruction of telephone kiosks, that it is a very wide group of individuals within society who are doing this, not simply adolescents. On the other hand, studies of other forms of urban destruction have been identified with young adolescent groups. The initial challenge of the work of Oscar Newman also led people to look more closely at where vandalism actually occurs. Like all other forms of human social behaviour it is not evenly and randomly distributed throughout our cities and countryside, but is linked to particular areas and particular types of location.

There are also in the presentations in this volume a number of indications of what can be done to reduce vandalism, which are having varying degrees of success. There is even now serious debate about what vandalism actually is. Most researchers put forward a definition that relates to the specific problem with which they are dealing and so no overall consensus has yet been accepted.

Against this range of fundamental questions still to be answered about vandalism and the essentially pragmatic concerns which led to it being studied in the first place, it does suggest that the most fruitful directions for the future are to be found in focussing on particular aspects of vandalism rather than attempting to answer the broad taxonomic and explanatory issues indicated above. What I would suggest is that there are two aspects of vandalism to which attention should be turned. One is what I would call the *process* issues, the other is the need for cross-national comparisons.

To deal with the cross-national issues first, the importance of this does seem to me to lie in the clarification of the extent to which vandalism is a unitary phenomenon, independent of culture and environmental context, and the extent to which various forms of vandalism are special to particular circumstances. This is absolutely fundamental to any future development of ways of dealing with vandalism. If it is a phenomenon which has very similar patterns and processes to it in all societies then it is likely to be very difficult to cope with, but fundamental ways of dealing with it are more likely to have widespread consequences. On the other hand, if patterns of vandalism relate to particular social or economic circumstances then it is more likely that specific solutions to specific incidents can be found. However, it is almost certain that some forms of vandalism will be common to most societies at the same level of technical development and other forms will be specific to particular contexts. It is clearly essential that we establish which forms of vandalism are which.

To turn now to the process issues, what I have in mind here is that, given that a central goal of research is to influence and modify patterns of activity, it is essential that research looks at the various processes, developments, changes over time which relate to vandalism. In other words, instead of being concerned with describing the frequency or distribution of acts of vandalism we should look more to the patterns of activity and processes involved in vandalism. Three processes can be identified which would benefit from further detailed explanation.

4.1. Precursors to vandalism

One process question which appears not to have been explored in any detail yet, is whether or not there are any identifiable precursors to vandalism. In other words, whether any activities can be identified which occur before vandalism occurs. There are really two temporal sequences involved here. One is the sequence of actions over a short period of time which may eventually lead into vandalism. For example, football hooligans who are fairly rowdy. Does their pattern of activities eventually develop and degenerate into something which is destructive? Does noisy play among children who push and shove sometimes go over the top and give rise to destruction? Can we, in fact, analyze the whole sequence of behaviours which occur before acts of vandalism and find some mechanisms there which give rise to it? Or is vandalism a sudden and distinguishable act that occurs without any such progenitors?

Another temporal sequence is really the longer term one within the life of the individual. Are there activities which are not uncommon at certain stages in growth and development, but which may, given the right context or the right combination of individual motivations, lead the individual into what almost might be called 'a career' of vandalism? Indeed, this raises the question as to whether vandalism itself is a stage along some other career into more severe anti-social behaviour and more recognizable forms of criminal activity. Or is it likely to be an activity which is quite separate from these other forms of criminal act? The third temporal sequence which is worth exploring are broad social changes over time. Can we see patterns and sequences of vandalism occurring in relation to social processes? Can we see changes relating to unemployment levels or to average wages or to the raising of the school leaving age? A number of criminologists have found such broad sociological trends in criminal behaviour, but the question remains as to how detailed these trends might be and whether or not specific aspects of the social system can be seen to relate to increases and decreases in acts of vandalism.

Behind all these questions of process is the assumption that vandalism occurs as part of a sequence of acts which may very likely be themselves part of other patterns and sequences of activity. It is particularly valuable to identify such precursors, for a number of reasons. One of these reasons is that such precursors are more likely to be open to public view. Minor incidents like boisterous play may be much more easy to record and to identify than acts which border on the criminal. It may also be more possible to get people to talk about these acts than about the criminal activities. But also, of course, the possibilities of prediction and modification are much more likely.

4.2. Attitude change

Another process which is relevant to the development of an understanding of changes in vandalism are changes in attitudes towards the objects and institutions which are vandalized. This process is very much part of studies of development and change in attitudes. Many researchers have also pointed out that attitude change and education are remarkably closely related both conceptually and practically. There are thus broader issues about attitudes towards the physical surrounding and how these might develop and change over time as well as more specific issues about what leads given groups and sub-groups in society to hold particular views of certain objects. This relates back also to our central issues of motivation. Do individuals realize the role of intention in legal proceedings? Do they themselves have any awareness of the intentions and reasons for their acts and how does this awareness relate to their beliefs and opinions about the significance of their act? Here is a point where the researcher's view as to what is serious or not is likely to be directly testable against the views of various respondents. Can a pattern of beliefs about what are serious acts of vandalism and what are minor acts be found in the general population? Do these relate to the frequency and significance of these acts? The question then is raised as to what educational processes will change these views and whether or not they do have legitimacy?

This last point of legitimacy cannot be passed over too easily. The famous examples of graffiti on New York subways being a form of vandalism which many people believed improved the subway system is an interesting example of how different sub-groups in the population can hold very different attitudes towards what are destructive acts and what not.

4.3. Forms of intervention

One aspect of vandalism which comes through all the presentations is that it needs to be considered a social and physical process. This is in direct contradiction of the earlier Oscar Newman perspective in which physical solutions were proposed as the major way of dealing with these problems. Perhaps the most significant view on Newman's work which comes from the contributions to this volume is the little reference that has been made to it. Clearly, few people find it of any real value, although its contribution in raising awareness of possible solutions to problems of urban crime, delinquency and vandalism shoud not be underestimated.

The combination of the physical and the social has strong implications for intervention processes. One of the major implications is that purely physical solutions are not enough. Indeed, on their own the provisions of physical attempts to defeat vandalism are liable to backfire, as well as producing an unacceptable physical environment.

The idea of 'target hardening' as it has been called needs to be contrasted with the concept of 'target softening'. Although it may be possible to reduce some vandalism by building extremely strong frameworks for notices or using shatter-proof and break-proof window glass, it also seems possible that by making potential targets of vandalism very easy to replace and by providing a maintenance system that will replace them quickly and cheaply it might have a more acceptable impact.

These physical solutions alone though, most contributors to this volume would probably agree, are not likely to be enough or even successful at all in the long term. As Hope pointed out, there is the very real, associated question of who actually owns the problem. The bureaucratic web which controls most cities can very easily lead to a confusion over whether vandalism is seen as a problem of maintenance, of design, of public education, or whatever. Each of the different decisions as to whose the problem is, is liable to give rise to different sorts of intervention procedures.

These thoughts lead to an emphasis on understanding what actually happens when intervention programmes are introduced. The more case studies we can have of the whole intervention procedure the more we will learn about the possibilities. There is, for example, already a growing view with some empirical support, that the rapid and repeated replacement of objects which have been attacked by vandals can eventually reduce the occurrence of the problem. The sequence is not fully understood but it would seem that in the early stages of replacing destroyed objects there will be repeated attacks on them but as the objects continue to be replaced so the vandals lose the motivation to attack them.

Studies of this type of intervention process are invaluable and the more of them that can be found to explore the better. They not only throw light on practical possibilities but also reveal some very important aspects of the central motivational issues which must be understood. Some types of motivational process would predict that the removal of the effects of the vandal's act would reduce the attractiveness of continuing to carry out such acts. Certainly vandalism as a means of self-expression would fall into this category. However, vandalism as a way of finding out how the system works and operates would be predicted to continue when replacements were introduced. However, if these replacements were produced standardly in an uncontroversial way then after it had happened once or twice there would be no interest to the vandal in seeing it being repeated again.

What is being introduced here then, are procedures and administrative frameworks within which to deal with and consider vandalism. This of course can be taken much further by the involvement of the citizens in considerations and actions that relate to particular anti-social issues. Using the individuals in the community themselves as advocates with other members of the community is a process which finds considerable support in socialist and communist countries, where the work force is often used as a major form of social control, but it is interesting to learn of parallel explorations in Los Angeles and other countries.

An extreme of this involvement is illustrated by the British approach to 'adopting a telephone'. The idea here is to make the potential target very much part of a community setting. French research has also revealed that considerable benefit can accrue from identifying individuals who are prepared to take a clear responsibility for objects which would otherwise be considered in the public domain. It is interesting to speculate how far these processes of ownership in an overt fashion by the community or by specific individuals of public objects can be taken. Instead of owning a phone box is there any future in the concept of owning a vandal?

5. In conclusion

By way of conclusion a few points may be emphasized.

First, the key to understanding vandalism is understanding its motivation. The reasons why people do it. This will include an understanding both of the explanations which individuals themselves will give as well as the explanations that might be provided by more distant observers.

Second, the role of the social in interacting with the physical components of vandalism need to be more fully explored and understood. We need to understand the way in which management procedures, social groupings, patterns of interaction between various sub-groups in a committee and so on, all operate in shaping the pattern of observed acts of wanton destruction.

Third, procedures of intervention and control need to be explored as they happen. Descriptive studies which do not allow the development of process information are not likely to be as productive as process studies which focus on changes over time within the individual, within groups, or within society.

Behind and beyond all these discussions will continue to be a debate as to what exactly vandalism is. This is especially important in a cross-cultural framework in order to understand whether we are studying similar processes, whether there is indeed a universal culture upon which we all draw, fed by television and the mass media. We have an important need to know what is common to different settings and what is particular to specific locations in order to more clearly identify the directions for future study.

A dictionary definition of a vandal is 'someone who destroys something beautiful'. As we all know, beauty is in the eye of the beholder, so the different perspectives of different sub-groups on what vandalism is, how it comes to occur and why it happens will remain important questions for this stimulating field of enquiry for some years to come.

Abstract: D. Canter, Vandalism: overview and prospect
The material presented in the volume is reviewed. It is argued that the central issue in the understanding and control of vandalism is the identification of the major motivations underlying it. Seven different motivations are identified from the various contributions. It is argued that by understanding these motivations a number of directions for action emerge. These directions all focus on the processes underlying vandalism rather than a description of its demography and frequency of occurrence. The main processes identified for further study are: the precursors to vandalism, public attitude change, and forms of intervention.

Notes on the authors

The notes are presented in alphabetical order of authors' names.

Vernon L. Allen, Professor of Psychology at the University of Wisconsin-Madison, USA, received the Ph.D. degree from the University of California at Berkeley and did postdoctoral work at Stanford University. He has held a Fulbright Fellowship in England and was a Fellow at the Netherlands Institute for Advanced Study in the Humanities and Social Sciences. His research interests include role theory, group dynamics, and environmental psychology. Ongoing research includes studies on vandalism, social interaction among children, and intergroup relations. Recent publications include *Role transitions: Explorations and explanations* (edited with E. van de Vliert), (Plenum, in press), *Human development: An interactional perspective* (edited with D. Magnusson) (Academic Press, in press), and *Children as teachers* (Academic Press, 1976).

Reuben M. Baron is a Professor of Psychology at the University of Connecticut (Storrs, CT, USA). Professor Baron is a social-environmental psychologist whose interests include the relationship between control and crowding stress, the nonverbal communication of emotion, the application of an ecological model of perception to social cognition, and dormitory vandalism.

Jacqueline Bideaud is Maître-Assistant at the Université René Descartes in Paris and has been both lecturing and conducting research at the Laboratoire de Psychologie Génétique since 1973. Dr. Bideaud's main research interests are the development of moral judgement and the development of elementary ideas with respect to logic and spatial relationships. She has published a book on the development of the logical concept of inclusion and a further 25 articles dealing with the aforementioned topics.

David Canter, Ph.D. FBPsS, is Reader in Psychology at the University of Surrey and Managing Editor of the *Journal of Environmental Psychology*. He has published widely on social issues, especially on those relating to human interaction with the physical surroundings. His most recent book, edited with Sandra Canter, is *Psychology in practice* (Wiley).

Harriet H. Christensen is a Research Social Scientist with the USDA Forest Service, Pacific Northwest Forest and Range Experiment Station, Wildland Recreation Research, Seattle, Washington. Her present activities include: developing administrative and management guidelines for prevention and control of vandalism, theft, littering, and other depreciative actions in recreation settings. Her recent publications include: 'Prevention and control of depreciative behavior in recreation areas: Managerial concerns and research needs' with Diane M. Samdahl and Roger N. Clark in *Forest and river recreation: Research update* (Miscellaneous Publication 18-1982, Agricultural Experiment Station, Univ. of Minnesota) and 'Bystander intervention and litter control: Evaluation of an appeal-to-help program' (USDA Forest Service, Research Paper PNW-287, July 1981).

Stanley Cohen is a sociologist working in the areas of crime, deviance and social control. He has written about subjects such as vandalism, juvenile delinquency, mass media and deviance, criminological theory and prison. His books include *Images of deviance*; *Psychological survival*; *Folk devils and moral panics* and *The manufacture of news*. After 15 years' teaching in England, most recently as Professor of Sociology at the University of Essex in 1980, he moved to Israel where he is now a Professor at the Institute of Criminology, Hebrew University of Jerusalem.

Pierre G. Coslin is Vice-Chairman of the Unité d'Enseignement et de Recherche de Psychologie at the Université René Descartes in Paris. He has both lectured and conducted research at the Laboratoire de Psychologie Sociale Appliquée. His main research interests are attitudes towards deviant behaviour, drug addiction, adolescent psychology and university level pedagogy. Dr. Coslin coordinated the special edition of the *Bulletin de Psychologie* on 'Approaches to adolescence' and has published some 26 articles on topics related to his research.

Joseph F. Donnermeyer is Director of the National Rural Crime Prevention Center, and Assistant Professor, Dept. of Agricultural Economics and Rural Sociology, The Ohio State University. He has a Ph.D. in sociology from the University of Kentucky. As its Director, he is primarily responsible for supervising the research and crime prevention programming activities of the Center (such as major studies of the extent and pattern of crime to farm operations and of the impact of crime on the rural elderly). Dr. Donnermeyer is author and co-author of numerous publications on rural crime and its prevention, and, with Dr. G. Howard Phillips, edited a reader: *Rural crime: Integrating research and prevention*.

Jeffrey D. Fisher is an Associate Professor of Psychology at the University of Connecticut (Storrs, CT, USA). Professor Fisher is a social-environmental psychologist whose interests include personal space, crowding, vandalism, recipient reactions to help, and responses to new technology.

Noëlle Girault read psychology at the Université René Descartes in Paris. She completed a DESS (French postgraduate degree) in Industrial Psychology in 1978 and has since been carrying out research into environmental problems. She is currently investigating the vandalising of public telephones, in collaboration with her thesis advisor, Professor Cl. Lévy-Leboyer. The subject of her 'troisième cycle' thesis is vandalism to school property.

Tim Hope is a Senior Research Officer in the Research and Planning Unit of the Home Office, London, which he joined in 1974. Initially trained as a sociologist, he has spent the last few years carrying out research into aspects of crime prevention. During this period he has been involved in organising and evaluating the action research project on the prevention of vandalism discussed in this volume. He has also completed a study of burglary in schools, paying specific attention to the environmental aspects of the offence. More recently he has carried out a study concerned with the prevention of disorder associated with the use of 'pubs and clubs' which examines issues of implementation.

Jean Lawrence took a first degree and a doctorate in modern languages at University College, London 1947-52. She began teaching in secondary schools and advanced study in education at the same time. She spent periods as head of modern languages in a mixed grammar school, research assistant, and head of the English department in a secondary modern school. She subsequently became headmistress of a secondary modern school, and of a London comprehensive school. She was awarded a Social Science Research Fellowship (1969-71), for work on disruptive school behaviour, at the University of London Institute of Education, Dept. of Psychology, taking her Masters degree in educational psychology during this time. Since then, Dr. Lawrence has combined teacher education with individual and collaborative research into disruptive behaviour, publishing many monographs and journal articles on the subject, including *Exploring techniques for coping with disruptive behaviour* (Goldsmiths' College, 1980). She currently holds the post of Principal Lecturer in Education in the Postgraduate Secondary Department of Goldsmiths' College.

Claude Lévy-Leboyer is Professor of Psychology at the Université René Descartes in Paris, Vice-President of the University and President of the International Association of Applied Psychology. She has been particularly active in the field of work psychology, notably with respect to group problems and motivations. Her current research interests include environmental psychology, particularly the psychological effects of noise and environmental stress, and environmental assessment. Among her more recent publications are an overview of research on psychology and the environment (Presses Universitaires) which has been translated into English, Spanish and Italian, and a field study on decision processes published in the 'Monographies du Centre National de la Recherche Scientifique'.

Charles Markus graduated from Cambridge and Paris Universities gaining a 'diplôme d'études supérieures' with mention 'très bien' and a 'doctorat de troisième cycle' at the latter. He has written several papers on geomorphology and statistics, the subject of his thesis. He currently works with British Telecom and was in charge of payphones for five years. It was at this time he became interested in vandalism as one aspect of payphone management.

Rob Mawby was employed as a researcher on the Sheffield Study of Urban Social Structure and Crime from 1972 to 1975. Since this, he has lectured in sociology and crime and penal policy at the Universities of Leeds and Bradford, and is currently Principal Lecturer in Social Policy at Plymouth Polytechnic. He is the author of *Policing the city* (Lexington, 1979), *Asians and crime* (with I.D. Batta; Scope Communications, 1981) and numerous articles on among other things crime, policing and victimology. He is currently involved in research on the Plymouth Nightshelter for Vagrant Alcoholics and on the use of volunteers in the Criminal Justice System. With A.E. Bottoms and P. Xanthos he is completing the final report on the Sheffield project, focussing on residents' perceptions of life in contrasting residential areas, and is particularly concerned with the experience and perceptions of the victim, most notably the elderly victim of crime.

Gabriel Moser holds a Ph.D. in Social Psychology and works as a researcher at the Université René Descartes, Laboratory of Applied Social Psychology. He lectures at the same university. His main interests are environmental stress and aggression, and research on vandalism and the behavioural effects of noise (man/environment interaction).

C. Nilsson has a Bachelor of Arts degree and works as a research assistant in the Department of Sociology of the University of Lund, Sweden. She has been head of the research project 'Vandalism in residential areas', briefly reported on here, which resulted in six working reports (mimeo). The final report on this research project will soon be published in English. A new research project, for which the author is also project leader, concerns vandalism in urban environments and will be a study of vandalism in schools and in residential areas. In this project, the method of self-reported criminality will be used to elucidate the youths' level of delinquency and especially of their vandalism. The project will be completed in the course of 1986.

Kaj Noschis, Ph.D., is a psychologist working as a researcher at the Architecture Department of the Federal Institute of Technology in Lausanne, Switzerland. He is editor of the *Journal of Architecture & Behaviour/Architecture & Comportement*.

G. Howard Phillips is founder and former Director of the National Rural Crime Prevention Center, and Professor Emeritus, Department of Agricultural Economics and Rural Sociology, The Ohio State University. Dr. Phillips also has a Ph.D. in Rural Sociology from that university. He has been recognized as the father of rural crime research and prevention in the United States. His pioneer research in the early 1970s represents a unique contribution to the fields of Rural Sociology and Criminology. Dr. Phillips has inspired many other scholars to seriously examine the rural crime problem and to seek effective preventive strategies.

George Rand is Associate Dean of UCLA's Graduate School of Architecture and Urban Planning in Los Angeles. He has been involved in a variety of architectural design projects at different scales, from designing a 'country club' for a large suburban housing development, group homes for the developmentally disabled, new towns overseas for mining corporation employees and, as in this study, social housing for indigent people. Dr. Rand worked with Oscar Newman, the architect, in designing the research and conducting the analyses that led to the book *Defensible space*.

Eric Reade worked in local authority planning offices from leaving school, in 1948, until 1963, qualifying as a member of the Royal Town Planning Institute by correspondence course and evening classes. Studied sociology as a 'mature' evening student at the London School of Economics, from 1963 to 1968, graduating with specialism in political sociology. Taught at the College of Estate Management, University of London, 1963 to 1970, and in the Department of Town and Country Planning, University of Manchester, 1970 to 1983. Has published a number of papers on the theory, philosophy, sociology and politics of planning.

Hans-Edvard Roos is a researcher at the Department of Sociology in the University of Lund, Sweden. He lectures at that Department as well as at the College of Social Work in Lund. His research experience and publications cover such subject areas as social life, urbanisation, economic history, social problems, action research and community work in urban neighbourhoods. His present research concerns violence and vandalism in urban settings. He has carried out empirical work in this field in a number of communities in Sweden, among them major cities such as Stockholm and Malmö, but also in small towns such as Arvika, located in a rather isolated part of Sweden. He currently heads the three-year research project 'Vandalism in big city and rural areas' of the Swedish Council of Building Research.

Jacques Sélosse is Professor of Developmental Psychology at the Université de Lille III. He also teaches a course on adolescent behavioural problems at the Institut de Psychologie in Paris. He has had great experience of youth problems of all sorts, both in the field and as director, researcher and training manager: he was head of the abandoned children's department in Morocco from 1952 to 1958, and Deputy Director and later Director of the Supervised Education Department's Research and Training Centre at the Ministry of Justice from 1958 to 1980. From 1963 to 1972 he was a member of the Centre National de la Recherche Scientifique. As a specialist in the problems of juvenile delinquency he has served as consultant to the Council of Europe and to the World Health Organisation. His published research concerns gang delinquency, motorised vehicle theft and the social integration of delinquents. He sits on the editorial board of the *Journal of Adolescence* (Academic Press).

Lyle W. Shannon (Ph.D., sociology, University of Washington in 1951) has been director of the Iowa Urban Community Research Center, University of Iowa, since 1970. He is also a professor of sociology in the Department of Sociology, which he chaired from 1962 to 1970. His research on juvenile delinquency and adult crime in Racine, Wisconsin, began while he was a member of the Department of Sociology at the University of Wisconsin (1952–62). Shannon's first book, *Underdeveloped areas* (Harper, 1957), is an interdisciplinary approach to the problems of what are now termed 'third-world' countries. After some years of research and publication in this field, he turned to work on the problems of adjustment faced by Blacks and Chicanos who had moved to Northern industrial areas from the South and Southwest. *Minority migrants in the urban community* (Sage, 1973) describes early phases of the work. The results of a 1972 follow-up have appeared in numerous professional journals. The birth cohort research on delinquency and crime was first published as 'A longitudinal study of delinquency and crime' in Ch. Welford, *Quantitative studies in criminology* (Sage, 1978) and as 'Assessing the relationship of adult criminal careers to juvenile careers' in C. Abt, *Problems in American social policy research* (Abt Books, 1980). This work is more fully described in *Assessing the relationship of adult criminal careers to juvenile careers* (U.S. Dept., of Justice, 1982).

Paul van Soomeren is a social geographer. He works at the National Bureau of Crime Prevention in The Hague, The Netherlands. He has written a book and several articles on vandalism with Bram Van Dijk and four reports on their research in Amsterdam (with Bram Van Dijk and Martin Walop).

Jean-Claude Sperandio has degrees in Psychology and in Town Planning. He is currently a Professor of Occupational Psychology and Ergonomics at the Université René Descartes in Paris. He has acted as a consultant in various projects of urban and architectural design. The major part of his research deals with ergonomics of computerisation.

Bram van Dijk is a social geographer. He has worked for two years at the National Bureau of Crime Prevention in The Hague, The Netherlands, and in 1983 set up his own consultancy bureau, working in the field of crime prevention. He has written a book and several articles on vandalism with Paul Van Soomeren and four reports on their research in Amsterdam (with Paul van Soomeren and Martin Walop).

Willem van Vliet is a graduate of the Free University of Amsterdam and received his Ph.D. in the Department of Sociology, University of Toronto. He is currently assistant professor in the College of Human Development at The Pennsylvania State University. From 1977 to 1979 he was a fellow of the Social Sciences and Humanities Research Council and the Department of External Affairs of Canada, representing The Netherlands in a bilateral exchange. He received a Lady Davis Fellowship in 1979, and stayed in 1981–1982 as an Allan Fellow in the Department of Sociology and the Center for Urban and Regional Studies at Tel Aviv University where he conducted a study of Israel's housing policy for young people. In his research, Van Vliet has dealt with questions concerning neighbourhood planning, housing, and the relations between young people and their environment. He contributed *Habitats for children: Impacts of density* and has published in journals in the fields of planning, urban environmental studies, and sociology.

Martin Walop is a sociologist. He works in the Department of Youth Affairs of the City of Amsterdam. He is investigating vandalism in Amsterdam, together with Paul van Soomeren and Bram van Dijk. With them also, he has written four reports on this research.

Jack K. Wawrzynski graduated with a Masters degree in Architecture at Warsaw Technical University in 1966 and specialised in urban design. He was awarded a state prize for his work in Town Planning and worked in Finland on the development of Tapiola New Town (1967–68). In 1969, he came to Britain and since then has lectured on designing at Duncan of Jordanstone College of Art, School of Architecture, Dundee, and at the Mackintosh School of Architecture at Glasgow University. He also worked as a Job Architect and Planner in the Cumbernauld Development Corporation. Since 1976, he has been a lecturer in the Department of Town and Country Planning at Manchester University, teaching primarily urban design. His publications include a number of articles and papers on physical planning in Poland and Finland as well as on vandalism in residential areas in North West England. His recent activities involve working on environmental improvement schemes in Greater Manchester. Dr. Wawrzynski is an associate of the Royal Institute of British Architects and an associate of the Royal Incorporation of Architects in Scotland.

Barry Webb graduated at Portsmouth Polytechnic with a B.A. (Hons.) degree in Psychology and studied for an M.Sc. in Environmental Psychology at the University of Surrey. His special interests lie in social and environmental psychology and, in particular, with the concepts of therapy and the therapeutic environment. At present he is employed by Torbay District Health Authority as a Research Psychologist. His present research activities involve investigating the ways in which nurses and patients conceptualise the psychiatric wards and units in which they work and live. He expects this information to have implications not only for the design of future psychiatric facilities but also for policy concerning provision and organisation of psychiatric services on a wider scale. A recent interest of his has been with systems theories of communication, particularly as they apply to families and family theory.

Subject index